Work Organisations

Also by Paul Thompson

The Nature of Work: An Introduction to Debates on the Labour Process

Working the System: The Shop Floor and New Technology (*with Eddie Bannon*)

Work Organisations

A critical introduction

Paul Thompson
and
David McHugh

MACMILLAN

First published 1990

Published by
MACMILLAN EDUCATION LTD
Houndmills, Basingstoke, Hampshire RG21 2XS
and London
Companies and representatives
throughout the world

Typeset by Footnote Graphics,
Warminster, Wilts

Printed in Hong Kong

British Library Cataloguing in Publication Data
Thompson, Paul
Work organisations: a critical introduction
1. Work. Organisation
I. Title   II. McHugh, David
306′.36
ISBN 0–333–43706–3 (hardcover)
ISBN 0–333–43707–1 (paperback)

Contents

List of Tables and Figures

Tables

Figures

Acknowledgements

Our thanks are primarily due to our families for their support and forbearance during the lengthy process of our collaboration on this book.

Likewise to our colleagues at Lancashire Polytechnic who have borne the burden of our preoccupiations with 'the book'. We would especially like to thank Jim McGoldrick, Martin Gibson and Maureen Sloan of the School Of Organisation Studies for their comments, loan of books and general encouragement which helped us on our way. Many groups of students on the Combined Studies and Business Studies Degree courses have provided a vital audience through which to test ideas.

We would also like to thank Jennifer Pegg (now at Academic Press), Steven Kennedy and Steve Rutt at Macmillan for their advice and help at various stages in the progression of the project. Hugh Willmot, Chris Smith and also Martin Corbett provided a useful and constructive set of comments on the proposal. Sandra Frost and Liz Corcoran did a wonderful job checking the proofs.

We wish to express our gratitude to Lancashire Polytechnic and the Beijing Institute of Business for facilitating our final four months of frenetic but heroic excursions into transcontinental authorship during Paul's sojourn in China.

Lastly we acknowledge our indebtedness to the Amstrad 1512 and the Tasword and WordPerfect programmes, through which we negotiated the not entirely user-friendly world of computing that enabled us to make most of the process 'all our own work'.

PAUL THOMPSON
DAVID McHUGH

x

Introduction

There are an increasing number of courses under the heading of organisation studies or related titles, whose primary focus is on work organisations. The study of work organisations has traditionally been a meeting ground for contributions from a variety of disciplines and sub-disciplines. These include:

- *Industrial Sociology/Sociology of Work*: social relations, attitudes and behaviour at work, particularly those deriving from the division of labour; work experience, satisfaction and alienation; design and control of work; industrialisation processes, industrial institutions and the wider social structure.
- *Management Science/Theory*: industrial management techniques in relation to worker performance, efficiency and productivity; how organisations function and how they should be managed; management functions, notably the control of human and technical resources.
- *Organisational Sociology*: the nature and problems of large-scale organisations, including bureaucracies; the causes and consequences of various types and dimensions of organisation and organisational experience.
- *Industrial/Organisational Psychology*: the human factor at work and how managers and organisations can make better use of it; the effects of organisational processes on individuals and group behaviour and attitudes; fitting the person to the job and the job to the person.
- *Industrial Relations*: the employment relation and related institutions in the workplace; formal and informal systems

of bargaining and other structured relations between employers, managers and workers; patterns of industrial conflict and co-operation.

Of course, these are not detailed descriptions or historical explanations of such disciplines (see Rose, 1975, Hyman, 1982). Though each will have its own more specific interests such as motivation or skill and work satisfaction, there are a growing number of areas of overlap. If we take management strategy, it is clear that a considerable amount of research has been done from a labour process perspective, within an industrial relations framework and by management studies itself. Similar points could be made with respect to job design, labour markets and a range of other issues. We welcome this interdisciplinary framework and its effect on organisation studies and hope that this book reflects and encourages it. Our own experience includes teaching on these courses within business studies degrees, as well as those of a more specialist sociology of work and organisational psychology orientation.

But is organisation studies the sum of these and other parts? In practice the answer is no. Since the 1950s a particular approach normally labelled organisation behaviour (OB), or sometimes Organisation Theory, has become dominant. It is drawn mainly from management writings and organisational psychology, but enthusiastically borrows from sociology, economics, anthropology and other areas; thus laying claim to be genuinely interdisciplinary. While the borrowing of concepts may be eclectic, it is not random. Rather it is structured by specific problematics (a network of concepts oriented towards a core idea). OB focuses on social behaviour in the enterprise, directed chiefly towards problems of motivation and the performance of individuals and groups in relation to different structures and practices. Organisation Theory is, according to Donaldson, concerned with the trivariate relationship between structure, contingency and performance; or put another way it is 'mainly about the analysis of different designs, and their contingencies and their outcomes' (1985: 121). When both are taken into account, the result is that, 'These writers have attempted to draw together and distil theories of how organisations function and how they should be managed.

Their writings have been theoretical in the sense that they have tried to discover generalisations applicable to all organisations' (Pugh, 1971: 9). This approach is found in most American and some British textbooks.

Therefore, though organisation studies has always been by its very nature interdisciplinary, it has often been on a narrow management-plus-psychology basis. In some sense organisation studies is a misnomer. Most of the time it is not about organisations *per se*. Though comprehensive formal definitions may be retained, the overwhelming amount of writing and research is about work organisations and those of a business type in particular.

It is possible to duck that issue, but we prefer not to. We agree with the approach taken by those such as Salaman (1979) that organisations are not a coherent category of objects capable of being studied in a distinctive way. It is simply not possible to treat things as diverse as scout troops and transnational companies meaningfully within the same analytical framework. Work may take place within a charity or a political party, but its nature and purposes are different from those which operate under market discipline. Why then refer even to work organisations? It is certainly true that it is the profit-seeking nature of business organisations that creates their distinctive forms of management, control or other social relations. Such forms of organisation remain the structural core of advanced societies, even allowing for the decline in the proportion of those engaged in manufacturing activities. It is primarily for these two reasons that the bulk of the book is geared towards those events and experiences.

But in the end it is neither possible nor desirable to maintain a complete distinction between business and other forms of work organisation. Parts of the public sector have always operated in a market environment, and this tendency has rapidly increased in parts of the health service, local government and other public spheres in recent years. In addition, management methods or technologies may arise in a specific sector, but are frequently applied in modified forms in others. Finally, as Weber recognised, there are continuities of structure and practice deriving from the bureaucratic forms present within all large-scale organisations. For these reasons, whilst recognising the limitations, we prefer to retain work organisations as a broad framework. It does not mean that they are studied in isolation. Families and state structures are just two of the forces that interact with work organisations and whose links need to be examined.

The question of the scope of the study of organisations is not the only or main problem with the 'Organisation Theory' that Donaldson (1985) attributes to North American business and management schools. Indeed, it was dissatisfaction with the texts written from within or influenced by this tradition that led us to embark on the process of writing our own in the first place. Despite Donaldson's spirited defence, this literature continues to reproduce a taken-for-granted view of organisations with respect to their structures and processes, and notions of effectiveness and rationality. Texts remain a curious and confusing mixture of analysis and prescription. Emphasis on a stream of advice and solutions to managers consistently undermines the generation of valid and realistic knowledge of organisational processes. Admittedly it may appeal to many 'practitioners' or students seeking the 'right' answer, but in our view it has no place in a text-book.

Avoidance of prescription does not mean a lack of interest in the 'practical' or the applied. We have tried to approach this in two ways. First, by giving an account and evaluation of up-to-date empirical research into work organisations, rather than the make-believe simulations that accompany many conventional texts. This involves critically examining the interventions made by social scientists as researchers or consultants as an issue in its own right. Second, by always analysing theories and practices together and as part of specific economic and political contexts. Showing how theories are used by managerial and other groups may sound unexceptional. But the dominant tradition has been to treat the major theories of organisation and management primarily as ideas systems and historically sequenced. The result is that most students do not get a realistic and informed view of the practicality of theory. In addition, the impression is often given that theories developed in the past are outdated and 'wrong' compared to the latest favoured perspective. When these are inevitably replaced, cynicism about theory and organisational analysis is the likely result.

There have of course been alternatives. The main one, organisational sociology, has had a less than peaceful coexistence with mainstream approaches. One result has been that in the last 25 years there has been a shift in the study of organisations from sociology departments to business and management schools (Hinings, 1988). The orientation of OB and Organisation Theory are far narrower and more prescriptive. Donaldson (1985: 71–2, 119–20) defends this by reference to different levels of analysis. Issues of class and power, ideology and social stratification, and economic contradictions are the province of sociology. Organisation Theory concentrates on the problems of people working inside organisations. This approach seeks to deflect criticism of neglect of wider concerns by moving the analytical goalposts. It is impossible to satisfactorily study something like the division of labour or hierarchy of groups in a business without an understanding of the broader social division of labour and power structure.

Some sociologists have also accepted that they are studying different objects in distinct ways: 'The organisation theorist is concerned to help managers and administrators. By contrast, the sociologist is "impractical". His search is for understanding untrammelled by the needs of men of affairs' (Albrow, 1973: 412). While such a view may be in part descriptively accurate, it has dangerous consequences. It tends to legitimise the separation between a narrow perspective which is only interdisciplinary to meet the needs of management problem-solving, and a broader analysis that neglects the dynamics of day-to-day practices in organisations. Our view is that there is a basis for a reformulated organisation studies which has a specific competence in the sphere of work organisations, retains the capacity to cross discipline boundaries, and which combines theoretical and practical emphases. This contrast between existing and alternative approaches will be examined in far greater detail in Chapter 1.

The other major problem bedevilling traditional texts is the relation between the psychological or behavioural material, and that from a more sociological orientation. Frequently there is very little connection between the two. The former is dealt with under a 'topics' approach, with separate chapters on perception or personality – often with few links with each other – with organisational life, and to the chapters on structure or management theories that follow. A dualistic analysis is implicitly or explicitly the underpinning, which separates an analysis of the individual from that of the structural in the form of groups, society and the like. We accept that different modes of analysis are needed to deal with complexities and levels of human behaviour in organisations. Clearly people are constituted as individual subjects at the level of their identities, emotions or self-directed actions. But that process is informed by the same 'structural' phenomena that shape management strategies or job design, such as the social relations of production between capital, labour or gender.

The links between different levels of analysis are highlighted by debate over the potential for a critical social psychology. Mainstream theory has long included a psychological component as part of the explanation of organisational behaviour. Its opponents have objected to the treatment of people in organisations as 'psychologically determined entities' with abstractedly and individually defined needs. This has led some critical writers to firmly reject any psychological orientation. Clegg and Dunkerley argue that people should be considered, 'not as subjectivities, as unique individuals or social psyches, but as the bearers of an objective structure or relations of production and reproduction which are conditioned not by psychology but by history' (1980: 400). Whilst sharing the critique of psychological orthodoxy, we reject the view that people can be considered only as bearers of objective structures.

A purely structural analysis, even where it allows for human action and resistance, fails to get sufficiently inside those routine everyday experiences in which people react, adapt, modify and consent to work relations. While concepts of motivation, perception and the like inadequately address the problem, some account of subjectivity and identity is necessary. Nor is the question of subjectivity significant solely at the level of the individual. A critical psychology also

identifies the way in which organisations act as 'people pro-
cessors', whether through informal cultural practices or formal managerial strategies, to mobilise consent. As subjectivity
and psychological theories are the province of later chapters,
we will say no more at this stage.

With this in mind, our aim with the book at this stage is
more one of complementarity of analysis and issues than close
integration and solving of underlying theoretical questions.
For example, we do not intend to attempt a comprehensive,
historical integration of psychological theories of personality
with critical sociological accounts of individual subjectivity.
What we can do is examine how such theory and research
becomes incorporated within managerial strategies for processing and directing employees.

We should make clear that our project does not involve a
rejection of the idea of organisation theory, merely a particular conception of it. As a critical text, we seek to balance
exposition and evaluation of mainstream theory and research
with the large body of alternative writings that have developed
in recent years within radical organisation and labour process
theory, feminism, industrial sociology, management studies
and social psychology. The current period is one of tremendous change in organisational life. It may not be quite the
'paradigm shift' that some commentators are talking of, but
we hope to bring together contributions from these variety of
sources to illuminate the important change processes taking
place.

STRUCTURE OF THE BOOK

Part One focuses on the areas traditionally dealt with by
organisation theory and more sociological and structural
writings. The first chapter seeks to explore three main questions. Why are we interested in studying organisations in this
way? How should they be studied? What are the conceptual
foundations and theoretical resources for a critical organisational perspective? It does so by contrasting the diverse
strands of mainstream theory with the growing body of critical
alternatives, including those deriving from radical Weberian

and labour process theories. A great weakness of much
organisational writing is the failure to locate theory in its
historical context. Chapter 2 seeks to show how the major
characteristics of large-scale organisations in the twentieth
century – control, hierarchy, bureaucracy – came into being.
We particularly try to identify the origins and development of
the best-known theories of organisation, including Taylorism,
Weber and the human relations movement. The focus is
firmly on the attendant practices and use by management,
both in the periods when the ideas emerged and the legacies
left for the modern era.

Everyone agrees that the environment work organisations
operate in is fundamental to their nature and activities. Yet
such environments are often dealt with in a limited way,
certainly once markets and technologies have been discussed.
Chapter 3 outlines and evaluates the mainstream literature,
including contingency theory and the more recent contributions from a population ecology perspective. Most discussions
of the environment ignore or pay lip-service to the political
context. We compensate by giving an historical and contemporary account of the role of the state in labour markets and
processes. This is linked to a contrast with the environment
that public sector organisations operate in.

The study of management rightly occupies a central place
in the study of work organisations. But much of the writing
has a narrow conception of its nature and activities. Chapter 4
connects the extensive body of knowledge on management in
mainstream literature to the neglected dimensions of control
and power. Again a contrast is provided by examining more
recent research on management strategies and managerial
work as a labour process. Those who own and run organisations are continually looking for ways to design them more
effectively, whether in terms of jobs, structures, communication systems or values. Chapter 5 therefore examines the full
range of organisational design issues. It picks up from the
discussion in Chapter 2 of the bureaucratisation of production, focusing on attempts to extend, renew and challenge the
dominant patterns of bureaucratic work organisation. But
current debates have shifted to the terrain of learning from
Japan and the need for flexible working. The second half of

the chapter gives a full account and evaluation of these and other contemporary developments.

Corporate cultures are a major talking-point in current management iterature and are put forward as a crucial factor in business success. Chapter 6 looks critically at the merchandising of corporate cultures and examines whether it is an attempt to constitute a form of 'organisation man' for the 1980s and 1990s. Links are made to other processes such as Organisation Development and human resource management. We see this chapter as one which draws together themes such as management strategy, power and subjectivity, and provides a point of transition between sociological issues and psychological material to follow.

In Part Two the next three chapters shift to issues of a more behavioural and psychological nature. These chapters seek to present an exposition and redefinition of how behaviourally oriented approaches have constituted the experience of organisational life and work. The aim is to move towards a conception of psychological issues which is complementary, rather than oppositional, to the range of issues developed in Part One.

Chapters 7 and 8 represent in some ways an equivalent to the opening chapter. There is a detailed contrast between conventional organisation behaviour perspectives (Chapter 7) and a variety of critical social psychologies (Chapter 8). Chapter 7 examines the foundations in social and organisational psychology of the mainstream agenda presented in OB. The analytic focus is on the assumptions, strengths and weaknesses of the concepts and research in the areas such as perception, learning, personality and motivation which form the typical main chapter headings of most textbooks.

Chapter 8 develops these arguments by opening with the general case for taking subjectivity and identity as focal points through analysis of their limited treatment in mainstream theories. Interventions by psychologists in the role of consultants or researchers complements the theoretical evaluation which goes on to extend the argument that an emphasis on identity can be a different and often better starting-point than the mechanisms of behaviour and interaction.

Chapter 9 looks more closely at organisational practices

and is concerned with how management and other groups shape and regulate the identities and subjectivity of employees. But the 'identity work' that goes on in organisations is not just initiated in a top-down fashion by management. We try to examine the full range of such activities as individuals and groups struggle for secure identities inside the structures of power and domination characterising organisational life.

Part Three consists of a short concluding chapter. Its aim is not to summarise what has gone before, but rather to reflect on issues of theory and practice relevant to changing organisations. From a discussion of how management theory has been involved in change processes, we move to consider how critical theories can act as a resource for rethinking organisational forms and to empower employees.

PART ONE

PART ONE

1

Organisation Theory

STUDYING ORGANISATIONS

As citizens of an industrial society we tend to have a love-hate
relationship with large-scale organisations. We frequently
berate them for being bureaucratic and wasteful and for
placing us under the shadow of big brother. Yet we take them
for granted as providers of employment, public welfare,
private services, and even charity or other voluntary activities.
In the not-so-distant past, information, leisure, economic
needs and other basic life processes were more likely to be
directly and locally produced or consumed. Now, complex
economic, social and political organisations provide a network
of individual and social relationships through which we
participate in society.

Organisations, as consciously created arrangements to
achieve goals by collective means, have therefore become a
focus for academic analysis. The same paradox that affects
public attitudes is often reproduced. Those very 'efficiencies'
which derive from the scale and structure of organisations
create conditions of domination over human liberty and
democratic institutions. But even as trenchant a critic as
Perrow, who notes that organisations are tools that can
mobilise immense ideological and practical resources for those
who control them, argues: 'If we want our material civilisation
to continue as it is ... we will have to have large-scale
bureaucratic enterprise in the economic, social and governmental areas. The development of industrialisation has made
this the most efficient way to get the routine work of a society
done' (1979: 56).

This latter view derives partly from the work of Max Weber, who, at the turn of the century, was most responsible for drawing our attention to the significance of large-scale organisations, which he labelled 'bureaucracies'. As the division of labour in society and at work became more complex and difficult to manage, the responsibility and means of co-ordination of core activities became focused on special-ised units. The essence of organisation is the creation of regular, standardised behaviour and orderly structure. For Weber the characteristic features of the *organisation society* would be complex and highly developed administrative structures governed by rules, hierarchy and experts. Most people would work for or become clients of such bureaucracies.

Some modern writers came to believe that such an organ-isation society reached fruition in the post-1945 period (Kerr *et al.*: 1960; Bell: 1960). The dominant themes were that corporations and other organisations had helped to usher in a new era where politics, ideology and conflict had been super-seded by rational, scientific decision-making, guided by a new enlightened, if powerful, administrative élite. A special sort of person – organisation man – was even evoked who could be relied on to be one of the vehicles of such techniques, given that their personality and commitment was subordinated to the corporation (Whyte, 1956). It was pointless to desire significantly different arrangements as all industrial societies were destined to converge into a single, similar type. The hierarchical and bureaucratic large-scale organisation, with its particular form of technology, was placed at the centre of mature industrial society. We cannot agree that this perspec-tive is an accurate description of what is, or an analysis of what could be. Rather, it is an ideology masquerading as science. Organisations and 'organisation man' are part of an imagery where:

> all the major institutional landmarks of modern industrial society – the factory, the welfare state, the business corporation, representative democracy, an independent civil service, universal education and medical care – were firmly set in place and equipped to manage any new

problems which were likely to emerge in the foreseeable future. Institutional fine-tuning and technical adjustment were all that was necessary to maintain social stability and economic development. (Reed, 1985: 99–100)

Grouping developments under a catch-all label of organisation society or 'complex organisations' became a means, however unintended, of stopping asking questions about how such arrangements had come into being, how they were maintained, and whether they were necessary. In particular, it obliterated real differences between organisational experiences such as being a worker and consumer of public or private services, organisations in a capitalist or non-capitalist society, and the origins and effects of different types of technology in varied cultural settings.

Whether existing organisational structures and practices are necessary and efficient, it is demonstrably the case that organisations are exerting greater power over our lives. Organisations mediate between the wider society and the individual, and joining an organisation as an employee exposes the individual to substantial direction and control. Despite the self-activity of their members, organisations as corporate bodies do have economic and political powers above and beyond those of the particular individuals that comprise them. In fact, there is every indication of a concentration of those powers in a small number of organisations that is far from enlightened in its effects on us as workers or citizens.

This was a perspective raised by C. W. Mills (1959) who dubbed those who commanded major organisations the 'power élite'. In the late 1980s takeovers and mergers continue unabated, whether the beneficiaries are tycoons like Rupert Murdoch or faceless financial institutions. This is not one-sided. Work organisations remain a crucial meeting-place of contending social forces – owners, managers, professions and workers – which generates and reflects contradiction and change. It is these senses of an organisation society which make the concept still relevant and provide crucial reasons for the study of organisations.

MAINSTREAM PERSPECTIVES

This section seeks to spell out the component parts of the mainstream perspectives underlying organisation theory. While there are varieties and differences, a number of dominant assumptions can be identified. These are first set out in general terms, then we examine the major theoretical influences before going on to a critical evaluation. We will, of course, return to the themes and theories in more detail in subsequent chapters when focusing on specific issues such as power or organisational environments.

Organisations as Goal-Seeking

An emphasis on organisations as consciously created instruments necessarily leads to defining their purpose in terms of goal-seeking. This is unexceptional, but further definition is more controversial. Goals are preferred states which organisations and their members attempt to achieve through collective and co-ordinated action. Not only is the process seen in a consensual way: the starting-point tends to be located within rather than outside the organisation: 'there is an assumption that the organisation has some capacity to resist environmental constraints and set its own pattern' (Benson, 1977: 5). Obstacles and variations are naturally acknowledged, which we will return to later. However, one obvious limitation is that emphasis on goals in general doesn't enable distinctions between different forms of activities. Therefore, the *type* of goal-seeking becomes a means of definition and classification and a way of identifying the determinants of particular patterns of structure and practice in organisations.

There are many schemas of this type. We will briefly mention three to illustrate the general point.

Parsons (1960): classification based on types of goal which lead to different *outputs* to the wider social system. Four major types are distinguished; those oriented to economic production, political goals, cultural/educational types concerned with 'pattern maintenance', and organisations such as those in the legal field concerned with social integration.

Blau and Scott (1963): differentiation based on *who benefits* from the organisation's existence and activities. Four types identified: (i) members – mutual benefit organisations such as trade unions, (ii) owners/managers – business enterprises, (iii) clients – service organisations such as hospitals, (iv) public – commonweal organisations, for example, the fire service.

Etzioni (1961): typology based on *structures of compliance* in which those who control organisations utilise types of power to secure the involvement of other members. A framework for an effective fit between organisational goals and compliance structures is advanced through a threefold classification; (i) order goals – coercive structures such as prisons, (ii) economic goals – utilitarian structures, for example, workplaces, (iii) cultural goals – normative structures such as political parties.

The latter two schemas are helpful means of differentiation but beg the question of whether such diverse forms can be understood through common frames of reference regardless of the fact that they are all forms of goal-seeking. There are forms of classification based on a range of other factors. For a more detailed look at the issues, see Eldridge and Crombie (1974) and Clegg and Dunkerley (1980).

In Search of the Rational-Efficient Organisation

The emphasis on collective goal-seeking can only be sustained by a vision of organisations as rational tools. When we talk of rationality it normally refers to the logical nature of beliefs or actions. This is an aspect of mainstream perspectives but the basic feature concerns the development of suitable means to reach specific ends. It therefore becomes inseparable from a notion of *efficiency*. The emphasis is on rationally designed structures and practices resting on processes of calculated planning which will maximise organisational effectiveness. Some traditional theorists have described this in terms of the 'one best way' to run organisations. While later writers often

deny that there is one formula to fit every situation, the search
for blueprints and formulas has not been forgotten. This can
be seen by the rash of books imitating the American bestseller
In Search of Excellence (Peters and Waterman, 1982).

All examine the activities of companies to find the winning
formula. At the level of the individual the equivalent is the
endless exhortation to become the 'successful manager', the
'one-minute manager' and so on. Interestingly, Peters and
Waterman attack the 'rational model' embodied in the classical
theoriests such as Weber and F. W. Taylor. But their objection is actually to a particular type of rational action that is
based on following rules, techniques and structural devices.
They approvingly quote Selznick: 'It [organisation] refers to
an expendable tool, a rational instrument engineered to do a
job ... the transformation of an engineered, technical arrangement of building blocks into a social organism' (1982: 98). For
them the key role is played by the distinctive values or culture
of an organisation, for this has the effect of binding the various
participants together. This is what has apparently made
Eastman Kodak, MacDonald's, Texas Instruments and other
companies successful (see Chapter 6 for a full discussion). The
magic formula may differ, but the framework of rational
action=efficiency remains the same.

Managerialism

Common to all versions of rational efficiency is the premise
that the logical basis of action is held to reside with the
manager. Employees who restrict or oppose such action are
frequently held to be acting irrationally, governed by 'logic of
sentiment' rather than one of efficiency. The more overtly
managerial writers are understandably full of references to
what management *should* do and in this sense are clearly
prescriptive in nature. For some, the role of organisational
analysis is to 'help managers in organisations understand how
far their behaviour can positively influence their subordinate's
productivity' (W. Clay Hamner, quoted in Karmel, 1980).

Effectiveness becomes synonymous with management effectiveness, and options in debates are situated within that

framework. Donaldson (1985: 86) disputes this by arguing that though both are concerned with systems effectiveness, their viewpoints are distinguishable. After all, if they were the same there would be no point in supplying prescriptions. This is true, but the parameters are strictly circumscribed, as in the example supplied, that an organisational analyst might advise greater or less socialisation into company beliefs, with no questioning of the legitimacy of the beliefs themselves.

Not all mainstream writing is openly managerialist. But the underlying assumptions seldom stray too far. In the preface to a recent popular textbook (Buchanan and Huczynski, 1985), Lupton remarks that social scientists should not attach themselves to any one organisational group or its problems. But he then gives two examples of key 'puzzles'. Why and in what conditions do workgroups restrict output? What are the origins and costs of impeding technical innovation? Similarly Karmel (1980) identifies key questions. Why do people sabotage equipment? Why does the introduction of a computer make many people unhappy? Why don't subordinates obey? Alternative 'puzzles' such as why are alienating technologies designed in the first place are conspicuous by their absence. In addition, the way such problems are defined and the recurrent use of the term *practitioners* can only refer to management practices.

Part of management's job is to maintain the maximum degree of harmony and generate feelings of belonging in the workforce, reflecting literally the definition of organisation as 'form into an orderly whole'. Translated into theoretical terms, mainstream perspectives believe that the natural state of affairs for organisations tends towards equilibrium. This, in turn, rests partly on a notion that organisations are or should be *unitary* bodies combining the activities, values and interests of all their participants and rationally organised by managers.

A Science of Organisations

In terms of methodology, many mainstream writers take what Benson (1977) refers to as a 'simple positivist view', that is, they tend towards the use of methods and a view of reality borrowed from the natural sciences. There are two particularly important features involved. Firstly, there is great emphasis on *measurement* of organisational phenomena, for example, types of structures, technologies, leadership styles and even the fit between them. Secondly, there is an attempt to discover clear cause-and-effect relationships, Donaldson (1985: 84) stating the need to 'reaffirm the commitment to valid general causal laws as the goal'. He asserts the superiority of science over lay accounts, which is hardly the point. It is a question of the nature of the scientific approach, particularly the mistaken emphasis on laws. The fact that no one can actually identify any doesn't seem to worry Donaldson, as this is no proof that they may yet be discovered in the future! Inevitably, under the mantle of science – whether administrative, organisational or behavioural – these generalisations are intended to apply to *all* organisations. On this basis, analysis and intervention can be used to predict and control events and make prescriptive recommendations. Stress is on *technique* rather than values, and this reflects the attitude towards the scientific intervention into the organisation itself which tends to be taken for granted rather than treated as problematic.

THEORETICAL RESOURCES

Weber and Rationality

Weber has been a key resource for mainstream perspectives, especially on questions of rationality and efficiency. His ideas in this area have to be considered as part of a broader conception of *rationalisation* which was considered to be the key modernising characteristic of the development of industrial societies. For Weber, social stability was established through acceptance of *authority* as a form of control which people regarded as legitimate. Previous societies had been dominated by limited forms of authority based on charisma (personal qualities of leaders), or tradition (established rights and customs of dominant groups). Authority in industrial societies was rational because it was formal and based on precise and predictable rules, calculation and accounting. For these reasons the bureaucratic organisation and administration best permitted the development of appropriate attitudes, structures and practices in public and private sectors: 'More and more the material fate of the masses depends upon the steady and correct functioning of the increasingly bureaucratic organisations of private capitalism. The idea of eliminating these organisations becomes more and more utopian' (Weber, 1984: 36). Weber's theory went beyond economic life. Rationalisation was held to encompass processes as diverse as law, politics, religion and scientific method itself. All were becoming governed by impersonal objectives, procedures and knowledge, embodied in structures and processes which 'confront individuals as something external to them' (Brubaker, 1984: 9).

However, rationalisation was acknowledged to be a morally and politically problematic development. Weber makes an important distinction between *formal* and *substantive* rationality. The former refers to the calculability of techniques and procedures. In contrast, the latter emphasises the values concerned with the desired ends of action. The key point is that while formal techniques are of a specific type, such values and ends inevitably differ. Thus space is opened up for recognition of contested rationalities between groups and individuals. Indeed, Weber acknowledged that the formal and substantive were always potentially in conflict, frequently making pessimistic comments about human needs being subordinated to the former. The formally rational, such as the pursuit of profit by merging and 'asset stripping' companies, may be substantively irrational in terms of its social consequences. In this sense, Weber does make some separation of rationality and efficiency as there could in principle be different views of what constitutes either category. For example, workers' co-operatives and private ownership could both be regarded as efficient on the basis of different value criteria.

These kind of points form part of the basis of a defence of Weber by some writers (e.g. Albrow, 1970) against the normal way ideas are used in mainstream theory. But though this has some validity, it is not clear how significant it is. Aside from the fact that Weber is not always clear about the separation and its consequences (see Storey, 1983: 26–34), from the viewpoint of evaluating mainstream perspectives as a whole most theorists influenced by Weber have acted as if rationality and efficiency are the same thing. As a result they have tended to be rather uncritical of existing organisations. Reed notes:

> The causal link which he is thought to have identified between rational bureaucracy and technical efficiency provided a substantive focus and theoretical bone of contention from which a general theory of organisations, based on a systems frame of reference, could be constructed in the course of the 1950s (1985: 17).

What some followers of Weber – dubbed *neo-Weberians* – have done, however, is to build from the distinction between formal and substantive rationality in order to uncover the neglected aspects of the functioning of bureaucratic organisations. Empirical research reveals two key processes. First, the inefficiencies arising from the following of impersonal rules, such as the displacement of the original goals by obsession with narrow interest and ritual by the office holder. Second, the dependence of bureaucratic organisations on informal, innovative behaviour and consensual human relations. Issues concerning Weber and bureaucracy are taken up in more depth in Chapters 2 and 5.

Taylor and Management Science

The ideas of F. W. Taylor, the founder of 'scientific management' at the turn of the century, complement those of Weber (we discuss his theories and practices in detail in Chapter 2). Despite his emphasis on rationality in the enterprise, Weber did not explicitly deal with the role of management. In contrast, Taylor was a management practitioner concerned directly with the efficient performance of work. In developing schemas for the potentially 'scientific' character of management he was echoing the themes of rationality and formal control. Emphasis, as with Weber, was put on a series of techniques, in this case to measure and control work and define clearly the relative tasks of management and worker. It fits clearly in a positivist framework of belief that there are objective means of measurement which can help discover laws governing work activity. Again paralleling Weber, Taylor saw management by 'scientific' methods as a move away from traditional authority where owners and managers attempted to control by inefficient, personal means. Today, among organisational writers there is considerable controversy about the nature and value of 'Taylorism'. But by 'invoking science as its foundation' (Kouzmin, 1980: 68), Taylor's ideas were a crucial ingredient in legitimising the conception of management as a rational, scientific activity, and this has been an enduring feature of mainstream analysis ever since.

Durkheim, Human Relations and Social Needs

The other 'founding father' of sociology to have a significant impact on organisational analysis has been Durkheim, though there is a marked contrast to Weber. Durkheim's contribution centres around the significance of the *division of labour* in sustaining the social solidarity necessary for the survival of the 'organism' of society or enterprise. Writing in the late nineteenth century, he observed that the more complex division of labour in industrial, urban society was undermining traditional values and mechanisms of social order. But at the same time it was laying the basis for a more effective integration of individuals in society which was labelled 'organic solidarity'. This advanced industrial, technological division of labour was inevitably based on specialisation, hierarchy, and functional interdependence between tasks and occupations. Durkheim recognised that the new arrangements and formal structures contained sources of social disorganisation, conflict and harmful individualism, summed up in the term 'anomie'. Any effective division of labour could therefore only take root and bind people together when it was sustained by new social values, by moral communities such as professional or occupational groups, and when workers had an understanding of their place within the overall scheme of production.

This kind of formulation was later interpreted through mainstream theory in terms of the permanent tension between the technical and formal needs of the organisation and the social needs of those who worked in it. It was therefore management's role not just to organise the former but to carry out running repairs on the latter. This necessitated paying specific attention to the *informal* side of the organisation, particularly to the primary groups that people belonged to, such as workgroups. In the 1920s and 1930s this theme was taken up and popularised by Elton Mayo, who had identified problems arising from the breakdown of traditional skills and values associated with the rise of mass production. Researchers could help management to reintegrate the worker by identifying social needs and relating them to common values which led to identification with the company. This was the beginning of the *human relations* tradition.

Barnard (1938) extended the analysis with emphasis on how organisations could become 'cooperative social systems'. He more clearly defined the role of the executive and the specialised managerial function in terms of defining and communicating goals and securing workforce effort. A key feature of the human relations approach is the social engineering role given to management through maintaining equilibrium and integrating the parts of the organisation. The vehicle is not formal structures of co-ordination and command, but values, informal practices and the 'logic of sentiment'. Though a subordinate aspect of organisational analysis for considerable periods, it has recently reappeared within a new socio-economic context and new management writings referred to earlier, such as Peters and Waterman's *In Search of Excellence*. Attention is being focused once again on the employee's needs, the human side of the enterprise, and to creating and sustaining unity through organisational cultures.

The human relations tradition, with its emphasis on social needs, also provided the basis for the beginnings of *psychological* intervention. In its early days, in the first quarter of this century, industrial psychology complemented scientific management by being concerned with workers rather than work structures. Its practices were centred primarily on processes of selection, measurement and testing, and vocational guidance. A narrow orientation towards manipulative techniques through emergent personnel departments led to some disrepute. But a basis was laid for the later development of an *organisational* psychology proper. In the post-war period, emphasis began to be put on more sophisticated behavioural science techniques and issues centred on motivation and group behaviour. A humanistic school of psychology consolidated around figures such as Maslow and McGregor, who explored the full implications for management of responding to all members of organisations as a human resource. Though they offered different and more challenging solutions, the basic themes of efficiency, satisfaction and productivity remained the same (see Hedy Brown, 1980). Organisational psychology is now an integral part of mainstream perspectives and the issues it raises will be dealt with in Part Two of this book.

Systems Theory

The classical theories previously discussed had a number of widely acknowledged weaknesses. In particular, they tended to have a rather static view of the organisation in which structures and practices could be internally regulated, with little reference to the outside world. Organisations were conceived of as *closed systems* balancing the various human and technical components. Later mainstream theorists greatly extended and modified the notion of organisations as systems. In doing so they drew from the basic organic analogy used by Durkheim and others, in which all social systems have to adapt to the environment to survive. This became a theme of *functionalist* social theory (Parsons, 1951; Donaldson, 1985) which regards social systems as self-regulating bodies, tending towards a state of equilibrium and order. Each part of any system plays a positive functional role in this process, for example, by generating binding social values. Thus the organisation is a system of interrelated parts or sub-units, for example, departments, groups and individuals, each functioning to mobilise resources towards meeting wider goals. These parts are at the same time differentiated and interdependent, aiding processes of integration and co-ordination.

The great influence of such thinking on the major organisational writers of the 1950s and 1960s can be seen in the comment from Woodward:

> Even more important from the point of view of ultimate theory building is the fact that various schools of thought are beginning to see themselves as concerned with the study of systems ... the starting-point is the identification of a system and the subsequent questions asked are very much the same: what are the objectives and strategic parts of the system under review and how are these parts interrelated and interdependent? One result is that those concerned with the study of organisation are beginning to develop a common language, on whatever discipline their work is based. (Quoted in Eldridge and Crombie, 1974: 93)

A crucial development, however, has been the acceptance of the importance of interaction with the environment; for the survival of an organisation depends on its capacity to adapt to markets, technologies and other situations. An *open systems* approach became the characteristic feature of mainstream theory, organisations coping with uncertainty through exchange and transaction with the external environment. Systems theory is therefore an explanation of the pattern of functioning of organisations in terms of inputs, outputs and transformations, encompassing the variety of social, psychological and technical variables. The most popular current variant is *contingency theory*, which deals with designing the appropriate structures of co-ordination and control to fit different environments (see Chapter 3 for detailed discussion).

AN EVALUATION OF MAINSTREAM PERSPECTIVES

Mainstream perspectives are not homogeneous and there are tensions between concepts derived from Weber, Durkheim and other key figures. There is much of value in the body of ideas, both in terms of the issues raised and empirical work generated. Nevertheless, we can identify the outline of a number of interrelated criticisms, many of which are followed up in other chapters. *Rationality* and *efficiency* have been important themes and no one should deny that they are legitimate aspects of organisational analysis. But in mainstream theory they are presented largely in neutral terms as if rationality was a simple determinant of organisational structures, processes and goals. Later writers have lost sight of the critique of formal rationality raised by Weber. In doing so it reduces these processes to a matter of technique, devising the appropriate kind of structure, or best fit with a particular environment. A picture is developed of a functional relationship between rational organisations and a rational society.

This perspective removes issues of politics, power and control from organisational choices and critical questions concerning means and ends. Donaldson (1985: 101) tries to get round this by separating the latter: 'The concern with rational means rather than values is part of what makes such studies apolitical'. But there are as many contestable choices to be made about how to design jobs or authority structures as there are about the ends to which they are put.

A rational *model* emphasising features such as calculability is further confused with rationality or reasonableness *as such*. As Fischer and Sirriani put it: 'For the critical theorist, mainstream writers have confused the rational model of efficient administrative behaviour with organisational rationality itself ... organisations must be conceptualised as tools for the pursuit of personal, group or class interests' (1984: 10–11). Furthermore, traditional notions underestimate the role of rationality and efficiency as *ideological constructs* which help to legitimise the positions, rewards and activities of dominant groups (Salaman, 1979: 177–82). For example, when changes take place, such as mergers or closures, they are often described in terms of *rationalisation* as if the decision of managers or boards of directors are inevitable and the only way of doing things. Acknowledging the contested nature of these processes is not made any easier within mainstream theory because, 'Weber attempts to use richly value-laden terms in a value-neutral manner' (Brubaker, 1984: 36).

Such perspectives are underlaid by an assumption of harmony of interests. This is reproduced in another crucial sphere, that of the division of labour. The way that tasks,

functions and jobs are divided, with the consequent specialisation and hierarchies, is all too often regarded as an unproblematic technical or functional necessity. The origins and
workings of the division of labour is neglected as an issue,
influenced by Weberian, functionalist and Durkheimean
analyses which emphasise differentiation and interdependence.
As a consequence many deep-rooted features of organisational
life – inequality, conflict, domination and subordination,
manipulation – are written out of the script in favour of
behavioural questions associated with efficiency or motivation. Some of these features may be seen as *pathological* or
temporary phenomena arising from breakdowns in organisational systems, rather than a fundamental product of the
structuring of the division of labour. This is also the case in
human relations analysis deriving from a Durkheimean tradition which 'defined the anomic consequences of capitalism as
abnormal, as a deviation from the ideal circumstances of
organic solidarity' (Hamilton, 1980: 70).

Notions of social harmony have also influenced understandings of *goals*. Nevertheless, mainstream writings have made
some progress towards acknowledging goal diversity and
uncertainty, particularly between formal and informal, official
and operative goals and actual policies (Perrow, 1961). This is
welcome, but there are still weaknesses. Members of organisations may have goals which are contradictory to the official
organisation and which they share with others, not just
'personal' ones: 'There is no notion of rational structural
sources of opposition being generated in the normal processes
of organisation' (Clegg and Dunkerley, 1980: 317). A sense of
reification is still present, in which the organisation is treated
as a thing and the only legitimate goal-seeking collectivity.
The notion that formal organisations, made up of different
members, are constituted to co-ordinate wider goals as if it is a
form of social contract (Albrow, 1973: 408), underestimates
the extent to which dominant power-groupings have set those
goals and shaped the appropriate structures. In practice, co-
ordination or co-operation may reflect pressure, constraint or
acquiescence to power as much as shared goals. This cannot
be avoided by the use of the 'stakeholder' model (Donaldson,
1985: 24), which postulates a spurious pluralism in which

goals are held to be the result of a relatively equal trade-off between the preferences of competing groups.

There is a sense in which we can refer to *organisations* having policies or goals, but they have to be clearly recognised as frequently the property of particular individuals or groups. For example, in the late 1970s the then Chairman of British Leyland produced the Company Plan. The extent to which they were not the product and property of the employees as a whole can be seen from the subsequent events. It was put to the workforce in a ballot and rejected. Edwardes then implemented it anyway. A final broader point on this issue is important. To define or classify organisations in terms of goal-seeking distorts the difference between them. As Salaman notes:

> a genuine sociology of organisations is not assisted by the efforts of some organisation analysts to develop hypotheses about organisations in general, lumping together such diverse examples as voluntary organisations, charities and political organisations ... It also obstructs the analysis of those structural elements which are dramatically revealed in employing organisations, but not necessarily in all forms of organisation. (1979: 33)

We need to differentiate between different types of goal and the wider economic and political influences upon them, how they are constructed and in whose benefit they operate.

The failure to adequately analyse these processes underlines the extent to which organisational analysis remains consciously or implicitly *management* oriented. Two qualifying points to this criticism need to be made. First, there *is* a need to study management as an activity. Second, an open 'management science' servicing the needs of such groups inevitably reflects existing socio-economic relations. But such an orientation is particularly dangerous to a broader organisational analysis. As Watson (1980b) points out, management requirements are likely to focus on short-term pragmatic relevance related to task achievement, or towards the ideological expedience of unitary and consensual views of organisational life. Theorists can become in Baritz's (1960) words 'servants of power', enmeshed in restrictive client relationships within the business firm. The problem is less that of the corruption arising from lucrative contracts (though it is worrying when yesterday's advocates of participation become today's advisors on union-busting) than that of knowledge and problem-solving on management terms. Thus Organisational Theory is helping to constitute a particular reality without critically analysing it, and runs the risk of reducing theory and practice to a technology of social control.

Not only does this limit the ability of analysis to be a resource for a wider range of participants, it has the negative consequence of ignoring lower-level employees except as objects or in their defined 'roles' (Salaman, 1979: 47). Limitations arise from the service role itself. Reed observes, 'organisation theory has presented management with a stock of "moral fictions" (such as "managerial effectiveness") that disguise the social reality of contemporary management practice' (1985: 95). Despite or perhaps because of that role, there are frequent complaints that official theory propagated to business students and managers is out of touch with the 'real world'.

In conclusion, we would argue that mainstream perspectives have often functioned as theories of regulation and are bound up in the purposes and practices of organisational control. This has prevented the development of 'any coherent or consensual theoretical object of the organisation' (Clegg and Dunkerley, 1980: 213). Instead, organisational and societal reality has tended to be taken for granted, with emphasis on that which is prescriptive and short-term. Viewing organisations as natural systems and as largely autonomous bodies has produced a limited capacity to explain historical changes and the political and economic contexts in which organisations operate. The overall objections of critical theory are summed up by Fischer and Sirriani:

> Common to all of the approaches is a concern over the conservative/élitist bias of organisational theory, a general absence of social class analysis, a failure to connect the organisation to the political economy of the larger social and historical context, a general neglect of political and

bureaucratic power, and the ideological uses of scientific organisational analysis (1984: 5).

CRITICAL PERSPECTIVES

Like its mainstream counterpart, critical perspectives are based on a variety of ideas and theoretical sources. Its starting-point is obviously critique itself; the identification of the weaknesses, limitations and ideological functions of orthodoxy. The two traditions are not always different on every point, and there are some partly overlapping objectives for some of the strands of thought, including humanisation of work processes and non-bureaucratic forms of organisation. Nevertheless, through the critique an outline of a different agenda begins to emerge, with a concern for issues of power, control, domination, conflict, exploitation and legitimation. What of the more positive alternative? What do we mean by critical?

General Principles

Any alternative perspectives necessarily start from different guidelines and assumptions about organisations and society. They must first of all be *reflexive*, that is, have the capacity to reflect upon themselves so that values, practices and knowledge are not taken for granted. We have referred previously to unproblematic conceptions of phenomena such as goals and productivity, but a key example would be that of *gender*. Existing analyses have largely treated gender divisions as irrelevant, or in practice invisible, despite 'the persistent fact that women's position in any organisation differs from men in the same organisations' (Woolf, 1977: 7). In addition, instead of reflecting the concerns of established power-groups, organisational theory should critically reflect on and challenge existing attitudes and practices, drawing on the distinction between practical and technical rationality originally identified by Habermas (1971) and subsequently espoused by many other radical writers. Technical rationality is based on the instrumental pursuit of taken-for-granted goals such as 'efficiency'. In contrast, practical rationality emphasises conscious and enlightened reflection which would clarify alternative goals and action based on the widest communication and political dialogue.

A further guiding principle is the necessity to be *historical* and *contextual*. Organisational theory and practice can only be understood as something *in process*, otherwise the search for general propositions and instant prescriptions becomes disconnected from reality as it has done in conventional ahistorical approaches (Littler, 1980: 157). It is also necessary to counter the tendency to see organisations as free-floating and autonomous, and the concentration on the micro-level of analysis, or single enterprise. This means locating organisational processes within their structural setting, examining the interaction with economic forces, political cultures and communities. To return to the gender example, it is impossible to understand the emergence and development of the sexual division of labour in organisations from within. We have to go outside to the family and patriarchal structures in society as a whole in order to reflect back.

This approach means more than diffuse references to the environment. In more specific theoretical terms, organisational issues cannot be comprehended outside the totality constituted by capitalist society and the mode of production in particular (Burrell: 1980a). Donaldson objects to this on the grounds that locating explanations within the wider social system denies that organisational phenomena are topics of enquiry in their own right. But no convincing argument is put foward to justify the desirability or possibility of such a degree of analytical autonomy. Furthermore, he argues that 'the notion of totality is a reference to everything – nothing is left out' (1985: 124). It is indeed important to avoid reducing totality to a meaningless level of generality. We hope to show that it is possible to refer to specific relations between work organisations and their social, economic and political contexts.

Many critical theorists (e.g. Benson, 1977a; Storey, 1983) utilise the notion of dialectical perspectives as a crucial means of explaining the dynamic of organisational change. In abstract terms a dialectical process refers to a movement from thesis, to antithesis and synthesis and derives from Hegel and

Marx. It is not always usefully employed. Morgan (1985, 266) produces a list which places 'oppositions' as varied as capital and labour, young and old and even sales and production on the same level. Understanding these so-called dialectics can therefore aid the management of change. This is an example of the way that the use of the term 'masks differences in both scope and meaning' (Neimark and Tinker, 1986). There are common interrelated themes. Often it is in practice reduced to a notion of reciprocal interaction between structure and human agency. Benson and Storey both refer to three themes, the first returning us to the concept of situating organisations in the wider totality of capitalism. Not all relationships and developments within the totality are compatible, for example, between private ownership and collective social needs. These are contradictions, antagonistic relations which are built into work organisation and society, and which in turn generate conflict and change. A third aspect is the social construction of reality through individual action. The fact that managers and workers find themselves caught up in structural processes does not mean that they are merely passive agencies. Any circumstances are experienced inter-subjectively, reconstructed and modified.

The most direct application to work organisations is expressed in the idea of a reciprocal relation between managerial control and worker resistance. Management control strategies are fundamentally a means of dealing with contradictions, uncertainties and crises in their socio-economic environment. New methods of control inevitably provoke and shape forms of employee resistance and sometimes counter 'strategies'. Over a period of time, management responses are likely to develop into alternative control methods, blending with and going beyond the old. For example, piecework was introduced as a means for management to set targets and control through monetary incentives. But the shop floor frequently devised ways of asserting their own controls over output and earnings. In the 1970s employers in the motor industry responded by establishing new payment systems based on 'measured day rates', but still using control techniques based on work study and measurement. Over a period of time, workers developed their own methods of adaptation and resistance and so the

cycle continues. This kind of perspective puts more substance
into the traditional idea of an interaction between formal and
informal dimensions of organisational life. However it is
formulated, we can view organisations as continually having
to respond to and counter *disorganisation*. Those who command organisations are required to mobilise a variety of
resources, including power, control and persuasion or consent.

Benson adds a fourth aspect of a dialectical perspective,
that of *praxis*, drawing on the previously discussed notion of
practical rationality. Praxis involves developing analytical
resources which go beyond reflexivity and can help members
of organisations constrained by existing relations of ownership
and power to critically reflect on and reconstruct their circumstances. Though some critical theorists advocate the
prioritisation of 'philosophically informed armchair theorising'
(Burrell, 1980a: 102), we would agree with Benson's emphasis
on theory as an emancipatory guide. A final general principle
of critical theory should therefore be a concern with social
transformation, and specifically with *empowering* a wider
range of organisational participants, though this implies no
particular form of politics or intervention. It may be argued
that this reproduces a one-sided partiality that is the reverse of
the management orientation of mainstream theories. There is
always that danger. But the existing realities and power
relations in organisations will, for the foreseeable future,
enable critical theory to maintain a certain distance and
intellectual independence. Furthermore, any critical theory
not testing its ideas through empirical investigation or practical intervention is ultimately arid. We now turn to look at
some of the specific theoretical contributions themselves,
starting with one that is linked to the above discussion in that it
represents more of a different way of seeing organisations than
a macro-model of work organisations in their societal context.

Social Action Theory

The most significant sign of a major alternative to mainstream
perspectives emerged with an attack on the dominant systems

theory by Silverman (1970). He brought together elements of an approach described as the *action frame of reference* or social action theory. It was not new, drawing on the phenomenological writings of Schutz (1967) and Berger and Luckman (1967). In fact, its methods can partly be traced back to Weber's conception of a social science, if not his actual writings on bureaucracy. For Weber, such a science begins from interpreting social action and the subjective meanings and purposes attached to it. This rests on a distinction between the natural and social worlds, but retains an attempt to situate individual action within material structures. In renewing this perspective, Berger and Luckman popularised the concept of *social construction of reality*. Rather than conceiving of people as products of systems and institutions, they are 'actors' who create these patterns through their own meaningful activity. However, it was accepted that the products of their action, for example, organisational structures, appear to them as 'things' with an independent existence. Social construction was one of the aspects of a dialectical approach discussed earlier, and it puts a necessary stress on the possibility of change through purposeful reflection and action.

Silverman was able to apply these kinds of idea more specifically to organisations, considering them as social constructs produced and reproduced through their members' activities. This was largely neglected in systems theory, which regards organisations as part of the 'natural' world governed by 'laws' concerning their structures and effects on behaviour. Hence, as we have argued, they have reified organisations and taken their basic features for granted. Silverman did not ignore structure, recognising that *roles*, as systematic patterns of expectations, were developed in the interplay between organisations and their environments. His study was largely theoretical but others were of a more empirical nature, utilising the concept of organisations as *negotiated orders* (see Day and Day, 1977). By the early 1960s, Strauss *et al.* (1963) had been analysing the negotiated order in hospitals, while other notable studies included those concerned with police and legal practices (Bittner, 1967; Cicourel, 1968), and welfare agencies (Zimmerman, 1971). A recurring theme was that controls exercised through rules in formal organisations were inevitably incomplete and unsuccessful. Any degree of effective co-ordination and co-operation is dependent on constant reworking of rules and goals, and formal and informal negotiation processes involving all participants. The subsequent customs and practices in any workplace act as a constraint on management.

The critique developed through action theory challenged the consensual and objective images of organisations that were often based on 'favoured' managerial definitions. By focusing on the realities of multiple goals and competing groups, dimensions of organisational life, such as work patterns and practices, could be demystified. It shed light on why organisations don't operate as they're supposed to. This latter emphasis tied into empirical work by *neo-Weberians* who were also concerned with the bending of bureaucratic rules through the value-systems of employees (Blau, 1955; Gouldner, 1955). Indeed, Silverman utilises some of these studies extensively. He notes, for example, how Gouldner shows that industrial relations in a gypsum mine had been based on an 'indulgency pattern': implicit rules rooted in give-and-take rather than formal codes. When management attempted to introduce changes which clashed with the established values and practices and reasserted formal rules, it generated grievances and strike activity.

During the 1970s, Silverman and other writings (e.g. Silverman and Jones, 1976) shifted the action approach in the direction of *ethnomethodology*. Though 'translated' as people-centred, it is actually only concerned with the production of a commonsense world and eschews any attempt at analysis of causation which would impose external categories. Nor is it concerned with the relation between ideas and interests or social and organisational structures present in the Weberian tradition. It restricts itself to accounting for the processes through which members construct their everyday life. Structures tend to be viewed at best as temporary patterns created by interpersonal action and based on available stocks of knowledge. Any notion of *organisation* in the traditional sense ceases to have any meaning. Phenomena such as power or control, which are expressed through relatively durable structures beyond specific situations and face-to-face interactions and meanings, are simply outside its frame of reference.

Though taken to extremes in ethnomethodology, these weaknesses were inherent in action theory. In Silverman's earlier work he argued that technological and market structures were meaningful only in terms of the understandings and attachments of participants. Though structures require the involvement of actors in their reproduction, something like a product or labour market does have a structural existence partly independent from how particular individuals think or act, as anyone who has lost their job or a fortune on the stock exchange will testify. Concepts such as role which were used to link subjective action and structure are useful but not substantial enough to carry the burden of explaining organisational behaviour. The more disconnected action theory became from wider concerns, the more it became 'buried in an obsessive concern for the minutiae of "everyday life" as exemplified in the intricacies of organisational routines' (Reed, 1985: 48). This is linked to a further problem limiting its capacity to act as a critical resource. Despite the emphasis on empirical studies, as we raised earlier and as has Silverman admitted, the approach is aimed at providing a *method* of analysis rather than a theory of organisations. Such a theory must move beyond how organisations and their environments are subjectively constituted to some kind of structural explanation of the dynamics of organisational development within capitalist societies. This can be achieved in part by reworking and extending the concepts provided by Marx and Weber.

Marx and Labour Process Theory

Marx had little to say about issues of administrative or even political organisation, and even less about the specific question of bureaucracy. Goldman and Van Houten noted that, 'Systematic study of the sociology of organisations is almost absent in the classical and modern Marxist traditions' (1977: 110). Those wishing to generate a discussion from Marx have had to rely on fragments of a critique of the Prussian bureaucracy and writings on the Paris Commune of 1871 as a model of the possibility of elimination of bureaucracy through a fully democratic administrative system (Marx, 1984). Marxist theory has tended to focus on the dynamics and contradictions of capitalism as a whole and issues concerning the distribution of the surplus product, neglecting changes in productive processes, organisational forms and occupational structures. Some Marxist concepts have been influential, if often misunderstood, notably his account of the alienation of labour. But they have remained unconnected to any systematic organisational analysis.

This general point is picked up by Donaldson (1985: 127) who argues that, 'Marxism is a theory of society therefore it cannot be a theory of organisation'. Clegg (1988: 10) makes the apposite response that applying the same criteria to Weber would place his work on bureaucracy outside the level appropriate to organisation theory. More importantly, the situation has now changed. During the last decade or more, Marxist or Marxist-influenced theory and research has had a profound effect on all of the disciplines concerned with work organisation. There has been a revival of Marxist scholarship generally, but the major vehicle has been *labour process theory* set in motion by Braverman's (1974) reworking of Marx's analysis of capitalist production (for a full account of labour process debates see Thompson, 1989).

Though more obviously influential in industrial sociology, labour process theory has provided conceptual tools observable in a wide range of critical organisation writers such as Clegg, Dunkerley, Salaman, Storey and Burrell. The former two begin *Organisations, Class and Control* by defining the theoretical object of organisational analysis: 'For this volume we have proposed as such an object the concept of organisation as control of the labour process' (Clegg and Dunkerley, 1980: 1). What enables such an argument to be made? Marx may not have been interested in an understanding of organisations *per se*, but he was centrally concerned with issues of work organisation and organisation of work. By this we mean a combined emphasis on work organisations as the site of key economic processes and contradictions, and the meeting place of capital and labour, as well as organisation of work in terms of questions including the division of labour, relations of authority and control and the distribution of rewards.

Marx defined the form of a society and economy in a manner strongly conditioned by an understanding of work relationships. Each mode of production gives rise to class relations which, under capitalism, are based on the sale and purchase of labour power. The partial antagonism between capital and labour as collective classes arises from the exploitation and appropriation of the surplus labour by capital, based on its ownership and control of production. This is a far cry from the notion of fair exchange implied in mainstream theory. Work relations therefore cannot be analysed in general, but only as they are shaped by the demands of a specific system of production. All societies have labour processes, but under capitalism it has specific characteristics. The most significant is what Marx referred to as the transformation of labour power into labour. In other words, when capital purchases labour it has only a potential or capacity to work. To ensure profitable production capital must *organise* the conditions under which labour operates to its own advantage. Naturally there is a tendency for workers to do the opposite as evidenced by informal job controls, restriction of output and the like. This is the necessary framework within which to understand the more modern concept of the *employment relationship* which has at its core the exchange of effort for reward, or 'wage-effort bargain' (see Palmer, 1983).

The above processes cannot be understood within the confines of one organisational unit. Competition between enterprises and the conflict within the employment relationship creates an accumulation process which compels capital constantly to reorganise production. Certain general features of work organisation and organisation of work tend to follow.

1. Employers need to exercise control over labour, both at the level of general directive powers and over working conditions and tasks. At the same time it is necessary to motivate employees and gain some level of consent and co-operation. Meeting these diverse and sometimes contradictory needs is the function of management systems and agents.

2. There are constant pressures to cheapen the costs of production, notably labour. This may take place through deskilling, relocation of plant, work intensification or some other means; though subject to constraints, including worker resistance and market variations.
3. A division of labour must be structured around the above objectives, involving the design of work and division of tasks and people to give the most effective control and profitability. This is sustained by hierarchical structures and the shaping of appropriate forms of science and technology.

Let's restate this and spell out the consequences with more specific reference to organisations.

1. Work organisations are distinct from other organisations and can only be properly understood within a theory of capital accumulation and labour processes. This 'political economy' must take in relationships to regional, national and international environments.
2. 'Organisations are structures of control' (Salaman, 1981: 143). This involves more than control over uncertainty, monitoring objectives or means of getting work done. They are administrative apparatuses concerned with control over productive activity in order to maximise the surplus. Appropriate managerial strategies are developed in this context.
3. In advanced capitalist societies large-scale organisations are strategic units acting as mechanisms which integrate economic, political, administrative and ideological structures (Burrell, 1980a: 99).
4. Organisational structures and processes, including management and worker organisation, control and reward systems, and job design, therefore involve *political* issues, decisions and choices.
5. Organisations do not embody any universal rationality, but rather contested rationalities arising from the partly antagonistic relation of capital and labour. Organisational change will reflect the subsequent dialectic of control and resistance.

This is not merely a question of the 'seamy side' of otherwise excellent organisations as Morgan appears to believe (1985: 316–17). Relations of exploitation and domination are integral to capitalist and other class-divided forms of work organisation. Nevertheless, the underlying principles of the relations between organisations and capitalist society are at a very general level. They involve no laws or functional imperatives concerning *specific* forms of control, organisational structures, management strategies or job designs. Nor does reference to class necessarily incorporate particular models of consciousness or social change. All these and other matters are empirical questions to be determined by research and the unfolding of real events. The renewal of Marxist and labour process theory *has* generated or influenced a tremendous amount of historical and contemporary research at a more 'micro' level. This is particularly true in areas such as managerial strategies (Friedman, 1977; Edwards, 1979); technology and work design (Wilkinson, 1983a; Child, 1985; Thompson and Bannon, 1985); and the sexual division of labour (Pollert, 1981; Cavendish, 1982; Westwood, 1984); issues which we will return to in subsequent chapters.

There are many gaps in explanations of key organisational processes in the work of this form of critical organisation theory. Some of this can no doubt be remedied by further research, but it is important to recognise the *limits* inherent in the perspective. It sets organisations in the context of *capitalist production*, and this raises some major problems.

1. Though the labour process is the core of productive activity, it does not encompass all aspects. Any theory of the role of organisations in capitalist society must deal with the *full circuit of capital* (Kelly, 1985; Nichols, 1986), including its realisation through the sale of commodities on the market, financial issues and the prior purchase of labour (see Chapter 4 for full discussion). It would be very misleading for any critical theory to proceed on the assumption that organisational processes and managerial activities were based solely on the control of labour, neglecting factors such as sales and marketing, financial controls, supply of components and product quality. Even

the employment relationship, though intimately connected to the labour process, is constituted on a far wider basis (Littler: 1982). Institutions such as the state and the family, plus different cultural values and patterns in a given society, shape the distinctive character of employment relationships, as can be seen by observing examples from Japan or farm work. Labour process theory is thus only a partial contribution to such analyses, though paradoxically it is in some ways ideally suited to organisation studies given that the dominant managerial theories are also overwhelmingly concerned with 'the labour problem'.

2. Not all work organisations are based on commodity production, or are capitalist in character. Those in health, education or other parts of the public sector are, at least for the moment, concerned with services for use not profit. It is possible to construct a Marxist-oriented analysis which shows the links between the various types of public and private sector within the totality of capitalist society (Heydebrand, 1977). But it remains the case that not all organisational processes or forms of work activity can be understood solely through a theory whose categories are geared to explaining capitalist production, despite distorted attempts to do so, such as Bellaby and Orribor's (1977) analysis of the health service.

3. Non-profit making organisations in capitalist societies and forms of administration and enterprise in 'socialist' ones such as the Soviet Union also show evidence of bureaucracy, power hierarchies and work fragmentation: 'contemporary socialist societies appear to be at least as bureaucratic and with as much of a self-perpetuating bureaucracy as capitalist ones' (Dunkerley and Salaman, 1986: 87). This suggests that the dynamic of bureaucratisation is *partly* independent of capital-labour relations, and that critical theory requires concepts that enable us to focus on that problem.

This is where Weber comes in. For he perceptively predicted that state socialist systems would be *more* bureaucratic than capitalism because of the absence of countervailing power structures between the state and markets. Interestingly,

however, though Weber's analysis aimed for applicability
across any system, it was not designed to explain the kind of
situation in Soviet-type societies where there has been a
totalitarian bureaucracy whose fusion of administrative, economic and political powers is outside the assumption of
separation of power and the rule of law (Polan, 1984: 112–13).

Radical Weberianism

Many critical theorists, particularly those of a Marxist persuasion, have been hostile to the Weberian tradition (Marcuse,
1971: Johnson, 1980). Their objections relate to many of the
points raised earlier in the chapter. This includes the tendency
to argue that there is a bureaucratic imperative obliterating
organisational differences within and between societies; that
there is an inherent rationality of technique; and the identification of rationality with capitalism and the market. Also
there are genuine limits to Weber's own categories, for
example, the emphasis on the bureaucratic hierarchy of offices
has far less relevance to shopfloor employees. Nevertheless,
there are *radical Weberian* perspectives and critical writers
who aim at some kind of synthesis of key aspects of Marx and
Weber's analysis of work organisations (Salaman, 1979, 1981;
Littler, 1982).

They point to certain common concerns with control and
domination by management and bureaucratic élites: 'For both
Marx and Weber the major elements of the structure of
modern large-scale organisations stem from the efforts of those
who own, manage and design the organisation, to achieve
control over the members' (Salaman, 1979: 20–1). Weber
recognised that control rested on the 'complete appropriation'
of all the material means of production by owners. In addition, both represent an attempt to explain organisational
dynamics within wider social and political structures rather
than as independent, isolated phenomena, subject to their
own 'laws'; though clearly the analysis of structural contexts
differed. Marx's account of alienated labour and Weber's
emphasis on the 'iron cage of industrial labour' share a
concern for the fragmented and dehumanised nature of work.

Weber saw that maximum formal rationality favoured economically powerful groups and their ability to use superior
resources to dictate terms and conditions in what may appear
as a freely made contract or legal equality (Brubaker, 1984:
42–3). Social tensions and sectional conflicts between different interest groups were therefore inevitable.

Where radical Weberians differ from orthodox interpretations is a rejection of Weber's fatalism about the relations
between bureaucracy and industrial societies. They do not
believe that bureaucracy is necessarily universal or inevitable,
but rather a pervasive tendency which can and must be
countered. Like some contemporary labour process theorists,
there is more emphasis on bureaucratic control as a *management strategy* (Edwards, 1979; Burawoy, 1979; Clawson,
1980). Though not unique to any system of production,
bureaucracy has to be explained through its relations with
that wider formation. Capitalist social relations dictate the
need to appropriate the means of production from workers,
not some law of bureaucratic rationalisation.

In these discussions of syntheses and overlaps between
critical perspectives, we should not lose sight of some of the
more distinctive Weberian contributions. Modern states and
enterprises involve complex functions, management of competing interests, and performance of problematic tasks according to observable rules and norms. Some of these processes are
created by and reflect specific relations of production, as in
layers of supervision whose sole function is labour control and
discipline. Certain functions may be artificially expanded and
new ones absorbed by bureaucrats themselves as a form of
self-preservation. But as Polan notes, bureaucratic forms are a
necessary object of analysis in their own right: 'Only as a
result of conceding to the bureaucracy its genuine, legitimate
and distinct functions can one begin to determine the boundaries of its powers and construct political control procedures
that may successfully police those boundaries' (1984: 71).

Weber's insights allow us to focus on a number of key areas.
Power is frequently constructed and legitimised through
'rationalisation', particularly through the expertise associated
with science and technology and what Weber described as
'control based on knowledge'. Weber identified the problem of

concentration of power through the *means of administration*: 'The bureaucratic structure goes hand in hand with the concentration of the material means of management in the hands of the master. This concentration occurs, for instance, in a well-known and typical fashion, in the development of big capitalist enterprises which find their essential characteristics in this process. A corresponding process occurs in public organisations' (1984: 33). Finally, work organisations operate on different levels and in some of these, formal control procedures are important. As Littler (1982) points out, Weberian categories are especially important in understanding the employment relationship and the career structure of officials in particular. More generally, bureaucratic procedures and rules are relevant to the analysis of processes such as recruitment, reward and promotion.

CONCLUSION

This far from exhausts available theoretical resources and overstates the degree to which analyses can be packaged under neat labels. Additionally it would be difficult to argue that the various components of a critical approach could, or even should, be synthesised into a coherent explanation of work organisations. However, despite these problems and differences, the theories discussed can be drawn on as a basic critical resource for understanding the complexity of issues involved. This view will be opposed by those who believe that 'their' theory can be hermetically sealed. That is not the view we take. In part, this is because there is some common ground. Referring to action theory and the more radical structural perspectives. Dunkerley and Salaman observe: 'Both seek to undermine the notion of inevitability in organisational structure; both seek to insert active human beings and groups and their values and interests into the complex processes which give rise to organisational structures' (1986: 93). Just as important is the extent to which, because they address different issues with different assumptions and methods, the perspectives can be *complementary*. We have seen examples of this in the way which labour process and Weberian analyses illuminate power and control through the discussion of means of production and of administration.

It is necessary to treat mainstream theory in a partly similar way, that is, as a series of overlapping perspectives sharing certain ideas and methods whilst differing on others. Some concepts and research are useful and compatible with a critical approach, others are not. None can be considered simply as 'tools of management' or embodying the values and interests of the dominant class. Such a view wrongly assumes that there is a clear set of interests that can be reflected at a theoretical level. The tortuous history of organisational theory and practice in fact reveals a consistent tension between technical-administrative perspectives such as systems theory and approaches of the human relations type. This in turn reflects the conflicting pressures to control and engage the workforce. All but the most unreflexive perspectives require some distancing from existing practices in order to act upon them in a way that will be a resource for management. Subsequent chapters in Part One aim to examine critically the complexities of those relations between organisational theories and practices, beginning with the historical development of large-scale organisations.

2

The Emergence of Large-Scale Organisations

ORGANISING THE NEW WORK FORMS

By the turn of the twentieth century, business organisations were beginning to be, 'transformed from chaotic and *ad-hoc* factories to rationalised, well-ordered manufacturing settings' (Goldman and Van Houten, 1980a: 108). This was not just a product of growth, merger and technological innovation. It was also a question of *management*. Though the trend was in its infancy, firms were beginning to move away from particularist and uneven practices towards the beginnings of an industrial bureaucracy. Indeed, the two were intimately connected given that the increasing scale of work organisation meant that it was no longer possible to rely on personal or unspecified forms of direction. Changes involved systematising and stabilising both the practices of management and the organisation of the labour process. Job hierarchies, new patterns of work supervision, measurement and reward, and greater specialisation and detailed division of labour became more characteristic of organisational life. It is important to trace the genesis and development of this industrial bureaucracy, reflecting on the theoretical issues through the writings of Weber, Taylor and others. Mainstream writings largely lack this kind of historical and comparative character. Moreover, they tend to treat managerial and organisational

47

theories as ideologies with universal effects. Of course, we haven't the space to provide a detailed business history that captures all events, variations and issues. The aim is to give a broad picture that locates ideas in context and focuses particularly on employment and labour process issues.

The Rise of the Factory System

Work processes prior to the factory system were not characterised by an extensive division of labour, nor by directly imposed coercive authority. In handicraft and domestic production, small producers were typically involved in independent commodity production, often based on the family structure. They owned their own means of production, worked according to their own patterns and sold the goods at markets. Some trades or crafts were organised through the guild system. This combined employer and employee, normally within the framework and traditional authority of apprentice, journeyman and master. Neither system was flexible enough to be an adequate basis for responding to the needs of an emergent market economy. Industrialisation and emergent capitalist production relations developed from a variety of organisational structures, including artisan production, cooperatives, centralised manufacture and the putting-out system (Berg, 1985). We want to focus mainly on the latter.

Though the site of the work remained the 'cottage', workers continued to retain their own tools and capacity to organise their own work and there was little division of labour; a relationship of wage labour was established and merchants supplied the raw materials and owned the finished product. Some historians see the putting-out system as a phase of *proto-industrialisation*. Rural workers were the ideal labour force as they were worked for less than their urban equivalents and were too isolated to organise against the merchants' pricing. New markets, sources of capital accumulation and training grounds for entrepreneurial skills also constituted important features. Berg rightly notes that this 'phase' was not universal and took different regional and other forms and had varied outcomes. But the point of transition from cottage to workshop and then factory raises crucial organisational issues.

Mainstream theory commonly asserts that the new and more complex forms of organisation, with the associated detailed division of labour and hierarchies, developed largely because they were *technically* required by the scale of production, technology and related factors. A number of writers, notably Marglin (1974) and Clawson (1980), have used specific historical evidence on the factory system to challenge this general explanation. It is directed at helping to explain why workers were deprived of control of the process and product through the centralised organisation of the factory system. A common response is to argue that the impetus was the necessity to shift from hand production to power-driven machinery located in a central source. In addition, there were the benefits of division of labour pointed to in Adam Smith's famous pin factory example.

Both Marglin and Clawson show that bringing workers together in workshops and later in the factory – for example, in the weaving and spinning trades – did not necessarily involve power-driven machinery or any other technical innovation. In fact, contrary to technological determinist arguments, '*organisational* change precedes, both historically and analytically, the technological revolution which is the foundation of modern industry' (Clawson, 1980: 57). The issue of the division of labour is more complicated. Marglin does not argue that it or hierarchy were brought into being by capitalist organisation of work. But a distinction is made between the specialisation of occupation and function that is present in any *social* division of labour, and the specific forms of specialisation involved in the putting-out system and then in the factory. The minute division of work was not necessarily more efficient; rather, it provided a role for the capitalist to play in organising production and to take a greater portion of the rewards: 'The social function of hierarchical work organisation is not technical efficiency, but accumulation' (Marglin, 1974: 62).

Given the time lapse, the evidence on this question is inevitably patchy. What, however, is beyond doubt is that though the new framework provided an impetus for technical

innovation, efficiency and technical superiority were not the
only, or even primary, reasons for the rise of factory organisation. The putting-out system allowed workers a great deal of
control over their hours, rhythm, intensity and quality of
work. Furthermore, there was a high level of embezzlement of
raw materials, as workers sought to secure a fairer return for
their labour. Historians have provided a large body of evidence that the workshop and factory were utilised as a means
of exerting discipline and control in order to facilitate capital
accumulation (Pollard, 1965; E. P. Thompson, 1967; Landes,
1969). Coercive authority could be more easily applied,
including systems of fines, supervision (for instance, the
overlooker system in textiles), the paraphernalia of bells and
clocks, and incentive payments. The employer could dictate
the general terms of work, division of labour and overall
organisational layout and design. It is not surprising that
many workers bitterly resisted entry to the factory and the
associated forms of discipline. In those early periods, employers were frequently forced to resort to groups such as
convicts, paupers and child labour.

To break such resistance, new *work habits* had to be created
appropriate to the discipline of labour, time and cash nexus at
the heart of the wage relation. Employers' concern with the
moral issues of sexuality, drink, bad language and theft was
directed less by fidelity to religious doctrine than to the
behavioural characteristics – obedience, punctuality, responsibility and performance – linked to capitalist rationality and its
new forms of organisational culture. As Clegg and Dunkerley
observe, the triumph of the formal factory organisation was
strongly determined by its 'moral machinery' (1980: 62). This
term was used by the economist Andrew Ure, noted for his
pertinent advice to employers. He and other such advisors
were, however, clear that neither the division of labour nor
work values were sufficient for the purpose of achieving the
goal of creating 'factory hands'. *Mechanisation* was necessary
to destroy old work-habits and to tie the worker to the
'unvarying regularity of the machine'.

Marx showed how workers were able to use the employers'
continuing dependence on their handicraft skills and knowledge as a weapon of resistance. In turn, Ure recognised that

the unity of capital and science was necessary to try to reduce skills to dexterities, create a technical framework independent of the producers, and reduce labour costs by *intensifying* work rather than the limited option of raising hours. Marglin's notion of the factory as a social control device independent of technology is therefore incomplete (Clawson, 1980: 54). Without these kinds of development, the formal control developed in the factory could not have been adequately realised. It is always necessary to resist the temptation to describe these processes of organisational change in finished rather than relative terms. Employer control remained at a very general level and still had to be accommodated to high levels of worker skill, knowledge and self-organisation. Work was still often labour-intensive and there were few or no bureaucratic or management structures. To explain the further development of large-scale organisation we need to focus more closely on the evolution of forms of control.

Modes of Control in the Transition to Bureaucratic Organisation

There were a number of obstacles to the development of a more bureaucratic work organisation during the nineteenth century. Even a more mature factory system rested on control structures that were inimical to moves in that direction. As Littler (1982: 69) argues, British industry presented a *spectrum* of modes of control that, despite differences, were fundamentally non-bureaucratic in nature. Using a range of evidence, three basic modes can be distinguished.

Entrepreneurial or simple control. In early factories at the beginning of the nineteenth century owners could exercise a large degree of power and control *personally*. Referring to the famous foundry owner, Bendix observes, 'Boulton maintained a personal relationship with his workers, knew their names and their families, and relied upon this relationship to ensure the discipline and work performance needed in his enterprise' (1956: 57). Exercise of authority under entrepreneurial control was therefore simple and direct, and sustained frequently by legal coercion and harsh market conditions. Even at this stage, however, it was not always possible to exert control personally. Foremen could be utilised but also, 'an important preliminary solution to the control dilemmas of divided authority was to rely on family ties' (Rueschemeyer, 1986: 57). At the required minimal level of co-ordination, the family or close friends of the entrepreneur proved sufficient. Middle managers were virtually absent; in fact, many employers were hostile and suspicious about the idea of a separate 'class' of managers.

Of course this situation could not survive a growth in the size and complexity of operations. Littler (1982) notes that the familial framework was rapidly discarded under such conditions, particularly in the USA. Nevertheless, some writers argue that direct and often despotic entrepreneurial authority remained at the centre of what Edwards (1979) describes as *simple control*. There are important qualifications to be made to the model of entrepreneurial or simple control, particularly Edwards's version. It is extremely doubtful whether it was representative of the economy until the end of the nineteenth century as he claims, rather than confined to a minority of firms (Littler, 1982: 64). In addition, though despotic authority was certainly a pervasive influence, it often had to accommodate to the power of other figures in the enterprise such as craft workers. Hence the image of the all-seeing, all-knowing employer underestimates the struggles at the frontier of control in the workplace. There is also considerable evidence that a more significant mode of control involved contracting arrangements.

Contracting. One of the main reasons why management was so slow to develop was the tendency of employers to delegate responsibility for work organisation to sub-contractors, around whom the employment relationship was constructed. We are concerned here with the internal contractor rather than the independent sub-contractor who was involved, for example, in outwork trades such as clothing and boots and shoes. Evidence from historians such as Pollard (1965) on the UK, and more recently Clawson (1980) on the USA, show that internal contracting was in extensive use in a range of industries including textiles, iron and steel, mining and transport. What did the organisation of work consist of?

> The inside contractor made an agreement with the general superintendent or owners of a company to make a part of their product and receive a certain price for each completed unit. ... Inside contractors had complete charge of production in their area, hiring their own employees and supervising the work process ... were employees of the company, and in most cases they received a day wage from the company as well. (Clawson, 1980: 71)

They accumulated considerable status and power, both in the community through patronage and in the workplace through their high income. In some cases this meant a social position and standard of living higher than company officials, and a capacity to actually pass on much of the detailed work delegated to them by the employer to assistants! Nevertheless, the intended advantages to employers were clear. Responsibility, risks and costs should be partly shifted on to contractors, thus creating greater flexibility in circumstances where managerial skills and knowledge of work operations were limited. In effect, contracting functioned as a means of transition through a period of growing enterprise, complexity and scale. It was certainly hierarchical but not bureaucratic in the sense of centralised authority, rules and record-keeping. Yet it proved capable of handling expanded output and technical innovation (Clawson, 1980). It did not encompass all industries or all labour within the firm. Newer industries such as service, process and railways were based on direct employment relations (Littler, 1982: 68).

Craft Control. Contracting is often seen as overlapping with the 'helper system', on which skilled workers were assisted by a small number of less skilled operatives. In some cases craft workers hired and paid them, thus reproducing contractual relations. However, the scale of operations was small with often just one helper; the practices were exercised by craft workers normally within a trade union framework and operated often in conjunction with foremen. In fact, the helper system is the basis for a model of craft control utilised by writers such as Stone (1973) and Montgomery (1976), in which skilled workers had the power to plan and direct immediate work processes. It is important not to exaggerate this 'partnership in production', for we are talking about a system of worker-directed *job controls*. But though not the equivalent of employer systems, such controls had a significant capacity to resist and constrain employer authority. This was put succinctly by F. W. Taylor in 1911 about his experience in the steel industry:

> As was usual then, and in fact is still usual in most shops in this country, the shop was really run by the workmen, and not the bosses. The workmen together had carefully planned just how fast each job should be done, and they had set a pace for each machine throughout the shop, which was limited to about one-third of a good day's work [i.e., the maximum possible]. Every new workman who came into the shop was told at once by the other men exactly how much of each kind of work he was to do, and unless he obeyed these instructions he was sure before long to be driven out of the place by the men. (1911: 128)

This was somewhat exaggerated in order to prove the need for Taylor's scientific management system, and particularly neglected the role and powers of the foremen. Though it varied from industry to industry there was a far more extensive range of powers and functions than for contemporaries today. The foreman's empire included substantial influence over the manner and timing of production, the cost and quality of work, and responsibility for employees often including hire and fire. They operated under similar delegated authority as inside contractors and enjoyed parallel status within and outside work. But that role must be seen within the framework of craft controls. A foreman would sometimes be a master of his trade or chief skilled worker, and would have to share or at least accommodate to the powers of craft workers and contractors.

Decay and Decline of Traditional Controls

Despite the *variety* of control relationships, each in its own way functioned as a constraint to management and bureaucracy. The shift further in this direction in the last quarter of the century again must be seen not merely in terms of gradual evolution and advance of technique. There were social contradictions as well as inefficiencies in traditional methods. Simple control is a clear case. During the period in question, the size and complexity of industrial firms increased considerably. During the last third of the century the average plant in the USA more than doubled in size and by 1900 there were 443 with more than 1000 wage earners (Nelson, 1975: 4). The impetus for change included mergers, concentration of resources, technical innovation, and shifts away from local and regional markets. In the USA this leap was particularly marked given its late entry onto the industrial stage and the relative freedom of business from social reform traditions and strong union organisation.

Such processes inevitably affected existing social relations characterised by an increasing separation of entrepreneurs and top managers from the daily activities of the workforce. Organisationally the crucial issue was a growing gap between the structures and expertise of management, and a more extensive division of labour with its requirements for new forms of control and co-ordination. For capital, the solution had to go beyond the employment of more managers, towards transforming the structures of managerial activity itself.

Problems associated with internal contracts had more to do with contradictions than straightforward inefficiencies. According to Clawson, these were in two major areas. The very fact that the company had entered into sub-contract arrangements meant that it was difficult to evaluate such activities. Contractors therefore used that power to keep employers as much in the dark as possible, aided by the fact that companies seldom kept many formal records. In addition to the income, the consequent social position of contractors was also a problem in that it was difficult for employers to motivate their own officials, who often felt inferior in power, status and rewards to the larger contractors. Craft job controls

were also a serious obstacle to employers taking full advantage
of mechanisation and expanded but more competitive markets.
As Stone notes of the steel industry:

> At the same time that their labour costs as a percentage were
> rising, the labour system also prevented employers from
> increasing their productivity through reorganising or mech-
> anising their operations. The workers controlled the plants
> and decided how the work was to be done. Employers had no
> way to speed up the workers, nor could they introduce new
> machinery that eliminated or redefined jobs. (1973: 26).

This again may be a somewhat exaggerated description,
but it helps to explain why both contracting and craft
arrangements came under increasing attack. Employers began to abolish internal contracting in order to shift income to
the company and create a hierarchy under their own control
and acceptable to their own officials (Clawson, 1980: 119).
Companies often tried to convert some of the contractors into
foremen, but many preferred to quit. The power of craft
workers was also increasingly challenged in the 1880s. A
minority of firms tried to formulate a system of co-partner-
ship, in the UK and France based largely on profit-sharing
schemes geared explicitly to ensuring loyalty to the company
(Brannen, 1983; Doray, 1988)). There were other head-on
clashes in the 1890s, including those between the Amalgamated Society of Engineers and their employers in the UK,
and major conflicts in the US steel industry, such as the
Homstead strike of 1892 (Stone, 1973).

Employers began to assert their general right to run production as they saw fit. This took a particularly virulent form
in the USA with its weaker unions, as manifested in the 'open
shop' campaign run by some employers. The predominant
measures used by capital there and elsewhere to challenge and
change existing modes of control were, however, less dramatic. An important area was to modify the role of *supervisory
labour*. This often involved breaking up the foremen's empire,
with a shift away from traditional functions such as hire-and-
fire and work organisation, towards the narrower but vital
sphere of task supervision and discipline. As Littler (1982)

shows, this was accompanied by considerable sub-division of the foreman's role. Examples include supervisory labour carrying out quality control, rate fixers, and 'feed and speed' functions. A further interrelated change was in *payment systems* which became more centrally determined, undermining the bargaining role played by foremen and contractors. In addition, piecework and bonus arrangements spread rapidly.

Significantly, the new systems required some formal standards of effort and labour management record-keeping. Payment through the office indicated a move towards a more direct employment relationship. It should, however, be noted at this stage in the battle for control of output that management techniques were generally not sophisticated enough to include time study or job analysis and were constrained by workers' initiative and knowledge. Companies frequently had to rely on the cruder measures of rate-cutting and employment of 'rate busters' to prove to the workforce that quotas could be increased.

We have already noted that such changes required an increase in *record-keeping* given the need to specify objectives and keep track of results. The administrative aspects of a management system thus began to be set in place, including that of simple cost accounting. In some companies simple organisation manuals began to appear, complete with management principles and charts (Edwards, 1979: 30). Technological changes also accompanied administrative ones. Further increases in the detailed division of labour and mechanisation were facilitated by the greater knowledge of productive processes that capital was gaining. Not only was greater output achieved, but the capacity of employers to dispense with skilled workers and exert greater controls over labour generally through standardised procedures was enhanced. As one employer remarked, 'I want machines so simple that any fool could run them' (quoted in Goldman and Van Houten, 1980a: 116). Engineering principles oriented towards treating workers as simple costs of production were therefore becoming more important than personal and direct controls.

Of course these developments were part of a broader process of the creation of the modern business enterprise.

Chandler (1977) stresses that viability was only achieved
when the 'visible hand of management' replaced the market as
a means of coordinating the flow of materials through the
economy. In other words, a managerial hierarchy was able to
supervise a large number of operating units and to co-ordinate,
monitor and plan their activities. The path to the new forms of
enterprise began in the USA with the railroads and the need
to manage their vast regional operations, but gradually spread
to other sectors. Some developed from the internal growth of
small single-unit firms who developed national and global
networks, others from mergers. The new consolidated enterprises centralised the administration of production and research facilities, and established vertical integration, attempting to control supplies and markets.

Management as a conscious and specialist activity was
enhanced by the spread of associations and journals dealing
with management methods (Clawson, 1980: 167–8). Entrepreneurial ideologies were complemented or challenged by
more professional concerns with the 'labour problem', and
direct recruitment from colleges grew, though specialist technical training was still relatively limited. In addition, a
growing army of clerical, technical and administrative employees were necessitated by new payment systems, record-
keeping and mechanisation, as well as the other growth
functions of purchasing, sales and finance. It was not just a
case of management hierarchy. By the turn of the century the
workforce was subject to structures of what Edwards (1979)
refers to as *hierarchical control*. As other writers put it:
'differential job statuses and wages for workers were an
integral component of the hierarchical nature of the industrial
pyramid' (Goldman and Van Houten, 1980a: 122). Job
ladders and individuated reward systems were also a means of
compensating for the growing homogenisation of labour by
artificially dividing the workforce (Stone, 1973).

It must be stressed that these measures were experimental
and varied in nature. Different countries and even sectors had
their own unique characteristics and influences which added
to the incoherence of transition processes (Littler, 1982). For
example, Rueschemeyer (1986) notes the significance of public
administration as a bureaucratic model for private enterprise in

Germany and other countries. In more general terms, the USA was a seed-bed for managerial capitalism primarily because of the size and the nature of the domestic market (Chandler, 1977: 498–500). It was not only faster growing than other nations, but more open and less class-divided. This encouraged the techniques and technologies of mass production and distribution. In contrast, domestic markets in Western Europe were smaller with slower growth. This limited the same kind of development and kept greater reliance on middlemen to handle goods. Even where integrated enterprises did appear, they often remained small enough to be dominated by owner-managers.

There are also specific *institutional* factors which can shape industrial development. In Britain's case, rigidity was introduced through a combination of factors. These included atomistic economic organisation, often dependent on single-plant family firms in industries such as cotton and steel; entrenched employee job controls; the separation of the banking system from finance of industry; and educational provision that failed to provide adequately trained managerial and technical staff. As a result, managerial structures and expertise were underdeveloped and 'the British only adapted patchwork improvements to their existing organisational and productive structure' (Elbaum and Lazonick, 1986: 7).

Finally, though there was a great advance in managerial organisation compared to the earlier period, even in the USA it was still very much in its infancy. There was still little systematic and long-term planning and as for work organisation, management 'was unable to make the qualitative leap to a different system because it had no alternative conception of how production should be organised' (Clawson, 1980: 168). That situation was soon to change.

CLASSICAL THEORIES AND BUREAUCRATISATION OF PRODUCTION

Taylorism and Systematic Management

The major means of change was through the work of Frederick Taylor and his 'scientific management' system. Not that

Taylorism was unique or totally new. Only time and motion study could genuinely be put in that category. A trend towards *systematic management* was already identifiable, as we have seen with instances of more formal management methods, cost accounting, standardisation of work, and use of less skilled workers. Nyland (1987: 56) comments that, 'The "systematisers" were a diverse group of engineers, accountants and works managers who argued that US firms had grown to a size where the internal functioning of the enterprise was becoming increasingly chaotic and wasteful'.

When Taylor proclaimed his new system as a 'science', some British engineers described it as common sense masquerading under a high-sounding title (Brown, 1977: 158). Understandable though the reaction was, it missed the point. Taylor was not just in the right place at the right time, he played a crucial role in *theorising* and *popularising* the new ideas. Furthermore, it was intimately connected to a body of practice, with Taylor 'Napoleon of the war against craft production' (Clawson, 1980: 202). Taylorism was therefore the most conscious part of the systematisation of management, and of the regulation and control of production.

Such developments met the needs of capital in that period (Rose, 1978: 58). This was particularly the case in the USA where larger corporations were developing higher levels of product and labour specialisation to cope with rising demand (Littler, 1982). A shift away from skilled labour towards unskilled immigrant workers was taking place, but still within the context of a relatively high wage economy. This required new forms of co-ordination, integration and control, and methods of keeping down labour costs. The orientation of larger firms towards professional managers, engineers and consultants additionally provided a supportive framework for the rise of Taylorism. Engineers were central figures and carried out wide-ranging activities, including refinements in accounting procedure (Nelson, 1975: 50). In the 1890s, Taylor began to publicise his ideas about time study and piece rates, mainly through the American Society of Mechanical Engineers, and gathered round him a group of enthusiastic adherents.

His own work was first carried out at the Midvale Steel

Works (owned by a friend of the family), in a variety of 'detective' roles ranging from unskilled labourer, machinist, clerk, gang boss, foreman, master mechanic, chief draughtsman and chief engineer. Experiments were also carried out in a small number of other firms in old and new industries. It was not just in the USA. By the First World War, 1 per cent of French as well as American firms had introduced schemes, often in new sectors such as electrical manufacturing and automobiles (Fridenson, 1978). There were similar initiatives on a smaller scale in Britain and other European countries.

Principles

Taylor was adamant that his system was a total package – one best way of organising work. Though affecting the activities of management and workers, the ideas were developed directly out of his obsession with combating the kind of workers' control of output – labelled 'soldiering' – observed at the steel works. He distinguished between natural and systematic soldiering: the former referring to the tendency to want to take it easy, the latter to practices deliberately geared to maximising rewards and job security. To solve the 'labour problem' a number of basic *management* principles were advanced.

1. Develop a science for each element of work.
2. Scientific selection and training of workers.
3. Co-operation between management and workers to ensure that the work is done according to the science.
4. Equal division of work and responsibility between management and workers, each side doing what they are best fitted for.

These sound rather bland, but their significance can only be understood when set against Taylor's description of inefficient practices. Included under this were 'rule of thumb' methods of deciding on the nature of work tasks, workers choosing their own methods of work and training and worker's knowledge being the basis of productive technique. He was particularly critical of managment by initiative and incentive where workers were given inducements to use their skills and know-how in the most economical way, *without* strict managerial determination of tasks.

Scientific management started from the belief that management had to reverse existing power relations in production: 'The management assume, for instance, the burden of gathering together all of the traditional knowledge which in the past has been possessed by the workmen and then of classifying, tabulating, and reducing this knowledge to rules, laws and fomulae' (Taylor, 1947: 36). The continual concern with rules and laws in Taylor's writings show why it can be located firmly within a process of bureaucratisation of production. As Braverman (1974: 119) makes clear, it can also be seen as a control system based on the monopolisation of knowledge by management and its use to control each step of the labour process. This 'separation of conception and execution' is clearly echoed in Taylor's comments such as, 'all possible brain work should be removed from the shop floor and centred in the planning and lay-out department' (quoted in Braverman, 1974: 113).

Other aspects of the above principles are not so prominent. Take selection. Taylor's search for workers who would follow his instructions to the letter is legendary. But despite the interest of some of his followers, explicit techniques to place the right worker in the right job remained an underdeveloped part of scientific management. What about the traditional emphasis placed in organisational behaviour on Taylorism as the model of 'economic man'? This is largely misleading. Like most of his contemporaries interested in management reform, Taylor *did* believe that workers were motivated by the pursuit of rational self-interest and incentive wages – in the form of a differential piece-rate system – were the solution to most labour problems. The tendency to restrict output, however, was seen as an unnecessary product of the absence of any scientific authority for work standards. Management could ensure co-operation on the basis of a consensus established by objective work measurement. Economic incentives could be used to overcome the hostility of workers to giving up traditional job controls. This exchange proved to be a limited and fragile basis for co-operation and certainly didn't ever eliminate restriction of output. But an instrumental view of human labour was a far cry from a complex theory of motivation. Taylor was far more concerned with breaking the power of the workgroup and removing the basis for collective bargaining through individualistic payment systems (Littler, 1982: 55).

Ideology and practice

The consequences of the operation of such principles were explicitly recognised by Taylor. There would be a need for extensive work measurement to predetermine tasks; the employment of cheaper, deskilled and substitutable labour in more fragmented jobs; a large increase in the number of non-productive employees to enforce, monitor and record new work arrangements; and functional foremanship that subdivided traditional responsibilities and involved reporting to the all-powerful planning department. It would, of course, be foolish to believe that all of this smoothly came to pass. In fact, there are a number of writers who believe that Taylorism was a *practical failure* and was not widely implemented owing largely to worker resistance and employer suspicions (Palmer, 1975; Edwards, 1979; Goldman and Van Houten, 1980a). This is often complemented by arguments that its significance is as a management *ideology* which was itself later discredited (Rose, 1978; Burawoy, 1979).

What is the balance of these two processes? We should certainly not underestimate the ideological purposes. Taylor himself emphasised the pressing need for a 'complete mental revolution' in the attitudes of the two parties. Whatever success was achieved can largely be attributed to the stress on the *scientific* character of the system, which trades on the predominantly uncritical attitudes to knowledge under such a mantle. Its technical orientation was of particular appeal and use to engineers in their struggle to establish themselves as the core management group in US industry (Armstrong, 1984). But there was a potential appeal to workers and unions from the same source: 'Under scientific management arbitrary power, arbitrary dictation, ceases; and every single subject, large and small, becomes the question for scientific investigation, for reduction to law' (Taylor, 1947: 211). The theoretical separation of authority from hierarchy was an attempt to construct some level of consent in the employment relation, and, with the increased productivity and wages from the system, was to be the basis for the co-operation promised in Taylor's principles.

In practice it never quite worked like this. As an ideology of science it strengthened management by providing 'the technocratic rationale for authority in formal organisations' (Kouzmin, 1980: 68). It was also flawed and contradictory in nature. It is strange that a science of management had to be based on knowledge and skills appropriated from workers. Of course it never was a science, but rather a control system, and has tended to be seen as a set of techniques to be countered and contested by generations of shop stewards. Even the stopwatch was admitted by Taylor to have an element of 'guesswork' in one of his weaker moments.

Most of the misunderstandings concerning the practical success of Taylorism stem from confusion of what *criteria* to employ. Many of those who see it as a failure are viewing Taylorism as a coherent and total package. This is understandable given that it coincides with Taylor's own views and his tendency to withdraw co-operation when companies refused to follow all the complexities of the schemes. But it is wrong. We need to redefine the criteria in two ways. First, as already indicated, we must consider it as part of a broader movement of systematic management that was implemented in a variety of forms. Second, it was also implemented in a *selective* manner: 'employers looked upon scientific management exactly as Taylor insisted that they should not: as an arsenal of devices designed to simplify and improve the management of labour' (Bendix, 1956: 286). All the elements were juggled about by companies according to their needs and prejudices. A close analysis of the early literature on 'Taylor firms' by Nelson (1975: 68–78) showed that none fully represented the principles set out in *Shop Management*. References to time study can be found in every firm and planning departments were widespread. But incentive payment schemes were patchy and employers found that functional foremanship embodied too many layers of responsibility.

Once these factors have been acknowledged we can recognise

a widespread, if uneven, diffusion of key aspects of Taylorist practices in industrial societies in the 1920s and 1930s (Brown, 1977; Clawson, 1980; Littler, 1982; Nyland; 1987). Taylor's death in 1915 opened the door to a variety of consultants to introduce further versions of scientific management. Some were short-cut emulators, others were Taylor's disciples such as Gantt, and the Gilbreths with their extension of Taylor's early emphasis on the study of fatigue and their advances in the use of cameras to record and time movements. This factor and changes in the external environment guaranteed that scientific management did not spread in pure form. One of the most significant combinations was with *Fordism*. Henry Ford's innovations in technical control through the flow assembly line had been directly influenced by Taylor from an early stage. But the new form of work organisation extended Taylorist principles such as job fragmentation and allowed for a greater level of intensity of labour through speed-up of the line and other measures. The scale of Ford's operations and his willingness to introduce the 'five dollar day' as a means of combatting labour turnover, enabled another of Taylor's principles – high wages for high productivity – to be realised.

Meanwhile, the most extensive implementation of neo-Taylorite schemes came through the *Bedeaux system*. Charles Bedeaux was a French full-time management consultant whose schemes were based on his 'discovery' of a universal measure for all work, given the name 'B unit'. He aggressively sold them as a cheap and quick method that did not need to have major consequences for existing management structures. Like the Gilbreths, he entered the unexplored territory of fatigue through basing the measurement on the proportions of work and rest required for completing a task. Though he had considerable international success, Bedeaux had his greatest impact in Britain where employers used the circumstances of the 1930s depression to install the system and utilise it for the purposes of rate-cutting and speed-up (Brown, 1977, Littler: 1982). This example illustrates the way that scientific management varied in both form and timing between and within countries. While Britain's late adoption differed from the American and French models, other economies such as

Germany and Sweden followed distinctive paths, for example, combining rationalisation measures with greater use of psychological testing (Fridenson, 1978).

Lack of uniformity was undoubtedly influenced by the pattern of resistance from a variety of groups. There has been well-documented resistance from craft and non-craft workers, using every method from strikes to informal disruption (Nadworny, 1955; Brown, 1977; Montgomery, 1976). Workers were particularly opposed to effects such as deskilling and speed-up because, as one put it, he 'never knew a rate to be raised after a time study' (quoted in Baritz, 1960: 98). But the plain fact is that resistance did not succeed in stopping the long-term diffusion of scientific management, though it certainly delayed and mediated it. This is often put down to the gradual shift in union attitudes from opposition to reluctant accommodation and occasional enthusiastic co-operation. There is a great deal of truth in this assessment, though some unions had always had a conciliatory attitude, and the behaviour of official structures should not be confused with rank-and-file members who continued resistance. Indeed, the very institutionalisation of scientific management guarantees that it is accompanied by a low-intensity war at shopfloor level.

Changes of this kind were influenced by later progressive Taylorites who lacked his hostility to trade unions and were prepared to give them an institutionalised role in work study and bonus schemes. Scientific management could also be given a progressive aura by its association with planning, Nyland (1988) showing that some of its adherents advocated the extension of the system to the whole society constraining the role of markets. He also correctly points to the neglect of Taylorism's wider capacity to improve work efficiency in the spheres of scheduling, stores management and purchasing, and plant lay-out; though whether this is enough to commend Taylorism despite the control dimension is more arguable.

Supervisory and managerial resistance also continued to be a considerable constraint both in the USA and Britain (Nelson, 1975: 75–6; Littler, 1982: 181–2). New schemes tended not only to change traditional roles, but eroded decision-making powers. Employers and managers often found it hard to embrace Taylorism wholly. Taylor was often bitterly critical of their competence. It challenged their traditional judgement, discretion and powers, to say nothing of straining their patience through contract stipulations that the company must do as exactly as he told them. The high costs, disrupted routines and social antagonisms meant that failure was more often linked to managerial opposition than that of workers.

Given the evidence, the problem of Taylorism is not *whether* it was introduced but its *limits* as a control system. Right from the start many employers realised that Taylor's neglect of 'the human factor' and of what Friedman (1977) calls 'the positive aspects of labour' such as know-how and goodwill, made it impossible to use it on its own. We will return to the combination with psychological methods later, but even as a means of bureaucratisation of production, Taylorism was insufficient.

Weber and Administrative Theories of Management

For some writers, the concept of bureaucratisation of production is a problematic one. Braverman (1974: 120) objects that it endorses the mistaken view such work arrangements are endemic to large-scale organisation rather than a product of capitalist social relations. We have already made our position clear in Chapter 1. Bureaucratisation *is* a universal tendency but can only be understood through the specific forms it takes in different modes of production. But there is a different point at stake. Braverman's influential theory of the labour process is constructed on the implicit assumption that what we have been describing as bureaucratisation could be fully represented by Taylorism. What Taylorism provided was a system of detailed control over work, aided by a set of bureaucratic rules. Clawson (1980: 248) argues that this is in contrast to Weber's stress on the remote and impersonal qualities of bureaucracy.

We will return to this question later. For now it is sufficient to observe that Taylorism had far less to say about the *employment relationship*: 'those structural conditions which surround the appointment, promotion and dismissal of individuals' (Littler, 1982: 37). While scientific management was meant to be applied at any given level of task or technology it 'left management in the position of having a set of principles laying down how to make its workforce more productive, whilst possessing no body of knowledge that specifically applied from supervisory levels upward in the organisational hierarchy' (Clegg and Dunkerley, 1980: 99). This was particularly important in the context of the previously observed growth of middle management, who were monitoring the performance of the operating units under their command but were not subject to systematic evaluation themselves. It is Weber and other theorists of formal management and administration who can give us a greater understanding of developments of this nature.

In common with most other writers, we do not intend to list all the complex features of bureaucracy which Weber includes as defining characteristics, but instead group them under two headings:

The employment relationship. The office is a vocation and a full-time undertaking. Officials are selected on a basis of technical qualification, education and expertise. Separation of office and office holder: it is not his property and the employee does not possess the means of administration. Thorough and expert training as part of the conditions of employment.

A career structure is provided based on the organisational hierarchy. Tenure is for life, fixed salary, pension rights and appropriate social status. Officials are appointed by higher authority, not externally elected, and promotions similarly regulated, for example, through seniority.

Work structures and relations. A hierarchy of offices: continuous and regulated activity within a fully ordered system of super- and subordination. Within the chain of command, a division of labour based on defined responsibilities, rights and duties. Calculable rules and regulations, impersonal modes of conduct and a common control-system governing the conduct of work. Written documentation as a basis of management of the office.

From these characteristics it is understandable that some may question their links to the *bureaucratisation of production*. After all, the impetus for Weber's analysis came primarily from the organisation of the state and the regulation of administrative employees. The historical context is also important for under-standing the significance of measures such as full-time work as a vocation. In the period under consideration, it was still important to break away from patrimonial, charismatic and other relations whereby people could be placed in a position through inheritance and similar 'private' attributes. The emphasis on calculable rules and regulations may also seem a bit abstract. But both examples remind us that the ideal type of bureaucracy is linked to the wider theory of rationalisation (discussed in Chapter 1) in which bureaucracies are a specific type of rational-legal authority. Officials work within a frame-work in which command and task are based on authority derived from impersonal rules.

But Weber's theories are not as separate from production as they may appear. He made it clear that they referred to bureaucratic *management* as well as administration. The Weberian 'causal chain' (Collins, 1986: 21–9) links the concept of rationality explicitly to the emergence of capitalist enterprise and markets. These were held to be rational because of their capacity for calculability, predictability and routinisation – through production, distribution, accounting and market-pricing mechanisms. Preconditions for this 'rationalised' capitalism started from the complete private appropriation of the means of production, which Weber said must be un-hampered by 'irrational obstacles' such as workers' rights to participate in management. In addition, there was the need for common management, free labour under the compulsion of the 'whip of hunger', mass markets, minimal trade restric-tions, and institutional, legal support from the bureaucratic state.

Weber also argued that large capitalist enterprises were becoming 'unequalled modes of strict bureaucratic organisa-tion' (Weber, 1984: 32). He was aware and approved of the role played by scientific management in this process. It was 'completely' the ideal vehicle for the necessary imposition of military discipline in the factory given its capacity for dehumanisation and conditioning of work performance. Techniques such as Taylor's 'shop cards' which specified the daily routines of employees were ideal vehicles of bureaucratisation. On reflection, it is therefore possible to see that Weber's schema is not only compatible with Taylorism; the associated practices can reinforce systems of work control. Formal structures of management enhance centralisation of power. Hierarchical organisation aids functional specialisation, task fragmentation and labour discipline, while emphasis on predictable performance minimises the discretion of employees.

But, as Littler (1982) argues, it is in the sphere of the employment relationship that Weber adds something new. The career structure linked to the bureaucratic hierarchy strengthens a commitment to the organisation absent from Taylorism. A specific form of bureaucratic motivation is also sustained by the identification of job security, status, rewards and performance to organisational structure. Employees may react against the bureaucratisation of control embodied in rules prescribing the way a task is performed, but welcome rules governing selection, training and promotion within the employment relationship. Nor is it necessarily confined to office administration. As we indicated in Chapter 1, some modern radical theorists argue that employers are increasingly turning to strategies of bureaucratic control for the shop floor. Edwards's research on companies such as Polaroid, IBM and General Electric points to two crucial features of the strategy. There is a finely graded stratification and division of the workforce, the hierarchical structures devised to divide and conquer, tending to 'break up the homogeneity of the firm's workforce, creating many seemingly separate strata, lines of work, and focuses for job identity' (1979: 133). In addition, impersonal rules form the basis of company policy. Detailed and specified criteria for job descriptions and performance are monitored by supervisors, rather than work tasks being directly enforced. The stress is on positive incentives in performance, not negative sanctions. Taken together with the job security and 'career' structure through job hierarchies, long-term identification with the company can be built.

Hence, contrary to Clawson's view, impersonality and 'remoteness' can be an effective control mechanism. This kind of use of Weberian categories as explanatory tools indicates their continuing relevance, but also their limitations. Clearly bureaucratic structures have no universal rationality. Rather, they are in part consciously constructed by employers for specific purposes that cannot be reduced to 'efficiency'. A further qualification needs to be made in relation to the *legitimacy* arising from bureaucratic systems. Undoubtedly they can generate loyalty and commitment. But the position of shopfloor workers is not comparable to the higher officials of a public organisation such as the civil service, which provides long-term security and stable career structures with a minimum conflict of interests. Private companies are seldom able to match those kinds of condition and the centrality of the wage-effort bargain will always tend to introduce uncertainty and conflict into the employment relationship.

Insights derived from Weberian theory have been applied in Britain and the USA from the late 1940s. But companies were able to draw on parallel developments in classical management theory in the inter-war period. Other theorists of formal organisation were, like Weber, concerned to tackle the administration of the whole enterprise. By far the most significant was Fayol, a Frenchman who shared the engineering and management background of Taylor. 'Fayolism' inspired, amongst others, the reorganisation of railway and engineering companies, and department stores in France (Fridenson, 1978), and translation of his short text enabled wider influence. His main concern was to establish the validity of studying and training management itself, not just the management of others. Emphasis was put on formulating general features of management, first in the form of five elements – planning, organising, commanding, co-ordination and control: – then through fourteen principles. The themes contained in the latter echo and extend Taylor and Weber, including division of work, stability of tenure, authority of command and subordination of the individual interest to the general (for the full list see Pugh, 1963: 66). One principle, that of unity of command, differed sharply from Taylor's belief in functional authority.

The basis of the approach in Fayol and other similar theorists such as Gullick and Urwick was oriented to rationalising management structures, often through centralisation and specified spans of control; emphasis on the managerial role in setting and securing goals; and planning for the optimal use of resources. Meanwhile, the 'visible hand' that had brought the new corporate structures into existence was being extended to defining the role and specific tasks of top management (Chandler, 1977). The context was a further centralisation of administration, often within new multidivisional structures such as those at General Motors. This process included uniform accounting and statistical controls, evaluating managerial performance and long-range planning.

Modern management takes many of these things for granted, which leads some to invest Fayol's theorising with a high status and lasting effect. In fact, his work was more of a practical guide with simple 'plan-ahead proverbs' (Perrow, 1979: 70) akin to today's numerous management handbooks. Later writers are more likely to prefer the judgement of Clegg and Dunkerley that 'the "principles" are neither universally empirically applicable, nor theoretically coherent' (1980: 103). But even in their own time the continuing neglect by classical theories of the informal dimensions of organisational life left gaps that had to be filled.

SOCIAL SCIENCE AND INDUSTRY: A COURTSHIP

'Increasingly the men who manage and direct industry, find themselves incapable of effectively controlling their organisations'. This is how Baritz (1960: 3) begins his brilliant account of the historical uses of social science in American industry. Managers had, by the early part of the twentieth century, already drawn on the expertise of people like Taylor and other consultants. But there had been little sign of embracing the emergent social sciences. This began to change in the period after the First World War when some major US corporations began financing industrial psychology and endowing business schools as part of a process of research and experimentation. Moves towards co-operation with social scientists arose from the same process as links with Taylorism; the vulnerability of management to the appeal of *planning* and *science*.

Enter the Human Factor

The instrumental attitudes of employers to any theories perceived to be of immediate use can be seen in the favourable attitude adopted towards the battery of tests and measurements offered to fit people to jobs (see Chapter 8 for more detail). This kind of intervention represented a version of Taylor's 'scientific selection of the worker' by other means. In fact, the *Bulletin of the Taylor Society* carried articles discussing issues of human personality and arguing that newly recruited workers should be tested for personality, character and temperament (Doray, 1988). Far from being different academic species, it is arguable that human relation's thought partly derived from a form of Taylorist revisionism. Nevertheless, the battle cry of 'neglect of the human factor' was directed against the costs of scientific management in terms of resistance and disenchantment. The simple appeal and apparent applicability of the variety of tests convinced a growing minority of employers. Problems arose when naive enthusiasm and unrealistic expectations quickly ran up against the crude nature and limited results arising from the techniques. By the mid-1920s, and in changed economic circumstances, the tests had been abandoned by most companies (Baritz, 1960: 71).

Accounts of the development of British industrial psychology (Rose, 1975: 65–87; Brown, 1977: 213–28) show it to be more sober, centralised, less consultancy-based and affecting even fewer firms. It took a particular interest in monotony derived from experiences of the Industrial Fatigue Research Board during the war. Fatigue was, as we have seen, an issue which also concerned the scientific management movement, linked as it was to the need for the successful measurement of work. Common interests and client relations again meant, as in the USA, 'a large proportion of their problems had to be taken over from the scientific managers' (Rose, 1975: 86). But despite sharing some common assumptions about efficiency, productivity and work organisation, British researchers established a distance from Taylorism.

Myers perceptively noted the hostility generated among workers by scientific management through its attack on skills, and the effects of speed-up and time and motion study. He made attacks on the notion of 'one best way', rightly pointing to the greater complexity of behaviour and industrial conditions. This critique was linked to a more sympathetic consideration of the need to convince the trade unions of the validity of social science interventions, and to win more generally the consent of the workforce. The relatively progressive stance of British industrial psychologists is further illustrated by their alliance with a small group of employers centred on the Quaker families, such as Rowntree, who shared their enthusiasm for 'scientific planning' and dislike for the harsher aspects of Taylorism. When those companies began to utilise psychologists, however, there was still considerable suspicion and resistance from employees, particularly when it was introduced at the same time as scientific management methods (Brown, 1977: 216). The Quaker tapestry firm, Lee's, divided the managerial responsibility for 'psychology' and Taylorist 'mechanics' between the owner's two sons (Johnson and Moore, 1986). Most British employers, however, still preferred to cut costs simply by squeezing wages and exploiting favourable market circumstances.

But industrial psychology was not as isolated a phenomenon as it appeared. Particularly in the USA it was part of a wider period of experimentation involving human relations and Taylorist management, as employers chose within and between the new techniques. Edwards (1979: 102) gives an interesting example of the Bancroft textile company employing a consultant to introduce welfare work in 1902 and Taylor's follower Gantt to reorganise production in 1905! *Welfarism* was a significant part of that context. A paternalistic concern for the well-being of employees in return for loyalty and hard work had a long pedigree in some companies. Company towns were one manifestation, as employers provided houses, schools, stores, sanitation and lighting in order to attract an adequate labour force.

But welfare work was also present in conventional circumstances. An increasing number of firms began to employ welfare secretaries whose role ranged from encouraging a 'proper moral atmosphere' to the provision of social and medical facilities. This interest was not philanthropic –

'Capital will not invest in sentiment' as one leading employer put it (quoted in Nelson, 1975: 104). It arose from attempts to grapple with the recruitment and motivation problems deriving from the increasing size of the labour force and a new industrial relations situation shaped by declining loyalty and rising unrest. There was a parallel development in the growth of employment or personnel departments as a means of dealing 'scientifically' with such issues – again showing an overlap with Taylorism. In the USA and Britain professional personnel bodies grew from the seeds of welfare work.

But in the latter country, welfarism was strongly connected to the study of fatigue in the laboratory of wartime factories. As in the USA, British welfarism was described by one of its leading members as combining 'pity and profit' (quoted in Brown, 1977: 185). Lee's issued 'partnership certificates' to employees who had shown a genuine interest in the company. Many workers, particularly the women who were its prime object, saw its motivation as directed primarily towards the latter, given the emphasis on improving conditions for the sole purpose of maximising output. After the war, changing economic circumstances saw the decline of welfare initiatives. But in the USA, to a greater extent than Britain, there was a broader framework of 'welfare capitalism'. Companies such as General Electric, International Harvester and US Steel continued policies of off-the-job benefits in the form of insurance, health, pensions, social clubs, profit-sharing schemes and other measures (Edwards, 1979: 91–7).

But the process took many different forms. Take Ford, for example. The company had only limited social provision, but it had social control potential. The 'Sociological Department' had investigators who were empowered to visit homes to check on absentees and monitor an employee's family, values and habits. But this social control mechanism did not exist in abstract. To act as a counterweight to the assembly line and associated problems of labour turnover and unionisation, Ford had profit-sharing schemes and the famed five-dollar-day. The Department could therefore ascertain the 'fitness' of workers for these generous rewards!

In a period in which space was opened up for employers by defeated industrial militancy and repression of socialist organising, welfarism in the USA also had close ties to the development of *company unions*. This was different from the kind of enterprise unions initiated more recently by Japanese employers. The former arose primarily from wartime attempts to institute limited forms of worker representation such as works councils. After the war many large companies, often utilising their new personnel departments, were quick to consolidate this trend by initiating company unions as a focus for formal grievance procedures which alleviated the need for independent union representation (Edwards, 1979: 106). There was some success in delaying or undermining unionism and employers learnt some significant lessons on the import-ance of controlled employee involvement and formal pro-cedures. But as in Britain, little survived the economic changes associated with the growing depression with its sharpening social polarisation. Company unionism and wel-farism did not provide an adequate means of pursuing collec-tive interests of workers, while at the same time they became a financial burden for employers without solving any of their fundamental control problems inside the factory.

Hawthorne and Beyond

The Hawthorne studies occupy a pivotal place in organisational theory. Begun in the mid-1920s, the research was carried out in the large Hawthorne plant employing 29,000 workers and making electrical appliances for Bell as a subsidiary of Ameri-can Telegraph and Telephone (AT&T), Management re-garded themselves as progressive, but this was with regard to a willingness to experiment rather than their general attitudes for they were strongly anti-union. The significance of Haw-thorne is not because of the results of the research as such, for both its findings and methods are widely regarded as highly questionable (Carey: 1967; Silver: 1987). Rather, it reflects two factors. First, the *sustained* nature of the intervention itself, combining psychologists, sociologists and anthro-pologists. In this way the courtship between social science and industry became something of a formal engagement. Second, the *interpretation* of the results became the core of *human relations* theory and subsequent managerial practices. This was partly due to the propagandising work of Elton Mayo (1946), despite the fact that he did not join the team properly until 1928 and was much more peripheral than those who actually wrote up the detailed research, such as Roethlisberger and Dickson (1939) and to a lesser extent Whitehead (1938).

Let us retrace these steps briefly. Early experiments centred on varying the lighting for two small test groups of women workers. The purpose was to identify conditions affecting worker performance. Unfortunately no firm conclusions could be drawn, as productivity increased under *every* level of illumination and even for the control group that was not being subjected to any changes at all! At the time this caused great puzzlement, but it was later theorised that the real change had been the segregation of a small group, which blossomed under special attention and treatment. Thus the 'Hawthorne Effect' was born, through which it was recognised that the research intervention itself is an independent variable in its effects on human behaviour. Initially the puzzlement led to a further stage of experiments on groups of women selected for their degree of friendship with one another. Again the emphasis was on manipulation of environmental variables, this time of a greater variety: rest pauses, length of working day, group bonus schemes and so on. Observers, initially placed in a test room, were gradually encouraged to act like supervisors and become more friendly with the group. Until 1929, in almost *all* cases output rose, with the only consistent factor again being the effects of creating a special group with its identity strengthened by the replacement of two 'unco-operative' members. However, worker interest in experiments declined and output fell with the onset of the depression. Furthermore, additional experiments with two other groups to test further the effects of incentives and rest pauses had inconclusive results, both experiments being discontinued amidst some discord.

All this confusion might appear to be grounds for giving up. But a more positive line was taken, that a constant factor was the significance of employee attitudes and the influence of supervisory techniques upon them. Even while the above experiments were going on, the company and researchers had initiated an interviewing programme to explore the relations between employee morale and supervision. 'Counsellors' were trained by researchers to play the role of the observers in the illumination phase. Over a long period of time a variety of formal and more open-ended techniques of interviewing were utilised as a means of gaining information and of detecting, diverting and redirecting dissatisfactions. The counsellor was told by the company 'to watch constantly for signs of unrest and to try to assuage the tension of the worker by discussion before the unrest became active' (quoted in Fischer, 1984: 182). Management did not act on complaints and were mostly not even told of them. Aside from letting off steam, the process could also be used to adjust employees to the work situation and screen out effective counsellors as management material.

A final phase of research linked together the concern with employee attitudes and the earlier focus on the group. The famed 'bank wiring room' experiments were based on an existing workgroup who were carrying out wiring, soldering and inspecting tasks with a supposedly unobtrusive observer present. What was 'discovered' on the face of it was no different from Taylor's observations in the steel industry: the workgroup systematically controlled and restricted output on the basis of their own conception of a fair day's work and enforced group norms on any fellow workers who deviated by overproducing (ratebusters) or underworking (chisellers). The interpretation and reaction was, however, sharply different. Despite the restrictions, cliques and hostilities, a more accommodating picture of group identities was endorsed. Instead of suppressing the group and attempting to individualise its members, the human relations approach is concerned to cultivate its sentiments and switch its loyalties to management. Roethlisberger and Dickson note, 'It is as well to recognise that informal organisation is not "bad", as it is sometimes assumed to be' (1984: 93). As it is fruitless to try and destroy it, management's task is to achieve a greater harmony of the informal and formal organisation. This can be done through controlled participation, effective communication and socially skilled, humane supervision. Referring to the experience of one of the Hawthorne experimental groups, Mayo commented that 'Before every change of program, the group is consulted. Their comments are listened to and discussed; sometimes their objections are allowed to negative a suggestion. The group undoubtedly develops a sense of participation in the critical determination and becomes something of a social unit' (quoted in Baritz, 1960: 88–9).

As an alternative managerial *tactic* this makes a lot of sense; indeed, a minority of British employers were reaching similar conclusions (Brown, 1977: 243). Today, it is applied in a new and more sophisticated way in current Japanese management techniques (see Chapter 5). The problem arises from how Mayo and the human relations tradition theorised their understanding of Hawthorne. They were determined to fashion a general theory of behaviour in organisations. Later management theorists have dubbed a key element of this approach 'social man' (Schein, 1965). For Mayo, this started from a critique of the so-called 'rabble hypothesis' he attributed to economists and management theorists such as Taylor, in which individuals act solely according to rational self-interest. In contrast, 'social man' proceeds from the assumption that the major human need is for social solidarity which can be satisfied through group association. Naturally, this downplays the role of economic incentives. Such associations are seen to create social routines which substitute for logical and individual self-interest. Mayo preferred the term 'non-logical' to irrational, but the essential message is clear: workers act according to sentiments and emotions.

Contrary to some accounts, he did not believe that management was by definition and contrast rational, for all individuals were held to be governed by the same abstract instincts and needs. Rather, managers and administrators could *become* rational precisely because they can free themselves from social routines and the accompanying emotional involvements. This is an extremely curious notion as any analysis of management shows that it has *its own* routines and 'illogicalities'. But it indicates the uncritical attitude of human relations writers towards the economic élites. Interestingly, the new theorists of corporate culture (see Chapter 6) manage to maintain the emphasis on emotions, symbolism and 'irrationality' without separating management and workforce in the same way.

It must also be said that the empirical basis for Mayo's

assertions in the Hawthorne experience is very shaky. Group solidarity was carefully engineered through the selection and treatment of those workers involved, even to the point of replacing 'unco-operative' workers. Even this did not sustain co-operative activity. Mayo interpreted restriction of output as a combination of group sentiments and lack of trust in management. But there are alternative and simpler explanations: 'Restriction of output by voluntary norms was a rational response by primarily economically oriented agents to the increasingly likely prospect of unemployment' (Clegg and Dunkerley, 1980: 131). This neglect of the socio-economic context was also due to the 'closed-system' nature of human relations analysis discussed in Chapter 1. Environmental influences on employee attitudes are recognised; however, it is held that the consequences could be dealt with and 'adjusted' inside the enterprise.

The denial of economic factors led to some absurd psychologisms. Mayo used the curious term 'pessimistic reveries' to account for industrial unrest of any kind. Put another way, strikes and other actions that restrict output are obsessive preoccupations and signs of maladjustment, even to the point of identifying industrial unrest with mental breakdown and casting trade union leaders as psychological deviants! Not surprisingly, unions very rarely get mentioned in Mayo's writings. That didn't stop later followers. The psychologist McMurry argued that unions were unnecessary when management acted fairly and workers joined unions not to protect their jobs and improve pay but because of unconscious cravings to improve the emotional situation at work (Baritz, 1960: 175).

It would, however, be misleading to view human relations through its excesses. To add to 'social man', a second highly influential level of theorisation emphasised the essentially co-operative nature of the enterprise. In fact, the two were linked as Mayo continually referred to the supposed eager desire of workers for co-operative activity. It is easy to dismiss this kind of analysis, particularly given the capacity of human relations researchers to systematically ignore or reinterpret conflictual processes. But they *had* identified significant changes in the socio-economic sphere that brought the issue of

co-operation to the fore. They pointed to the disparity between the attention paid to technical efficiency and economic
functions, and the absence of 'the development of skills and
techniques for securing co-operation' (Roethlisberger and
Dickson, 1984: 87). The need to improve the latter was
especially important because, as Mayo recognised, the
balance between technical and social skills had been disrupted
as workers' traditional forms of craft socialisation and identity
had been undermined by mechanisation and the assembly
line.

Emphasis is therefore put on the role of management to use
the *formal* organisation to intervene in the *informal* in order to
create and sustain consent. Only in this context can we understand what appear to be the superficial solutions of human
relations practices, with their prescriptions of 'democratic'
supervision, good communications, teamwork and socially
skilled leadership. Mayo's 'lifelong obsession with social harmony' (Rose, 1975: 115) was not based merely on his distorted
empirical observations but was underwritten by an organic
model of society in which equilibrium and stability are the
natural order of things, while structural divisions and conflicts
are pathological. This is based on the Durkheimean tradition
discussed in Chapter 1, and, like Durkheim, Mayo is concerned more with what society *should* be like than what it is in
reality. Just as Durkheim observed anomie due to the form
taken by the division of labour, so Mayo worried about the
'extensive maladjustment of our times' as a *later* period of
rapid change also transformed values and atomised individuals. The task was to recreate a sense of community
inside the workplace, a call we are again hearing from
advocates of corporate culture.

During the same period, Chester Barnard, the President of
New Jersey Bell Telephone Company, was developing an even
heavier emphasis on the basis for human co-operation that
was to have a major impact on later mainstream theorists
(Perrow, 1979). Co-operation necessary to the survival of
society could be most clearly observed in organisations.
Unequal power and resources were irrelevant against the
'fact' that individuals voluntarily entered and submitted
themselves to a common goal unachievable without collective

effort. Organisations were rational and individuals were not. But this virtual deification of the formal organisation, like Mayo, still reserved the key role for management. The rationality of the 'non-personal' organisation was in practice again located with the executive élite who, as decision-makers, had responsibility for what Peters and Waterman, in praising Barnard, describe as 'managing the values of the organisation' (1982: 26). For co-ordination was still required to *make* a system, particularly as a sense of common purpose was not always present amongst the 'lower participants'. Barnard therefore reinforced the emphasis, not just on co-operation, but on the balance of formal and informal. As Perrow points out, this is the most extreme identification with the formal organisation, devoid of the concern shown in Weber for the negative effects of power and domination, and the stress in human relations on sympathetic supervision and controlled participation.

Evaluation

Recognising the significance of co-operative activity was an advance, but it was wrong to transfer the analysis from the workgroup to the organisation as a whole. The fundamental contradiction at the heart of human relations and of Barnard is that co-operation, even of the 'spontaneous' kind, has to be created. Reed refers to an intellectual schizophrenia whereby 'a theoretical framework is forced to reconcile the contradictions generated by a metaphysic that assumes collective moral consensus as a social given and at the same time advocates the adoption of techniques whereby this may be engineered' (1985: 6). There is, therefore, a wide consensus among the critics we have discussed that the significance of the tradition is to be located in its *ideological appeal*. Rose (1975: 124) puts this most succinctly in his memorable comment that Mayoism is the twentieth century's most seductive managerial ideology in which social scientists and managers fashioned each other in their own image.

There is a great deal of accuracy in the view that one of its major functions was to legitimate the power and authority of both emergent professional 'classes' of managers and industrial consultants. The problem is that such an analysis can slip into giving the impression that human relations was a gigantic, if dangerous, con-trick with no purchase on reality. In part the reverse is true, for it only makes sense as a reaction to and means of shaping new realities. The depth of economic and political crisis meant that 'by the 1930s corporate America felt under siege' (Neimark and Tinker, 1986: 25). Congress had passed corporatist legislation allowing companies greater control over markets and pricing in return for acceptance of codes governing minimum wages and maximum hours, plus guarantees of union membership and collective bargaining rights. In addition, the country was experiencing a huge strike wave of sit-down strikes and factory occupations. Large corporations bitterly resisted the 'New Deal' institutions and the union organising drive. But the more perceptive of them also realised that 'the crisis generated critical problems of social control and legitimation for management' (Boreham, 1980b: 25). A second front was opened, drawing extensively on the human relations package of better communication, democratic leadership, co-operation and social integration. This went hand-in-hand with early versions of the managerial revolution thesis, General Motors claiming that the organisation was a community of stakeholders for which management was a trustee.

The success of strikes and union-organising drives only consolidated a recognition of the importance of consent and attention to employee attitudes in the more general writings of human relations theorists such as T. N. Whitehead in his *Leadership in a Free Society* (1936). Despite the weakness of the tradition in Britain, Whitehead's book was well received in progressive management circles who were worried about the changing position of business in a more democratic community. Human relations was able to provide greater legitimation of management authority than Taylor because it went beyond the narrow confines of 'science' and formal organisation to address issues more in tune with the times. But it would not have made the same impact merely as a body of ideas. It had to help generate new *practices*.

Though still confined to a minority of even the largest

employers throughout the 1930s, Bendix, Baritz and other researchers show that an increasing number of firms such as General Electric, General Motors and Procter and Gamble developed programmes influenced by human relations. Greater emphasis was placed on training of managers and supervisors in the arts of intensive communication, social skills and non-authoritarian leadership that would motivate as well as command. Personnel departments grew further alongside more use of attitude surveys. General Motors managed neatly to combine them with spying on union activists by employing Pinkerton detectives to carry out the tests! As previously, the war acted as a spur, large companies and the state finding the use of tests an invaluable means of dealing with the problems associated with sudden employment of thousands of new workers.

Despite a sustained attack by more critical academics, the diverse applications and effects of human relations had established a bridgehead for the social sciences in industry. The 1950s saw that relationship blossom further. Not that there was always an exact and direct relationship between theory and practice. Perrow, for example, has written sceptically of the 'thirty year history of the effort to link morale and leadership to productivity' (1979: 97). Nor were the practices or solutions necessarily any less superficial than Hawthorne. Bendix (1956: 326–7) remarks that the National Association of Manufacturer's new-found attachment to 'two-way communication' was based on the assumption that employers relayed *facts* to the workforce to promote co-operation, whereas what workers say is *information* which management can use to 'eliminate understandings'.

But an extensive body of research and to a lesser extent practical intervention did build up, extending key human relations themes in areas such as leadership styles and group dynamics. They acted to provide, in Bendix's words, a new *vocabulary of motivation*, and as language is a fundamental part of social practice, it is a further indication of the significant role of human relations, whatever limits there have been to its ideas and results. Furthermore, the tradition which had lain dormant and often been abused for its naivety suddenly became fashionable again in the 1980s. The influence in particular of Japanese management techniques, with their emphasis on teamwork, workgroups and corporate cultures, brought human relations back into focus. That story is told in Chapters 5 and 6.

3

Organisations and the Environment

The previous chapter provides plenty of evidence that the *contexts* in which organisations operate, whether they be the rise of monopoly capitalism, the ups and downs of the trade cycle, or political circumstances such as the New Deal, profoundly shape their nature and development. But does this figure prominently in conventional organisational theory? Salaman argues that it does not:

> The society in which these organisations occur, and its relation with these organisations, has been very little studied. To the extent that the outside world does impinge on the structure and functioning of organisations, it is conceptualised not in terms of interests, values, class loyalties, ideologies, market developments etc., but as the organisation's 'environment'. (1979: 32)

Given that environment can be taken to mean external conditions which could encompass all the above, there is nothing in principle distinctive or problematic with the concept. Clearly, however, environment means more than that in Organisation Theory, and the main purpose of this chapter is to trace those meanings and to discuss the issues they raise.

It is conventional wisdom in such theory to argue that early or classical perspectives took no account of the environment. Instead, they were concerned with manipulating the internal variables of an organisation in the service of goal attainment.

Specific emphasis tended to be put on the development of rules or principles maximising the rational and efficient application of resources embodies in work design and other aspects of formal structure. Because this treats organisations as self-sufficient entities, or systems in and of themselves, it has been retrospectively dubbed *closed systems theory* (see Clegg and Dunkerley, 1980: 191–6). Human relations theory too, has been criticised for suspending the firm in a social vacuum and ignoring the degree to which its problems were results of outside pressures (Albrow, 1973: 406). This is somewhat unfair. Researchers such as Mayo and Roethlisberger and Dickson did recognise the effects on employees from membership of wider collectivities such as communities. The problem was more that they and their less discriminating followers tended to believe the *solutions* could be found through internal adjustment.

If anything, the supposedly more sophisticated *neo-human relations* perspectives of Maslow, Herzberg and others were more 'guilty' of closed system thinking. Their emphasis on a model of universal psychological needs that, once identified by the intelligent manager, could be harnessed through new forms of organisational design, completely isolated the individual and the firm from social structure (see Chapters 5 and 7 for further discussion). Since the 1960s, closed systems approaches have largely been frowned upon. However, that does not mean that they have gone away. Because the focus is overwhelmingly on the *individual* organisation, there is a tendency for theorists to highlight internal and predictable goals-means relationships that can, in fact, operate as a 'buffer' to the environment. (Hall: 1977). The search for the magical ingredient to organisational success which can be internally controlled also increases the likelihood of a constant reworking, or accommodation to a closed system approach. The latest is the fashionable concern for organisational culture, expressed through the writings of Peters and Waterman (1982) and their many imitators on both sides of the Atlantic.

Peters and Waterman utilise a schema derived from Scott (1978), in which four stages of theory proceed through closed system/rational actor (Weber/Taylor); closed system/social actor (human relations of all kinds); rational actor/open system (e.g. Lawrence and Lorsch – see later); to the favoured open system/social actor. We have already argued in Chapter 1 that the authors do *not* depart significantly from a rational model, and would make a similar point with reference to closed systems. The whole selling point of the excellence genre is that the strategy and structure themes discussed in this Chapter are out, and culture, style, symbols and values are in (see Chapter 6 for a more detailed assessment). Successful companies are those which create and manage a distinctive culture that satisfies employees and customers alike. If we examine their four elements of new theory (Peters and Waterman, 1982: 102) – people's needs for meaning, elements of control, positive reinforcement and behaviour determinant of belief – they are largely psychologistic in character. The cultural solution is secured *within* the organisation.

Now this is admittedly not the whole picture. The environment *is* recognised through the notion that successful companies emerge through purposeful, though unpredictable, evolution. Though the Darwinian imagery of experiment and evolution is invoked, the message is simple. Companies survive and stay fit and well by adapting to their environment. It appears that the essence of that environment is the customer. The logic is that successful companies are those which have a large market share, long-term growth and high profits. They have adapted to the (customer) environment. Success is therefore simply read-off from a diffuse concept of the environment. But we are still returned to internal organisational processes, for what made them successful in the first place 'was usually a culture that encouraged action, experiments, repeated tries' (1979: 114). This is what Peters and Waterman mean by 'intentionally seeded evolution within companies'.

One final point needs to be made about the issue of closed systems. The use of the term *systems* is not accidental. It refers to systems theory discussed in Chapter 1. Such theory utilises biological analogies in which system parts are interconnected and each are functional to the viability of the organisation. Yet this model is not really closed, for the system transacts with and adapts to the environment to survive. The description 'closed system' is therefore partly a label of convenience, true only to the extent that the organisation as a whole and the relation between its parts (technical and social, different departments and functions) could be seen as itself analogous to system–environment relations. True systems theory is open and adaptive in character and we need to spell this out in more detail.

ADAPTATION THEORIES

There are a number of different approaches and types of research that treat organisations in terms of adaptation and as open systems. But before considering them in detail, we need briefly to examine basic assumptions concerning who is adapting and what they are adapting to. Systems theory derived from the broader functionalist model (Parsons, 1956) is multi-layered. At its simplest, this can be expressed as society – organisation – sub-unit (e.g. department). As Elliot (1980: 96) notes,

> This boundary can be drawn anywhere for the purpose of analysis. If the system one is studying is the whole organisation then the boundary is between the organisation and its environment; if the system being studied is the work group, then the boundary is between this group and the rest of the organisation, which in this case is its environment.

But most writers treat the organisation itself as the system, and although the wider environment determines the general goals such as economic survival in a stimulus-response manner, the environment still tends to be defined in terms of the single unit of organisation. As Hannan and Freeman note, 'In the adaptation perspective, sub-units of the organisation, usually managers or dominant coalitions, scan the relevant environment for opportunities and threats, formulate strategic responses, and adjust organisational structure appropriately' (1977: 929–30).

Although organisations are frequently seen as adapting to *the* environment, this is qualified and filled out by many writers. Mullins (1985: 12) claims that organisations are viewed in their *total* environment. Unfortunately this does not mean that they are situated within a coherent *totality*, but rather that lists of multiple influences are provided. Child (1969) in examining a variety of classification schemes, notes that some utilise a narrow conception of *task* environment based largely on economic factors such as customers, suppliers, competitors and self-regulating groups (e.g. Dill, 1962). Child prefers a broader categorisation taking in product markets, factor markets, technical knowledge, political and socio-cultural (e.g. communities, social memberships and values). An even wider and influential set of factors is employed by Hall (1977): technological, legal, economic, political, demographic, cultural and ecological. A realistic analysis of the contexts of organisations take such factors into account. But in practice, as we shall see later, most research has tended to focus on the narrower frame, particularly on markets and technology.

Open Systems

The most well-known adaptation perspective is the *open system* approach pioneered by J. D. Thompson (1967) and Katz and Kahn (1970). As indicated earlier, the starting-point is the need for the organisation to transact with the environment, more specifically, to take inputs from the environment and convert them into outputs. The operation of the system in markets, and among other organisations, gives essential feedback about its performance measured by realisation of corporate goals. Attention is particularly given to achieving a proper balance of system parts. This would involve integration, co-ordination and differentiation of structures and processes, not just functions such as production or research, but activities of leadership, innovation and the like. It would be wrong to give the impression that these 'boundary exchanges' are characterised by smoothness. While the organisation generally adapts and finds an equilibrium by responding to opportunities and risks in the environment, a central concept of open systems is that of *uncertainty* and related terms: stability, turbulence or indeterminacy. This uncertainty can arise in relations with the environment itself, through clashes with surrounding cultures, or rapidity of technological change, or internally in the organisation's members or sub-units. The interdependence of the system parts includes a measure of specialisation specifically to deal with this problem: 'we suggest that organisations cope with uncertainty by creating certain parts specifically to deal with it, specialising other parts in operating under conditions of certainty, or near certainty' (J. D. Thompson, 1967: 13).

An early conceptualisation of the conditions of uncertainty was the emphasis of Emery and Trist (1965) on the significance of the *causal texture* of environments. They developed ideal types ranging from a placid/randomised environment through to a turbulent one. The key differentiating feature is seen as the interrelationship of parts of the environment. Where they are causally interconnected in a complex and changing way, this increases turbulence and can inhibit or encourage different types of action by the organisation. For example, a government might suddenly introduce new rules under which a state industry has to open up a proportion of its tenders to foreign companies. This introduces considerable turbulence in the product markets affecting their traditional suppliers, which is also connected to major changes in the rate of technological advance. This is roughly what happened in the telecommunications industry in the early 1980s (Thompson and Bannon, 1985). The categories used by Emery and Trist are now regarded as rather outdated. More recent approaches are summarised by Child (1984). From open systems research (which will be examined later under contingency theory), he identifies *variability* and *complexity* as key processes. Variability refers to the difficulty of predicting changes and departures from previous conditions that will induce uncertainty. Complexity is linked to the degree of diversity in organisational activities and the environments it is operating in. This may mean difficulty in gathering and monitoring information necessary for effective performance. Each organisation needs to design the structures or processes in a manner which reduces uncertainty or adapts to the degree of environmental stability.

Aside from uncertainty, the other major factor shaping boundary exchanges is held to be *dependency*. Indeed, they may be linked; for example, when dependency takes an intra-organisational form, whereby the ability of sub-units to cope with uncertainty is shaped by the degree to which a sub-unit's activities are central, substitutable, or when it relies on others (Hickson *et al*.: 1973). Outside the organisation, dependency is conditioned by the fact that the environment is a source of scarce resources which have to be competed for. Dependency is the reverse of power, 'As the resources increase or expand the organisation increases in power ... since other organisations become more dependent on the resources' (Clegg and Dunkerley, 1980: 381). These issues have stimulated the development of the *resource dependence* model (Aldrich and Pfeffer, 1976) and *exchange theory* (Blau, 1964).

In the latter, organisations exchange with each other and negotiate the environment, seeking to exert power on the nature and rate of exchange. A classic case is the 'Just-in-Time' system used to control the flow of stocks and materials between large corporations and suppliers in Japan. It works on the basis that small sub-contractors are flexible on the terms of their larger 'partners'. Toyota, for example, relies on 35,000 small businesses, who are mostly in a totally dependent relationship (see Chapter 5 for more detail). Alternatively, they may minimise dependency by seeking alternative sources. This can be seen in the 'world car' strategy pursued by Ford and GM. By co-ordinating design, production and marketing across national boundaries, companies can ensure that components can be acquired from a considerably larger number of locations.

There is a danger with theories of constantly talking as if organisations were things adapting to the environment. However, in practice, open systems theory gives the central role to *management* to maximise a bounded rationality, in other words to predict and design appropriate structures and responses, and to manipulate resources and sub-units effectively. To some extent these processes depend on the access to and nature of information. *Uncertainty* affects the perceptions of management and increases the likelihood of them maintaining flexible structures and methods. In a recent study, Newman and Newman go as far as claiming that 'Information is that which destroys uncertainty' (1986: 503). Large organisations do not necessarily have stable control over their environments and the consequent management of diverse activities drives the growth of information work. To avoid information over-load, top management require assistance in utilising filtering mechanisms, for example, 'technology' such as Decision Support Systems. The aim of such mechanisms is to make sure that decisions about alternative courses of action take place under conditions of calculable risk rather than uncertainty.

This highlights the connection of environmental uncertainty and dependency to issues of *decision-making*, which has long been a significant aspect of research literature (March and Simon, 1958; Cyert and March, 1963). Because of unevenness in the informational, technological and other environmental conditions, and in internal power relations between sub-units, decision-makers frequently have to cope by forming *dominant coalitions* (J. D. Thompson, 1967). As a result, 'Organisational decision-making becomes much less a matter of unquestioned command or rational appraisal and much more a process of political bargaining and negotiation in which the exercise of power plays a key role' (Reed, 1985: 41–2). The positive aspect of this type of thinking is that it begins to see the organisation in a more pluralistic light, with some, albeit limited, recognition of power, bargaining and change pro-ceses. Given that dominant coalitions have to exert choice about alternative actions, it also qualifies the emphasis in systems theory on structures as a functional imperative arising from given environmental conditions (Child, 1972).

Open systems theory has also been extended by the de-velopment of the concept of *socio-technical systems*, particularly associated with Trist and the work of the Tavistock Institute (1963). Primarily it is a way of identifying the key sub-systems and the relations between them in the 'conversion' process. Three sub-systems are identified: technical, formal role struc-ture and sentient (individual feelings or sentiments). Working broadly within the human relations problematic of integrating the formal/technical and informal/social dimensions of organisation, an additional twist is given by putting greater emphasis on the technological environment. This environ-ment of the workgroup, in the form of equipment and lay-out, is seen as a basic constraint on the shape of work organisation.

However, it does not simply reflect the technology, as the organisation has independent social and psychological properties. Management's task is to create a socio-technical system in which the two dimensions are jointly optimised and mutually supportive. There is some choice at the organisational level, but there are defined limits set by the need for 'economic validity'.

Research support has been particularly associated with Trist and Bamforth's (1951) study of the mining industry. Traditional methods of 'hand-getting' the coal had involved limited technology, short coalfaces, high workgroup autonomy over the pace and distribution of work, and an egalitarian ethos. New 'longwall' methods bore similarity to mass production, with work fragmentation and more specific job roles. Not surprisingly this led to lower work commitment, higher absenteeism and a host of other standard problems. The researchers' solution was to accept the technology and layout, but to vary the methods of work to a 'composite' approach in which groups performed whole tasks, were paid collective bonuses and had a degree of self-regulation over job allocation. The results convinced them that management choice could be exercised in favour of methods which took grater care of socio-psychological needs, whilst accepting economic and technical constraints. Working within a similar framework, Miller and Rice (1967) were less optimistic about the capacity to match task and sentient systems, given that the latter can encourage attachment to routines which inhibit technological innovation and the 'primary task' of profit-making.

Like its human relations predecessors, the Tavistock writers adopt a unitary and socially harmonious view of the enterprise, taking for granted that the primary task is shared by all. It is also consistent with that tradition in taking technical and formal structures for granted, the difference lying in the language of management choice rather than worker adjustment. As Rose notes, once the above constraints have been accepted, even that choice is within strictly determined managerial limits and 'the socio-technical systems concept may be seen as a device for helping production engineers to discover better "best ways",' (1975: 216). For Trist and his associates, workers' choices are seen as non-existent in the face of a determinate environment. Resistance to management plans runs up against 'uncontrollable forces in the external environment' (quoted in Rose, 1975: 216). In fact, the mining study hardly utilised the wider environment in the analysis at all. Where the environment is mentioned, it is that of the 'seam society' immediately surrounding the workgroup.

Contingency Theory

The most noted application and extension of the open systems approach is grouped under the heading of contingency theory. As Reed puts it: 'Eventually the theoretical developments taking place within the systems tradition culminated in a 'contingency theory' of organisation which attempted to specify the aproppriate "functional fit" between environmental settings and the internal organisational structures which they required' (1985: 100). In terms of the ideas discussed so far in the chapter, this does not sound very remarkable. Its appeal, however, is in part because of a powerful *normative* dimension in which the emphasis is on practical applications (Legge: 1978). A situational approach requires a 'reading' of the firm's environment by managers and their academic helpers. Furthermore, it appealed because the 'if-then' formula constituted an explicit break with the 'one-best-way' orientation of existing theories, whilst *retaining* powerful guidelines for what power-holders should actually *do* to sustain effective organisation. By the mid-1970s, contingency theory was the dominant approach and had been applied to specifics such as payment systems as well as to general structures (Lupton and Gowler, 1969).

Curiously, as a theory it rested primarily on research that took place largely prior to its own development. The most noted of these was that of Burns and Stalker (1961), who studied twenty firms in Scotland and England drawn mainly from the textile, engineering and electronics industries. Management systems and structures were classified according to a range of environments differentiated by degree of predictability and stability. They found that firms operating in an environment with relatively stable and predictable markets and to a lesser extent technologies, such as those in textiles, tended to have what they called *mechanistic* systems. This broadly resembled bureaucratic models where there is centralised knowledge, clear hierarchy, task specialisation, vertical communication and a general emphasis on formal structures, decision-making, values and rules. By contrast, in environments where there is more rapid change, uncertain markets and complex technologies with a requirement for constant innovation, such as in electronics, a more *organic* system predominated that was less bound by traditional structures and roles. Instead, though structures remained within a general hierarchy, they utilised dispersed information centres; lateral communication; meritocratic and expert positioning, ethos and practices; and more flexible tasks and rules.

Rather than getting embroiled in arguments for and against bureaucracy or any structural arrangements, Burns and Stalker were able to argue that both systems were suitable and rational for specific market-led situations. Successful companies were precisely ones which had adapted their strengths to environmental requirements. They did recognise that they were discussing ideal types and that relationships were not rigid. Organisations facing changes in the environment might have to move along the spectrum or mix particular characteristics. Though normally noted less, Burns and Stalker also recognised constraints to changing structures away from mechanistic models, even where it was environmentally desirable. These arose particularly from entrenched interests and routines, consolidated through the operation of internal political systems (Wood, 1979: 353).

The American writers Lawrence and Lorsch (1967) extended this type of analysis by showing that it is wrong to treat firms as homogeneous structures. Sub-units are likely to have different environments and therefore require specific structures and management to be successful. As a result, a crucial problem for organisation is finding a balance of differentiation and integration. Their research was based on a smaller number of firms in plastics, food and containers. So, for example, whereas the research departments of the plastics companies operated in dynamic, innovative environments that were reflected in long-term orientations and the least bureaucratic arrangements, production had a stable, technical environment and was dominated by short-term concerns and more bureaucracy. Sales departments were somewhere in between. High performing firms were those that not only manifested a high degree of differentiation of structures and goals but had coped by developing adequate means of integration such as specialist teams with such responsibilities. Of course, those organisations where the sub-units do not have to vary significantly can be co-ordinated through conventional command structures. As with Burns and Stalker, the emphasis is not on which theoretical model is 'out-of-date' but on a continuum of models suited to alternative environments.

The final piece of notable contingency research by Woodward (1958, 1965) shifts the emphasis away from market environments to *technology*. She started the research as a means of testing traditional propositions popular in administrative theory, such as relation between formal structures or size and performance. But in studies of around 100 firms in South-East Essex in the mid-1950s, no consistent correlations were found. Instead, a relationship between 'technological complexity' and organisational structure was claimed. Technologies were grouped developmentally according to supposed complexity under a variety of broad categories, eventually reduced to unit and small batch production, large batch and mass production, and process production. Woodward commented: 'While at first sight there seemed to be no link between organisation and success, and no one best way of organising a factory, it subsequently became apparent that there was a particular form of organisation most appropriate to each technical situation' (quoted in Rose, 1975: 203).

Among the aspects of formal organisation found to have a direct association with the technical production system were length of line of command, the extent of the span of control of Chief Executives and of supervisors, and the ratio of managers and clerical workers to production personnel. Problems of running organisations with different technologies varied. Unit and process technologies were both found to have little bureaucracy and simple organisational structures based on line specialisation of basic task functions. This is linked to the

predominant problems of product development and marketing for such technologies, which put the emphasis on innovation. Woodward can be situated within a range of technological determinist writings popular in this period (Walker
and Guest, 1952; Sayles, 1958; Blauner, 1964). As Rose notes
(1975: 202), such studies utilised fairly unsophisticated conceptions of technology as hardware and as the taken-for-
granted physical aspect of production, with little or no
recognition of social shaping or choice.

One of the attractions of the theory generally is that any
contingency can be posited as the key to structural variation
and business performance. Hence *size* is seen by some researchers such as the Aston Group (Pugh and Hickson, 1976)
and Blau (1970) as the major factor. The Aston Group
accepted the significance of technology in circumstances such
as smaller companies or directly for production, but argued
that increased size produced structural patterns based on
impersonal control mechanisms, formal procedures and higher
numbers of administrative staff. Though there are associated
problems, increased size also confers benefits through capacity to take advantage of specialisation. Reference to size
illustrates the point that contingency theory is not necessarily
based on environment–organisation relationships, though
markets are the most constant feature of later research (see
Wood: 1979; Child: 1984). To an extent the same can be said
of technology, of which there has been some disagreement
over whether it can be seen as part of an organisation's
environment. As the dominant approaches have treated it as a
factor 'out-there' determining the features of companies, it is
perhaps justifiable to accept that it has to be discussed in that
framework without accepting its theoretical rationale. We
return to these issues with a critique after the next section.

SELECTION THEORIES: THE POPULATION ECOLOGY APPROACH

The population ecology aproach is a mainstream theory of
organisation–environment relations that shifts the emphasis
from adaptation to *selection* (Hannan and Freeman, 1977;

Aldrich, 1979). In their seminal contribution, Hannan and Freeman do not deny that adaptation takes place, but argue that it is not primary and that there is limited evidence that 'the major features of the world of organisations arise through learning or adaptation' (1977: 957). There are substantial constraints to organisations changing in order to adapt to the environment. For example, failing churches do not become retail stores and vice versa. Such constraints are based mainly on structural inertia, including non-transferable investments in resources and people; information blockages; the type of internal political systems identified by Burns and Stalker; conservative organisational ideologies and normative systems; plus external constraints such as legal, fiscal and political barriers. The stronger the process the more the logic of environmental selection is likely to predominate over adaptation. A further criticism is of the emphasis on the single organisation as a focus of analysis. Instead, the appropriate unit of analysis is taken to be populations of organisations; theoretical abstractions relating to classes of organisation that share some common features in terms of their relations with the environment.

What is this logic of environmental selection? Over a period of time, environments are held to select some organisations or classes of organisation for survival and others for extinction. Those that have survived are proof of a 'best fit'. As can be seen, the emphasis on natural selection involves borrowing, like systems theory, extensively from biology; transferring a Darwinian survival of the fittest to organisational life, with survival paths within each sector of competing firms. There is even a species analogue for organisations, blueprints which consist of rules and procedures inferred from formal structures, patterns of activity and normative orders, for transforming inputs into output (Hannan and Freeman: 934–5). One 'law' is that of requisite variety; organisations need to be as complex as their environment. If they are less complex they are not likely to be adaptable enough. But over-complexity would probably mean that too much slack is being carried; 'populations of organisational forms will be selected for or against depending on the amount of excess capacity they maintain and how they allocate it' (Hannan and Freeman, 949). Furthermore, the environment is an ecological system populated by sufficient organisations to allow for selection. The full process involves three stages. First are planned or unplanned *variations* from which appropriate structures or behaviours are drawn; second, natural *selection* which eliminates undesirable variations; and third is a *retention* mechanism which ensures the reproduction of those variations that have been positively selected.

The borrowings do not stop at biology but draw from neo-classical or free-market economics. Perfect market competition tends to underlie the 'rationality' of natural selection: 'Organisational rationality and environmental rationality may coincide in the instance of firms in competitive markets. In this case, the optimal behaviour of each firm is to maximise profit, and the rule used by the environment (market in this case) is to select out profit maximisers' (Hannan and Freeman: 940). These 'natural laws' are shaped by the kind of competitive struggle over limited resources identified by the resource dependency school. Competition also produces a crucial process for population ecology theory, that of *isomorphism*. When equilibrium conditions obtain, the structural features of organisations – for example, the appropriate degree of specialism or generalism – will correspond to the relevant features of the resource environment. Those organisations that fail will be selected against, though organisations can also purposefully adapt. Of course, equilibrium models can be too simplistic. To help deal with this the concept of *niche* width is used. A niche consists of the combinations of resource levels at which the population of organisations can survive and reproduce themselves. It is difficult for new organisations to enter already-filled niches where they cannot compete with existing social and economic resources.

Despite the use of some sophisticated historical models to handle data, population ecology analysis frequently remains at a highly abstract level. Hannan and Freeman admit to a frustration with the level of empirical information (1977: 959), a problem which arises partly from the choice *not* to focus on particular organisations but on populations over long periods (Clegg and Dunkerley, 1977: 376). But the problems also derive from the theory as well as the method. As Perrow

(1979) argues, ecological perspectives are attractive to some theorists because behaviour and events can be interpreted as natural. Evolution through natural selection gives the impression that patterns of activity that serve society are maintained, while those that are dysfunctional fortuitously disappear. Though contingency theories generally allow more scope for individual actors to learn from processes of adaptation, the remarkable thing is not the distinctiveness of population ecology but how much it has in common with adaptation approaches. We are still in the world of 'best fits' with organisations responding to environments. Hannan and Freeman (1977: 929) admit that processes involving selection can usually be recast at a higher level of analysis as adaptation processes.

Environments are not only given determinate power, as in all systems theory, but they are literally reified through the language of environments acting on passive organisations. Somehow managerial actions to change work rules, create dual internal labour markets or hire temporary workers instead of full-timers can be elevated to a principle of natural selection which rewards flexible organisational forms (Staber and Aldrich, 1987). Perrow (1979: 243) notes that such reification makes it difficult to for workers to say 'I was fired by the environment', adding that:

> the new model of organisation–environment relations tends to be a mystifying one, removing much of the power, conflict, disruption, and social class variables from the analysis of social processes. It neglects the fact that our world is in large part made by particular men and women with particular interests, and instead searches for ecological laws which transcend the hubbub that sociology should attend to.

This neglect of choice is at the heart of the general critique that can be made of the approaches discussed so far, and it is to this that we now turn.

CRITIQUE AND ALTERNATIVE

We have already made a variety of criticisms on our journey through mainstream perspectives. Of course, it would be

foolish not to recognise that such research on organisation–
environment relations has generated some useful knowledge
of structural differentiation within and between organisations.
The best of it, drawing on perspectives such as resource
dependency, has introduced issues of bargaining and power
partially on to the agenda. The appeal to 'practitioners',
particularly of contingency theory, can be located in the more
realistic clarification and yet expansion of managerial role and
of organisational success. Indeed, at one level the general
argument is correct. Clearly organisations do face environmental constraints and often need to adapt to new markets or
technologies to survive. For some people, the 'if-then' formula
became difficult if not impossible to criticise precisely because
it was based on a 'horses for courses' argument. Wood notes:
'Thus ironically an approach which began by dismissing
previous work as "panaceas" became itself the new panacea,
the "situational approach to management"' (1979: 336).

Contingency theory and wider adaptation and selection
perspectives have, however, rightly been criticised for their
environmental determinism. The starting-point of such
critiques has often been John Child's (1972) influential concept of *strategic choice*. Strategic choice can operate with
reference to the context of the enterprise, performance standards or organisational design. Most emphasis is, however,
given to restoring the significance of the *internal* environment
and particularly the degree of discretion available to
power-holders and decision-makers within the dominant
coalitions identified earlier. Contingency and other mainstream perspectives neglect the role of policy formulation and
intervention, or see it only in terms of adaptation to the
environment. One of the crucial factors this ignores is the
existence of multiple contingencies which affect the capacity
to achieve internally consistent responses and any potential
correlation between structure and performance. There is
sufficient 'slack' in most organisations' position and resources
to allow different strategies to be considered and pursued
without occurring performance penalties or diseconomies.

Child sees his own insights as indebted to the work of the
business historian Chandler (1962, 1977) on strategy, previously discussed in Chapter 2. Chandler showed how a new

multidivisional structure was created as a strategic response to short- and long-term market trends and technological innovations. The refashioned structures allowed for an improved internal division of labour and resource allocation based mainly on the separation of longer-term strategic planning from operational decisions and practices. A decentralist strategy established market-type conditions within firms. Though the focus is on strategy and the 'visible hand' of management, the extent to which it can incorporate real choice is open to question, and an adaptation perspective seems just as compatible. However, Chandler also shows that the thrust of emergent giant corporations was to intervene in and shape economic environments, an issue we will be returning to shortly.

The conceptual schema used by Child allows for important breaks with determinism compatible with a radical analysis. He explicitly distances himself (1972: 6) from technological determinism by stressing the role of decisions relating to control of work. The empirical evidence in this area has been provided in later post-Braverman studies, including those by Noble (1979) and Wilkinson (1983a). Noble's work allows us to focus on the neglected issue of choice of technology itself, in this case the development of numerical control in engineering which allowed management to replace the direct input of craft workers by tapes that were externally programmed. He shows that an alternative technology for automating machine tools existed in the form of a 'record playback' system which retained operator skills. This was passed over in part because management preferred a system which enabled them to transfer skills from shop floor to programming office and shift authority and control.

The latest forms of Computer Numerical Control include machinery that can utilise a manual data input (MDI) system through which programming can be carried out by the operator at the machine. One of Wilkinson's case studies shows how a machine tool company bought in one MDI machine and eight which had been conventionally designed with the intention that programming should take place away from the shop floor. No significant performance differences were found, but senior management indicated a preference for the latter on specifically *organisational grounds*. The other cases of automation in the West Midlands focused on the more usual issue of the design of work organisation around the technology. Two of the companies concerned with plating and rubber molding followed the conventional path of attempting to eliminate worker discretion and intervention. However, an optical company preferred a strategy of compensating for deskilling effects by a comprehensive system of retraining, job rotation and enhanced responsibilities which gave management greater flexibility. In all cases, there was no determinate relationship between the technological environment and work organisation, nor technological 'impacts' independent of human choice and negotiation.

At a wider level, Child's analysis moves beyond the dominance of technical criteria in organisational practices, 'recognising the operation of an essentially political process in which constraints and opportunities are functions of the power exercised by decision-makers in the light of ideological values' (1972: 22). How far does Child's early work take us? There is a good deal of ambiguity as to whether he is seeking to modify or supplement contingency and systems theory or significantly depart from it. Wood notes, 'Put simply, he is arguing theoretically for the inclusion of managerial ideology as an intervening variable between the environment and organisational design' (1979: 350). This orientation has heavily influenced an action theory (Silverman, 1970) which had contested the 'metaphysical pathos' of perspectives that produced pessimism and fatalism about structures and choices in organisations. It challenged models of goal consensus and social engineering based on neutral knowledge, shifting the emphasis to internal processes and the diverse behaviour of organisational members. In addition, action approaches stressed the wide variety of environments beyond the economic, particularly the orientations to work developed in community life.

However, at this stage Child tends only to consider strategic choice as a variable and within management terms. Options that involve contesting existing power relations are made largely redundant. As Whittington (1988: 532–3) argues, property rights and structures of class, gender and ethnicity endow a limited circle of actors with command over resources to make strategic choices. Furthermore, we need to break from the idea that environments produce situational imperatives, or the equivalent population ecology argument that environments can only select out a specifically appropriate form. Child's recent work (Child and Smith, 1987) from a 'firm-in-sector' perspective recognises that changes are primarily triggered by markets, but choices still remain and new strategies require an intellectual or cognitive reframing among management.

To illustrate the general anti-determinist point, take the 1980s wave of privatisation in Britain. There is no evidence, even from conventional economic indicators, that an organisation such as British Telecom was inefficient or ill-adapted to markets as a public enterprise. The decision to privatise was a strategy shaped by the hostility of the Conservative Government to state ownership and the material interests of senior management who wished to substitute market disciplines for public accountability. Under privatisation, new structures and practices could be followed, notably an orientation away from the householder to the business customer, the development of a market-driven corporate culture and the extension of decentralised profit-centres.

Changes in organisational forms, structures or practices may be legitimised by reference to the vocabulary of efficiency or fit with the market environment, but they remain social and political choices. Population ecologists take bankruptcy rates as a major indicator of 'natural' selection. Yet this can be a direct result of government monetary policies, as in Britain in the early years of the first Thatcher administration. The general point can be illustrated in more detail with reference to the British coal industry, drawing on the research of Hopper *et al.* (1986b). Traditional structures in what was then the National Coal Board (NCB) were based on 'loose coupling' between the financial, production, marketing and other parts of the organisation. This allowed management to localise and contain contradictions arising from the diverse demands of those parts, and to deal with short-term uncertainties. One of the most significant effects was to isolate the long-term plans and interests of the technical and productive core of the NCB from environmental change and financial pressure. Two further influences on structures and practices need to be recognised.

First, the degree of job regulation exerted by miners in conditions in which conventional managerial controls are difficult to establish (Kreiger, 1983). Second, the relative dominance of professional engineers among management who were production-led, interested in stable long-term planning and partly tied to mining communities and cultures. Strategies pursued by the NCB in the 1980s, particularly after the appointment of Ian McGregor as Chairman, were aimed at breaking these patterns. Decentralisation was a major theme, with specific emphasis on 'economic pits' and 'economic' instead of 'production' centres, as part of a national 'rationalisation' of resources. The Government and Treasury particularly encouraged the enhancement of financial controls as a link between state policies and enterprise practices. This included the use of Financial Information Systems as a monitoring device and the strengthening of the NCB's own Financial Department who were wedded to an ideology of market fitness. Such controls were complemented by the development of strategies of technological control through the MINOS system, which gives management far greater capacity to monitor and direct the labour process underground.

Once again this is an example of the kind of research within, or stimulated by, labour process theory that has deepened conceptions of strategic choice. Earlier contributions on managerial control strategy (Friedman, 1977; Edwards, 1979; Burawoy, 1979) had established an analytical framework (see Chapter 4 for more detail). Child in his later work (1984: 231) refers in detail to Friedman's ideas of strategies of direct control and responsible autonomy. Direct control corresponds broadly to the scientific management tradition of close supervision, minimal responsibility and treating workers as machines. In contrast, responsible autonomy is mindful of the negative effects of worker resistance and the potentially positive gains from worker co-operation and involvement. Hence the stress on enlarged responsibilities and status, lighter controls, greater security and sometimes enriched jobs. These are not abstract choices. Responsible autonomy is more applicable to well-organised workers with controls over external or internal labour markets, who therefore need to be treated as central or core. Workers who are poorly organised, less skilled and working for companies in highly competitive product markets are more likely to be directly controlled and treated as peripheral. This distinction, however, is too crude and does not fit all sectors. We return to issues of core and periphery in Chapter 5.

For Child, Friedman's analysis appears to confirm the relevance of managerial choices within market environments. But this neglects the wider nature of radical explanations. No matter how strategies are described, and Friedman is only one variant, they are shaped not just by markets but by the capital–labour relation itself. As was outlined in Chapter 1, management is caught in the contradiction of needing to exert control and authority over labour to secure profitability in competitive conditions, while requiring workers to be motivated and co-operative. These contradictions are also conditioned by the general dynamics of capitalist production, either in a particular sector or in the economy as a whole. The development of monopoly capitalism has enabled large firms with power *over* markets and access to 'scientific' planning and management to experiment without being under undue pressure for short-term profits. Friedman rightly argues that *any* strategy will generate its own contradictions and tensions as it provokes resistance, facilitates worker organisation and power, or becomes inflexible in new circumstances. For example, during the 1940s and early 1950s most motor industry workers were treated as core, reflecting powerful shopfloor organisation, favourable markets and need for post-war co-operation. But management was put under pressure by intensified competition to challenge the resultant wage systems and rigidity of workgroup practices and manning levels.

Following intense struggles in the late 1960s and early 1970s, management at Ford, Leyland, Chrysler and other companies have been able to take advantage of recession and restructuring to shift power relations, often involving a return to more direct controls. Similar variability in managerial strategies, conditioned by capital's contradictory labour requirements and changing economic and political contexts, can be observed with reference to other dimensions of organisational life such as job design, industrial relations or worker participation schemes. A notable example is Ramsay's (1983, 1985) studies of participation which show that employer interest in participation and job reform follows *cycles* mainly determined by challenges to managerial authority from below. When economic and political circumstances become less favourable to such challenges, as in the 1980s, managerial concern normally fades from view. This is examined in more detail in Chapter 5.

A further form of choice open to management is over the *nature* and *sources* of labour. Labour markets are clearly part of the organisational environment, and decisions about who to recruit are important ones. Employers may not always have much discretion, but the basic criteria of controlled costs, stability and minimisation of risk has been well documented (Jenkins, 1982). Hence employers may look for workers with characteristics such as family men with commitments, as at Ford (Beynon: 1975), or draw on informal Protestant family networks in Northern Ireland telecommunications plants (Maguire, 1986). In the former case the company hopes that mortgage and other responsibilities will mean financial dependence and unwillingness to strike, while in the latter, employment of people from the same family can increase the sense of social obligation and act as a social control over behaviour such as absenteeism. But a more significant choice is over the *location* of a workplace. Radical labour market theorists (Garnsey, Rubery and Wilkinson *et al.*, 1986) rightly regard the firm as a social organisation acting collectively. In locating a plant to utilise a specific form of labour, it is *segmenting* the market, though such effects can also occur when employees seek to build 'shelters' round their own jobs (Freedman, 1984).

There is plenty of evidence to show that large companies have often made their location decisions with specific cheap or controllable labour sources or stable industrial relations in mind (Whitaker: 1986). Modern 'high tech' companies have consciously tended to select young, female labour in places such as Edinburgh's 'silicon glen', or the telecommunications industry on Merseyside (Thompson and Bannon, 1985). Locational decisions can additionally shape environments in a broader way. When GM finally chose Spring Hill, a small town outside Nashville, Tennessee, for its Saturn plant, it was the end of a process which began with a public specification of decision criteria. The subsequent beauty contest had 38 out of 50 states offering a total of 1000 sites which could be created to the requirements (Meyer, 1986: 78). Tennessee has laws outlawing union closed shops. Locating new plants in small towns has been an increasing policy of GM, with the effect that the company *becomes* the environment.

Recruitment and location policies are examples of the power of organisations to *enact* environments. This capacity to set limits to environments was a sub-theme of Child, who drew on Galbraith's (1967) analysis of the 'new industrial state' to argue that any significant countervailing powers to big business had broken down (1969: 54). This stands in sharp contrast to the complacency of conventional open systems theory (Thompson and McEwan, 1973, 158) which only conceives of organisations dominating their environment in extreme circumstances, and which in turn will generate the countervailing powers dismissed by Galbraith. Cook (1977) has approached the issue through analysis of organisational networks which can structure the environment, but it has not been followed through to change the prevailing models of organisation–environment relations. One of the key processes affecting the transactions in networks is *mergers*, which increasingly create environments, and other organisations and sections of the community have to adapt to them. For example, there has been a tremendous concentration of media resources through mergers and takeovers such as those initiated in many countries by Rupert Murdoch. This does not only create a new business conglomerate, but gives enhanced power to shape cultural and political environments and the ideological climate of a whole society.

We have already referred to Chandler's analysis that the growth of managerial power in large corporations coincided with the declining influence of the market economy. In an updated version of that analysis, Teulings notes that 'large corporations do not comply with the laws of every market, but rather the other way round' (1986: 146). An organisation with a monopoly or semi-monopoly position can, for instance, create a product market through its own sales policies, or displace parts of its costs on to the environment, as with unchecked industrial pollution. The most obvious case of the capacity to control and change environments is that of the transnational company. Increasingly they can call on re-sources and structures which are superior to many nation states. One of the crucial powers is mobility of capital across national and international boundaries, enabling an evasion of laws on taxes and profits in a particular country. Markets can be shaped and their ebbs and flows ridden by cross-subsidisa-tion and transfer-pricing of goods, services, technology and loans between related activities in their global structure. Domination of a product market can reduce dependence on external sources of finance. Clairmonte and Cavanagh (1981) illustrate the process with reference to textile transnationals, adding the point that those in oligopolistic positions can act as pricemakers, thus subordinating markets through cartels and other mechanisms. In the case of the Third World, many countries such as Sri Lanka and Malaysia have actually created an environment in the form of 'Free Trade Zones' in order to attract foreign capital. They offer virtual freedom of operations, cheap labour, bans on unions and maximum repatriation of profits (Mitter, 1986).

Such dependency, however, is not just a feature of those regions of the world. The capacity of governments in advanced nations to control transnationals is often limited. During the 1974–9 Labour Government, a planning agreement was drawn up with Chrysler which the company later uni-laterally broke, with the Government being unable to impose any penalty or constraint (Coventry Trades Council *et al.*, 1980). The theme of enacted environments enables Perrow to make a related and further criticism of population ecology theory. He argues that to begin with, the question why are there so many kinds of organisations? is to ignore reality. When we are dealing with the big corporations such as the auto giants, it is simply not the case that there is evidence of significant differences. Furthermore, the large firms very seldom die and they dominate the environment of the host of small organisations around them, as we saw in the example of the Japanese 'just-in-time' system currently being copied in the West. Perrow (1979: 243) concludes, 'If there is little variation, and little negative selection, then, what is the value of the theory?'

The other major theme to come out of this discussion is the need to take large firms seriously as economic actors in their own right. Though there are a variety of competing options or rationalities within organisations, the subsequent actions frequently constitute market environments more than they are constituted by them. As Whitley notes (1987: 140), the capacity of such firms to determine their own market 'niches' requires a level of analysis of the political economy of international and stage agencies, yet this is seldom recognised in organisational analysis. Before looking at some of those factors, it is worth making one general concluding point about the debate. There has been a tendency to counterpose organisational choice and environmental constraint. Some writers are beginning to argue that population ecology and strategic choice perspectives are different aspects of organisational adaptation, the former being able to supply more detailed information about how environments constrain options (Zummato, 1988). Whittington (1988) makes a similar point without endorsing the dubious ecological theory. Such constraints cut down the range of feasible actions, forming the preconditions for choice and shaping its content.

THE STATE AND THE POLITICAL ENVIRONMENT

Given the importance of the state as a political and economic actor in the environment of work organisations, it is remarkable how little attention it has received in the mainstream literature. The political environment may occasionally be listed among the variables but it is rare for it to be followed through. Radical texts such as Clegg and Dunkerley (1980) do discuss the issue in some detail, but even research on the labour process often simply takes the state as a shadowy background factor acting in the interests of capital without specifying how or why. With both sets of perspectives, these issues are often left in practice to other branches of social science, notably political theory. This section tries to redress that balance a little by raising some of the issues that any more detailed analysis would have to deal with.

Theorising the State

We take the state to comprise a set of institutions based on the government and legislature; the executive and administrative branches; the coercive apparatus of military and police; the judiciary; and the arms of the local state and the advisory bodies known as quangos. The definition goes beyond the government simply because processes of power and decision-making cannot be contained within a single focus; though neither can they be contained within the state, as we shall see.

Two poles constitute the major theoretical alternatives. For a *pluralist* analysis (Dahl, 1957, 1978) groups in the political élite have to compete for electoral support among citizens and interest groups. The latter and pressure groups are the main ways through which participation in government and decision-making takes place. As a consequence, power is widely distributed and the state acts as a kind of referee or neutral arbiter between rival interests and claims. As Held (1984: 40–1) notes, more recent pluralist writings recognise uneven resources, access and treatment, but still within a Weberian belief in multidimensional sources of power. Though mainstream theory cannot be explicitly linked to such a conception, it is compatible with it, as McCullough and Shannon identify (1977: 74):

> it may be noted that in so far as a view of the state is implied by organisation theorists, it is usually that the state is itself a characteristic organisation that operates regulatively in the interstices of other organisations and is checked both internally by the aims of its members and externally by those of other organisations whose interests it ultimately safeguards.

Most theoretical work on the state has been done within or in response to a *Marxist* tradition. An orthodox Marxist view takes its lead from Marx's statement that the state is but a committee for managing the affairs of the whole bourgeoisie. Hence the state is an instrument of the dominant class and the political environment is firmly subordinate to economic power. Such a straightforward 'instrumentalist' view is seldom expressed today, though Holloway's (1987) analysis of industrial trends, which claims that managerial strategies *lead* state policies, is a recent example. Contemporary Marxists are more likely to refer to the state having a *relative autonomy*, a concept originally developed by Poulantzas (1975). Paradoxically this is required because the state must manage the affairs of the *whole* of the dominant class. Capital is divided by different and potentially conflicting factions and interest groups, such as finance and manufacturing. The state can in theory act as a collective capitalist: attending to long-term interests even against particular business demands; providing facilities such as a national transport network or housing that single capitals cannot; and regulating and incorporating demands from subordinate classes through concessions and institutional channels which do not threaten existing class power.

Why is there this emphasis on *must*? Although some writers (Miliband, 1969) put additional stress on the common class origins, experiences and values of political, economic, administrative and judicial élites, the basic argument is a *structural* one. The state's activities are constrained by having to operate within the existing market framework. Particularly in a world system of interlocking manufacture, trade and finance, no nation state can ignore the requirements of capital accumulation and reproduction. Capital can utilise its resource power to place unique pressure on the state's economic management processes.

But it is possible to recognise that the state has a high level of dependency on capital accumulation for its economic resources and success, *without* accepting that its form or activities can be derived solely from the class relation to capital. Writers such as Offe (1984) and Crouch (1979) recognise that though the prime function of the state is to create the conditions for successful *accumulation*, state institutions have to respond to popular pressures, even where that

might create conflict with business interests. Gains made by
labour or other social movements may thus be genuine
advances, rather than conspiratorial concessions to maintain
class domination. In a more general sense, system stability,
including state institutions, requires a level of loyalty, consent
or even just acquiescence from subordinate classes and groups
(Clegg, Boreham and Dow, 1987: 286). Taken together, the
conditions are created for the state to have a *legitimation*
function.

The problem is that the two functions may be antagonistic,
particularly when the state is involved in its standard crisis-
management practices. Offe (1984) uses the example of the
growth of the welfare state, with such institutions developing
in part because the state need to compensate for the inability
of the market to meet social needs. To the extent that welfare
provision is a response to popular demands, it sustains public
legitimacy. Yet at the same time the welfare state threatens
the accumulation process by expanding the range of social
activities met by non-commodity forms, or by generating
fiscal crises with an expanding social wage and budgets.
Though Offe's options for the state and political solutions are
beyond our scope, such contradictions can certainly be
observed in the escalating conflicts about public expenditure
in the UK and other advanced industrial societies. In examining other issues, we shall suggest that the accumulation/
legitimation framework provides a useful analytical tool.

Dimensions of state economic activity

Five interrelated dimensions of state activity can be identified
that affect the environment which work organisations operate
in.

State as economic manager. The state's most crucial role has
been to provide a macro- and micro-economic framework
favourable to business operations, especially in the more
interventionist post-war period. This can range from traditional forms of demand management, control of the money
supply and interest rates, to wage regulation and tax structures. Take the example of *enterprise zones* in the UK, which

were set up in two batches on inner city and urban conurba-
tion sites by the Government in the early 1980s (Shutt: 1985).
Using a model of economic regeneration influenced by third
world zones in which capital is allowed to operate without
restriction, the British version includes rates and tax exemp-
tions, 100 per cent tax allowances for capital expenditure,
freedom from training levies, and simplified planning regimes.
This illustrates how state practices have been focused on
managing the process of industrial rationalisation and reconstruction, a task beyond the market alone. Sometimes this has
been through special interventionist bodies set up by Labour
Governments, such as the Industrial Reorganisation Corporation in the 1960s and the National Enterprise Board in the
1970s, or straightforward government departments under the
Conservatives. Considerable resources have been poured into
sectoral planning, encouraging mergers and industrial concentration, and funding plant modernisation. If anything,
state intervention in the UK has been underdeveloped compared to France, or MITI in Japan, which Clairmonte and
Cavanagh describe as 'a superbly honed state instrument
which, in conjunction with the corporate leadership, periodic-
ally rationalises Japan's chemical and textile industries'
(1981: 20).

In certain conditions these processes have taken a *corporatist* form, where the state seeks to regulate both polity and
economy and reduce uncertainty by bringing in capital and
labour as formal interest groups. Under the Heath and
Wilson/Callaghan Governments of the 1970s, tripartism involving the CBI and TUC was a consistent feature until
broken by the Thatcher administration (Grant, 1983). But
economic management is not necessarily the result of rational
planning. It frequently takes a reactive form, reflecting state
dependence on the resources of capital. The most obvious
manifestation is the continual subsidisation of investment,
such as the £148 million in aid to Ford for its Bridgend plant
and the estimated £100 million to Nissan in the North-East.
Subsidising capital appears to be the main feature of successive governments' regional policies, with no guarantees
that companies will not simply close down grant-aided plants,
as Plessey did in the late 1970s without even informing the

National Enterprise Board. The state also indirectly sub-
sidises investment costs through social management and
collective provision. With reference to new town policies,
Cochrane and Dicker note that this was 'part of the state's
response to the needs of private industry for better facilities.
As in so many other areas of the economy, the provision of
new sites and an associated labour force could not be organised by individual firms and the state had to intervene'
(1979: 9).

State as employer. With the spectacular growth of state services
and public corporations such as the National Coal Board in
the UK, the state has become *the* key employer. Even in the
US environment of low intervention, public employment has
grown by eight million between 1952 and 1980 (Cousins,
1987: 123). In theory this gives the state the possibility of
creating distinctive organisational models. In practice, public
corporations at least have been firmly required to act according to market criteria, with no essential differences in management structures, though the nature of service work itself
generates different employment relations. What the British
state *has* done is to use its position as major employer to 'set
standards' in its general regulation of incomes and industrial
relations. Wages have been specifically kept down, leading to
a rise in public sector unionism and militancy. During the late
1970s and the 1980s, in the public corporations of steel, coal
and British Leyland there have been a state-directed management offensive, led by Michael Edwardes and Ian McGregor,
which has had a wider 'demonstration effect'. Under Thatcher
the state has also been able and prepared to finance long set-
piece confrontations with miners, teachers and civil servants in
a way that private employers would find difficult (MacInnes,
1987: 93). Clearly a recent objective has been to break the
power of public sector unions by squeezing expenditure,
decentralising bargaining and by contracting-out services.

State as persuader. While legitimation is a facet of all state
activities, its communicative power and resources gives the
state unique persuasive capacities. In the UK and US the
state has frequently acted to 'sponsor' particular managerial

and organisational initiatives, aimed at spreading them beyond the advanced sectors of capital. During the First World War, President Wilson used the War Labour Board to push arbitration mechanisms and works councils as an alternative to independent unionism (Edwards, 1979: 105), whilst in the Second World War, Stafford Cripps, the Labour Minister of Aircraft Production, used his powers to spread new work study techniques, human relations, welfare and personnel methods, and psychological testing (Brown, 1977: 272–4). Royal Commissions such as the Donovan Report (1968) are a favoured method. This had an important influence on the institutionalisation of collective bargaining. In the early 1970s, governments in many countries produced reports advocating work humanisation as an antidote to dissatisfaction and disruption. More recently the Conservatives have been exhorting companies to develop participation and involvement schemes as a response to the threat of EEC legislation on industrial democracy (MacInnes, 1987: 104), as well as using the Department of Trade and Industry, the Treasury and quangos such as NEDO to spread the word about the value of flexible working practices (Pollert, 1988a).

In a democratic society, the state's persuasive role is normally subject to some constraint and certainly pales into insignificance compared to the massive social engineering programme undertaken by the state in Singapore, for example. Wilkinson (1986) reports that the government has gone beyond the normal use of state bodies and incentives to encourage training and skill development by also directing its attention to desirable attitudes and behaviour. A Productivity Movement is charged with 'inculcating the productivity will' through every form of media under the imprint of Teamy the Bee. In part this is an attempt to spread a paternalistic version of human relations techniques for managers, whose companies get subsidies for sending them on courses. But the general campaign reaches its peak with the Social Development Unit's attempts to encourage graduates, and more recently 'O' and 'A' level holders, to 'meet, marry and breed'. One year of exhortation, however, including all-expenses-paid trips to exotic beach resorts, produced definite evidence of only two marriages!

State as legislator. As with legitimation, legislation accompanies most forms of state activity, yet it has been a core function of the state to provide a legal framework governing industrial relations and employment practices. Hyman (1986) shows that the historical commitment of British employers and the state to a system of minimal labour law was conditional on the former's economic strength and the relative weakness of trade unions. When the material basis for voluntarism was eroded by economic decline, more assertive workers and crisis management by the state, we saw the beginnings of intervention through the abortive Industrial Relations Act of the Heath Government in 1971, revived in more favourable circumstances in the 1980s. Since then there have been successive waves of legislation which have severely restricted the rights to strike and picket, narrowed the definition of lawful industrial action and undermined the enforcement of the closed shop. Though employers have seldom had to *use* the Acts outside celebrated instances such as the Wapping dispute, a legal framework has been established supportive of managerial prerogatives and capable of easing problems in the reorganisation of production. As Sir Jeffrey Stirling, Chairman of P&O Ferries, noted when using that framework during the 1988 dispute: 'This Government has given companies like ours the right to manage' (*The Guardian*, 29 April).

Of equal importance has been Conservative legislation in the wider employment field. In the 1980s we have seen the abolition of the Fair Wages Resolution, dating back to 1891, which obliged governments and private contractors to pay the going rate; some Wages Councils which set minimum wage rates disbanded, or their coverage restricted to adult workers; and abolition of aspects of Labour's previous employment protection legislation with respect to union recognition, rights on unfair dismissal and maternity leave, and for part-timers (Standing, 1986; MacInnes, 1987). Such meaures have been part of an explicit attempt to deregulate labour markets, ensuring the freedom of employers to set wages and organise work as they see fit. Though it is not always connected to legislation as such, the other relevant state action with respect to labour markets has come through policies ostensibly directed towards training.

The major arm of this intervention has been the Manpower Services Commission (MSC). Begun in the mid-1970s, a decade later the MSC had a budget of over £2000 million, a staff of over 20,000 and there were 670,000 people in Special Employment Measures (Standing, 1986). At first, MSC schemes were little more than *ad hoc* responses to youth unemployment. Though critics continued to charge that the object was to massage the unemployment figures and provide make-believe jobs with no permanent prospects, a longer-term strategy was beginning to develop. The Holland Report in 1977 had already revealed that employers valued behavioural qualities such as appearance, manners and adaptability to work more than qualifications that were of little relevance to the mass of semi-skilled jobs.

Evidence shows (Thompson, 1984; Finn, 1986) that through the various schemes, from the Youth Opportunities Programme to the Youth Training Scheme, trainees have been taught generic or transferable skills which were geared to performance and flexibility in low-skilled jobs in the manufacturing and service sectors. This was backed up by behavioural and 'personal effectiveness' training in the form of Social and Life Skills packages with the aim of providing a work ethic for this new reserve army of semi-skilled labour. At the same time, direct intervention in youth labour markets was explicitly geared towards the lowering of wage rates. Central to this process was conditioning people to low training allowances, the destruction of expensive and union-influenced apprenticeship schemes and abolition of many of the Industrial Training Boards with traditional responsibilities in these areas. These were allied to a range of subsidies to employers – through the Young Worker Scheme, the New Worker Scheme and the Temporary Employment Subsidy – if they would take on young workers below wage rates specified by the state.

State as policeman. Weber defined the core function of the state in terms of its monopoly of violence and coercive power; indeed, this was the basis of its autonomy. As the use of such powers to maintain industrial order is likely to undermine the legitimacy of the state and capital if used on its behalf, there are obvious constraints. This was felt less in the nineteenth and early twentieth century when the use of police and the military in disputes was a regular occurrence in the US and UK (Edwards, 1979; Hain, 1986). The notion of the police force as an arbiter and protector of the general interest is central to pluralist notions of the modern state. Yet coercive powers are still used in disputes, as we have seen during 1980s disputes in the UK: at the Wapping print plant and during the miners' strike. In the latter there was every indication of a nationally co-ordinated police effort to undermine the effectiveness of the strike (Geary, 1985).

Geary uses historical comparisons to argue that there has been a shift to more repressive police tactics which are less subject to informal community controls. Yet compared to Reagan's repression of the strike by the Professional Air Traffic Controllers Organisation, in which the state dismissed the employees, scrapped PATCO and carted its leaders off in irons, this seems small beer! Constraints still remain in all complex societies. Degrees of tolerance and repression depend strongly on the perceived political consequences both for the police themselves and the wider state apparatus. Most police involvement in disputes is not marked by intent. Rather, it is a reflection of the legal framework under which they are expected to guarantee property rights on picket lines or in other circumstances. We should also remember that the state's policing role has a social dimension. A notable example was the law on social security used in the miners' strike. This assumed that unions paid strike pay regardless of whether they did so in practice and even to non-members, with a resultant large reduction in benefits payable to dependants of strikers.

Retheorising the State: a Reflection

The range of examples in each of these areas *appear* to support an instrumentalist view of relations between capital and state. They certainly indicate that the political environment shaped by state practices in a capitalist society is likely to be favourable to business organisations. It is a more unequal competition for access to the state and its resources than allowed for in most versions of pluralist theory. However, most of the examples were from the last decade where we have seen highly distinctive political and state frameworks. The *outcomes* of state interventions in the economic environment are conditioned by three main factors: the balance of power between classes and related interest groups; the prevailing ideological climate; and the dominant political project within the various state apparatuses.

Though these conditions can be localised in time and space, they are normally part of broader changes in relations between the main political and economic actors. In the UK, USA and some other industrial countries, the last decade has seen a sharp move away from corporatist and 'social democratic' practices that had formed the basis of what commentators call the post-war consensus. Such a state accomplished its tasks by putting a premium on ideological and social cohesion, integrating and organising various interests through wage and price controls, social compacts, arbitration and conciliation procedures, regional employment premiums and the like (Lehman and Tinker: 1985). The direction has been towards 'neo-liberal', market-driven practices in which

> Political efforts at neo-corporatist institutional design have come to a standstill almost everywhere ... many governments now seem to place little hope on negotiated adjustment and no longer see it as their responsibility to protect the principle of joint regulation from the disruptive effects of a severe power imbalance. (Streek, 1987: 286–7)

As an example, the kind of tripartism between the state, CBI and TUC has been cursorily jettisoned by the Conservative Government. Such constellations of practices constitute different modes or ways in which interests can be represented and organised by and through the state (see Jessop, 1982: 228–41, for a detailed discussion).

The point of outlining these changes is to emphasise that they *are* changes. There is no evidence to show that there is any permanent or *essential* relationship between capital, labour and the state, or between the political and economic environments which business organisations operate in. After all, the recent changes are not universal. Austria still has its corporatist 'Economic and Social Partnership' with a high level of insitutionalised co-operation between the state, unions and employers' organisations; Sweden retains a well-entrenched social democratic state apparatus with high levels of control over the labour market and high levels of welfare expenditure; and the co-determination system of works councils in West Germany gives employees a level of involvement in the management of industrial change markedly higher than in the UK or USA.

Just as importantly, we cannot assume that the 'neo-liberal' state strategies are necessarily and unambiguously of benefit to capital, even when acting in its name. Let us return to some of the examples we used earlier. The first wave of enterprise zones were a spectacular failure, with the main effect being to transfer existing small businesses short distances from places where the state gained revenue from their rates and taxes (Shutt: 1985). In many parts of the country the opposition to the zones was led by business interests such as local Chambers of Commerce. Yet the government's response was to create a new set of zones! If we turn to industrial relations legislation, a number of measures described earlier went too far for the CBI and influential groups such as the Engineering Employers' Federation. They have complained in written evidence and on delegations about the dangers to stable industrial relations from excessive restrictions on the closed shop and on the rights of unions to discipline their own members, as well as the proposals to make a 70 per cent affirmative vote necessary for strike action. Finally, consider the MSC and training policies. Despite the massive expenditure on training schemes, employers all over Britain are complaining of skill shortages. These schemes are of poor quality and have an extremely dubious record in relation to the provision of trained manpower (Standing, 1986). This is not surprising when the major considerations of the state have been to manage the political crisis of mass unemployment, the emphasis being on placing sheer numbers on schemes and removing others off benefit in order to get official statistics down; being seen to be *doing* something about unemployment; and providing a work ethic, even when no regular work was available.

One of the things all three examples have in common is a tension between the accumulation and legitimation functions of state practices. The political project articulated by the Thatcher Government has to be seen as capable of maintaining its ideological coherence and dynamism to its social bases of support and indeed to itself. That is likely to undermine or at least mediate its practices geared to providing conditions for successful accumulation. Nor are these the only relevant examples of policies that had at last partially negative effects on business interests. In the early years of Thatcherism, the effects of monetarist measures such as high interest rates and low public capital spending led to a bitter clash with leaders of the CBI, with a feeling that the state was favouring finance rather than manufacturing capital. As MacInnes (1987: 94–5) points out, the business sector tolerated Thatcherism in this period because they associated themselves with the general project compared to any alternatives, and because they gained the benefits from the shift in power relations *vis-à-vis* labour.

Finally, in drawing out some theoretical conclusions we would endorse a number of the factors which Pierson (1984) identifies as characterising post-Marxist theories of the state. The concept of relative autonomy solves few problems. The state does not function unambiguously in the interests of a single class; it is a state *in* capitalist society rather than *the* capitalist state, and it is an arena of struggle constituted and divided by opposing interests rather than a centralised and unified political actor. National differences are an important factor in the specific evolution of state structures and practices. In trying to explain why the British state has traditionally failed to pursue effective policies for economic restructuring and growth, Hall (1986, 278) observes that 'the precise form it [political responses] takes is strongly influenced by the institutional setting within which the state finds itself'.

A further factor is highlighted by Skocpol (1979) who argues that states have their own distinctive structures, histories and interest groups developed from transactions with increasingly complex, transnational environments. While such state-centric theories may overplay the degree of independence, there is a need for an *organisational* perspective which recognises that, 'all states are composed of complex and often internally contradictory and inconsistent organisational apparatuses' (Clegg, Boreham and Dow, 1987: 281). There are obvious tensions between the Treasury and other ministries arising from the former's organisational dominance in Britain, and there may be certain contradictions within structures. So, for example, within the MSC empire of over 20,000 people there are varied groups of functionaries carrying out state management tasks. In a complex bureaucracy different groups inevitably develop their own resources, values, interests and funding practices, mediated by which ever client group (enterprise agencies, colleges) they transact with. Goals set by the core state apparatus have to be filtered through these layers. Not surprisingly there have been reports that the Department of Trade and Industry under Lord Young wished to cut back on the MSC empire and its power.

THE PUBLIC SECTOR ENVIRONMENT

We have already spoken of the significance of the state as an employer, even allowing for governmental erosion of large parts of public provision. That part of the sector normally referred to as public corporations, such as British Coal, operates largely under conditions comparable to other commercial operations. But to what extent does the public *service* sector constitute a distinct environment for organisations? The answer sheds some important light on a comparative analysis of work organisations and their contexts. We seek an explanation by focusing on recent trends in British Government policy towards public services, drawing extensively on Cousins's (1987) *Controlling Social Welfare*. She identifies four main policies – tighter financial controls such as cash limits on the total budget of each service; recommodification through privatisation or contracting-out; changes in internal management and control, notably through the introduction of private sector practices; and a shift of decision-making to the central state apparatus.

This can be illustrated by focusing on the National Health Service (NHS) and recommodification and management processes in particular. Attempts to introduce tighter managerial controls are not new. From the 1960s onwards, steps have been taken to move away from consensus or collaborative styles of decision-making and administration which rested heavily on the power of medical professionals over resource allocation (Dent, 1986; Glover *et al.*, 1986). A number of reports were vehicles for rationalisation processes which sought, among other things, to establish the dominance of management. The Griffith Report played a particularly important role. It argued that the NHS required a central directing force which could allocate and monitor resources. Hence a dual strategy was to be pursued. General managers were to be appointed who could assert managerial prerogatives and make 'technocratic' decisions about the health service, such as equipment and manpower.

In addition, medical professionals such as consultants would be drawn into managerial activity, mainly through involvement in clinical budgeting. A new Management Board was also established to strengthen central control over strategic resources. Griffiths was also important for its emphasis on private sector practices. He was previously Managing Director of Sainsburys, and considerable (though largely unsuccessful) attempts were made to recruit general managers from private industry. In other parts of the public sector such practices took the form of financial scrutiny under the auspices of the Audit Commission, the Raynor efficiency drive in the Civil Service and the use of performance indicators in higher education.

Through the 1980s these policies took on a more sharply political tone. A convergence could be noted between a longer-term shift from administration to management shaped by the fiscal crisis of the state, and the ideological thrust of 'new right' politics that are in principle hostile to public and collective provision. Privatisation and contracting-out are favoured by the latter as they are direct means of introducing market mechanisms and profitability criteria. Managers are given greater leverage to rationalise labour-intensive forms of work organisation. As Cousins (1987: 177) points out, 'If an in-house tender wins, however, the service has still been subjected to the discipline of competition and although labour is not conducted for the extraction of profit, the labour process is organised *as if it were*' [our emphasis].

It would be tempting to see these trends also in terms of a convergence, this time in the nature of public and private sector organisations. State organisations *are*, as marxist writers emphasise (Carchedi, 1977), intimately connected and often subordinate to capitalist political economy. It is also the case that the rationalisation and intensification of service work makes the experiences of workers increasingly comparable to those in the private industry. But, as we argued in the previous section on the state, such measures are primarily the result of specific political choices and practices rather than any law of capitalist development. In addition, Cousins uses the work of Habermas (1971) and Offe (1984) to show that there are still different *modes of rationality*: 'state welfare organisations are not governed by the logic of maximising profits, although they are dependent on the revenues derived from profits and the prosperity of the private sector' (1987: 4–5).

Operational criteria lack the clear parameters deriving from the capital-labour relation and are still likely to be shaped by policy and budget decisions arising from the political apparatus. The Director of Personnel for the NHS, Len Peach, has stated that Griffith is his Bible, 'We recognise that the politicians will make the strategic decisions. The management decisions are about how to implement them' (quoted in *The Guardian*, 9 June 1986). A similar point is made by Batstone *et al.* in their study of the Post Office. They argue that

The essence of the distinction between public and private lies in the fact that though they may be encouraged to act commercially, state enterprises pursue politically determined objectives which complicate the process of strategy formulation and implementation. (1984: 7)

In the state service sector such processes are even more open to public discourse and interest group pressure. Hence the constraints on the Conservative Government simply dismantling the NHS, as well as the decision to fund pay rises fully for nurses in 1988. We can see in these examples a version of the previously discussed tension between the state functions of accumulation and legitimation. Compare that to the events surrounding the takeovers affecting firms such as Rowntree. Despite considerable public disquiet and intense lobbying, the 'logic of the market' took its course as institutional shareholders looked for the highest returns.

Public and private are also distinguished by the distinctive role played by professional groups. Like professions everywhere, those in state services such as medicine have pursued strategies of occupational closure, controlling entry and access to knowledge and positions. But whereas professions in business have to 'prove' their reliability by carrying out functions on behalf of capital (see Chapter 4), in many state services the unmediated power of higher professions is greater and the state has had to act as partners or sponsors of key groups such as doctors. As Glover *et al.* (1987: 13) observe, 'Unlike engineers and salaried accountants in industry, the work and employment situations of doctors approximate far more closely to those of the traditional independent service-to-individual-client'. That is not to say, of course, that such circumstances are transferable across all professionals in all state services. It also applies far less to female-dominated and semi-professions such as nursing, which have also pursued occupational closure strategies, but which remain more vulnerable to managerial control and domination by medical élites (Cousins, 1987: 110).

Those élites may also face pressure from government and general management for reorganisation of their work. But doctors can utilise their socially constructed expertise and power over employment conditions to 'claw back' measures such as clinical budgeting. Dent shows this in the case of one particular tactic – the medical audit which is based on qualitative and medically defined criteria, rather than financial. The profession began to 'recognise the potentiality of medical audit could be utilised to thwart what they considered the unwarranted encroachment of the administration, or the health commissioner, or the patient, into the area of medical autonomy' (1986: 17).

Though privatisation in its varied forms continues to undermine the basis of public provision, the factors discussed above place significant difficulties on the strategies of state managers to reorganise work processes and assert greater controls.

Evidence collected by Cousins shows that managers have to balance the cost benefits from measures such as contracting-out against the ceding of control over staff to an external firm and the loss of commitment and cohesion from existing teams, to say nothing of potential declining standards which they may be blamed for. Employees, both manual and professional, can also use the ethic of service and welfare to challenge the legitimacy of managerial decisions purporting to be based solely on technocratic rationality. Employee organisations themselves, of course, have to seek legitimacy for their actions in the political environment. It has taken the unions a considerable period of time to recover from the damage done by the 'winter of discontent' of 1979, in order to mount more recent and effective public campaigns.

There may also be tensions between state managers and central government control. Glover *et al.* (1987: 19) point out that the Management Board set up in the wake of Griffith was never given the formal space or authority to act in a manner independent of political interference and necessary to implement the Report effectively. Hence the whole process of management is a complex bargaining and balance act. While this may be true of all management, the factors which shape it in public services are both distinctive and more widely ranging. The problematic nature of management strategies of control form a major feature of the following chapter.

4

Management, Power and Control

We saw in Chapter 2 that the first quarter of this century marked the emergence of professional management as a social force, specialist occupational category and with a set of distinct work practices. This development was integral to changes in the organisation of capitalist production, with the modern bureaucratic enterprise increasingly based on the joint stock company, often in the new multidivisional form with its separation of ownership and management. In this type of structure, middle managers headed autonomous divisions which integrated production and distribution by co-ordinating flows from suppliers to consumers in the more clearly defined markets (Chandler, 1977). Such divisions administered their functional activities through specialist departments. All this encouraged the professionalisation of management and the rapid spread of administrative techniques. Management thought became intimately linked to the appearance of a distinct occupational grouping; organisational theory being used as a resource to understand the complexities of the large-scale organisation and management's role within it.

A key theme underlying the contradictory and partial organisational prescriptions, strategies and tactics was the belief in principles and even 'laws' concerning the nature of managerial activities and functions. As Child observes:

> Management's claim to professionalism, for instance, was only plausible if it could be shown to possess some uniform

and generalised body of knowledge upon which its practitioners could draw. The so-called 'principles of management' could be presented as a theoretical base upon which
the subject of 'management' rested (1969: 225).

Much of this development was during the inter-war period of
'classical' writers such as Fayol, Taylor and Barnard, discussed
in Chapter 2. As we saw there, Fayol was the most concerned
to elaborate common characteristics of management. These
consisted of *planning* general lines of action and forecasting;
organising human and material resources within appropriate
structures; *commanding* the activities of personnel for optimum
return; and *co-ordinating* of varied activities and *controlling* to
ensure consistency with rules and command. These were
situated within a detailed set of principles reflecting the
division of labour and hierarchy of the bureaucratic enterprise, tempered by equitable treatment and personal responsibility. One of the effects of this way of thinking was to define
managerial functions by a process of abstraction from specific
activities into a conception of *general* management (Armstrong: 1987b). Managerial work would differ not in kind but
only in the proportion which is actually 'managerial'. This
would have a profound influence on management thought,
spreading the idea that knowledge, skills and experience are
common and transferable.

Meanwhile in Britain, Mary Parker Follett was producing
prescriptions for a science of behaviour informed by the
concerns of the human relations tradition. Management could
learn this science because it was derived from *situational* laws
governed by the needs of the system. As such, management
could represent and integrate all interests through its capacity
to apply optimal solutions through depersonalised authority.
Classical writings have now been superseded in the post-war
period by a body of more detailed studies of management.
Indeed, as was made clear in Chapter 1, the study of organisation has become synonymous with that of management.
Management Studies has emerged as an 'intellectual field'
sustained by an extensive network of educational and training
institutions (Whitley, 1984). The more confident asserted
the viability of a Management Science whose methods and

knowledge could support rational activities and decisions. This chapter aims to examine such claims through an analysis of the nature of management. It will argue that though recent research offers important insights, the perspectives are partial and flawed. In particular, they neglect important dimensions such as power and control, as well as the divisions and contradictions embedded in the managerial labour process itself.

THE NATURE OF MANAGEMENT

The modern literature (e.g. Drucker, 1955; Stewart, 1967; Mintzberg, 1973; Kotter, 1982) shared the central concern of the classical writers to identify common functions and criteria for effectiveness. There has been an even greater emphasis on the individual as a unit of analysis, a problematic of 'what do managers do?' (Hales, 1986). The answer given is a positive one. Drucker starts his well-known text by saying that 'The manager is the dynamic, life-giving element in every business ... the only effective advantage an enterprise has in a competitive economy' (1955: 13). Texts continually invoke as examples captains of industry such as Lee Iaocca the ex-Chrysler boss. In this elevated role, the manager is presented almost as a free-floating centre of power. Organisations are still frequently treated as closed systems with the assumption that 'it was largely within management's own powers to fashion behaviour and relationships as might best suit their own purposes' (Child, 1969: 168). Paradoxically, by focusing on the individual, management can be analysed as if it was homogeneous, leading to the conception of the 'universal manager' carrying out a generalised set of functions standing above any specific context (Mintzberg, 1973).

Theorists could agonise about whether management was science, art, magic or politics (Watson, 1986: 29), but all options rest on the analytical and practical skills of 'successful managers'. An emphasis on skills was boosted by the influence of human relations perspectives in the 1950s, with the notion of training managers to learn how to exercise social and leadership skills. The constant struggle for competency is further linked to the assumption that management *effective-ness* is tangible and identifiable (Hales, 1986: 88). To this end anything can be quantified and learned, including the qualities of managerial excellence (see Hitt *et al.*, 1986, 10–11).

These various assumptions underwrite the more fundamental view of management practices as a neutral, technical resource, the central task of which is deciding what should be done and getting other people to do it. In this view that we describe as *technicist*, managers can embody and carry out the central mission of the organisation and secure its desired objectives. Managers are also seen as functionally necessary in a deeper sense. The functions are 'indispensable' and are ones which 'no one but the manager can perform' (Drucker, 1977: 39). As Willmott observes (1984: 350), this view confuses the general process of management of resources with the role of managers empowered to command others within specific institutional frameworks. Put another way, it wrongly assumes that 'the management function must, of necessity, reside with a particular category of agents who manage or administer other agents' (Hales, 1988: 5).

It would be wrong to think that such conceptions of management developed purely within the organisational field. Though it is seldom acknowledged, the wider theory of a 'managerial revolution' played a crucial role (it is linked to the theory of an 'organisation society' discussed in Chapter 1). This rests on a particular interpretation of changes in the nature of the large corporation. As the dominant form, joint stock companies are held to be characterised by a separation of ownership and control, share dispersal and a corresponding rise in the importance of a professional managerial élite who run the new corporations. For some adherents of the theory (Berle and Means: 1935), this enabled the corporate system to be a 'purely neutral technocracy', with managers of a different background and experience exercising social responsibilities. Tougher versions (Burnham, 1945) envisaged a managerially planned and controlled society beyond the workplace, with management becoming the dominant class of *all* industrial societies.

The managerial revolution thesis had a wider significance for social theory often influenced by *systems* thinking (Reed,

1984: 278). At its core was the view that capitalism as a system based on individual private ownership was being supplanted by a post-capitalist society in which old political disputes about ownership were irrelevant (Dahrendorf, 1959). But these theoretical developments enabled management writers such as Drucker to assert that 'we no longer talk of "capital" and "labour", we talk of "management" and "employees"' (1955: 13). Some scepticism was expressed by senior managers who referred to 'claptrap' about social responsibilities, reminding their colleagues that they remained the servant of their employers (Child, 1969: 152–3).

Managers as Leaders and Decision-Makers

Having set out the basic assumptions of mainstream approaches, it is useful to highlight some of the further dimensions of the research which shapes the broader view of management activities. From the 1950s onwards, considerable attention has been paid to the interrelations between management, leadership and decision-making. Textbooks are normally quick to point out that all leaders are not managers and not all managers have or even need leadership abilities. Indeed, there is a modest sub-literature on leadership qualities as such; for example, on whether successful leaders all have or need particular personality traits. We are concerned, however, with the way in which leadership studies frequently merge with those of management by virtue of a focus on effective management *styles*. In fact, most texts not only use management and leadership styles interchangeably, they refer to the same research.

A common starting point is often McGregor's (1960) famous theory of X and Y assumptions that management have about people. The former leans towards Taylorist notions of employees who dislike work and initiative and therefore have to be directed and coerced, while the latter accepts that they have self-direction and self-control if committed to organisational goals and involved in decision-making – people need whipping versus people are better at whipping themselves, as someone once mischievously put it. McGregor's theory is clearly part of the human relations tradition and follows through the perceived results of the Hawthorne Studies in terms of the beneficial effects of participatory leadership and sympathetic supervision. A variety of subsequent studies developed categories based on a comparison between democratic and autocratic management or leadership styles. The dominant message is that democratic leadership is better, both for increasing morale and productivity and for improving the quality of decisions. How democratic it is remains open to question. Most new styles have always left management command structures intact. Nichols and Beynon quote one manager at 'Chemco', 'Democratic leadership is the only way. But you'll know that won't you. Psychologists have proved it with children' (1977: 123). Those evaluating the results of such styles have also been sceptical, with Perrow noting that 'the history of research in this area is one of progressive disenchantment with the above theses' (1979: 98).

Some of the studies are careful to allow for combinations of styles or particular ones in appropriate circumstances. In addition, Fiedler's (1967) research offers a thoroughgoing contingency approach in which effectiveness is linked specifically to organisational context. By developing a 'least preferred co-worker scale', the suitability of a task or relationship oriented leader was shown to be dependent on the degree to which the task is structured, the leader's position power, and the relations between leaders and led. But even this has a relatively limited notion of the context of management practices and rests on individualistic and small-scale scenarios. The literature on leadership and management styles has failed to integrate a deeper analysis of how management strategies develop and their interrelationship with the political economy of the firm and society. We will return to this question later.

A crucial part of leadership is decision-making, Simon (1960) regarding the latter as synonymous with management. It is therefore not surprising that this has been another focus for researchers. For example, organisations have been analysed as decision-making systems, while Mintzberg (1973) has used 'decisional roles' as one category of classification of management activities and functions. Traditional approaches tend to start from a *rational choice* model which, having assumed consistency of goals, requires the setting out of decision-making alternatives and assessment of likely outcomes. Once again the emphasis is on skills and techniques to aid the optimal or 'one best' decision. Assessments must take into account the technical and human requirements, one text recommending a balance of the skills of Captain Kirk and Mr Spock from Starship Enterprise!

Social scientists can help managers to design appropriate centralised or decentralised structures; identify stages in the process such as generation, evaluation, choice, implementation and follow-through; and ensure an awareness of the behavioural dimensions of decision-making in groups. This may include specific techniques, the best known of which is brainstorming. Another important area is access to information and the design of Management Information Systems. One of the purposes is to separate routine, 'programmed' decisions, and enhance the ability of management to concentrate on strategic decisions (Stewart, 1970). The above emphasis reinforces a technicist view of management processes and activities. It further neglects the inequalities in access to information which structure decision processes that are frequently legitimated by reference to technical expertise (Child, 1973). The *politics* of decision-making is also highlighted by Pettigrew (1973), who points to the hierarchy of powers shaped by the control of resources.

Researchers *are* aware, however, of limits to rationality. March and Simon (1958) introduce the concept of 'intended rationality', recognising that there are considerable constraints to the capacity to access and evaluate a full range of options. The existing structures of specialisation and hierarchy in organisations, as well as the routine practices identified in a Weberian analysis, will limit the content and flow of information and set agendas for decision-making. As a result there is 'limited search' and 'satisficing' rather than rational and optimal choices. Cyert and March (1963) point to similar processes such as 'uncertainty absorption', whereby in order to maintain stability of operations, rules and processes are geared to short-run decisions and frequent reviews. What emerges are policies and decisions by 'incremental comparison';

not a rational science, but a 'science' of muddling through (Lindblom, 1959).

Management Practices: A New Realism?

The glimpses of realism displayed in decision-making research helped to extend the study of management. But discussion of the core issue of defining and classifying activities has now moved on to a more detailed 'realism'. Textbooks do remain influenced by prescriptions from Fayol, and the narrow preoccupations with *new* lists of functions can still be described as variations on a classical theme. Some of the variations reflect managerial *ideologies*, with modern writers in a more democratic era preferring to describe command as motivation (Mullins, 1985: 121).

Though the number of studies dealing with the real work of managers is relatively small, the actual choice of new lists is extensive. Many writers recycle a limited number of activities under new and more exotic titles, such as jungle fighter and gamesman. By getting a large and varied group of managers to fill in diaries, Stewart (1967) drew up classifications based on how they spent their *time*. This produced emissaries, writers, discussers, troubleshooters and committee men; while a later study (1976) focused on *patterns of contact*, this time identifying hub, peer-dependant, man-management and solo. In contrast, Mintzberg (1973) confined himself to five chief executives and classified ten roles with three headings. Under *interpersonal* came figurehead, leader and liaison; under *informational* – monitor, disseminator and spokesman; and under *decisional* – entrepreneurial, disturbance-handler, resource allocator and negotiator. We would agree with Hales's observation that many of the categories used in these and other studies are largely interchangeable, for example, leader/figurehead/spokesman. New terms such as network building and setting agendas correspond in substance to old favourites such as planning. He produces a composite list (see Table 4.1) from six of the best-known studies, which 'exhibit striking parallels with the supposedly outdated "classical principles of management"' (1986: 95).

Table 4.1 Managerial functions

---

(1) Acting as figurehead and leader of an organisational unit
(2) Liaison: the formation and maintenance of contacts
(3) Monitoring, filtering and disseminating information
(4) Allocating resources
(5) Handling disturbances and maintaining work flows
(6) Negotiating
(7) Innovating
(8) Planning
(9) Controlling and directing subordinates.

Source: Colin P. Hales, 'What Do Managers Do?: A Critical Review', *Journal of Management Studies*, 23, p. 95.

Accurate though this is, it remains the case that the new empirical studies do partly break with traditional approaches and those found in popular management books. Once the complication of producing labels and lists is set aside, more realistic insights are available. We have already referred to Cyert and March's findings on the short-term incrementalism in the sphere of decision-making. But the significant breakthroughs are aided by a willingness to use a greater variety of research methods than those used in broad-brush analyses of managerial functions. Structured or unstructured observation methods, time–budget studies and self-report questionnaires can capture a greater sense of fluidity and processual factors (Horne and Lupton, 1965; Stewart, 1967, 1976; Mintzberg, 1973; Kotter, 1982; Burns, 1982).

Such studies reveal that the image of the reflective strategist, thinker and planner is a myth. An alternative picture is indicated through the language of realism. Though there are variations between the studies, management practices are said to be opportunistic, habitual, tactical, reactive, frenetic, *ad hoc*, brief, fragmented and concerned with fixing. This arises primarily because the manager has to adapt to contradictory pressures, not least on time and energy. As a result, routines are shaped by short-term spans, the domination of face-to-face interaction and lateral communication in gathering and using information. For Mintzberg, this actually corresponds to managerial preferences for use of informal structures, gossip and speculation. A picture of this nature overlaps with the emphasis in *action theory* on managers investing meaning in the 'organisational work' of reinterpreting stocks of knowledge and routine practices (Silverman and Jones, 1976). It also reflects the fashionable post-modernist perspective, in which 'all organised human activity is essentially reactive or defensive' (Cooper and Burrell, 1988: 106).

Nor are such activities necessarily bad for effectiveness and efficiency. Though energy can be dissipated in conflict and power struggles between cliques, Kotter (1982) points out that patterns do emerge based on establishing and maintaining *networks* vital for co-operation and a flow of information. Finally, though the focus is on the internal world of the organisation, the new realism is not incompatible with an analysis of environmental pressures. Loveridge's (1982) study of manufacturing companies in the Midlands showed that marketing and financial pressures, plus the need to accommodate to the power of workforce job controls, led in the direction of federal structures, short-term reactive policies and a concern with implementation rather than planning.

The realist challenge to the idea of the science and rationality of management is useful, but there are limits and even drawbacks. It is as Hales (1988) notes, an *internal* critique, and at the heart of the problem is the fact that it is at the *empirical* level only. It can show us that management is not what it is made out to be. Instead it portrays the activities of managers 'as a quite arbitrary set of roles with little suggestion as to why they are as they are' (Armstrong, 1986: 19). The pervasive image of ad-hocery and muddling through seems to deny both purpose and coherence. Hales (1986) rightly observes that by focusing on individual jobs, rather than management as a process, behaviour is unsituated and neglects the institutional context and functions. This is worsened by the tendency of behavioural analysis to concentrate on observable activities in a non-problematical way. For all its limitations, responsibilities and functions were the focus of classical theory. In this sense 'realism' marks a retreat from a broader framework of analysis. Understanding managerial work requires questions to be asked not just about what managers do, but what they have to ensure others do; in other words, an emphasis on the control of particular organisational units in the labour process, though Hales later qualifies this by referring to control as one *phase* of the management process (1988: 5).

CONTROL AND POWER IN MAINSTREAM PERSPECTIVES

Yet it is precisely issues of control and power that are neglected in mainstream perspectives: 'the commonsense, technical images developed by managers to acount for their activities get returned to them in the form of apolitical descriptions of the reality of their work' (Willmott, 1984: 350). Control *is* discussed explicitly in standard textbooks, though the chapters devoted to it are sometimes of a rather bizarre nature in almost omitting any reference to conflicts between groups. The talk is of technical inputs and outputs in a self-adjusting system, performance standards and feedback mechanisms. Control is reduced to a *monitoring* device, with management's role being to check progress, ensure that actions occur as planned and to correct any deviation. It is also seen in a unitary way: 'controlled performance' with an assumption of goal-consensus. Some writers (Lawlor, 1976) put an emphasis on people *desiring* control, for example, getting enjoyment from dependence on higher authority. Resistance is smuggled in occasionally when discussing the *behavioural* implications as people 'react' to control processes, requiring management to adjust strategies accordingly.

We do accept that not all control processes arise or are structured by antagonistic interests. Stock inventories and financial budgeting are necessary and not always conflictual features of any system of work organisation. A written job description may under certain conditions actually allow employees to assert power or control. But most control processes remain difficult to separate from the social relations of work, even when they appear to be neutral. This was the important conclusion of Blau and Schoenherr (1971), who used the concept of *insidious* controls to highlight the way in which management can utilise impersonal and unobtrusive means. The power dimensions are not easily identifiable compared to chains of command backed by sanctions. Examples include selective recruitment of staff whose sense of professionalism or expertise enable them to work without direct controls; use of resource allocation as a financial discipline; and controls embodied in technology. Thus even those staff who exercise considerable work autonomy, such as those in higher education, have a series of indirect constraints over their actions.

In contrast to control, most organisational behaviour textbooks simply don't have chapters on power, or if they do, admit that it has been largely ignored (Luthans, 1981: 387). Sometimes power is subsumed under chapters on leadership, or raised only as a factor in classification schemes through Etzioni's structures of compliance (discussed in Chapter 1). Power relations may be simply written out of the picture, for example, by redefining 'subordinates' as 'non-managers' (Mullins, 1985: 238). They then have a shadowy existence, hidden within discussions of why management finds it 'difficult to delegate', focusing on personal disposition rather than the structures of power that shape them. Debates on management style will contain occasional advice on *when* to use authoritarian methods, Hitt *et al.* writing that in today's large corporations 'fear must be used cautiously' (1986: 43). Furthermore, power is the hidden agenda when managerial prerogatives are stressed, though the ideological needs of management may blunt the directness of language. But what else is meant when the phrase 'management must manage' is used?

Some of the roots of the neglect can be traced to the historical association in organisation theory between rational, formal organisation and legitimate authority (Clegg and Dunkerley, 1980: 433–4). Theorists such as Parsons see authority as granting a consensual 'power to' structure the behaviour of others (Storey, 1983: 54–5). Alternatively, power is linked to the breakdown of authority and the growth of informal practices. This can be seen in a standard definition of organisational power quoted in Luthans, 'the management of influence to obtain ends not sanctioned by the organisation' (1981: 389). As a result, any research that does exist on power concentrates on its *exercise*, taking, as we shall show later, the formal organisation and deeper power relations for granted.

There is a small literature on power within mainstream perspectives. Its orientation is towards an analysis of the *internal* politics of organisations, which Pfeffer defines as: 'Those activities within organisations to acquire, develop and use power and other resources to obtain one's preferred outcomes in a situation where there is dissension or uncertainty about choices' (1981: 10). A narrow focus on power in a solely organisational setting was itself indicative of what Hinings (1988) refers to as the continuing divorce of organisation theory from sociology. Within this framework one of the best-known contributions is from French and Raven (1959), who start from the concept of 'bases of power' located in organisational resources. They are available for use singly or jointly by the manager, but depend on the perceptions and responses of those 'targeted'.

Reward: The use of resources as rewards, where the target values the chosen method and believes it can be delivered. Can include not just money, but promotions, increased job satisfaction and social recognition.

Coercive: The capacity to enforce discipline. Rests ultimately on the fear of the likelihood of psychological or material punishment, whether loss of overtime bonuses or humiliation in front of the peer group for poor sales figures.

Referent: The personal characteristics of the manager are perceived as attractive by employees, generating feelings of identification. Similar to Weber's concept of charismatic power.

Legitimate: Power is made acceptable by subordinates acquiescing in the right of power-holders to influence them. Linked strongly to the idea of authority.

Expert: The existence of power as knowledge or other forms of expertise attributed to individuals or groups, which others feel obliged to accept. It is in itself a type of legitimacy.

There is some evidence concerning the application and effectiveness of these sources of power (see Luthans, 1981: 395–401).

Not surprisingly it shows that non-formal sources such as expert power impact most favourably on organisational effectiveness. But given the questionnaire methods used, this may tell us more about cultural expectations than actual work practices.

That is not the only problem. The French and Raven categories are widely regarded as too individualistic. In practice, organisations are composed of *coalitions* which compete for resources and influence. Individuals seeking sources of power normally have to work within sectional interest groups, such as departments or specialist occupations. Pettigrew's (1973) research showed computer programmers locked into a power struggle with systems analysts. Their weapons were ideologies of expertise, exclusivity of technique by avoiding written records and control of recruitment policies. Political *skills* are vital in these processes. We have already referred to how these are used by managers to build alliances and informal networks that are sometimes dubbed 'dominant coalitions' (Kotter: 1982).

This political view clearly starts from realist assumptions which 'see the manager not as a servant of the owners nor as a technocrat serving the system, but as a manipulator trying to compete and co-operate with others in order to pursue his own ends' (Lee, 1985: 206). It is also a *pluralist* perspective in that it recognises multiple and competing goals as well as internal bargaining processes. The resultant internal political systems do, however, tend to stabilise themselves through the stake in the survival of the whole system held by the competing parties and the extra power wielded by top management. Political skills such as advocacy may even be useful to the company in a competitive environment. What are the dynamics of the internal power structure? A coherent explanation synthesising a range of other studies is provided through the *strategic contingencies* model of Hickson *et al.* (1973). This starts from the observation that it is necessary to treat power as the property of a social relationship, particularly the departmental division of labour between purchasing, marketing and so on, rather than individual action. These social relations are shaped by external and internal factors.

At the external level, we return to the open systems model

discussed in Chapter 3. Coping with uncertainty is a crucial feature in transactions between organisations and the environment. The internal institutions charged with this responsibility are the *sub-units*, such as departments. Power enters the picture because those sub-units which can cope with uncertainty will be able to exercise power in their competitive struggle for resources with their rivals. Hickson and McCullough (1980) use the example of purchasing agents who were trying to expand their limited power base, trying to move from merely placing orders and ensuring delivery, to the provision of information to management and planning new products. The tactics used involved building alliances with contacts in other departments and manipulation of rules. But power could only really be gained when the customer environment contained a variety of suppliers, thus increasing the dependency of other sections on purchasing.

Such examples indicate that structural contingencies constitute a number of variables which shape power. Ability to deal with uncertainty is complemented by the degree of *dependency* on other units, the extent to which activities are *substitutable* and on the overall level of *centrality* to the organisation. Therefore power is gained through the process of exchange and control of strategic contingencies. Though the point is not often made, this kind of analysis can be extended to shopfloor employees. 'Lower participants', as Mechanic (1962) describes them, can also utilise power derived from control over uncertainty. Amongst his examples were hospital orderlies who exploited their skills and access to information in order to control waiting lists for operations against more senior medical staff disinterested in administration. In a more industrial relations context, Marchington (1982) has explicitly used the strategic contingency framework to analyse the power of workgroups in the production cycle.

A Critical Evaluation

The literature on internal politics and power is very useful, particularly when set against the traditional conceptions of rational management. Its limitations flow from being confined to a particular *level* of power relations. Power is analysed through its symptoms, by what is observable through behavioural exchange and by identifying who the players are. This is linked to the focus of strategic contingency theory being primarily *horizontal* power relations. Vertical power hierarchies are set aside by the interpretation of the division of labour as consisting of relations between sub-units. Such neglect is reinforced by the tendency to see managerial authority and goals as always accepted by workers, or at least subject to joint regulation and negotiated outcome through the interplay of power. Substantial power differences and sources of dissension are therefore underestimated. We need to deal with 'power over' as well as 'power to', and treat managerial authority as a *form* of organisational power.

Clegg's (1977) critique is pertinent here. French and Raven and the strategic contingency theory can show how managers use resources to exercise power. Neither explain the prior distribution of power, how some people come to have access to these resources while others do not. The exercise of power is premised on institutional frameworks and rules, 'the "power" of the sub-unit has to be grounded in the prior *capacity* to exercise power which managers possess' (Clegg: 27). Furthermore, managerial power has to be located within deeper structures of economic domination which underpin its use and legitimacy. A prime example is the concentration of ownership and control in the transnational company. The power to switch resources and relocate operations simply cannot be explained at the level of the single enterprise and its sub-units. Without such a structural framework, we are left with a micro-level analysis capable only of explaining the skills of 'politicking' rather than political power. We are also left with a view of managers solely as self-interested manipulators and power-seekers with little understanding of the broader dynamics and constraints that dispose *management* to use power in the first place.

These differences in perspective can be clarified by reference to the wider debate on power, taking the three-dimensional model of Lukes (1982) as a framework. The behavioural literature is primarily one-dimensional in that it focuses on the observable activities of particular 'subjects', seeking proof of power in processes such as decision-making. But organisational studies draws on a definition of power developed by Dahl (1957), which itself is based on Weber (1968). Power is seen as the ability of A to get B to do something they would not do otherwise, despite any resistance. Note that this formulation is specifically linked to intended effects and imposition of will: 'Power is only relevant to our understanding of behaviour and organisation, when there is conflict' (Dawson, 1986: 148). On this basis rests the behavioural assumption that power can always be observed and measured.

In the broader debate the one-dimensional view has been criticised by writers such as Bachrach and Baratz (1962), utilising the concept of 'non-decision making'. This may sound odd, but refers to the capacity of power-holders to limit those issues which are contested or even discussed. By controlling agendas and mobilising the bias inherent in greater access to institutional resources, values and even the language of legitimacy, they can keep to safe issues and exclude others that threaten their interests. Though the research deals with political actors, there is no doubt that management actions can be seen in this light. Crucial decisions regarding investment or the introduction of new technology very seldom reach normal bargaining, except perhaps to deal with the consequences. In industrial relations terminology they are 'non-negotiable', particularly when market trends favour employers. Even with worker-director schemes such as those at British Steel in the 1970s, management could manipulate the rules of the game and socialise workforce representatives to the extent that their interests were not seriously contested (Brannen, 1983).

Lukes (1974: 21) pays tribute to this 'two-dimensional' analysis, but argues that it remains too much on the terrain of observable behaviour. Elite power can prevent grievances, and therefore conflict, from ever arising by shaping the very wants and preferences of subordinate groups. This is not a question of brainwashing. Market mechanisms and the distribution of wealth and property constitute power relations – such as ownership rights – which frequently come to be taken for granted. Though there are concrete practices that arise from such relations, they are not always observable in the traditional sense. Power does not necessarily need a subject. As Clegg and Dunkerley observe: 'Much of the time the power of capital does not have to be exercised to be present ... because this exercise is grounded in a structural "capacity" which frequently obviates the need for its exercise' (1980: 495).

Though the processes cannot always be measured, the outcomes can in terms of structural inequalities between groups. For Lukes, this indicates that a latent conflict exists, 'which consists of a contradiction between the interests of those exercising power and the *real* interests of those they exclude' (1974: 284). His three-dimensional explanation of power in general therefore coincides with radical perspectives on organisational power, which would draw on Weber and Marx's analysis of the deeper economic roots of domination. This involves a different understanding of 'dependency' in which there is a 'fundamental asymmetry of power between employers and workers' (Rueschemeyer, 1986: 76), based on workers' lack of control of the means of production. The propertyless have to 'seek access to resources owned or controlled by the few' (Fox, 1974: 284). When Nissan opened their factory in the North-East of England, they had 30,000 applications for 300 jobs. Not surprisingly this enabled them to pick workers and a union wholly on their own terms. The lesson of this discussion should therefore be that, rather than seeking an all-encompassing definition of power, we require an analysis that can deal with all three dimensions.

CONTROL: RADICAL PERSPECTIVES

Despite their critique that mainstream theories neglect or misunderstand power, radical writers on organisation and management begin from an analysis of *control* relations. Most use a broadly Marxist framework, in which 'power is expressed in organisations through the control of the means and methods of production ' (Clegg and Dunkerley, 1980: 476). This can be contrasted to managerial revolution theories which divorce management power from property and production relations. Dahrendorf reverses the formula, 'control over the means of production is but a special case of authority' (quoted in Johnston, 1986: 35).

The theorisation of control over the labour process was explained in Chapter 1, but can be briefly restated. Competition between capitals requires employers to seek control over the conditions under which work takes place. Control is not an end in itself, but *a* means to transform the capacity to work, established by the wage relation, into profitable production. It is a term, 'summarising a set of mechanisms and practices that regulate the labour process' (P. K. Edwards, 1987: 17). Richard Edwards (1979: 18) distinguishes three elements in any system of control:

(i)   direction and specification of work tasks;
(ii)   evaluation, monitoring and assessment of performance;
(iii) the apparatus of discipline and reward to elicit co-operation and compliance.

Such elements may, however, be best described as *detailed* control, in that they are normally connected to immediate work processes, whereas *general* control refers to management's capacity to subordinate labour to their direction of the production process as a whole. This distinction made by P. K. Edwards (1987) and other writers is of significance in that it allows for recognition of tremendous variations in how detailed control is exercised. Such a model can even allow for employers giving workers significant discretion over tasks, as in work humanisation schemes, *if* it maintains their overall control. Control is also not absolute but, at least at the immediate level, a contested relationship. Conflict is built into the wage-effort bargain, with even mainstream writers recognising that an employment contract outlining required performance runs up against employees with their own goals and wants.

What about the role of management? Claims of independent actors carrying out a neutral role are disputed by evidence concerning the top strata of management (Zeitlin, 1974). By their motivation, social background and connections, rewards and share-holdings in corporations, most are

part of the capitalist class. While a useful corrective, this
'sociological' analysis is not the crucial point. For example, a
number of entrepreneurs, such as Alan Sugar of Amstrad, are
from a traditional working-class background. But what matters is the structural location and *functions* in the organisation.
If anything, entrepreneurs from this background tend to
identify even more closely with their new role.

Proceeding from an analysis of process and functions,
radical theorists (Carchedi, 1977; Edwards, 1979) argue that
management perform a *dual* function in the enterprise. Managerial practices are a necessary means of *co-ordinating*
diverse activities and services, particularly as production
becomes a more collective process. However, they also bear
the imprint of the antagonistic social relations within the
capitalist labour process. These require management to carry
out functions of *control* and surveillance, exercising hierarchical
authority over workers separated from the means of production. While it is not always clear that it is possible to
distinguish between a 'neutral' co-ordination and an 'antagonistic' control, managers do act as agents carrying out the
'global functions' of capital, functions which, as we observed
in Chapter 2, were delegated as part of the process of bureaucratisation of production. Though Marxists talk in terms of
managers being the 'personification of economic categories',
the idea of agency should not conjure up images of conspiracies
and empty vessels, but rather active and diverse means
through which the requirements of capital are brought about.

Such analyses often get tangled up in attempts to designate
managers to precise class positions. This theme does not
concern us here (though see Johnston, 1986, for a critical
account). What is important is that we have available a
framework for understanding management practices which
provides an alternative to the dominant combination of
behavioural and managerial revolution theories. The fact, for
example, that executives of a large corporation have the
formal status of *employees* is, as Braverman observes, merely
the form given to the domination of capital in modern society:

Their formal attribute of being part of the same payroll as
the production workers, clerks and porters of the corporation

no more robs them of the powers of decision and command over the others in the enterprise than does the fact that the general, like the private, wears the military uniform, or the pope and the cardinal pronounce the same liturgy as the parish priest. (1974: 405).

Instead of the separation of ownership and control, radical writers distinguish between *real* or *economic* ownership and agents holding actual *possession* (De Vroey, 1975; Carchedi, 1977). Managerial agents are governed by the external constraints imposed by the dynamics of competition and capital accumulation, with profitability remaining the crucial criteria through which the successful management work is judged. If anything, this is enhanced by property ownership and related forms of control becoming increasingly depersonalised with the rise of finance, pension funds and other institutional shareholders. Individual enterprises become 'simply units in a structure of intercorporate relations' (Scott, 1985: 142), the division of ownership and possession resulting in greater vulnerability for managers who know they may be removed from office (Holland, 1975).

A structural analysis does not imply that the growth of new forms of managerial labour is irrelevant. The heterogeneity of management has increased with the sheer extent and diversity of delegated functions and the competing groups, such as accountants and engineers, who lay claim to them. Within an increasingly complex hierarchy, middle- and lower-level managers occupy 'contradictory class locations' (Wright, 1976), carrying out functions as agents of capital *and* as salaried employees. They are likely to exercise 'partial' possession; operational rather than allocative control to use the language of organisational analysis (Carter, 1985: 122). We will return to the significance of these divisions later. All this has taken us a long way from the opening point of this section: that radical theories begin with control rather than power. In the enterprise, 'power will be exercised to re-assert control' by management (Clegg and Dunkerley, 1980: 481). This should not mean that power is marginal or subsumed under control. The ability of employers to exert controls over labour is conditioned by a variety of different power relations. In particular

companies or sectors, crucial factors will include those arising
from product and labour markets, the state of employer and
worker organisation, and factors identified by strategic contingency theorists such as management dependence on
specific occupational and workgroups. Such issues should not
be relegated to the sphere of industrial relations, but regarded
as an integral part of organisational analysis.

We must also recognise that control structures are shaped
by broader non-industrial power relations, such as those
embodied in employment laws which sustain the power of
capital, or relations of social dependence in the community
which are transferred into the workplace. Broader power
relations are significant in another sense, in that they may
reproduce themselves in the workplace independently of control systems. A prime example is that of *sexuality* (Hearn and
Parkin, 1987). Sexual harassment at work, whether at the
office party or in promotion processes, is a means through
which individual men exert their power over women. The
difficulty of women entering management and male occupational preserves is connected to perceived threats to masculine
identity as well as to conventional material interests. Of
course, sexuality and gender *can* be used as a collective
method of control, as numerous studies show (see Thompson,
1983: 196–7), but power relations are not reducible to them.
Thus in this example, as in general, processes of control and
power are both independent and interrelated inside and outside the workplace. More concrete discussion should reveal
those complexities, not treat them as synonymous or analogues.

Management Strategies

Radical perspectives on management and control were given
more concrete form by the work of Braverman (1974). He is
noted for his argument that the twentieth century has seen the
tightening of managerial control, primarily through the application of Taylorist and scientific management strategies.
Detailed evidence is provided of the extension of such methods
from simple to complex production and its use in the transformation of clerical labour. When allied to managerial shaping

of science and technology through mechanisation and automation, work design and organisation continue to embody key Taylorist principles such as task fragmentation and the separation of conception and execution. Braverman provided an important corrective to the widespread view that Taylorism was a failed system, superseded by more sophisticated behavioural theories to be used for motivational and job design tools (see Rose, 1975). But it is widely recognised that Braverman overestimated the dominance of Taylorist strategies and practices and underestimated the varied and uneven implementation, influenced by worker hostility, management suspicion and appropriateness to given environments.

This was shown in Chapter 2 and a similar assessment can be made of more modern circumstances. If Taylorism is taken to be part of a broader movement towards 'scientific' management focused on fragmentation of tasks and their subjection to increasing job measurement and evaluation, as well as the structuring of work processes so that skills and planning activities are located off the factory and office floor, then particular elements remain a highly significant component of control strategies, though seldom on their own. Even the most advanced 'Japanese' systems of work organisation such as those in the US auto industry, which embody variability of production, reskilling and flexibility between tasks, and use of workers' knowledge in job design, rest in some writers' view on a 'superTaylorism' of precise specification of tasks and the cycle time to complete them (Slaughter, 1987: 5–6). We will look at these issues of job design in more detail in Chapter 5.

Precisely because Braverman confused a particular system of control with management control in general, the question of strategy was put firmly on the agenda because of the resulting debate on *alternatives*. This is not to say that issues of strategy had no place in the existing organisational literature. We have already seen in Chapter 3 how Chandler (1962) regarded strategy, defined as long-term planning and resource allocation to carry out goals, as the characteristic feature of the modern multidivisional firm. But control over employees was not systematically dealt with. Strategy has also been increasingly part of the agenda of the business policy and corporate management literature (Steiner and Miner, 1978).

Radical perspectives differ from both in avoiding the prescriptive search for the 'best way', remaining free to analyse what management *does*, rather than what it *should* do.

What of the alternative strategies raised in the labour process debate? Some of the best-known contributions have already been discussed in previous chapters. Richard Edwards's (1979) model is based on historically successive dominant modes of control which reflect worker resistance and changing socio-economic conditions. A nineteenth-century system of *simple* or *personal* control by employers exercising direct authority gave way to more complex *structural* forms with the transition from small-business, competitive capitalism to corporate monopolies. The first of these forms was *technical* control typified by the use of the assembly line which can pace and direct the labour process. The contradiction for management is that it created a common work experience and basis for unified shopfloor opposition. In contrast, a system of *bureaucratic* control (see Chapter 2) embedded in the social and organisational structure of the firm rather than in personal authority, offers management a means of re-dividing the workforce and tying it to impersonal rules and regulations. With his co-thinkers among radical economists (Edwards, Reich and Gordon, 1975; Gordon, Edwards and Reich, 1982), Edwards has also argued that employers consciously create *segmented* labour markets as a response to economic crises and as a divide-and-rule strategy, particularly using gender and race.

In contrast, Friedman (1977) rightly eschews the notion of stages, preferring to set out ideal types or strategic poles of responsible autonomy and direct control which run parallel throughout the history of capitalism (for a description see Chapter 3). Each strategy generates its own inflexibilities in areas such as hiring-and-firing and task specification. The choice of strategy is governed by variations in the stability of labour and product markets, mediated by the interplay of worker resistance and managerial pressure. There is, however, an element of common ground in the belief that there has been a gradual historical tendency towards more consensual, integrative strategies, utilising internal markets, institutionalised rules and, in some cases, work humanisation schemes.

This is also the view of the other major control theorist, Burawoy (1979, 1985). He periodises the development of capitalist work organisation in terms of the transition from *despotic* to *hegemonic* regimes. The former involved relations of dependence and coercion that did not prove viable for capital or labour. Workers sought collective representation and social protection from the state. Capital also had an interest in state regulation of conflict and a minimal social wage that would boost purchasing power. The shift to hegemonic regimes was also based on an internal state in the workplace that provided an 'industrial citizenship', utilising grievance machinery and regulated bargaining that minimised likely resistance and class solidarity.

This kind of judgement of long-term trends has not looked quite so accurate in a period where many companies have used the recession to restructure the workplace. While some writers (see MacInnes, 1987) doubt whether the basic features of industrial and employment relations have significantly changed, there is certainly considerable evidence that in Britain and the United States many employers are consciously reconstituting employment practices. In the latter (Parker, 1985) there have been aggressive deunionisation campaigns and 'concession-bargaining' which forces workers to renegotiate worse pay and conditions. While Britain's deeply rooted union tradition largely prevents the deunionisation and concession-bargaining, there has been a strong emphasis, particularly in the newer industries, on single-union and 'no-strike' deals; reduced demarcation and increased flexibility; more direct management communication with the shop floor, bypassing shop stewards; as well as new human resource initiatives like quality circles (Morgan and Sayer, 1984; and see Chapter 5).

Events of this nature have led Burawoy to define the new dominant factory regime as one of *hegemonic despotism*. This is not a return to arbitrary tyranny but the apparently 'rational' power of a capital that is mobile across the globe, over the workforce (1985: 150). But regardless of the pervasiveness of such trends, new conceptual categories of this nature merely illustrate the fundamental problem of the control theories we have been examining. Alternative strategies have been put on the map but too often within what has been described as the 'panacea fallacy' (Littler and Salaman, 1982) or 'monism' (Storey, 1985), that is, the idea that capital always seeks and finds definitive and comprehensive modes of control as the solution to its problems. Admittedly, this is somewhat less true of Friedman, who in his own defence argues that responsible autonomy and direct control have in-built contradictions and are 'two directions towards which managers can move, rather than two predefined states between which managers choose' (1986: 3). But there is still a sense of a search for all-embracing categories which have their parallels in behavioural theory, such as Etzioni's (1961) structures of compliance, or Schein's (1965) linear models of economic, social and complex man.

Nevertheless, the control debate has sparked off an extensive and useful amount of empirical work within the parameters of labour process theory. Early case studies tended to focus on reaffirmation of theses of deskilling and tighter controls (Zimbalist, 1979), or critiques of them highlighting mediating factors such as markets and worker resistance (Wood, 1982). More recent efforts have been concerned to establish trends in their own right. Studies dealing with the introduction of new technology have stressed that deskilling and direct control represent only one of a range of management strategies. We have already discussed the variations shown in Wilkinson's study (see Chapter 3). Child's (1985) research shows even more clearly how ideas of strategy can be used, whilst recognising variations in goals and environments. He identified a variety of strategies including elimination of direct labour, sub-contracting, polyvalence or multi-tasking, and job degradation. These were connected to an even wider set of influences, including those of national economic cycles, government policy and the culture of organisations.

Some research has tried to apply models to specific industries, but without any claims for universality. A good example is the use by Murray and Wickham (1985) of Richard Edwards's theory of bureaucratic control. They studied two Irish electronics factories employing mainly female semi-skilled workers, showing that direction, discipline and evaluation are all carried out according to explicit rules rather than direct controls. Supervisors do not monitor production performance and enforce discipline. This is left to inspectors on the basis of statistical records that can identify the operators responsible. Supervisors, however, are central to processes of evaluating the social character of the 'good worker' in order to facilitate promotion through the internal labour market. The elaborate and artificial hierarchy created at the plants meant that one third of workers had been promoted from the basic assembly grade, thus confirming Edward's view that employees are given positive material reasons for complying with bureaucratic rules.

Other studies have focused on specific strategies and processes of control such as recruitment policies (Fevre, 1986; Maguire 1986; Winstanley, 1986) neglected in an exclusive focus on the labour process. The most extensive research has been carried out on *gender*. Socially defined notions of femininity as a form of control have been observed in multinationals operating in the third world (Pearson, 1986). Plant management consciously exploit cultures of passivity and subordination by combining an image of the company as a patriarchal family system, with the manager as father figure, western-style beauty competitions and classes (Grossman: 1979). In the West, Grieco and Whipp's overview argues that 'managerial strategies of control make use of and enhance the sexual divisions in society' (1986: 136). Studies of office and factory workers (Glenn and Feldberg, 1979; Pollert, 1981; Westwood, 1984; Bradley, 1986) show that management use women's marginality to work, arising from the family, to frame their labour control policies. Strategies of paternalism and restrictive controls on supervision and piece rates are frequent, though not always successful or uncontested.

In reflecting on the above debates, a degree of common ground emerges. Product and labour markets, worker resistance and a range of other external and internal factors are recognised as mediating control strategies and shaping power relations in the frontier of control between capital and labour. The variations in strategy that result are not random but reflect the fundamental tension we have talked of between managements' need to control and discipline whilst engaging workers' commitment and co-operation. Strategies therefore

contain inherent contradictions (Storey, 1985; Hyman, 1987).
These are enhanced by the difficulty of harmonising the different managerial functions, sites of intervention and decision-
making, that include technology, social organisation of labour
and relations with the representative bodies of employees.
Hyman notes that 'there is no "one best way" of managing
these contradictions, only different routes to partial failure'
(1987: 30). Management of large organisations are therefore
likely to try *combinations* of control strategies and practices
appropriate to particular environments or sections of the
workforce. As one of us has remarked elsewhere:

> The most consistent weakness of existing theory has been to
> counterpose one form of control to another ... No one has
> convincingly demonstrated that a particular form of control
> is necessary or inevitable for capitalism to function success-
> fully. (Thompson, 1983: 151)

Questioning the Idea of Control Strategies

The above 'consensus' does not satisfy those within and
outside the radical perspective who are critical of the explanatory power of concepts of management control strategy. They
go beyond the previously noted criticism of 'panacea fallacies'
to object to the treatment of management as omniscient,
omnipotent and monolithic. Based on her study of chemical
plants, Harris mocks the image of managers who have the
attributes of deity and 'papal inerrancy' when dealing with
workers, commenting that radical writers assume senior management 'always know what is in capital's interests and
unfailingly order things so that they work together for its
greater good' (1987: 70). There are conflicts within management reflecting contending interest groups and the difficulty of
carrying out integrative functions. Nor is it always possible to
draw a neat dividing line among workers, given that managers
are also wage labourers subject to controls. The distortions in
such analyses are held to derive from a wider determinism and
functionalism in which 'managers are regarded as unproblematic agents of capital who dispatch their "global functions"

in a rationalistic manner' (Storey, 1985: 195). Capital's interests are not given and management practices cannot be 'read-off' from them. Assumptions of a 'tight-coupling' underestimate the diversity and complexity of such practices and the significance of decision-making processes within the enterprise. As a result there are too few insights into what 'flesh and blood' managers actually do.

At a general level some of these criticisms would be accepted across a wide spectrum. But some would carry it much further: 'current uses of the terms "strategy" and "control" are somewhat misleading guides both to actual management conduct and to the causes of particular outcomes in work organisation and industrial relations' (Rose and Jones, 1985: 82). We can break this down into two issues: do identifiable management strategies exist and are practices centred on controlling workers? Those who argue against the idea of coherent strategies with a fixity of purpose believe that management activities are more likely to be piecemeal, uncoordinated and fragmented, with at best a striving for logical incrementalism. Management is concerned primarily with 'keeping the show on the road' (Tomlinson, 1982: 128), corresponding with the 'realist' views discussed earlier.

Supportive research exists in areas such as work reorganisation schemes (Rose and Jones, 1985) and new technology and skills in engineering (Campbell and Currie, 1987). Any strategic capacity is held to be inevitably undermined by a plethora of sites of decision-making; varied objectives among different management specialists and interest groups; the need to smooth over diverse and contradictory practices; and the requirement of sustaining a consensual accommodation with employee organisations. The result is an unpredictable variety of managerial intentions characterised by a 'plant particularism' (Rose and Jones, 1985: 96) and control structures as merely 'temporary outcomes' (Storey, 1985). Campbell and Currie plump for the idea of 'negotiated preferences' and there is a general orientation towards explanations based on *practices* rather than strategy.

Some of these differences may reflect the sector being researched. For example, engineering is well-known for its 'seat-of-the-pants' approach to management, whereas other sectors such as food or chemicals are noted for a more strategic approach. Nevertheless, this kind of approach is confirmed by some writers on industrial relations (Purcell and Sissons, 1983) who note the problems created by the absence of management strategies towards their own employees, particularly ones that are integrated into overall business objectives. Instead, there is a continued dominance of reactive and opportunistic practices directed towards immediate problem-solving (Thurley and Wood, 1983: 209). What *kind* of strategy is said to be absent is not always made explicit. But the basic model used is similar to that popularised by Chandler. That is of a detailed and co-ordinated plan of campaign in which conscious, long-term planning based on corporate goals is supported by appropriate courses of action and allocation of resources; management by structured foresight. This is very much in line with the *business* policy debate (Steiner and Miner, 1978) in which the burgeoning number of MBA students are warned of the negative consequences of the absence of corporate strategy.

But conceptions of management strategy in the above frameworks are in themselves problematic. While it is wrong to attribute rational intent to management, it is equally mistaken to assume that strategy has to be seen as always consistent, systematic and without contradiction. Strategies may not always be effectively followed through at the implementation stage, as with the introduction of new technology. They may not constitute a coherent package for the whole operations of a company, perhaps manifesting a disjuncture between job design plans and employee relations. Coherence is an important variable but it has to be set against the knowledge of inevitable contradictions and the likelihood of 'loose-coupling' between planning and practices. Strategies are likely to be accompanied by bargaining within management and with the workforce, so making the end result uncertain. As Friedman rightly notes: 'Irrationality, inconsistency, lack of system certainly exist and must be allowed for; however, a more useful concept to introduce is failure' (1987: 294). Even where changes are introduced without clear intent they can establish the preconditions for subsequent strategy (Hyman, 1987: 47).

While managers frequently act on the world with poor information, they can and do act strategically. It is only necessary for researchers to show a degree of intent or planning and to infer a logic over a period of time from the frequency and pattern of action, or from 'emergent outcomes' (Hales, 1988: 12). The same criteria apply to the activities of workers. Groups such as printers or doctors do not always behave in a fully conscious or coherent manner. But observation reveals a clear pattern of operation of occupational and job controls, strategies of closure aimed at excluding competitors, often women (Cockburn, 1983; Witz, 1986a). The mistake the critics have made is to set criteria for strategy so stringently that it becomes impossible to meet them (Child, 1985). Of course, the capacity for strategy is not random. Certain external conditions are likely to push management in that direction. Streek (1987) puts forward a persuasive case that economic crisis and rapidly changing market environments have created a 'general strategic problem' whose core element is the need for *flexibility*.

However, the very nature of uncertainty and varied conditions in sectors and countries produces different strategic responses. For example, countries such as West Germany and Austria with traditions of tripartite state, union and employer bargaining have seen moves towards flexibility that retains a strong union role and corporatist regulation of wages and labour markets. Streek's analysis not only builds in an explanation of such variations, it provides a framework for understanding the *general* conditions under which strategies develop. At times of crisis and readjustment, 'the variety of strategies and structures within the collectivity of firms is bound to increase at least until a new standard of "best practice" has been established' (1987: 284). This is not the case at all times. More stable environments produce routinisation of decisions, with management practices governed by tactical accommodations rather than strategic thinking. Britain in the 1950s is a case in point. Economic expansion and new markets, combined with labour shortages, created conditions for the growth of powerful shop steward structures and localised bargaining. Industrial relations was characterised by short-term considerations and 'fire-fighting' which became a dangerous liability for employers as conditions changed in the next decade.

The second strand of critique questions whether the centrality given to control of labour is actually reflective of managerial behaviour. It is argued that we cannot view management strategies and tactics from the vantage point of the labour process but must consider the role of product and labour markets and technologies. Control proceeds in a complex cycle from planning to implementation, involving groups such as accountants and industrial engineers. Analysis should focus on the 'multiple constituents of management expertise beyond the confrontation of capital and labour in the control of the labour process' (Miller and O'Leary, 1987: 10). Such a critique can be presented in a 'Marxist' form. Accumulation and costs of production are what matters to capital and its agents, not control. If anything, managers are dominated by problems of the *outcomes* of the labour process, including sales, marketing, supply and cash flow. Kelly uses the concept of the full circuit of capital to argue that we must be concerned not only with the *extraction* of surplus value through controlling the labour process, but its *realisation* through the sale of commodities, as well as the prior *purchase* of labour. On these grounds, 'there is no sound reason for privileging any moment in the circuit' (1985: 32).

Morgan and Hooper use a similar framework in their research into the Imperial Tobacco Group in the 1970s to distinguish between three circuits of capital. *Industrial* capital refers to that used in the management and design of the production process itself; *commercial* to the sphere of buying and selling and therefore functions such as marketing, advertising; and *banking* to the process of capital used in lending and borrowing, governed by accountancy and financial controls.

These distinctions are used to argue that radical theories of the labour process have often lost sight of the role of capital and ownership because of the emphasis on *management* control. The case study shows a series of strategies pursued in tandem, representing the particular circuits. To break out of a static tobacco market, top management prioritised commercial and banking strategies rather than develop existing labour processes. In particular, companies such as Imperial were drawn into investments in the share and gilts markets. These proved successful but when the resultant money was invested in production they had disastrous results. Firms are thus conceptualised as 'sites of a complex integration of circuits of capital' (1987: 623) which management must integrate and control.

Other writers question whether control can be regarded as the factor which distinguishes between a dominant management and a subordinate labour. Management has non-control functions and characteristics of employees, while workers exercise job controls and may be involved in the regulation of others (Melling, 1981b: 249). At a more theoretical level, Cressey and MacInnes (1980) observe that workers have an interest in the viability of their own units of capital as well as resisting subordination, matching capital's dual relationship with labour as a commodity and as a source of co-operation necessary for profitable production. Some mainstream writers use their own research into the chemical industry (Harris: 1987) and those of chemicals, engineering and biscuits (Buchanan, 1986) to argue that workers basically accept managerial authority, give commitment and effort willingly, and have convergent interests with management, thus negating any preoccupation with control. This is likely to be linked to a rejection of 'zero-sum' conceptions of power in which one side necessarily gains at the expense of the other (Harris: 77). Even some radical writers believe that capital and management are not necessarily dominant, with unions having considerably more power, even in a recession, than usually acknowledged (Kelly, 1985: 49; Rose and Jones, 1985: 101).

It is certainly true that, as Hyman observes, 'If most orthodox literature on business strategy ignores or marginalises the conflict between capital and labour, most Marxist literature perceives nothing else' (1987: 34). This has a curious parallel with the virtual total emphasis in organisation behaviour on 'man-management'. So the full circuit of capital is a very useful and necessary concept for understanding the capitalist enterprise. Furthermore, change and crisis often arise from disarticulation of the moments of the circuit (Kelly, 1985), as we saw in the Imperial example. However, that does not invalidate a specific emphasis on relations of control between capital and labour. This is not *just* another process equivalent to marketing or financial accounting. The management of workers and work remains at the heart of the enterprise and, indeed, of economic reproduction as a whole. But such an orientation need have no marginalising effect on the analysis of other social relations. As P. K. Edwards (1987) observes, the problem of 'privileging' one part of the circuit arises only if the analysis assumes that this one part determines what happens in the others.

Nor are we saying that control is normally the *goal* of management but rather a *means* embodied in strategies and techniques. It is true that management strategies are not always developed with labour's role in mind. But it is ultimately difficult to separate a concern with 'outcomes', such as product quality or financial targets, from acting on labour in some way. Strategies towards markets or technologies will often be constrained or mediated by labour policies and the practices of workers (Friedman, 1986). In addition, as Child notes: 'strategies which are unspecific towards the labour process may still have relevance for it' (1985: 110). An example is the introduction of new technology, which much research shows is frequently used as a means of more general work reorganisation.

On the issue of the existence of co-operation and common interests we would wholly concur. In fact, we would go further. As one of us has observed, 'Workers do not always need to be overtly controlled. They may effectively 'control' themselves' (Thompson, 1983: 153). Participation in routine practices to create interest or increase rewards can generate *consent* to existing structures of control and power, as Burawoy's (1979) famous studies of production 'games' indicate. What is puzzling is why some writers insist on co-operative and consensual processes being *counterposed* to those of control and conflict. It is increasingly recognised that all have to be theorised as different products of the contradictory relations within the enterprise. Not only do consent and control coexist, 'the mobilisation of consent' forms an increasingly central part of management-employee relations strategies in the newer sectors influenced by Japanese practices.

We also accept that workers exercise controls, but it would

be a serious mistake to regard them as *equivalent* to those of management. This would fail to distinguish between *types* of control, particularly between the general and detailed dimensions referred to earlier in the chapter. At the general level of direction of production, managerial dominance is guaranteed by their stewardship of the crucial organisational resources. This is not 'zero-sum' because it cannot be 'added up'. Clearly, however, control of immediate work processes is largely zero-sum in that if workers control a given item, management cannot also do so (P. K. Edwards, 1987).

Analysing Management as a Labour Process

What is required is a structural analysis that can account for both the constraints on and complexities of managerial behaviour: a perspective that is neither deterministic or voluntaristic. *One* way forward begins from a remark made by Braverman that 'Management has become administration, which is a labour process conducted for the purpose of control within the corporation, and conducted moreover as a labour process exactly analogous to the process of production' (1974: 267). An offshoot is that the alienating conditions attached to the purchase and sale of labour become part of the managerial apparatus itself. Though little more than an aside, it has been utilised by a number of writers, notably Teulings (1986), to produce an analysis of management's role in the administrative aparatus of industrial organisations. The very fact that management is a 'global agent' carrying out the delegated functions of capital means that it is part of a collective labour process at corporate level. As we have previously indicated, this delegation in part reflects the transfer of functions such as co-ordination from the market to management and administration.

As that role has evolved, it has also become *differentiated*. So, for example, large administrative divisions are, in the case of accounting, 'producing nothing but elaborate mechanisms of control associated with the realisation of capital and its enlargement' (Johnson, 1980: 355). But it is not only a case of the emergence of specialised functions and departments.

Table 4.2 Institutionalisation of distinctive management functions at separate levels of management

function:	levels:
I the ownership function —accumulation of capital	institutional management —creation and preservation of legitimations
II the administrative function —allocation of investments	strategic management —development of objectives
III the innovative function —product market development	structuring management —new combinations of production factors
IV the production function —control of the direct labour process	operational management —direction and co-ordination of direct labour

Source: W. M. Teulings, 'Managerial Labour Processes in Organised Capitalism', *Managing the Labour Process*, D. Knights and H. Willmott (eds), Gower, 1986.

Differentiation also takes place in terms of *levels*. Teulings puts forward a model based on the existence of four distinct management functions: ownership, administrative, innovative and production (see Table 4.2). Two major consequences of the new division of labour follow. First, though the power of the administrative machinery of which management is a part has increased, the power of *individual* managers tends to diminish due to the rationalisation and routinisation of their activities. With the development of more complex managerial structures, new techniques have been introduced to integrate, monitor and control middle and lower management (Carter, 1985: 98).

> Years ago there might be five hundred fellas but you would only have one boss. Now everyone has a chief ... You can't discuss the job with them, everything is ticked in little boxes now. The boss is scared because if they don't treat everyone in a standard way they are afraid the other bosses will

report them. (Plessey engineer quoted in Thompson and
Bannon, 1985: 107)

Hales's analysis of management divisions of labour qualifies
Teulings by showing that some management functions – those
that the latter designates as operational – have their origins in
the labour process rather than the market, and that there is
not an exact correspondence between functions and levels.
Those divisions are vertically fractionalised so that 'there is a
differentiation within the performance of management work in
terms of the extent to which agents are involved in the
decision-making process' (Hales, 1988: 10). Most will be subordinated to senior management through merely providing
information from which decisions are made.

Managers managing other managers can take the form of
the multidivisional structure of modern corporations, where
decentralisation goes hand-in-hand with increased accountability and monitoring, or at a micro-level, techniques such as
management by objectives. Ironically, the latter is presented
as a form of control and motivation arising from the objective
demands of the task (Drucker, 1955), reproducing an aspect of
the relationship workers have with 'scientific management'.
In other cases managers became more literally victims of their
own devices (Storey, 1983: 93), as shown in studies such as
Nichols and Beynon (1977) on the chemical industry. The
latter additionally note the flattening out of career structures
and exposure to redundancy characteristic of many managers.
Even the detailed studies of management functions discussed
earlier in the chapter have the purpose of restructuring and
rationalisation. Both Mintzberg (1973) and Drucker (1979)
favour using techniques to split off routine activities from
senior layers, introducing separation of conception and execution within management itself. This can now be further aided
by computer technology and information systems.

The second consequence of changes in the managerial
labour process is the growth of structural conflicts and im-
balances between the different levels and functions. Teulings
argues that each level of management tends to follow a rational
logic of its own, enhancing the potential for defence of specific
group interests, for example, between production-oriented

operational management and the strata concerned with innovation in product markets. Such tendencies are worsened by the absence of, or limits to, formal mechanisms to resolve or bargain conflicts. Instead, they are likely to be dealt with at the operational level, leading to a disproportionate emphasis on changing the practices of shopfloor workers.

One effect not discussed by Teulings is on managerial *ideologies*. The legitimatory content in management thought has traditionally been directed towards two objectives: convincing non-management groups who challenged managerial goals and activities, and sustaining common aspirations (Child, 1969: 228–9). This becomes more problematic with the development of competing claims to fashion management theories and practices. Such competition cannot be wholly understood within the kind of framework which talks of levels. It neglects the role of what Armstrong calls *inter-professional competition* (1984, 1986, 1987a). It has long been recognised that professional groups pursue market strategies based on claims to exclusivity of knowledge and monopolies over a set of practices (Johnson, 1972; Brown, 1980). But the examples and models have mostly come from the older and 'social' professions such as law and medicine, with professions active in business seldom figuring as prominently.

One of the reasons for the neglect is that the sociology of the professions has emphasised the traditional 'role conflict' between professional autonomy and the bureaucratic principles of work organisation (Child, 1982; Rueschemeyer, 1986). Radical writers interpret these trends in terms of the conflict between acting for capital whilst increasingly taking on the characteristics of employees. Some refer to the growth of a new professional-managerial class (Ehrenreich and Ehrenreich, 1979), with others preferring to talk of the *proletarianisation* of the 'middle layers' (Braverman, 1974). While some insights can be gained from such perspectives, a primary focus on issues of class location is limited. Armstrong's model allows us to focus on the specific role of the professions in the managerial labour process.

However, Armstrong is critical of the latter concept. He agrees that lower management has been subject to greater controls and its own version of the separation of conception and execution, but is concerned that attention is drawn away from that basic contradiction between labour and capital, legitimising the existence of any form of unproductive activity by referring to it as a labour process in its own right. Armstrong prefers to talk of struggles for control within capital, reflecting the 'tensions and contradictions within the agency relationship' (1989: 312). In other words, employers and senior managers are inescapably dependent on other agencies to secure corporate goals and policies.

So, in practice, management functions for capital are mediated by competition between occupational groups. Each profession has a core of specialist knowledge and activities which can form the basis of advancement through a 'collective mobility project'. But the core can only be effectively used if it is sufficiently *indeterminate* to prevent parts being detached or routinised. While the general point might apply to all professions, those active in *business* have to face rival claims over the carrying out of control functions. For example, drawing on the work of Layton (1969), Armstrong (1986: 26) argues that scientific management's techniques and justification for the control of labour through the 'planning department' was an expression of an ideology of engineering. Industrial engineering rests on the design of operating procedures which monitor and control labour costs (Storey, 1983: 275). But the attempt to place engineers at the apex of the firm through the diffusion of such techniques has clearly not been fully achieved, given that engineers do not predominate in the higher levels of management. At the heart of the 'failure' lies the difficulty of maintaining a monopoly over control practices which could be carried out by others.

To make matters worse, British development has taken place based on a definition of management hostile to engineering. This is because of a combination of finance and marketing as favoured specialisms, and the tendency to define management as a set of general functions and skills divorced from productive expertise (see earlier in chapter). One commentator noted that a result has been 'a whole generation of MBA students who will not go near a manufacturing strategy ... They want to be in at the gin-and-tonic end with the financial strategy' (quoted in Armstrong, 1987a: 428). Other professions

have gained because of the popular belief that the education of
engineers does not equip them for dealing with people and
money. As a potential agency they therefore experience difficulty in establishing the vital commodity of 'trust' with those
in positions of power. It is therefore not surprising that many
engineers seek a route out of production into senior management through courses such as MBAs. The consequent low
status of engineering identified in the Finniston Report and
by Child *et al.* (1983) is in part, however, a peculiarly
anglo-saxon phenomenon. In contrast, West German management is dominated by professional engineers, owing in part
to the historical relevance of engineering techniques and
technical education, to competition with British and other
manufacturing goods, and to access to training in financial
techniques.

In the case of accounting and other financial specialisms
there has been a dramatic rise from the days of poorly paid
clerks and bookkeeping tasks. Some of the factors involved
include the development of *management* accounting as cost
control techniques in the industrial restructuring during and
after the depression of the mid-1920s. In the United States,
the control function of management accounting can be clearly
identified in the following definition from the National Association of Accountants:

> the process of identification, measurement, accumulation,
> analysis, preparation, interpretation, and communication
> of financial information used by management to plan,
> evaluate and control within an organisation and to ensure
> appropriate use and accountability for its resources (quoted
> in Wardell, 1986: 28).

Other factors include once again the need for co-ordination
and control over middle managers in multidivisional companies, and the legal requirements for control through audit-
ing. The cohesiveness of an accounting élite in business has
been facilitated by the acceptance of an inevitable 'horizontal
fissure' in the profession. This has allowed a range of routine
tasks to be delegated to 'accounting technicians' (Johnson,
1980; Glover *et al.*, 1987), thus maintaining indeterminacy

and monopoly over core practices. Accountants have also undertaken an aggressive campaign to encroach on the spheres of other professions through such measures as manpower audits and human resource accounting (Armstrong, 1986: 32). Though only a minority are closer to real power, the spread of a 'financial rationality' means that British board-rooms are increasingly dominated by those with a background in banking or accountancy.

Personnel has also enjoyed a major growth. From the days of its origins in company welfare workers, the Institute of Personnel Managers now has more than 20,000 members. Throughout that development personnel professionals have had a continual struggle to convince business power-holders that they could move from welfare to general management functions. They have consolidated a hold over administrative functions such as interviewing and record-keeping, as well as expanding into the newer areas of staff development and determination of wage rates and incentives (Carter, 1985: 102). In a partnership of mutual convenience the behavioural sciences have helped develop a mystique that 'the personnel manager is probably the only specialist in the organisation whose role can be distinguished by the virtually exclusive concern with the management of human assets' (Mullins, 1985: 129). But the problematic of 'dealing with people' has inherent limits in establishing a monopoly of knowledge or practice. It is therefore unsurprising that surveys (Daniel and Millward, 1983) have reported a lack of qualified and trained personnel staff in many companies. Fortunately for the profession some factors have been working in their favour, notably the spate of employee legislation and codes of practice in the 1960s and 1970s, and the recommendations of the Donovan Report (1968) that firms should centralise and formalise their bargaining procedures. Both measures have allowed personnel to extend and monopolise spheres of expertise, as well as exercise greater authority over lower line managers (Armstrong, 1986: 37). The recent spread of Japanese-style practices with an orientation towards 'human resource management' may also be helping, but there are contradictory tendencies (see Chapter 6).

This kind of analysis usefully adds to an understanding of

the complex levels and functions within the managerial labour process. As long as the connections to the dominant capital-labour contradiction are maintained, we see no reason why the latter concept cannot be usefully employed. A focus on competing agencies and professions also emphasises the specific *historical* bases and differences in the development of management theories and practices, particularly between different national traditions, though we have had little space to elaborate on them here. The discussion also embodies the general purpose of the chapter, that of developing a structural analysis of management that recognises the contradictory sources of influence over activity. Hence it becomes possible to utilise a conception of agency that accepts considerable variation in management practices. Of course, this is far from the last word on these issues. Chapter 9 attempts to develop an understanding of the individual and subjective orientations of managers compatible with the framework outlined here. Additionally, management practice needs to be further located within economic and social structures so as to identify the factors shaping major policy and organisational directions. This is an important theme of the next chapter.

5

Organisational Design

DEFINITIONS AND ISSUES

There may be room for legitimate debate over the extent to which coherent managerial strategies exist, as we saw in the previous chapter. But it is incontestable that the various dimensions of organisational life are subject to some degree of conscious planning and patterning through *design* processes. The accompanying issues have been central to the discipline, Donaldson arguing that, 'Organisation theory seems to be distinguishable as a body of thought by a concern for internal characteristics such as differentiation, standardisation, specialisation, integration, co-ordination and the like' (1985: 118). Indeed the notion of design is central to the whole idea of rational organisation. Structures, tasks or cultures are seen as manipulable by management, design being central to the achievement of corporate goals. It is also, therefore, the key to 'good' or 'effective' organisation (Child, 1984: 3). If you get it wrong, much of the investment in people or other resources will be likely to go to waste. For example, Cummings and Blumberg's case studies on the introduction of advanced manufacturing technology showed that ineffective use was primarily linked to a failure to *redesign* the work process and context when the technologies were implemented (1987: 54–5). Hence old task structures and functions were retained which undermined the potential for new interdependent relations and self-regulating groups.

In practice, discussion of design variables has proceeded from the assumption that correct *structure* is the key to good

171

performance. An organisation's structure refers primarily to the patterns and regularities in its division of labour by task or function, its hierarchies of authority and control mechanisms. There are, as usual, a number of ways in which the elements of structure can be conceptualised. For example, Child (1984: 3–4) makes a distinction between the *basic* structure which allocates and co-ordinates people and resources, often through job descriptions, organisation charts and formal bodies, and the *operating* structure which specifies more detailed activities and forms of behaviour, such as those embodied in performance reviews, work plans, and communication, financial or reward systems.

Emphasis has been traditionally put on design *techniques* and those concerned with planned change, in order to cope with and keep one step ahead of the environment. But the more significant design issues are *how* they should be operationalised. Again, the literature has identified a fairly consistent set of design dimensions (Pugh *et al.*, 1968), decisions (Child, 1984: 8–9) or parameters (Mintzberg, 1983: 27). These include the

- degree of job specialisation and formalisation;
- criteria by which units and activities are grouped, for example, by function or product, and the size of those groupings;
- nature of the general 'superstructure': tall, flat or otherwise, spans of control, and levels of management;
- type of integrative mechanisms and lateral linkages;
- decision-making structures, including degrees of centralisation and delegation.

There are a number of possible design configurations within these parameters. Generally there has been a shift away from singular 'one best way' solutions, often based on standardisation and rules. In its place, 'The organisation designer has been expected to mix good doses of long-range planning, job enrichment and matrix structure, among many other things' (Mintzberg, 1983: 2). The mix or choice is, of course, not a 'free' one. Account has to be taken of significant contextual or environmental factors. Not surprisingly, therefore, the design debate has been strongly underwritten by the contingency approach discussed extensively in Chapter 3. If we take some of the traditional 'show me your environment or technology and I'll show you what your structure should be' material from Woodward or Lawrence and Lorsch, then the scope for alternatives is fairly restricted. No matter how qualified by references to adjusting to uncertainties and complexities in the environment, 'most of the literature on organisational design treats it as a purely technical matter' (Child, 1984: 9). Yet in practice, strategic choices by organisational power-holders are made with reference not only to efficiency and profits but the related requirements to uphold and express forms of discipline and command (Fox, 1980: 182).

It is, of course, possible to create more complex contingency models such as Mintzberg's five configurations which recognise a greater variety of design options in the context of multiple contingencies. We will return to these later. Other approaches such as the information-processing perspective of Galbraith (1984) remain informed by notions of contingency. The greater the uncertainty of task, the more that decision-makers have to process information before executing it. Therefore the variety of structures and forms are indications of the different strategies pursued by companies to act on uncertainty, by increasing flexibility or decreasing levels of performance in order to cope. Galbraith argues that although organisations can follow combinations of design strategies, the choice is likely to be that which has the least cost in its environment.

A further alternative and current favourite is to return to 'best way' models. Dawson notes: 'after twenty years of contingency and its limits as a basis for organisation design, a view is now gaining ascendancy that it is possible to identify principles of good management which will be universally applicable' (1986: 133). This is channelled primarily through the 'search for excellence' genre (Peters and Waterman, 1982; Goldsmith and Clutterbuck, 1985), the apostles of Japanese management techniques (Pascale and Athos, 1982), or a combination of both such as Ouchi's (1981) 'theory Z' organisations. How *much* they depart from contingency models is debatable, but we will return to the major contemporary design approaches in more detail later. It remains the case that those alternatives still take the bureaucratic work organisation as their reference point, so this is where we start from.

BUREAUCRATIC WORK ORGANISATION REASSESSED

In 1983 an influential article in the magazine *Business Week* heralded 'A Work Revolution in US Industry'. This 'revolution' is directed against the major pillars of bureaucratic work organisation: functional specialisation and the resultant narrowly defined, low-skill and low-knowledge jobs enforced by management and by contractual bargaining over work rules set up to govern the workplace. Chapter 2 traced the origin and consolidation of bureaucracy as the dominant form of work design through Taylorism, classical management and later Weber. Before we examine the challenges to that dominance, it is worth briefly specifying how such systems developed and what their essential characteristics are.

One of the most consistent themes of organisational literature is minimising uncertainty and this acts as a fundamental motif of bureaucratisation. Variables may be focused on the relations between the components of structure and the environment; between the components themselves; in decision-making processes or in the 'technical core' of the firm, for example, that of routinised tasks or mass production (Thompson, 1967). A traditional response has been to construct 'buffers' against uncertainties. These may take the form of stockpiling supplies, maintaining a surplus labour pool in the factory, or vertical integration by taking over companies up- or down-line to the organisation's core activities (Goldman and Van Houten, 1977: 114–15). The degree to which labour has been seen as a significant variable differs, but bureaucratic regulation of work has also been a recurrent theme.

Specialised division of labour, hierarchical authority, abstract performance standards, job specifications and rule-governed procedures are of course the things that come to mind. But it is worth remembering the point established by Richard Edwards that bureaucratic controls are not necessarily synonymous with close, direct or coercive authority. They rely more on *standardisation* of work processes, outputs and skills. By reducing the amount of stimuli, information and premises for decisions, behaviour can be formalised and regulated (March and Simon: 1958). The resultant indirect or unobtrusive controls are effective enough to enable the workforce to be trusted to make more decisions within established parameters without necessarily having to change their attitudes. Popular and expert opinion points to the costs of wasteful bureaucracy. But as Edwards observes: 'The core corporations survive and prosper on their ability to organise the routine, normal efforts of workers, not on their ability to elicit peak performances' (1979: 146).

We have been talking as if such bureaucratic work organisation only favours management. This is to miss part of the point. Many of its features benefit workers, or at least those who are long-term core employees. Such benefits include mobility through internal labour markets, seniority rules governing pay and lay-offs, grievance procedures, and job protection and demarcation. In well-organised workplaces, these are enforced through plant-wide collective bargaining or informal shopfloor power. As part of this process there is a limited movement towards positive benefits for co-operation rather than negative sanctions: 'a system of mutually binding rules, material and symbolic incentives, and eventually the emergence of an ethos that is impersonally oriented towards performance' (Rueschemeyer, 1986: 94).

Bureaucracy: the Internal Critique

Given that bureaucratic structures are strongly associated with Weber, it is not surprising that his work has borne the brunt of critique. But the famous 'Weber debate' was primarily an internal one. Taking place in the 1950s and 1960s, it was conducted largely by neo-Weberian writers within a sociology of organisations tradition. Though their case studies questioned whether the bureaucratic ideal type was fully rational and efficient, many of the assumptions concerning the functional imperatives towards specialisation and hierarchy were left intact, with the emphasis on the need for bureaucratic adaptation to social action.

These case study critiques have been reworked many times in texts, so we will simply highlight some key issues. A central feature has been the unintended consequences of bureaucratic modes of operation, for instance, in relation to *efficiency*. Writers such as Merton (1949) pointed to the dangers of rule-following becoming an end in itself, leading to the excesses of 'red tape'. Standardisation and predictability could easily degenerate into rigidity and defensive behaviour, a kind of 'trained incapacity' resistant to innovation. This was therefore proof of the dysfunctional effects of bureaucratic practices, though few went as far as Bittner's comment that 'the inventory of features of bureaucracy contain not one single item that is not arguable relative to its efficiency function' (1973: 269).

Rationality does not escape. There is a whole sub-literature stressing the rational propensity for employees to break, bend or modify rules in order to get things done more effectively. Hence the oft-quoted adage that a 'work to rule' is an extremely damaging form of industrial action. Blau (1955) exemplifies this kind of argument through his studies of a state employment agency and a federal law enforcement agency in the USA. In the former, employees bent centrally laid-down rules in order to place unemployed people, involving the setting aside of competitive assessment norms in favour of co-operative practices and altering the subsequent statistical records. At the law enforcement agency it was more functional to ignore rules such as those related to reporting attempted bribery, in order to be in a position of power over the perpetrators at a later date.

Nor is specialisation or hierarchy necessarily functional to the overall goals of the organisation. This is particularly because there is a potential association between bureaucratic structures and *power*, as shown in the studies of two French state organisations by Crozier (1964). Hierarchy and specialisation can encourage groups to extend their own influence and discretion, displacing formal goals and replacing them by sectional ones. For example, maintenance workers in the state tobacco factory used the remaining uncertainty linked to their role to develop informal powers over other workers. The television programme 'Yes Minister' also shows how senior civil servants oppose or redirect policies which run counter to their established interests. Selznick's (1949) study of the Tennessee Valley Authority illustrates how the tendency of specialised groups of officials to form power cliques can frustrate attempts to create forms of citizen participation. In keeping with a Weberian framework, however, Selznick sees these events as evidence of the inevitable triumph of bureaucratic rationality over democratic values (Reed, 1985: 29–30).

Finally, the case studies indicate the existence of alternatives within bureaucratisation. The most famous derives from Gouldner's (1954) examination of gypsum mines in a closed, rural community. This showed how a form of bureaucracy based on shared knowledge and consent to rules, characterised as a 'mock bureaucracy' based on an 'indulgency pattern' reflecting the nature of the community, was challenged by a new manager acting on behalf of a cost-conscious parent company. Control was reasserted in a 'punishment-centred bureaucracy' through highly centralised authority, formalisation of rules and new technology. A theme of the above debates was the 'costs' of control, predictability and purely calculative exchange. In part this echoed themes from the still-influential human relations movement, notably the tension between formal rules and informal practices, as well as the need for a human dimension in design. Thus connections were made to that part of the Weberian tradition that emphasises meaningful social action.

Alternative Designs in a Bureaucratic Framework

While Bennis was prepared to write off bureaucracy as a 'lifeless crutch that was no longer useful' (1966: 263), neo-Weberians and those working in a more managerialist tradition were more likely to seek to analyse or promote alternative forms of design within bureaucratic organisation. This was taken up particularly by those within a managerialist tradition rather than organisational sociology. Blau built on the existence of alternatives to advocate greater decentralisation, discretion and participation. More usually, writers simply recognised that bureaucratic organisation should be treated as a *continuum* rather than as a unitary phenomena (Hall, 1973). All the features of the ideal type do not have to be present and, in fact, some can function as substitutes for each other. The main illustration used is the distinction between control through centralisation and hierarchy, normally exercised over workers with routine tasks, and controls over professionals, experts and managers. Direct controls over decision-making are not suited to the work of the latter with its emphasis on autonomy. Though there is a tension between professionalisation and bureaucracy, Hall shows they are not incompatible. As we saw earlier, discretion and delegation can be allowed within a rule-governed framework.

A similar trajectory away from unitary conceptions was made in the Aston Studies, briefly discussed in Chapter 3. Their search (Pugh *et al.*, 1963, 1969) to identify causal relations between size, other variables and bureaucratisation led them to develop a structural taxonomy. Seven types were identified, distinguished through dimensions centred on how control over work activities was exercised. There were three main types. *Full bureaucracies* – closest to Weber's ideal type – were based on a high level of standardisation of activities, concentration of authority and impersonal control but were held not to exist in pure form outside central government. In contrast, *workflow bureaucracies* had highly structured activities such as production schedules but more decentralised authority within the command framework. This type was found to be characteristic of large manufacturing concerns. Finally, smaller branch plants or parts of local government manifested bureaucratised employment relationships but a low structuring of activities and control exercised in a more personal way. These were dubbed *personnel bureaucracies*. Some of the applications in the shape of structural profiles can be seen in Pugh and Hickson (1973), while a detailed critique of the highly formalised nature of the Aston studies is found in Clegg and Dunkerley (1980: 218–62).

Debates continued, of course, around old favourites such as tall or flat structures and on which criteria to group positions in units. The latter concerns horizontal *differentiation*, and design issues have been dominated by whether to organise by function or product (for a fuller list of possibilities see Buchanan and Huczynski, 1985: 306). Under a *functional* system the division is based on identifiable specialisms such as personnel, production and sales. One consequence is that the line manager in a particular product area is likely to have to accept the authority of the servicing functional department. Conversely, the specialist functions are reproduced a number of times in a *product-based* structure. This form is particularly associated with a divisional structure for large diversified corporations, whereas a functional arrangement is more relevant to smaller organisations with more specific activities. Hence it can be seen that a contingency-type perspective is being used, though all choices embody costs and benefits (Galbraith, 1984).

A costs and benefits approach may also be applied to *vertical differentiation*. More hierarchical structures in large organisations characterised by internal labour markets can enhance commitment and bureaucratic motivation. But costs often include large management overheads, distorted communication channels and narrow spans of control which restrict initiative. Child argues that there has been a shift in modern job design thinking towards flatter structures which break from the determinist assumptions that bureaucracy directly arises out of increased size and complexity. This 'implies that it is possible to contain and perhaps even reverse the growth of long organisational hierarchies' (1984: 58).

In the real world, structures are increasingly *mixed* in some way, for example, combining functional and divisional systems. The most promoted design of the 1970s was a *matrix* arrangement in which one mode of organising activities is overlaid by another. This involves a joint decision-making process which cuts across lines of authority, breaking with the 'unity of command' principle. Matrix structures are linked to the development of liaison roles, integrating units and project teams earlier identified by researchers such as Lawrence and Lorsch (1967). Such arrangements may exist for short-term tasks, or on a 'permanent' basis. In practice, it could mean someone reporting to both a project team and the functional department.

The advantages are held to be a capacity to balance different demands on the use of resources, a retention of the benefits of functional organisation whilst exposing specialists to a wider range of influences and increasing the potential for innovation (Child, 1984: 102). Some major companies have in recent times certainly been convinced of the potential and have adopted it for parts of their activities in the case of ICI, or the whole operation as in the case of the then British Aircraft Corporation in the 1970s. While there may be contingent reasons for adopting matrix structures, such as having to cope with more than one major focus of activities, it has been widely seen as a useful way of responding to an increasingly volatile environment by having instability 'built-in'. As ever, instability has costs too. Co-ordination in dual authority structures is considerably more difficult; highly complex structures may lead to more unwieldiness and senior management may have to accept a good deal more conflict and 'politicised' relationships between sectional interests.

Matrix structures are linked to Mintzberg's 'structure of the future' – *adhocracy*. This is part of his structure-in-fives concept, and as Mintzberg is probably the most influential writer on design, it is worthwhile ending this section by looking at his arguments. The arguments cannot be understood without some reference to the wider analysis of the growth of the component parts of large-scale organisation. Some of those parts are common to most analyses: an operating core doing the basic work in relation to products and services; a strategic apex of decision-makers and senior managers; and a middle-line management as a link between the two. Standardisation as a means of controlling work activities creates the need for various forms of analytical techniques for design, planning, training and the like. This forms the basis of a *technostructure* involving categories such as work study engineers, personnel and accountants. In addition, complex organisations require the provision of indirect services ranging from the printroom to public services which are designated as *support staff*. Given this context, the five basic configurations are:

Simple Structure: direct supervision based on the strategic apex.
Machine Bureaucracy: standardisation of work based on the technostructure.
Professional Bureaucracy: standardisation of skills based on the operating core.
Divisional Form: standardisation of outputs based on the middle line.
Adhocracy: rests on mutual adjustment/informal communication, with support staff playing the key role.

These configurations embody forms that pull organisations in different directions. Naturally hybrid forms can result, or different structures in different parts of the firm, but 'the organisation is often drawn toward one of the configurations in its search for harmony of structure' (Mintzberg, 1983: 288). This ties in with the research of Khandwalla (1973) into American manufacturing firms that found *internal consistency* had the most positive correlation with high performance. If the five configurations are examined, we can see that all but the adhocracy are indeed variations on bureaucracy. Borrowed from Toffler's *Future Shock* (1970), the latter's design parameters are based on organic structures, low levels of standardisation and formalisation of behaviour, decentralisation and matrix-like use of specialists. Mintzberg argues that none of the previous forms are genuinely capable of innovative responses to new environments. Adhocracy is also the only form that combines more democracy with less bureaucracy, avoiding, 'sharp divisions of labour, extensive unit differentiation, highly formalised behaviour, and an emphasis on planning and control systems' (1983: 254). He acknowledges that like matrix arrangements it carries with it a necessary increase in conflict, aggressiveness and politicisation.

In conclusion, we would argue that the traditional design debate has largely been concerned with 'fine-tuning' bureaucratic models. Some of the variations are influenced by changing contingencies and some because, 'not all managers agree on ways to overcome uncertainties' (Goldman and Van Houten, 1980b: 67). Overall the contributions work within what Peters and Waterman call the 'hard S's'. This is not just systems and structure but *strategy* as a means of co-ordinating and directing the structural elements from the apex (Hitt *et al.*, 1986). Again, only adhocracy appears to depart from the bureaucratic framework. Even formation of strategy is believed to develop implicitly from individual decisions, rather than handed down from the top. Adhocracy is a structural configuration that appears in essence to be anti-structure. It is in tune with the fashionable orientation towards flexibility and decentralisation in broader management theory. The claims made on its behalf will be evaluated later in the chapter.

THE CHALLENGE OF WORK HUMANISATION

Well before the anti-bureaucratic appeal of adhocracy, 'people like Argyris, Bennis, Likert and McGregor built their careers on the analysis of the psychological dysfunctions of highly formalised structures' (Mintzberg, 1983: 37). A group of 'structure critics' had emerged to parallel the 'structure designers' (Hickson, 1973: 113). Their calls for new forms of participative organisation and job design draw on a psychology that assumes universalistic higher order needs that can only be met by the provision of intrinsically satisfying work (see Chapter 8 for a full discussion).

In fact, the theoretical framework is more often attributed to Maslow (1954) and his hierarchy of needs, with Herzberg (1966) as the most effective populariser in the role of management consultant. This *neo-human relations* perspective seemed to be more in tune with the post-war period of rising affluence and levels of education, as well as a decline of traditional authority. But the ideas would not have advanced unless linked to a critique of the economic, technical and social 'costs' of traditional management methods and job design manifested in low motivation, morale and commitment. Employers and managers were prepared to live with those costs if they could be controlled or compensated for. Neo-human relations only really came out of the shadows when those costs were manifested in a publicly articulated 'crisis of work'.

This peaked in the early 1970s when, amongst other initiatives, the United States government commissioned the 'Work in America' report from the Special Task Force (1973); France appointed a Minister for Job Enrichment; the British Conservative Government published a report on the Quality of Working Life; the Swedes set up a Commission on Industrial Democracy; and the International Labour Organisation proclaimed the need to prioritise the humanisation of work. Behind this show of official concern lay tight labour markets and high levels of employment which gave firms problems in recruiting and retaining workers, and an upsurge in industrial unrest through strike waves and less formally through absenteeism, high labour turnover and sabotage. Assembly lines, particularly in motor plants from Lordstown Ohio to Ford Halewood, Fiat in Turin and Renault in France, seemed to epitomise the problem. The latest production technology and engineering went hand-in-hand with highest levels of disaffection and disruption.

By no means all companies responded by thinking about job redesign. Many, such as Plessey on Merseyside, simply attempted to tighten-up controls and introduce new pay and productivity deals (Thompson and Bannon, 1985). But the decline in management-labour certainties was sufficient to put the question on the agenda. This crisis was of course also felt *politically*. Industrial democracy, worker participation and joint consultation were also back on the agenda, though employers tended to see consultation as an *alternative* to the threat of more fundamental change (Brannen, 1983). As it happened, neo-human relations favoured task-centred, rather than power-centred participation. But it helps understand the kind of climate that led Herzberg to predict in 1973 to British managers that Taylorism would disappear in ten years as it was obsolete and inefficient.

Maslow and Herzberg were not the only ones with a critique of existing forms of capitalist work organisation. Radical writers also spoke of the destructive legacy of authoritarian control and alienation (Braverman, 1974; Gorz, 1976). But compared to the work humanisation package, they did not have a set of practices compatible with management needs. Though the package varied according to its designer, certain basic principles can be identified. Hackman and Oldham (1980) later summed these up as skill variety, task identity, task significance, autonomy and feedback. One of the problems in focusing on the practicalities is that work humanisation, quality of work life (or QWL) and job enrichment have all been used as generic terms for a variety of measures ranging from, 'allowing AT&T telephone operators to go to the bathroom without raising their hands, to fully self-managing and self-recruiting work teams in four of five different factories' (Zimbalist, 1975: 50).

This would not satisfy Herzberg, who dismisses anything like rotation as mere superficial tinkering with design. In essence he is concerned with vertical job loading. This involves enlarging the scope of jobs, not by adding more routine tasks but through the addition of responsibilities for planning or indirect elements such as inspection and extending the work cycle so that workers engage in as complete a task as possible. This might also include the development of semi-autonomous working groups, such as those at the famous Volvo truck plant in which the pace and progress of work was much more under operator control.

When focusing on the experiences of work humanisation, mainly in the peak period of the late 1960s and the 1970s, we face the further problem that many people have heard *only* of Volvo. There were dramatic early gains in productivity and other benefits deriving from the use of the static assembly method. But the company became the victim of the accompanying hype when subsequent difficulties, including suspicious management and new intakes of workers, meant constraints on the degree to which the experiment was extended (Blackler and Shimmin: 1984). But the real limit of the emphasis on Volvo was that it distracted from the wider nature of job design initiatives in that period. This should not be taken out of proportion. It was certainly not a 'third industrial revolution' as Hofstede (1977) claimed. But it did involve a significant minority of large companies. As usual the assessment of the extent of experimentation varies considerably. An article in the Harvard Business Review reported 2000 cases in the USA alone (Mills, 1975). This seems a gross exaggeration when compared to Bosquet's (1977) identification of 200–300 large companies in the USA and Europe, and even the Special Task Force Report (1973) only listed 30 firms and some of them were in the very different political circumstances of Yugoslavia. Where inflated claims are made, they are likely to be based on two main sources: the role played by management consultants with a vested interest in 'spreading the word', and the inclusion of *anything* that modifies traditional job design.

While accurate knowledge is therefore hard to come by, it is important to recognise that many participants were from large and leading firms; often those with a tradition of 'progressive' management methods such as ICI, Olivetti, Philips, IBM and Polaroid, as well as new players such as Ford, General Motors and Volkswagen. Like the period of experimentation in the 1920s, discussed in Chapter 2, work humanisation was often a *part* of a wider change programme or the latest in a series of management initiatives. When the New York Telephone Company introduced a job enrichment scheme in the early 1970s, its Training Director admitted that they had tried 'everything – human relations, sensitivity training, OD' (Carr Mill Consultants, 1973: 11) before the turn to Herzberg. Similarly, Philips undertook 'a vast array of initiatives' (Daniel and MacIntosh, 1972: 24), from simple job rotation, to improving the physical environment and sophisticated job enrichment exercises, facilitated by a high level of local management autonomy. ICI's experiments in the late 1960s took place in the context of a Weekly Staff Agreement that was as much a productivity bargain as anything to do with redesigning work, and also involved revamped consultative systems, profit-sharing schemes and briefing groups (Ramsay, 1985: 67).

Evaluating the Experience

The record of work humanisation is 'inconclusive on both efficiency and humanitarian grounds' (Dawson, 1986: 48). Using the managerial criteria of increases in productivity and quality, and reductions in absenteeism and labour turnover, there were consistent reports of gains, albeit uneven, in companies such as ICI, Philips and AT&T (Daniel and McIntosh, 1972). Interestingly, many of the more successful were in white-collar or craft jobs, arguably the least in need. It is easier to assign wider responsibilities and discretion to clerical workers without expensive technological change. Work redesign among manual workers has been facilitated by changes in product markets requiring more varied work forms (Kelly, 1982). But this has most application to batch rather than mass or process production. The former allows for machines to be grouped together in 'families' to produce a common component or product. This system of group technology is compatible not only with an enlargement of the task cycle but the use of semi-autonomous groups for problem-solving (Littler, 1985). While there has been restructuring of assembly lines around work stations (Coriat, 1980), applications of job enrichment to manual workers has generally focused on the trivial facets of work such as job rotation (Nichols and Beynon, 1977).

On the positive side, at least some of the initiatives have aided a further break with determinism concerning technology or structure. But it is difficult to identify any consistent success in terms of the original claims for a genuine transformation for work and work experience. Beyond the consultants and other professional advocates (Paul and Roberston: 1970, Roeber: 1975) most academic accounts are pessimistic in their conclusions. Blackler and Brown's survey (1978) showed that job enrichment functioned mainly as a different form of control device, while Kelly's (1980) cross-national examination showed any benefits to employees in immediate task autonomy tended to be offset by work intensification and increased general subordination to management. The latter can be observed through studies of white-collar workers in AT&T (Bosquet, 1977) and the Banker's Trust Company (Special Task Force, 1973), where the elimination of checkers and the expansion of financial responsibilities combined great cost savings with increased accountability *to* management.

However, the greatest proof of the limited character and effectiveness of work humanisation experiments is their short-lived nature. While there are still some initiatives in the West German motor industry (Dankbaar, 1988), Volkswagen ended their experiment in 1978 because it was utopian and too costly (Littler, 1985: 23), and General Motors dumped a QWL programme in the mid-1970s due to the oil crisis which led to redundancies and one-shift working (Guest, 1983: 150). At a more general level, Ramsay's (1985) survey of the international evidence concluded that with the onset of the recession, work humanisation had largely faded from view or stagnated, even in Scandinavia. In the USA, one enthusiast, Hackman (1978), argued that employers had turned back towards a route of adjusting workers to closely controlled and engineered jobs. Managers and management writers began to 'discover' that the work ethic crisis and demands for fulfilling jobs were greatly exaggerated. Some gained enough confidence to explicitly advocate 'close attention to work rules, manning requirements and other minutiae ... [which] can do as much for long-term productivity as a flyer with job enrichment' (Arnold Weber quoted in Goldman and Van Houten, 1980b: 86–7).

To help explain why the experience was so limited, we have to recognise that for all its good intentions neo-human relations lacked a realistic analysis of the constraints embodied in the capitalist labour process. In principle, task-centred reforms have been attractive *because* they 'appear to solve the problem of when to give workers more discretion in the performance of their work without weakening management control over the broad objectives of the enterprise' (Hawkins quoted in Clegg, 1980: 7). But that fails to recognise the threat any far-reaching changes could have on existing forms of hierarchy and control. One famous instance was Polaroid's worker participation project that was so successful that it had to be ended because the Training Director felt that they were getting to a position where supervisors and managers would not be needed (Jenkins, 1973).

This is reminiscent of the Pandora's Box scenario put bluntly by one of GM's Directors of Research and Training, where employees may want to go from 'safe' to dangerous topics in which 'management's present monopoly of control can in itself easily become a source of contention' (quoted in Edwards, 1979: 156). Herzberg (Herzberg *et al.*, 1959) himself shared similar views, arguing that it was unrealistic for 'lower-level' employees to exercise any control on overall goals (Herzberg *et al.*, 1959) and that participation in power structures would give workers 'the idea that they're all part of one big happy family' (Carr Mill Consultants, 1973: 7). It is therefore hardly surprising that the American Management Association found that most companies paid only lip-service to job enrichment (Zimbalist, 1975: 56) and combined Theory 'Y' *styles* with Theory 'X' *structures* (Storey, 1983).

Linked to the above is actual resistance from those managers and supervisors in the intermediate hierarchy whose positions are most directly threatened by elimination or redesign of *their* jobs. Those who use power as a resource within bureaucratic control have a material interest in opposing initiatives that break such systems down (Drago and MacDonough, 1984). There may also be a perceived threat to legitimacy, producing the defensive responses quoted in Jones, where managers 'pine for the days when "a manager's job was to manage" or see the new innovations as "just another confidence trick"' (1978: 14). The lesson for advocates of work humanisation is that you cannot be soft on power and expect at the same time that management will carry out organisational transformation as if it was in their rational self-interest.

The other factor which neo-human relations tended to ignore was the limits set by managerial uses of technological change, In fact, like most of mainstream social science they had a rosy picture of the potential of 'automation' to upgrade skills and enhance involvement. Unfortunately that was not generally to be the case. There is a wealth of evidence from the post-Braverman debate (Zimbalist, 1979; Thompson, 1989) which shows the widespread deskilling and strengthening of managerial control associated with the early form of new technology. It is not just true of manual workers but the clerical staff investigated by Crompton and Jones (1984), who found that 'computerisation deskills tasks, enhances the level of functional specialisation, and centralised control of the workforce' (1984: 53), and the computer 'information workers' employed by the Automobile Association, who need no formal qualifications and take eight hours to train. The very capacity of microprocessors to copy and incorporate human skills and intelligence often proved an irresistible attraction to managers looking for greater control over working conditions, reduced dependency on expensive skilled staff or simply to shed workers. Indeed, a standard selling-pitch of some manufacturers was that computer numerical control and similar machinery could be operated by children or the mentally handicapped.

Additionally, *job* design decisions are normally made *after* technological and organisational systems have been established (Davies and Taylor, 1979). The most influential groups in design processes are engineers, line managers and systems analysts who tend to look for minimal immediate costs and manual intervention (Lupton and Tanner, 1980; Wilson, 1988). For these reasons, Braverman came to the conclusion that Taylorism remained the basis for the organisation and control of the labour process, while human relations was 'the maintenance crew for the human machinery' (1974: 88). This is a rather over-simplistic view. But a more measured version can be seen in Hackman's prediction that with a move in the 1980s towards job design on technical and engineering principles, industrial psychologists would be left with the roles of specifying the required knowledge and skills, and developing techniques 'to minimise the personal and organisational costs of maladaptive responses to change' (1978: 15).

In retrospect it is now accepted that the simple deskilling and control thesis was limited. It failed to take into account the variety of intervening factors ranging from worker-resistance or employee-intervention to retain knowledge and skills (Wilkinson, 1983a); the size and structure of the firm (Sorge *et al.*, 1983); variations between and within sectors, notably those of product markets; and the strategic choices exercised by management. There may even be unevenness within firms, for example, loss of direct machining skills but acquisition of programming ones (Rothwell, 1987: 77). Additionally, the second wave of computer-based technology may be reversing some of the task and knowledge fragmentation common to the first (Baran, 1988). But the very minimum that is common ground in the debate is that frequently a *polarisation* of skills has taken place between a minority of highly trained and rewarded positions and the majority of those in routinised jobs

(Gill, 1985). This polarisation has often been overlaid by a gender dimension, with areas such as design and maintenance retained as masculine preserves, while women are confined to a range of operator tasks (Cockburn, 1985). On balance the evidence is enough to sink the idea that work humanisation could ride on the back of some natural technological progression towards the golden future of automation.

Some writers have taken the experience of work humanisation as a further illustration that managerial interest in job reform and participation is of a cyclical nature (Ramsay, 1983, 1985). This is not so much the result of 'fashion' but of periods which combine economic pressures and a challenge from below to the legitimacy of capital. Work humanisation rose in such a period and largely bit the dust in the recession. There is obviously a partial truth in this argument which is reflected in the disappearance of articles on job enrichment from management literature. But while the solutions of work humanisation proved unacceptable or unnecessary to capital, the issues it addressed of low commitment and the costs of routinised work did not go away. After all, they are part of the ongoing control-engage dilemma. However, the forms through which questions of consent and involvement changed as economic and political circumstances altered in the 1980s. This is the theme of the second half of the chapter.

CONTEMPORARY DEVELOPMENTS: FLEXIBLE FUTURES?

New buzzwords have surfaced during the 1980s. Popular management texts have stressed the need for 'change masters' that can handle innovation at every level (Kanter, 1984); new forms of 'transformational' leadership (Tichy and Devanna, 1986); the need for intrapreneurs (Pinchot, 1985) who can act autonomously and creatively across decentralised or federal organisations (Handy, 1985); and for flexible and committed employees (Martin and Nicholls, 1987). For Lessem (1985) this means that the first major paradigm shift in organisations is occurring since Taylor and Fayol. He dubs this a move from the 'holding' to the 'enabling' company, characterised by initiatives such as joint ventures, management buy-outs, contracting parts of the organisations and personal networking. Such requirements are not abstract. They arise from what might be called new *strategic contingencies* in 'post-industrial societies', linked to the dynamic environmental 'shocks' induced by slower economic growth, globalisation and intensification of competition, a rising rate of product innovation, and the impact of advanced forms of information technology.

The consequent forms of uncertainty and discontinuous change (Drucker, 1981) cannot be handled adequately by the bureaucratic structures and decision-making processes of traditionally designed organisations. Hence companies such as General Electric, British Telecom and Plessey are seen to be breaking up their bureaucracies by disaggregating to smaller or independent units, or developing new corporate structures where divisions operate as autonomous profit-centres with delegated decision-making powers. Integration will be provided by overall strategy, information technology and corporate cultures. More flexible arrangements that are recommended echo themes of Mintzberg's adhocracy discussed earlier. Such analyses have even impressed some on the Left. Mulgen (1988) refers to the replacement of 'strong power' under the Fordist corporations characterised by pyramidal structures, formal rules and close controls, by a post-Fordist order based on weak power controls and decentralised leadership, horizontal communication and self-regulating units.

Theorising Flexible Specialisation

Many of the above themes have been packaged in a far more sophisticated way by advocates of the theory of flexible specialisation (Piore and Sabel, 1984). This is the term given to the efforts 'to convert the traditional highly integrated, corporate structure into a more supple organisational form capable of responding quickly to shifting market conditions and product demand' (Piore, 1986: 146). In its earlier form, Sabel's (1982) analysis preferred to speak of corporate management attempting to maintain continuity with mass production, deskilling and labour controls whilst moving away from standardisation. This *neo-Fordism* was seen as coexisting alongside a new high tech cottage industry which combines craft forms of production with computerised technology (C. Smith, 1987: 1).

More recent work declared a general crisis of industrial systems or 'second industrial divide'. In this formulation, the Fordist system of mass production is held to be incapable of permanent innovation. Flexible specialisation works on a kind of *design chain* (see Figure 5.2). It starts with increasingly specialised demand for customised quality goods which renders the old economies of scale redundant. The shift to new market conditions is facilitated by production and information technology such as flexible manufacturing systems (FMS) and Manufacturing Automation Protocol (MAP) which are general purpose and programmable, allowing switches within and between families of products on more of a small batch basis (Williams *et al.*, 1987: 409). Once such choices are made, manufacturing economies are locked into a technological trajectory. Fragmented and repetitive work organisation characteristic of Taylorism is no longer compatible. Collaboration between designers, producers and managers is both feasible and necessary, while craft skills and 'the production worker's intellectual participation is enhanced' (Piore and Sabel, 1984: 278). This kind of analysis of the logical fit between flexible forms of technology and flexibility in skills and work structures is paralleled in Kern and Schuman's *The End of the Division of Labour* (1984), which talks of the re-professionalisation of production work and new production concepts and also finds support from some other writers on advanced technology (Gill, 1985; Francis, 1986).

Flexible specialisation even allows transnationals in some instances to begin to reverse the international division of labour, in which assembly processes are located in low-wage areas of the third world, whilst maintaining research and design at home. Technical innovation, capital-intensive manufacturing and far higher levels of productivity from smaller workforces enable redomestication of activities, though the developing countries are likely still to utilise the low-skill, mass production methods. In the advanced economies, decentralised production will be the order of the day as smaller plants can operate efficiently within the same range of products and be close to the customer to save transport and other costs.

Piore and Sabel admit that working economic models of flexible specialisation based on networks of small firms is limited to regions such as Veneto and Emilia Romagna in Italy. But it is certainly possible to identify firms or sectors which appear to qualify. General Motors's emergent Saturn Plant utilises flexible equipment to produce specifically tailored products without retooling and with a high level of worker participation (Meyer, 1986: 74). Technology such as computer-aided design systems have enabled clothing firms both to create and then speedily respond to customer demands for a greater range of design and colour. Standardisation and long runs are said to become uneconomical. Computerisation also helps large firms such as Benetton to centralise marketing and skilled processes like design and dyeing among its small core workforce of less than 2000 people, whilst decentralising its other production work to small sub-contractors and franchising its sales outlets (Fergus Murray, 1983; Mitter, 1986). Whether this justifies referring to *Benetton Britain* (Robin Murray, 1985), we can examine by looking at flexibility in more detail outside the confines of the theory itself.

The Flexibility Offensive

During periods of significant change in work organisation, attention is often directed towards a particular phenomenon that is seen as an obstacle to efficiency. In the past it has been 'overmanning' or unofficial strikes. Now, within the general reference to the defects of Taylorism and Fordism, it is *work rules*: regulatory mechanisms established by workers and managers to govern the workplace. The previously mentioned article in *Business Week* (1983) celebrated a revolution against rules that place constraints on management's right to allocate and organise work. Under systems of bureaucratic organisation and control, employers had gained from rules by being able closely to specify job assignments and operate internal

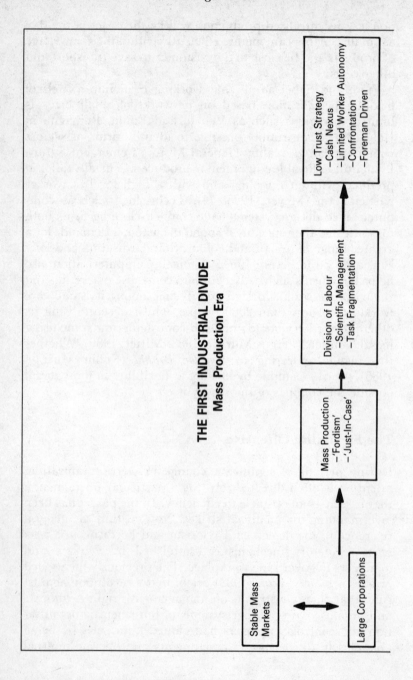

Figure 5.1 The flexible specialisation hypothesis

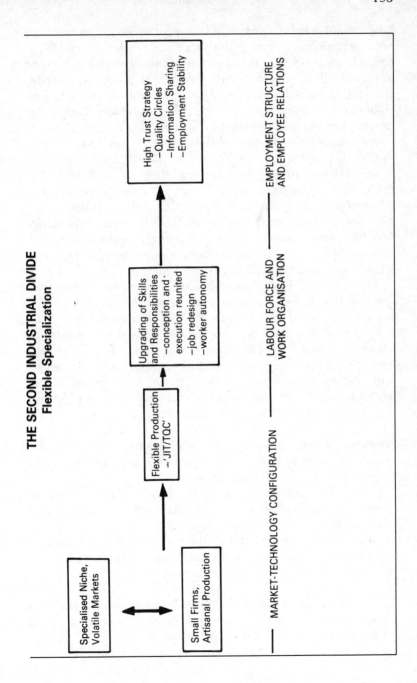

THE SECOND INDUSTRIAL DIVIDE
Flexible Specialization

Specialised Niche, Volatile Markets ←→ Small Firms, Artisanal Production

→ Flexible Production – 'JIT/TQC'

→ Upgrading of Skills and Responsibilities
– conception and execution reunited
– job redesign
– worker autonomy

→ High Trust Strategy
– Quality Circles
– Information Sharing
– Employment Stability

MARKET-TECHNOLOGY CONFIGURATION —— LABOUR FORCE AND WORK ORGANISATION —— EMPLOYMENT STRUCTURE AND EMPLOYEE RELATIONS

Source: Thomas Bramble (1988) 'Industrial Relations and New Management Production Practices', *Labour and Society*, vol. 112, June.

labour markets. Unions could restrict arbitrary power and enforce adherence to rules that benefited workers. In addition to such areas as task demarcation, seniority rules governing job protection, lay-offs and promotions were established. Because work rules were embodied in contractual relations rights and grievance procedures, they gave unions bargaining power. Employment protection in law also enhanced status rights which limited what employers could gain from contractual exchange (Streek, 1987: 241–2). The flexibility offensive is directed not just against the 'rigidities' of work rules but their high, often fixed, costs in terms of compensation and movement (Mangum and Mangum, 1986). When taken together with better pensions and other social and fringe benefits, senior management increasingly begin to see such arrangements not just as an unnecessary burden, but as a form of 'corporate socialism', as one American executive put it.

The most widely used analytical framework for understanding the new moves by employers to vary their workers and work is provided by the flexible firm model developed by Atkinson (1984) and the researchers from the Institute for Manpower Studies (IMS). (See Figure 5.2.) It is based on a break with existing unitary and hierarchical labour markets and organisation of internal labour markets to create a core workforce and a cluster of peripheral employment relations. Three types of flexibility are identified:

functional: Core workers gain job security in return for managers' right to redeploy them between activities and tasks as products and production require.
numerical: The capacity to vary the headcount according to changes in the level of demand so that there is an exact match between the numbers needed and employment.
financial: Pay and other employment costs reflect the state of supply and demand in the external labour market and support the objectives of functional and numerical flexibility.

IMS surveys show that most larger firms contacted claim to have increased flexibility: 31 out of 35 in one case, nine out of 10 increasing numerical flexibility in another, mainly through sub-contracting (Atkinson and Gregory, 1986). Sectoral

Figure 5.2 Model of the flexible firm

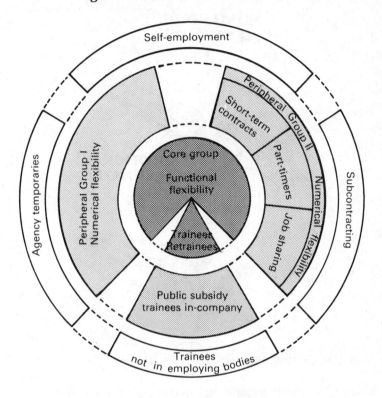

Source: G. C. Mangum, 'Temporary Work: The Flipside of Job Security', *International Journal of Manpower*, vol. 17, no. 1, 1986, p. 14.

variations indicate an emphasis on functional forms in manufacturing and numerical in service work.

In the area of *functional flexibility* it is admitted that no really reliable evidence exists on the extent of such practices. We therefore have to start from the pattern that arises from specific cases. Recent years have seen a significant growth in flexibility agreements. The most extreme, such as those at Nissan and at Sony, specify complete flexibility, even to the point of managers and clerical staff working on the production line if necessary (IPM Digest, 1986). Beyond general statements of manpower utilisation, agreements are mostly

Figure 5.3 'Numerical' and 'functional' flexibility

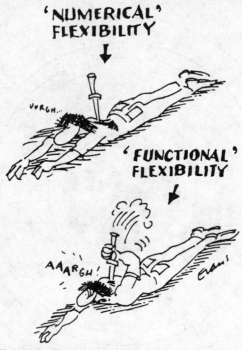

Source: CAITS (1986), *Flexibility, Who Needs It?*, London, p. 34.

directed towards removing 'barriers' between grades and categories. This may be achieved by merging production grades or ensuring job rotation. But a crucial goal is 'multi-skilling' and the erosion of distinctions between production and other categories such as indirect, maintenance and even craft work. For example, production workers at Cadbury and Findus have to carry out maintenance work, while skilled engineering construction workers on oil and gas platforms must undertake semi- or unskilled work if there is no craft work for them to do.

Emphasis is also being put on creating flexible craftsmen or 'crafticians' by focusing on the interfaces between crafts, and non-crafts, craft assistants, supervisors and other trades (Cross, 1985). Gulf Oil inserted a clause which requires skilled workers to learn seven other jobs (*Business Week*,

1983). Notable agreements in the UK include those at Esso, Babcocks, British Shipbuilders and Shell. In the latter case, management at the Carrington site negotiated (under threat of closure) an amalgamation of the craft workforce into four trade groups with no demarcations. All non-management jobs were brought together under one technician heading and a single set of terms and conditions (CAITS, 1986). Even clerical groups are not exempt. Lucas Electrical has amalgamated many clerical with manual tasks under a new grade of materials controller. One of the characteristics of flexibility is a turn towards teamworking, such as the composite groups at British Shipbuilders within which there is complete interchangeability. Problem-solving and diagnostic skills are also seen as valuable.

There are a number of related changes worth noting. Modification and reductions in gradings have allowed the simplification of *pay structures* and bargaining. Many companies such as Shell are also linking rewards and career progression to individual appraisal measured by supervisors or team-leaders. This often moves away from piecework and undermines the traditional notion of a specific rate for the job and towards performance-related pay (see Chapter 6 for more details). Not surprisingly this has the intention and effect of undermining trade union organisation. It is part of a more general trend associated with the flexibility offensive of creating an emasculated more enterprise-based unionism. This is based on single or reduced representation, local bargaining, a shift from an industrial relations to a 'human resource management' framework (Streek, 1987: 299), and the aim of workforce identification with its unit of employment. Finally, there are alterations in the use of *time*. It does not normally involve an extension of flexi-time chosen by employees, or the 35-hour week beloved of trade unions. It is an attempt by employers to vary attendance to meet fluctuations and workload and gain general control over time-scheduling. This includes buying-out overtime and breaks or ending them as rights and introducing round-the-clock, round-the-shift systems, with the use of part-time and temporary labour to cover peak demand: Yates, 1986; CAITS, 1986; Wainwright, 1987).

What about compensating factors? Clearly any increased

focus on a core workforce is likely to enhance the need for training and retraining, though this will be in-house and limited largely to firm-specific skills. The most touted carrot, however, is job security which is linked to 'the difficulty of implementing productivity programmes without the full co-operation of the employees' (Clutterbuck, 1985: 2). Given that we are in the early days of new arrangements, it may be premature to judge. The few definite examples are mostly from the USA. If workers are laid off, they have been promised retraining, relocation and income support by GM and Ford (Mangum and Mangum, 1986: 12). This also involves 'job banks' in which an equivalent number of jobs are created if production is outsourced. How firm or widespread such arrangements are, we will assess later.

Whatever the limits, any kind of security is considerably more than the growing army of *peripheral workers* is ever going to get. Indeed, the capacity to externalise uncertainty, costs and risks to a variety of holders of labour services is the explicit rationale for *numerical flexibility*, as well as a form of compensation for commitments to core workers. A number of overlapping peripheral categories have been identified that on some estimates total 34 per cent of those in employment in the UK and 25 per cent in the USA (Mather, 1987), accounting for most of the extra jobs created. Except where specified, most of the figures for the specific categories below come from surveys done in the UK for the International Labour Organisation (Standing, 1986) by the Confederation of British Industry (Yates, 1986) and ACAS (1988).

Sub-contracting: This is argued to be the most significant development, facilitated by and helping feed the decentralisation process. It can take the form of contracting out work or outsourcing the supply of components. Though not a new phenomenon, it is breaking out of traditional fields such as cleaning, and half of all large firms in the UK have increased the use of sub-contractors. In some instances, former employees are turned into suppliers of services, thus linking sub-contracting to the categories below.

Self-employment: This actually fell during the 1970s, but rose from 1.2 m. in 1979 to 2.6 m. in 1985. Any increase is difficult to disentangle from the effects of unemployment and the recession. But many firms are transforming specialist and skilled work from waged employment to the supply of services; sometimes re-employing their previous workers. This is known as linked sub-contracting (Clutterbuck, 1985). The building industry has put enormous pressure on workers to move into the 731 self-employed category.

Temporary contracts: Two thirds of the ACAS respondents reported using temporary workers. Some are employees re-hired on a temporary basis; this category of work growing at 16 per cent a year during the 1980s. The 5000 temporary help services make it the fastest-growing industry in the USA. In the UK, some firms such as Control Data are using 'supplementals' on short-term contracts with poor conditions to act as buffer to their permanent staff (CAITS, 1986: 32). Nor is it confined to manual workers in manufacturing or to seasonal work. Universities and colleges are increasingly employing teachers on one-year or renewable rolling contracts.

Part-time: Those working 16 hours or less have doubled in recent years, making the UK one of the highest users of part-time labour. Though mostly female and in the service sector, the CBI and ACAS estimate that the trend is spreading to manufacturing and other sectors. Managerial proposals to increase the use of part-timers has been at the root of industrial trouble at Fords and the Post Office.

Homeworking: This trend has received a considerable amount of glamorous publicity through Rank Xerox's networkers, F International, ICL and other professional and white-collar workers linked by computer in 'electronic cottages' (Control Data Corporation: 1985). But manufacturing homework, involving putting out to women domestic outworkers, in sectors such as textiles, electrical components and toys, is arguably more significant (Mitter, 1986; Allen and Wolkowitz 1987), though it remains a small number: one in twenty firms according to ACAS.

Franchising: This also appears to be rapidly rising and is spreading through retailing into service activity such as milk rounds (Labour Research Department, 1986b). The latter constitutes a classic example of transferring risk in an uncertain market and undermining trade unionism, while retaining control of supplies, prices and business style.

We will return to an evaluation of these arguments and figures in the final section of the chapter.

LEARNING FROM JAPAN

We have been talking as if the perceived need to respond to new market conditions has been the only 'learning experience' motivating Western business organisations. Yet the 'Japanese threat' has changed the terms of competition in the 1980s and in doing so has set in motion a major process of emulating or modifying the ingredients believed to be the basis of superior performance. What precisely is to be learned, however, from the Japanese model? Flexibility is a central theme, while specific tactics or techniques such as quality circles have been widely implemented (see George and Levie, 1986). But the overwhelming emphasis in the management literature, sparked off by the OECD Report (1977). Ouchi (1981) and Pascale and Athos (1982), has been on *management* skills, style and values. The latter set up a comparison between Matushita Electric and ITT, and specifically their two leaders. In terms of the hard S's of strategy, structure and systems the result was a draw. However, on the soft S's of style, skills and staff a spiritual knockout was attributed to the Japanese. Looking in the 'Japanese mirror' resulted in an image of a unique corporate culture and commitment to the management of human resources. A similar story emerged from a contrast between Rank Xerox and Fuji Xerox (Giles and Starkey, 1987). Senior executives talk of the same product and competitive and economic environment, the magic ingredient therefore has to be the Confucian-based culture, with mindset of Samurai Warriors being transferred to industrialists! Pascale and Athos also deal at length with the positive existential influences of Zen in living with uncertainty, imperfection and ambiguity.

These 'culturalist' explanations have been rightly criticised by other writers (Dunning, 1986; Wood, 1986). If there is a Japanese 'miracle', it has far more to do with the nature of industrial organisation and productive expertise. Central to this is the attention paid to product design, quality, labour utilisation, scheduling and stock control. Take for example the just-in-time system (JIT), discussed briefly in Chapter 3. Originally developed by Toyota it consists of a group of related practices aimed at ensuring the exact quantity and quality of raw materials, parts and sub-assemblies are delivered 'just-in-time' for the next stage of production. Compared to the normal 'just-in-case' practices, this keeps inventories and buffer stocks to a minimum (Tailby and Turnbull, 1987; Sayer, 1986). JIT is not merely an inventory system. To work properly it requires flexible labour utilisation and harmonising of tacit skills, close managerial involvement in production, multi-purpose machinery and reductions in set-up times. It feeds into the overall process of *kaizen* or continuous improvement (Wood, 1989). Such a system also frequently depends on a set of relations between large corporations and suppliers, normally characterised by tightly controlled multiple sourcing through layers of sub-contractors.

Culturalist explanations also vastly underestimate the role of state intervention; hardly surprising when the discourse is conducted through American management consultants. Historically the Japanese state has taken an interventionist role in shaping domestic markets and foreign trade, in contrast to the UK and USA where the concern has largely been for demand management (Ackroyd *et al.*, 1987). Particularly important preferential support is given for industrial banks and long-term, cheap credit, and for new technologies. The need for a specifically historical perspective is relevant to other areas too. Littler's (1982) study showed the significance of the particular forms of corporate capital that developed, the deliberate avoidance of the most destructive aspects of Taylorism and the shaping of industrial relations by the legacy of powerful labour-only sub-contractors. One feature of industrial relations – consultative councils – were developed, not out of an inherent orientation to participation but to head off the emergent trade unions (Broad, 1987). Following 1945 there

Table 5.1 Subcontracting levels of a major company (Nippon Kokam Steel)

Master company	First subcontractors	Second subcontractors	Third subcontractors	Dayworkers
Nippon Kokam Steel Corp.	Kokankogyo	Sugusute		
		Toshim		
		Kobayash		
		Fuji Kaium		
	Fuyo Kaium	Maruzen Showa		
	Kokam Tsuglio	Minaoto	Suzugem	
	Kokam Kikai	Rokkan Kogyo	Kawami	Mr Yamada
	Nichiel Unyu	Izumi Kigyo	Nambu	Mr Tamaka
	Sogi Kemsezsu	Nakajima Unyu	Aita	Mr Kimura
	Shinagawa Haku-Remga	Toshim		
	Tokyo Yogyo	Mochizuki		
	N. Kokam Koji	Kamto Juki		
	Nagato Kohyo	Suzuki Umso		
	Mori Kogyo	Aoyamgo Juki		
		Aomachi Juki		
		Omosniya Umyil		
		Miyaitara Kogyo		
		Toho Kohyo		
		Nippon Tekko		

Source: Y. Kato and H. Levie, TURU Occasional Paper no. 69 (1981)

was a sharpening of militancy and such councils were used alongside the creation of company or enterprise unions as a means of suppressing independent unionism and preserving managerial legitimacy and prerogatives. While economic and historical processes clearly have cultural dimensions, the above examples show that it is nonsense to refer to 'cultural imperatives' as a basis for the practices of Japanese corporations (Kelly and Brannick, 1987: 6).

Finally, it is worth laying to rest illusions concerning Japanese management itself. Six 'pillars' are commonly referred to – lifetime employment, company welfare, quality consciousness, enterprise unions, consensus management and seniority-based reward systems. Even taking this sympathetically as an ideal type, evidence suggests that it applies at best to the 20 per cent of core employees in large private and public corporations (Briggs, 1987; Dickens and Savage, 1987). The 80 per cent working in smaller firms and for sub-contractors are largely excluded from fringe benefits, company welfare and job security, as obviously are the large number of those on temporary contracts, or casual and part-time workers within both sectors. Such secondary labour-market characteristics are indeed found within the big companies themselves, as Kamata's (1982) graphic acount of life as a temporary worker at Toyota illustrates.

Even the much-vaunted consensus management has an authoritarian dimension underneath the paternalism. Much of the employee participation has a strong element of compulsion. Itoh's (1984) account of Matsushita brings out a common theme that 'voluntary' activity in quality circles is founded on being forced to give suggestions, in this case three a month ranked on a scale of 1 to 9. The company's 'seven spiritual values' are a feudalistic ideology which plays a great role in promotions. As Briggs notes, 'Japanese workers are explicitly rewarded for "desirable" behaviour, and ostracised should they display attitudes not in keeping with the company philosophy' (1987: 3). Loyalty is cemented not only through peer group pressures, but through cheap loans to buy houses and other financial inducements related to the process of creating a company man. As Peter Wickens, the Director of Personnel at Nissan UK, notes, 'If you cannot move to another company, you *have* to be loyal to the one you first joined' (1987: 27). Alcoholism, suicide and stress are serious prolems and women are systematically and openly discriminated against in the competition for secure jobs. Even the 'humble manager' is part of a rigid hierarchy marked by obsessions with rank, manifested subtlety in language and ritualistic behaviour.

It is also necessary to be careful of not overdoing the idea of the Japanisation of Western business. In the UK, by the mid-1980s, Japanese companies had reached between 50 and 60 and employed about 15,000 workers (Turnbull, 1986). This is tiny compared to the 450,000 employed by US multinationals, though Japanese investment is concentrated in specific regions (South Wales, West Midlands, North-East) and sectors (electrical, cars), and is projected to rise sharply by the end of the century as more companies seek to penetrate British soft markets (Dunning: 1986). Nor is there a simple or single pattern to organisation and employment practices. Within the diverse and pragmatic arrangements, only a minority have single-union deals and an even smaller number use quality circles (Morris, 1987).

Why then take it seriously, particularly given the prevalence of previous miracle models from Germany, the USA or Sweden? There are two basic reasons. First the *demonstration effect* of Japanese 'best practice' (Turnbull, 1987: 2). This can be best illustrated through the Nissan example. Set up in May 1986 in Washington, Tyne and Wear, Norman Tebbit even stated that 'We want them to demonstrate to our auto makers ... these aspects of Japanese industrial management' (quoted in CAITS, 1986: 20). A 'Nissan effect' has already been widely noted, drawing primarily from the single-union, no-strike deal. In fact, it is not a no-strike deal because the Amalgamated Engineering Union is not a negotiating partner! All matters of wages, conditions and company business are dealt with at plant level by a company council, with direct worker-representation conditioned by company veto. However, an initial deal was struck specifying complete flexibility and managerial prerogative. Teamworking, temporary workers and an intense work pace are also prominent features, the latter causing low morale and drop outs (*Daily Telegraph*, 6

May 1987). It is hardly surprising that union membership was less than 25 per cent in 1988.

But of more long-term importance is that Nissan has established the first British, and possibly European, example of a spatially concentrated production process (Crowther and Garrahan, 1987). A large site will enable the company to maximise influence over the industrial environment and the supply of components, moving towards a full JIT system. Employment and production practices are being built in, not grafted on. High levels of local recruitment are enabling Nissan carefully to select and train, in one case four supervisors from 4000 applications. Nor are they alone. Morris (1987: 12) found that the majority of Japanese firms in the UK used stringent tests, in one case a five-hour round of three written tests, a practical test and two interviews followed by a probationary period. As more inward investors set up on greenfield sites and are able to dictate a form of enterprise unionism and consciousness, the Nissan pattern is likely to be replicated.

The Nissan effect can also be identified in the second reason for taking the process seriously: the desire of British companies to *emulate* Japanese practices. This has been seen most prominently in the case of Ford, an early After Japan initiative based on quality circles, an 'employee involvement' programme and a new management culture and structure foundered on workforce opposition (Giles and Starkey, 1987). The second attempt to achieve a 'Japanese' restructuring of jobs and shop-floor practices culminated in the uncertain outcomes of the 1988 dispute. Explicit reference was made to Ford's plethora of grades compared to Nissan's two – manufacturer and technician. 'Participative management' is meant to be the running mate of employee involvement. Organisational change is also directed at challenging narrow functional specialisms and authoritarian attitudes (Starkey and McKinley, 1989). But Ford is by no means the sole example. Jaguar and Lucas have introduced extensive experiments featuring JIT and employee involvement (Turnbull, 1986: 19), while among the joint ventures, the Rover-Honda link-up is notable for its use of 'zone circles' and 'zone briefing groups' (D. Smith, 1987). Though Japanisation remains a highly problematic

concept, core themes linked to Nissan's tripod of flexibility,
quality and teamwork can be identified. A closer examination
of recent developments in the UK and USA allows us to link
this discussion to the general question of flexible working.

Japanisation on the Shop Floor

One of the most striking aspects of the more advanced forms
of Japanisation and flexible working is that they have allowed
a reappropriation of the language of participation, job redesign and even humanisation. Guest refers to 'the remarkable changes that took place ... as a result of the industrial
democracy effort known as Quality of Work Life' (1983: 140).
QWL is a likely vehicle for appropriation because it has
always been a generic or umbrella term subsuming anything
from job enrichment to participation schemes. Though beginning prior to the main wave of Japanisation, it has been given
force and coherence by initiatives such as GM's QWL and
Ford's Employee Involvement programmes in the USA.
These and other experiences have enabled flexible specialisation theorists to claim justification for ideas of flexible craft
workers, and management writers to refer to evidence of
parallel organisations with flatter structures, vertical communications and participative managers and workers (Cross,
1985). Arguments concerning the end of Taylorism and
Fordism have gained more power because they appear to be
based on mainstream practices rather than peripheral pre-
dictions.

The reformulation of QWL is defined by Drago and
McDonough as 'managerial efforts to involve workers in
management decision-making, to systematically empower
workers, to a limited extent, particularly as groups' (1984:
54). Team- or groupworking is indeed at the heart of Japanisation and has been introduced at 15 out of GM's 36 plants.
Involvement is based on problem-solving, quality and a range
of production decisions in such areas as use of tools, materials
handling and work layout. When Saturn, NUMMI and other
plants are fully operative with the team system, they will drop
formal worker participation programmes (Wood, 1986: 438).

To some extent, teamworking can be seen as interchangeable with quality circles which also work on a group, problem-
solving basis. But the change reflects attempts to shift away
from a narrow focus on quality to wider production issues and
a general level of involvement. Quality circles have always
tended to experience some tension between their dual functions as *technique* and vehicle for localised participation.
Many companies have always used quality circles in the latter
sense. Dunford and McGraw quote a Managing Director of
Reckitt and Colman in Australia who had initiated circles as a
catalyst for a period of organisational restructuring: 'With
hindsight I wouldn't call it quality circles. I would not try to
have it labelled' (1986: 25). In the UK Rover plant, the label
has been deliberately avoided, management preferring zone
briefings and circles. The latter work under management
'facilitators' who guide 'voluntary problem-solving groups'.
Techniques used include brainstorming and discussions based
on 'thought starters' such as 'every member is responsible for
the progress of a team' or 'strive to generate enthusiasm'
(D. Smith, 1987: 23).

It would be a mistake, however, to detach forms of involvement from the influences deriving from new forms of technology such as flexible manufacturing systems, and production
processes, notably JIT. While it would be over-deterministic
to ascribe 'needs', there is little doubt that both operate more
effectively with higher levels of co-operation, knowledge and
flexibility than previus configurations of technology and work
organisation. Under JIT, workers are expected to do on-the-
spot problem-solving. Indeed, they have little choice given
that reduced buffer stocks mean subsequent activities would
break down without such action (Tailby and Turnbull, 1987).
In more general terms, movement between jobs requires
multiskilling. This may take the form of merging of functions,
including the incorporation of inspection, maintenance and
support activities into production operative's tasks, or vice
versa. Dankbaar's (1988: 39) study of a West German motor
plant shows that when such skilled and unskilled activities are
combined in one person, management gain because there is
continuous work whether the line is running without problems
or at a standstill. These processes also require increased

knowledge, both of details of the work process such as quality control and a wider range of jobs. Pay for knowledge systems may be the form taken, in which learning of extra tasks is built in to the reward system.

It is also important not to neglect what Wood (1986: 432) calls *attitudinal restructuring*; in other words a much more explicit focus on shaping employee attitudes in spheres such as co-operativeness and self-discipline. As Sayer notes with reference to JIT, 'profitability can depend quite heavily on the performance of workers who are technically unskilled or semi-skilled but behaviourally highly skilled' (1986: 67). This helps explain the paradox that many companies are engaging in detailed and intensive selection and screening processes for relatively routine jobs, often recruiting young 'green' labour. We have already given examples from Japanese companies but at NUMMI all candidates for employment must undertake three days of interviews, job simulations and discussion on the firm's philosophy and objectives (Wood, 1986: 434). Attention to attitudes is also reflected in increased emphasis on communications. This is the purpose of Rover's zone briefing system in which supervisors stop the track to give information about output targets, sales performance and matters more specific to the 'zone'.

Communicating company goals can also take place outside the workplace. Part of GM's Hydra-matic Division's QWL programme includes week-long 'Family Awareness Training' sessions at education centres (Parker, 1985: 17–19). This does not refer to the employee's nearest and dearest but to the notion of company as family. Once outside the normal environment and in circumstances where everyone is individualised, psychological exercises and techniques are used to break down old identities. GM questionnaires rate those with limited scores on loyalty to the company as having a low quality of work life. Pressure can also be put on workers by their union, as the United Auto Workers is increasingly integrated in to the limited power-sharing mechanisms of GM's 'joint process' (Black and Ackers, 1989). In addition, the workgroup can be used to redirect collective goals towards the company in a way that fulfills the old human relations' dream. A number of firms put absentee lists up, while another favourite is encouragement of intergroup competition. In the USA this is called 'whipsawing' by unions and is facilitated internally by computerised data on productivity and externally through the threat of closure (Giordano, 1985: 18). Overall, the focus on behaviour, groupwork and personnel appraisal helps to explain the increased, though different role for supervisors. Japan has the highest supervisory density among the advanced economies (Broad, 1987: 16). Attitudinal restructuring speaks to a range of issues more explicitly related to organisational cultures. We will return to this question in the final chapter.

EVALUATING CONTEMPORARY ALTERNATIVES

It can be seen that there are a number of overlapping organisational themes from the 'models' established through Japanisation, flexible specialisation and the flexible firm that have tended to reinforce one another. The break from Taylorism and Fordism is one example. Each 'model' therefore needs to be evaluated both for their specificity and overlaps.

Japanisation. Given the misconceptions surrounding Japanisation, it is not difficult to reach a conclusion that it is a bad abstraction (Dickens and Savage, 1987: 2) which conflates unrelated and non-essential factors behind an inappropriate racial tag. As Marchington and Parker comment, 'there must be some doubt as to whether there is anything inherently Japanese about the practices employed' (1987: 28). They point to British companies with a history of consensual, paternalistic management and encouragement of enterprise unionism. But we would put it another way. Japanisation, like other sets of management ideas and practices, is a *resource* which is drawn on selectively. So the Japanese experience can be seen either as confirmation of the need to retain managerial prerogatives or for the expansion of worker participation, or indeed as both (Streek, 1987: 295). Even unions can draw on those aspects which are perceived as egalitarian, such as single status conditions. Interestingly, Wickens is bitingly critical of faddist managers, who 'have only an idealised,

often out-of-date, sanitised version of Japanese-style management based on constantly recycled versions of the human
resource and other management techniques of some of Japan's
larger companies' (1987: 37).

Selectivity, however, is more likely to be applied to technique. It is quite possible to detach aspects from their social or
organisational context as ICI has with its Quality Policy.
Whether this kind of approach with QCs or JIT will work is
another matter as the amount of time, training and planning
is often underestimated. The case of Reckitt and Colman in
Australia (Dunford and McGraw, 1987) mentioned earlier
highlights a parallel danger. After the QCs had achieved their
initial aim as change catalysts they were wound down as
management felt they were 'flogging a dead horse', leaving
behind a worforce cynical and hostile to any similar initiative
in future. Similarly, the zone briefings at Rover engendered
little enthusiasm from supervisors or workers given the limited
content and lack of genuine two-way communication. Researchers on Ford, Lucas and other plants make the point that
the relative failure of emulation partly reflects the difficulty of
grafting high trust practices on to low trust cultures and
environments, as well as 'an etiquette for managing power
relations which has little cultural support' (D. Smith, 1987:
28–9). British companies have shown little commitment to the
compensations of job security; in fact, the reverse. Threats to
job security have normally accompanied the introduction of
emulation programmes. The selectivity with regard to the
'pillars' of Japanese management can also be seen in moves
away from seniority-based rewards, given impetus by the
offensive against bureaucratic work rules.

The above suggest that Japanisation is often used as a
rationalisation or organising principle for changes that companies may have initiated anyway. It also provides a handy
motivational tool to counter the competitive threat itself, as
with the Philips managers sent on courses with the slogan 'zap
a Jap a day'. This judgement needs to be qualified when
discussing the motor industry programmes in the US discussed in the last section. As was shown, specific initiatives
take place within a wider productive context. In addition, the
job banks scheme has been seen by some as the 'final piece in

the Japanisation jigsaw' (Wood, 1986: 435), though it does not appear to have stemmed closures. But the main claim that the programmes have ushered in a new era of worker partici-pation is open to even greater doubt. Wood rightly notes that though QWL practices signal a move away from low-trust, low-knowledge systems they do not signal a transition to any form of industrial democracy. This would be to demean the concept and to detach it from any conception of power relations. Whatever participation does exist is within a man-agement decision-making process concerning issues of cost, efficiency and product quality (Giordano, 1985: 31). Though Meyer refers to real powers invested in workgroups at Saturn, this is qualified by the comment that they 'represent actions which have already been routinised to the point at which machines could execute the functions' (1986: 84). GM makes an explicit distinction between alternatives to current practices, which can emanate from the worker, and decisions to act and commit resources, which remains a management prerogative. Not only is this a highly constrained form of empowerment, QWL further signals the abandonment of the traditional terrain of job redesign associated with work humanisation.

Flexible Specialisation. This is not just a resource, it is rapidly becoming a new work organisation paradigm (C. Smith, 1987) and as such is more directly open to analytical critique. A number of studies, notably Williams *et al.* (1987), have convincingly argued that the conceptual polarity between mass production and flexible specialisation is misleading. Traditional mass production is still widespread, particularly where semi-skilled women workers doing labour-intensive assembly and packing jobs remain a cheaper or more reliable option (Pollert, 1988a). In addition, mass production does not always use dedicated equipment to make standardised pro-ducts but can handle diversification within flow lines. Wood (1987, 1988) has shown that the world car – the archetypal example of mass production within the international division of labour – remains prominent, albeit in modified form. Economies of scale have fallen, but the break-even point is still high. Japanese companies have established variety within mass production with the use of JIT and not always with

advanced technology (Sayer, 1986). In fact, flexible specialisation and JIT may be in contradiction as flexibility is
undermined by a range of factors including single sourcing
and the dependency between buyer and supplier (Meyer,
1986).

Nor, on current trends, are mass markets necessarily
saturated. There are a huge range of industries which are still
based on mass and large batch production and the pattern
with goods such as colour TVs and videos is for production to
be based on families of interrelated models. Fragmentation of
demand, or what companies call 'positioning strategies', is
more often an attempt to create a market rather than reflect
new consumer tastes. Part of the obsession with the Fordist
stereotype is ignoring the inconvenient fact that most plants in
modern economies do not contain assembly lines (Williams *et
al.*, 1987: 421). Even the identification of flexibility with
manufacturing itself neglects the service sector as the major
growth area of such practices (Hyman, 1988). The flexible
specialisation thesis also overestimates the use of programmable technology. Advanced machinery such as FMS is very
expensive, particularly for the small firms who should be in
the forefront of customised production. Neither is all new
technology inherently flexible or being *used* in a flexible way.
The emphasis is more likely to be on control and co-ordination of the labour process, quality and routing rather than
product flexibility (Wood, 1988: 9).

Overall, as the Williams critique proves, the statistical and
case study evidence used by Sabel and Piore is frequently poor
or non-existent. Even on their 'home-ground' in Emilia-
Romagna, the majority of production is still Fordist in nature,
while quality craft work is the preserve of the majority of
middle-aged men: 'Semi-skilled assembly work, plastic-
moulding, and wiring work is carried out by women, while
heavy foundry and forging work is done by Southern Italian
and North African workers' (Murray, 1987: 88). One of the
reasons may be that flexible specialisation claims to be both
an analysis of the causes of the crisis of the market system and
a projected solution to it. It is, therefore, never sure whether it
is talking about what *is* or what should *be*. Ironically, it is the
radical writer Hyman (1988) who has to point out that the

thesis represents a dangerous oversimplification of the strategic options open to employers, and that the practice is likely to be piecemeal application rather than an integrated package. Because the analysis treats the relations between markets, technology and work organisation in such an uncritical way, flexible specialisation is presented almost as a functional necessity (Wood, 1986: 416). In particular, by making technology subordinate to their demand-pull focus, choices remain limited and frozen, despite attempts to avoid a deterministic framework (C. Smith, 1987: 3–6).

The flexible firm. What about this less theoretical cousin? Pollert (1988a, 1988b) argues that both share vital commonalities. The notable features include a celebration of the market and consumer sovereignty; a legitimation of the view that the solutions to organisational and economic problems lies in altering the behaviour of labour; the resurrection of a dual labour market analysis; and a futurological discourse underwritten by a post-industrial analysis in which flexibility marks the vital break from the past.

It is certainly true that the idea that employers are introducing flexibility simply to respond to market demands neglects the strategic choice both to fragment product markets and to get the best of both worlds from core and peripheral workers. Both flexibility arguments fuse 'description, prediction and prescription' (Pollert, 1988a: 43). The latter tends to have a prominent and dangerous profile through the role of the IMS as an intermediary between employers and government policy in the labour market (Pollert, 1988b). But the commonalities can be overstated. Precisely because one is a management policy model and the other a grand theory, the flexible firm can be utilised in some instances as an explanatory tool without the burden of any wider conceptual and historical baggage. Looked at more cynically as a proclaimed ideal type that does not actually describe any actual organistion, the goalposts can be moved across sectors as circumstances require! Nevertheless, the empirical claims need to be scaled down before any effective use can be made of it.

Even before Pollert's highly effective 'deconstruction', the idea of a new *core* workforce had attracted a body of critical comment. A number of writers have challenged the novelty of flexibility agreements by making explicit comparison to the productivity deals of the 1960s which also reduced demarcation and restrictive practices in exchange for greater rewards (Towers, 1987; MacInnes, 1987). Others have pointed out that the evidence collected by the IMS itself, for example in the NEDO study (1986), found that changes were widespread but uneven by sector and there was little evidence for any extensive flexibility. The changes themselves were mostly the result of short-term cost-saving and threats of job loss, without sinking deeper roots or employment cultures at the 'core'. This coincides with scepticism in other commentaries (Labour Research Department: 1986a; Elger: 1987) which raises the possibility that talk of flexibility may often be a *post hoc* managerial rationalisation geared towards the valued goal of strategic planning. As with all attempts to transform labour power into profitable production, agreements are only a formal beginning and there is evidence of considerable worker resistance which may modify outcomes (Labour Research Department, 1986a; Slaughter, 1987; Turnbull, 1986). A precise differentiation between sectors is not always possible. Fast food chains like McDonalds are of the fastest growing parts of the economy. But this 'core' sector, employing mainly young people, blacks and women on part-time and unsociable hours, has workers with decidedly peripheral employment conditions (Transnationals Information Centre, 1987).

A critical examination of evidence in relation to the *peripheral* category has to rely more on Pollert's studies. She rightly points out that evidence has tended to conflate long-term changes and standard practices to vary production with genuinely new employment patterns. The rest of the critique uses a variety of sources to show that most of the figures for temporary, part-time, homeworking, self-employment and sub-contracted work are greatly exaggerated. Again, where there have been increases it is often on the basis of already established practices and on the basis of state sponsorship in the public sector rather than management strategy in the private. Finally, though it is probably too late to stop the terminology entering established discourse, the use of peripheral itself does not really do justice to the centrality of such forms of work, particularly that done by women, to a modern capitalist economy.

On the basis of these criticisms of the flexible firm, would it be right to concur with the judgement that this is a fad that will be forgotten in five years? While full flexibility is likely to remain a 'Holy Grail' that is desired but never quite attained (IPM, 1986: 11), we would argue that dualism is a reflection of increasing reorganisation of manpower resources and control over the headcount. The need is for more specific research to identify the relevant areas. Broad brush statistics make it difficult to disentangle real trends from the decline in manufacturing and uneven shifts between sectors. We should also recognise that while the much-hyped examples are unrepresentative, they are likely to be the beginnings of trends that will only show up fully in statistics over a longer period of time.

Overlapping themes. The dominant themes express an optimistic view of trends on work organisation. We have already indicated the limited progress towards any form of job security. In fact, as Standing (1986: 114) notes, labour flexibility is almost synonymous for workers with one or more forms of labour market, job or income security. So, for example, the British and American steel industries have both re-hired redundant workers under sub-contractors with significant loss of pay, benefits and health and safety protection (Fevre, 1986; Mather, 1987).

Most of the worst aspects are at the 'periphery'. Trends towards decentralisation in industries such as clothing are resulting in a modern 'burgeoning sweatshop economy' based on women and ethnic minority workers (Mitter, 1986). Nor would some of the developments have been possible or as favourable without action by the state to 'foster more realistic attitudes and action' (Economic Progress Report, 1986: 1) through removal of some institutional protection, deregulation of labour markets and weakening of union power that was discussed in detail in Chapter 3. In an interrelated way the purpose of some policies is not flexibility *per se*, but the avoidance of remaining legislation which protects employee rights. This pushes hiring practices in the direction of part-time work below 16 hours and temporary contracts, as the CBI admits (Yates, 1986: 34). Italian laws giving job security can also be avoided in firms of less than 15 on the payroll. The reality of homeworking is more likely to be super-exploitation and casualisation rather than the happy, autonomous employee in the electronic cottage (Allen and Wolkovitz, 1987; Phizacklea, 1987). In fact, flexibility analyses largely set aside the issues of gender and ethnicity by recasting the dual labour market as benign, progressive or inevitable (Pollert, 1988a).

But work intensification is also a major characteristic of much of the most advanced work arrangements such as JIT which rely on continual and controlled pressure (Turnbull, 1987: 13), internalising disciplinary pressure within the group (Sayer, 1986: 66) and conforming to new behavioural rules. Slaughter gives a vivid account of 'management by stress' at NUMMI, where the goal is to stretch the system like a rubber band. Breakdowns and stoppages of the line are encouraged as this can indicate where weak points are and how they can be corrected, fine-tuned and further stressed. Workers who fall behind may have video cameras trained on them to 'help' in this process. When *Business Week* (1983) discusses job flexibility, most of the examples are simply enlarging jobs by adding extra duties, cutting the size of workteams, or eliminating breaks.

This indicates that though *multiskilling* and multi-activity jobs are important, they may not quite be the end of Taylorism as we know it! The study of Shaiken *et al.* (1986) explicitly refutes the flexible specialisation thesis by showing that in only one out of ten firms using numerical control machinery did management grant workers the central role in innovation and debugging. Similarly, Kraft and Dubnoff (1986) indicate that computer programming work is characterised by increasing task hierarchies rather than more fluid work. Managerial ability to move across demarcation lines and combine tasks often reflects the reality of previously routinised and fragmented jobs. Putting these together, adding on further deskilled tasks (NEDO, 1986), or extra ancillary duties such as inspection, does not normally make a substantial difference to their content. As a worker at Lucas Electrical commented: 'The jobs are just the same, you just do more of "em"' (quoted in Turnbull, 1987: 17). Slaughter (1987) shows that teamworking at NUMMI involved specifying, measuring and timing every move in greater detail: describing this as 'super-Taylorism'. This would not be our description. Though workers' knowledge continues to be appropriated by management, the move away from narrow specialisation towards pay for knowledge and quality circles marks a significant break from those parts of Taylorism based on the separation of conception and execution. An increased emphasis on selecting and training the 'appropriate worker' shows that another part of Taylor's original agenda is being renewed (Wood, 1988: 11). The overall lesson is the same as learned in Chapter 2. Taylorism is not a package which management has to implement as a whole, though the elements selected have changed.

The study by Shaiken also showed that the primary managerial concern remained that of centralising control and reducing unpredictability. This is not the only study to throw doubt on the anti-hierarchical pretensions of contemporary developments in work organisation, in which organisations that remain centralised will become dinosaurs (Bumstead and Eckblad, 1985: 67). In fact, a consistent theme is the gap between potential for decentralisation and skill enhancement, and the reality of subordination to traditional functional structures, narrowly defined cost efficiency and conservative cultures (Cummings and Blumberg, 1987; Child, 1987; Williams, 1988). We have to distinguish between the delegation of operational autonomy and strengthened financial and other controls by the central structures. At British Telecom, the system of profit-centres relies on accounting structures and marketing forecasts to control and monitor costs: 'District managers, supposedly freer than ever in the age of devolution, complain of now being more tightly restricted by budgets imposed from above over which they have less influence' (Hallet, 1988: 35).

Similarly, information technology can allow for varied uses, 'particularly the development of an industrial organisation whose planning and financial decisions are centralised and whose operations are frequently decentralised and highly interdependent' (Giordano, 1985: 11). Though there may be a thinning out of the middle levels of command (Williams,

1988: 8), the power of strategic decision-makers is actually increased. The vast increase in information available on production activities can in itself reproduce managerial power to monitor, control and predict performance. Sections of the business community also remain sceptical. John Hunt of the London Business School comments, 'Despite the pleas of social scientists, centralisation is the current trend in authority relationships' (1984: 15), while in *The Economist* Stuart (1988) argues that 'big is back and beautiful'. The only people who thought centralised power went away were management gurus obsessed with heroic entrepreneurs.

It can be seen, therefore, that evidence surrounding contemporary developments in organisational design does not justify a new paradigm or general theory of work organisation, despite attempts to move from Bravermania to cybermania, as Wood (1988) puts it. This is not to deny that very important changes are taking place. But strong elements of continuity remain, both in capital-labour relations and the use of bureaucratic structures and processes. The changes can therefore be understood through the modified framework of radical organisation theory established in Chapter 1.

6

Reinventing Organisation Man

In 1956, William H. Whyte wrote the influential *The Organisation Man*, a vituperative attack on the 'social ethic' shaping the values of those in the middle ranks of private and public corporations. This oddly named ethic was a collectivist nightmare which morally legitimated the powers of society against the individual. Amongst those blamed was Mayo and his obsessive concern for belongingness and group adjustment. Whyte's solution was for the individual to fight a rearguard battle against the organisation, with the aid of some useful advice such as 'how to cheat at personality tests'. As Peters and Waterman note (1982: 105), the association with grey conformity made corporate culture a taboo topic. Though some continue to doubt the idea of people 'belonging' to the company (Lessem, 1985), by the end of the 1980s organisation man was back in fashion. IBM's 'corporate fascists' with their historic emphasis on conformity and commitment could get their overdue kudos as well as smile politely on the way to the bank (Pascale and Athos, 1982: 186). Despite all the hymns of praise to corporations, the credit for reviving the issue largely goes to American academics and management consultants, notably the two mentioned above, plus Ouchi (1981) and Deal and Kennedy (1988) (all except Ouchi connected to the McKinsey consultancy company), though it was filtered, as we began to discuss in Chapter 5, through a reading of the Japanese experience that located their success in the existence of strong cultures and 'turned-on workforces'.

Corporate culture, which can be defined as the way that management mobilise combinations of values, language, rituals and myths, is seen as the key factor in unlocking the commitment and enthusiasm of employees. To the extent that it can make people feel that they are working for something worthwhile, it is projected as part of the solution to the historic *search for meaning* in the study of organisations. For work humanisation theorists that search was connected to the provision of intrinsically satisfying tasks. The ground has now shifted to the psychosocial benefits from identification with the company and its superordinate goals. There may be characteristics which make companies successful, as in the famous lists of Peters and Waterman or Goldsmith and Clutterbuck – autonomy, zero-basing, productivity through people – but corporate culture is the core and the glue that binds the increasingly diverse activities together. When the project is defined as developing a non-deified, non-religious 'spiritualism', it is to be expected that advocacy often takes on a distinctly evangelical tone with managers and workers exhorted to love the company. Such acts of will can break the 'attitudinal barriers' that hold firms back (Goldsmith and Clutterbuck, 1985: 5).

More conventionally there is an emphasis on culture *strategies*, with senior management taking the process of value-shaping seriously. But perhaps strategy is the wrong word. For as we discussed in Chapter 5, corporate culture is part of a proclaimed shift fom the hard S's of strategy, systems and their quantifiable objectives to the soft S's of style and shared values. So, is this another fad of pop-management or a doomed attempt to transplant culture-specific Japanese systems? Maybe, but we should not underestimate the shift in management theory, and to a lesser extent practices, that is going on. Changing people's emotions or what they think has mostly been off-limits to the dominant strands in OB. It is summed up in Herzberg's answer to a question about the problems of employees at a seminar – 'don't worry about their attitudes or personality, you can't change them' (Carr Mill Consultants, 1973: 7). Similarly, when commenting on March and Simon's views, Perrow argued that 'to change individual behaviour, you do not have to change individuals' (1972:

147). Under systems of bureaucratic or unobtrusive control, what had to be changed was the structure of communication, rules or selection, along with provision of the appropriate rewards and sanctions.

Managerial and professional employees *were* subject to moulding and socialisation processes, though how seriously or effectively is open to question. But for all the unitarist rhetoric about goals, routine manual and clerical workers were not really expected to identify with the company. It was more a case of 'if you've got them by the balls, their hearts and minds will follow'. Put more politely, the problematic of motivation has been dominant which, as we shall argue in Chapter 7, can become a surrogate for meaning. It is not the case that questions of attitudes were wholly by-passed, merely that they were never satisfactorily dealt with from a managerial standpoint. Before we move to examining the contemporary corporate culture debate, it is therefore worth discussing some of the streams that led towards or are complementary to it.

ORGANISATIONAL DEVELOPMENT

Organisational development or OD was probably the most direct antecedent, Bennis (1966) arguing that the only way to change organisations was to change their cultures. But that change process should be conscious, systematic and planned; part of a collaborative effort between change agents in the guise of behavioural scientists armed with 'valid' knowledge and their corporate clients. It began in the 1950s, building on the human relations tradition of analysis of groups discussed in Chapter 2 but specifically directed towards management education and training. Many companies began to use T groups, a form of sensitivity training based on the assumption that 'improvements in the quality of interpersonal relations will produce appreciable improvements in organisational functioning' (Cameron, 1973: 10). Diagnostic, interpersonal and problem-solving skills could also be developed through other group processes such as team development. At the level of the organisation as a whole, techniques such as goal-setting and planning (of which MBO is a type), and survey feedback based on the controlled use of management and employee survey data can be used as a springboard for change (French and Bell, 1973).

Early OD was part of the same 'liberal' agenda as work humanisation. The prescriptions for a healthy organisation operated on similar assumptions about the capacity for human growth and the organisational blockages to it, as well as the same values of openness, trust and creativity (Argyris, 1967). Its techniques were participative and anti-bureaucratic but there was a certain division of labour. Though both started from 'people variables', OD took virtually no interest in questions of structure such as job redesign. In fact, it stayed away from such *content* issues (Roeber, 1975) believing that the process or form was the content. Nevertheless, to the extent that OD programmes were concerned with adjusting employees to the goals and structures in change processes, it was sold as methods for ensuring the 'best fit' between the social, technological and task-oriented cultures and can be identified as a contingent control strategy.

Those companies that used OD systematically rather than as one-off techniques – a familiar 'progressive' roll-call including IBM, Procter and Gamble, Shell and Philips – were often more concerned with facilitating general change processes. Checklists for implementing change share common elements, notably careful diagnosis of the problems and the options, support of top management, identification of key internal change agents, participative and consultative mechanisms among all parties, training and personal development, and monitoring and evaluation (Child, 1984: 291–2). ICI is a classic case of a pioneer and long-term user of OD (Pettigrew, 1985). OD complemented its productivity deals and job enrichment initiatives of the late 1960s and 1970s, unlocking the rigidities of attitudes and practice that are inevitably built into any organisation's management, its culture and history. Pettigrew rightly makes clear, however, that this is not entirely a rational planning process; it has to work through internal political systems.

In OD, processes of unlocking or 'unfreezing' are normally intimately connected to dealing with resistance to change. As OD is concerned with process not content, the change itself, regardless of its effects, tends to be taken as valid. The 'problem' is people's attitudes, behaviour and performance (Beckhard, 1969). Though social influences on employee attitudes are sometimes recognised, resistance tends to be conceived in purely psychological terms as a normal response to the threat to the stability of individual and group practices – 'people resist change'. Though a certain amount of conflict is inevitable, 'excessive' amounts are harmful, dysfunctional and anyway are unlikely in a healthy organisation (Hitt *et al.*, 1986: 439–42). Having discarded any recognition of structurally opposed conflicts of interest, emphasis is placed on techniques to overcome resistance and manage and resolve the conflict (Schein, 1969; Likert and Likert, 1976). Though formally neutral on the choice, the bias is towards democratic-consultative methods compatible with overall OD philosophy.

Fall and Salvation?

By the late 1970s the OD movement had suffered 'a collapse of professional confidence in itself' (Harrison, 1984: 12), marked by introspection and self-doubt, a decline in the British OD network and a dismantling of some of the largest internal company units. In part, it had gone the same way as other techniques in the history of management of human resources, 'enthusiastically introduced by managers who are keen to find solutions to their "people" problems only to be discarded and discredited by the same disillusioned and increasingly cynical managers some time later' (McLean, 1981: 4). Its critics were able to point to the failure of studies to yield any evidence of lasting change on job behaviour or performance effectiveness (Campbell and Dunnette, 1968). Where gains are made, it tends to be a result of managers being convinced by consultants that an intervention would succeed. This is communicated down through supervisors to workers and any productivity improvements are due more to the expectations raised through the studies than to the form of intervention itself (Evden, 1986).

It is certainly true that OD presents an easy critical target. There was, as Mangham (1978) noted, a reassuring and blandly optimistic tone in much of the writings, shored up by assumptions that change is always desirable and that resistance can be overcome by an able and intelligent manager. But as with its work humanisation running mate, changing conditions in the political and economic environment also played a part in undermining its appeal. Recession and competitive pressures have shifted public and managerial ideologies away from liberal-humanist values. There has been a rediscovery of managerial power and authority, and participation is 'wet' in an era whose tone was set by the Thatcher and Reagan administrations. Even traditionally paternalistic companies such as Cadburys sought an organisational transformation which largely jettisoned the consensual and evolutionary pattern, to say nothing of the Factory Council established in 1918, though other elements of OD such as identification of internal change agents played a key role (Child and Smith, 1987).

In a way which again parallels work humanisation, OD was always likely to underestimate structural constraints and organisational design archetypes (Greenwood and Hinings, 1987), particularly given its presentation as a neutral technology of planned change. Entrenched hierarchical power remained intact as OD attempted to create attitude change among first line supervisors. Meanwhile companies were finding that they could achieve change and secure corporate goals through technical and economic restructuring, with unemployment as an external discipline over the workforce. There simply wasn't a great deal of negotiation and consultation over major organisational changes such as those associated with new technology, as the survey by Daniel (1987) showed. The alliance with middle management as a client group therefore began to break down, particularly with management under increasing pressure from their own superiors, and with decision-making shifting towards financial and IT specialists.

Some, particularly in the USA, simply adapted to the pressure towards hard-nosed business results and 'bottom-line' evaluation criteria: 'the primary value is on financial results and people are treated as secondary' (Harrison, 1984: 14). This has necessitated a distancing from the traditional values of, 'openness, democracy, trust, authenticity and risk-taking ... competitiveness, political ambition, distrust and dislike are coming to be seen as endemic and enduring features of organisational life' (Maclean, 1981: 2). Some OD practitioners (Myers, 1976) have proved their more managerial orientation by acting as 'union-busting' consultants. This is a subsidiary part of what could be the partial salvation of

Figure 6.1 'Sign of the times'

Organisation Development Manager
...to lead a major culture change
c.£23K+car

This is an outstanding opportunity to break new ground. Reporting to the main board Human Resources Director you will be a leader in planning and implementing a culture change strategy involving all aspects of this household name fmcg company's activities.

To achieve their high growth goals our clients, national leaders in an ethically attractive natural products market, are committed to evolving from the successful paternalism of the past to a people centred, quality, performance and market orientated culture.

A thoroughly rounded professional is required with exceptional conceptual and practical skills. 'Streetwise' and business motivated, your experience will include OD, assessment centres, psychometric testing, process counselling, sales marketing and performance management training, leadership of a training team. Applicants should be action orientated. Administrators and behavioural theorists need not apply.

The Company offers a salary package dependent on experience and potential contribution, backed with full, large company benefits including a company car. Located in an attractive semi-rural area in the South benefited by relatively low housing costs.

Please write with full details. These will be forwarded direct to our client. List separately any companies to whom your application should not be sent. John Woodger, ref.SB2464.

HAY-MSL Selection and Advertising Limited, 52 Grosvenor Gardens, London SW1W 0AW.

Offices in Europe, the Americas, Australasia and Asia Pacific.

Source: advertisement from *The Guardian*.

OD – the growth of the 'new human resource management' in the new conditions discussed in Chapter 5. New production arrangements and sharpened competition have put a premium on increasing employee commitment. The working party for the GM Saturn plant developed a set of organisational principles which accord with an OD model (Wood, 1986: 437). Meanwhile companies are beginning to advertise for OD managers who can plan and implement culture strategies (see Figure 6.1). This is the new ball game: OD as specific techniques within a broader organisational culture and human resource context, and this time targeted at workers as well as managers. We shall return to this issue later.

THE CORPORATE CULTURE MERCHANTS

The Perspective

'In culture there is strength' is the ominous-sounding new law of business life proclaimed by Deal and Kennedy (1988: 19). But what is it that gives such strength? One of the most recurrent themes is *attention to employees*; ownership in a shared vision rather than changes in work or working conditions. The notion of 'pillars' occurs again, this time in creating a committed workforce. The British personnel writers Martin and Nicholls (1987) name three – a sense of belonging to the organisation, a sense of excitement in the job, and confidence in management. In general terms 'the notion of employee commitment is built on the internalisation of the norms and values of the organisation' (Kelly and Brannick, 1987: 19).

Interestingly, there is explicit recognition of the benefits of *emotional* engagement; affectiveness more than effectiveness. As 'man is quite strikingly irrational' (Peters and Waterman: 1982, 86), employees can be appealed to through symbolism and the ceremonies and awards of 'hoop-la'. In the new corporations it is the role of those at the top to act as symbolic rather than rational managers; scriptwriters and directors of the daily drama of company life (Deal and Kennedy, 1988:

142). By symbolising the organisation internally and externally, heroes become a crucial component of the leadership process. For Deal and Kennedy, John Wayne in pinstripes is an appropriate role model. Leadership is invested with a large burden in cultural management, reflecting in part research which has identified the founder's influence in shaping values (Schein: 1985). In addition, the focus is on disseminating values through stories, myths and legends about the company, its products and heroes, backed up by rites and rituals which reinforce cultural identification. The latter also helpfully facilitates the goal of a large dose of Skinnerian positive reinforcement, where *everyone* is made to feel a winner. Management in general is expected to use non-authoritarian styles to create a climate of trust. Some writers made a nod in the direction of feminism by referring to nurturing qualities and androgynous managers (Naisbitt and Aburdene, 1985: 207). Others are content to report the aim of shifting from an aggressive, confrontational and macho style at companies such as Ford and Rank Xerox (Giles and Starkey, 1987).

Personnel is seen by many as playing a more central role in these processes, but not the reactive and industrial relations orientation of old. It is being recast as the previously referred to *new human resource management* (HRM), though the latter will not be the property of a narrow functional department (Tichy *et al.*, 1982; Beer *et al.*, 1985). Instead, the emphasis is on the integration of 'personnel' issues within the overall business strategy, with employees becoming a 'resource' equivalent to something like finance. Strategic is a term continually invoked to refer to the management of employees at all levels directed towards the creating and sustaining of competitive advantage (Miller, 1989). Whether this harder-edged approach genuinely reflects substantial shifts of policy from the old personnel is open to dispute (Guest, 1989). But the intent to move away from an industrial relations approach is clear.

Collective bargaining and unions are bad words in the new world of *unmediated* relations between the organisation and the individual. An example of the new practices is that of direct communication with the workforce. Winning companies have a culture that enables 'a passion for disclosure of information' (Goldsmith and Clutterbuck, 1985: 73), hence the rash of briefings, videos, house magazines, open days and consultative forums. Trade unions are not given much of a part in strong culture companies. At best they are considered a recalcitrant junior member and at worst an unnecessary obstacle. The HRM advocates, Kelly and Brannick, deliver a blunt warning: 'The ability to organise will be curtailed, if not openly challenged by management, and the role of the trade union as an element of the communication network will lose its significance' (1987: 20). In fact, such employment practices already constitute a significant part of the strategies of a growing number of companies to make themselves union-free by removing or substituting any employee desire for collective representation (Basset, 1989).

Though the package of corporate culture is new, some of the ideas are not. Pop-management writers seldom discuss theoretical sources, but Peters and Waterman acknowledge that 'The stream that today's researchers are tapping is an old one started in the late 1930s by Elton Mayo and Chester Barnard' (1982: 5). Human relations influences can most clearly be seen in the focus on managing the informal organisation – workers as irrational creatures of sentiment, and social needs to belong – whereas the shadow of Barnard looms over conceptions of the organisation as a co-operative social system and on the role of the executive in articulating and disseminating values and superordinate goals.

But there are also deeper roots: 'it is in the various writings of Durkheim that a conceptual framework for discussions of corporate culture may be found' (Ray, 1986: 290). Ouchi is one of the few corporate culture writers to accept the need for a macro-sociological analysis that breaks from the interpersonal level so favoured by many organisational writers. His article with Johnson (1978) draws directly on a Durkheimean framework which sees a modern division of labour involving a loss of moral community and mutual obligation, with a decline in the role of the family, Church and other institutions. Durkheim believed that the necessary function of social control and cohesion could be played by professions and occupational groups, a theme echoed later by Mayo. Ouchi and Johnson argue that Japanese work organisations have provided the necessary primary relations. Ray (1986) extends the analysis by pointing out that the corporation is expected to take on the functions embodied in Durkheim's realm of the sacred, hence the emphasis, both on faith in the firm and binding rites and rituals. Most corporate culture books draw on such assumptions. Deal and Kennedy do so explicitly: 'corporations may be the last institutions in America that can effectively take on the role of shaping values' (1988: 16).

The Evidence

What is the evidence for the dual claim that strong cultures exist and that they constitute the primary reason for better or even excellent performance? Many of the same companies tend to appear across the range of US books – IBM, Procter and Gamble, Hewlett Packard, McDonalds, Delta Airlines. So do some of the 'baddies', notably Harold Geneen and ITT who seem to get it in the neck consistently. In the UK the roll-call includes Marks and Spencers, Plessey, Sainsburys, Burton and Schweppes. As for the information about the companies, the opening sentence of Deal and Kennedy begins, 'S. C. Allyn, a retired chairman of the board, likes to tell a story ...' (1988: 3). With partial exception of Ouchi, stories, vignettes and anecdotes about the dedication and commitment of corporate heroes and managers, or the devotion of ordinary employees, constitute a large proportion of the evidence presented.

Of course they are not the only sources. Across the books it is possible to find interviews with top management; testing the culture by conversing with the receptionist; profiles based on company documents; use of formal statements of objectives and philosophy and of biographies and speeches; and questionnaires filled in by Chairmen asked to rank their firm according to 'excellence' criteria. Occasionally, as in Goldsmith and Clutterbuck, there is reference to interviewing people on the shop floor but there is no sign of the results. A major consequence is that what executives and managers say in words or on paper is taken as proof. There is little critical reflection on this. Martin and Nichols get nearest:

> we cannot be sure of the extent to which the companies we studied were *actually* successful in creating that commitment or whether that commitment contributed to their success. All we can say is that the managers in question *reported* that their efforts to create commitment met with a positive response and produced a significant improvement. (1987: ix, our emphasis).

In addition, they present some useful, if brief and largely propagandising cases. As for most of the literature, much of the time even corporate slogans are taken as virtually incontrovertible evidence of culture and effects because they are taken to be synonymous with superordinate goals. There is considerable positive reference to slogans, such as Delta Airlines 'the Delta family feeling'; IBM's 'IBM means service' and 'respect for the individual'; GE's 'Progress is our most important product'. Apparently *everyone* knows and believes in Tandem Computers' slogans such as 'It's so nice, it's so nice, we do it twice' (Deal and Kennedy, 1988: 9). McDonald's has an extraordinary quality assurance and level of care for its people (Peters and Waterman, 1982: xix–xx).

These kinds of statement about 'qualitative beliefs' are then linked to a second set of quantitative information detailing the superior financial and economic performance of the given companies over 10 or 20 years. Strong cultures are the assumed link but there is no direct evidence or real discussion of other market or environmental variables. A rare statement of this kind comes from Deal and Kennedy: 'we estimate that a company can gain as much as one or two hours of productive work per employee per day' (1988: 15). No criteria or proof is ever given.

The Emperor's New Clothes?

With this kind of evidence, so much of it resting on bland management statements, unattributed quotes and plain assertion, it is tempting to dismiss the whole enterprise as a fairy-tale. Drucker, the best known management writer, pulled no punches in describing *In Search of Excellence* as 'a book for juveniles' and a fad that wouldn't last a year (quoted in Silver, 1987: 106). The lack of rigour in research methodology has been a persistent theme of critics (Hammond and Barham, 1987: 8–14). Samples of companies, for example, those used by Peters and Waterman, were selected and treated in a cavalier and uncontrolled manner, some being dropped from the original list and evidence from others not in the sample at all being used (Silver, 1987: 113). The tenuous link between cultures, excellence and performance turned out to be highly fragile. Companies were included whose performance was far from excellent and a significant number subsequently ran into difficulties, as *Business Week* reported under a headline of 'oops!' An important book on IBM (DeLamarter: 1988) – by a senior economist who had worked in the US Justice Department on the anti-trust case against IBM – pointed out that the company built up its dominance by undercutting its competitors in vulnerable market sectors and paying for it through excess profits from customers who had little choice. Commenting on *In Search of Excellence*, the author argues that

> According to the authors, IBM has benefited from a strong central philosophy that was originally laid down by its charismatic leaders, the Watsons. They present a simple, appealing model for IBM's success – excellence in management. But this view is dead wrong. IBM's success comes from the power of monopoly. (1988: xvii)

Follow-ups such as Peter's and Austin's *A Passion for Excellence* (1985) have failed to quell the doubts, particularly as the same author has apparently decided (Peters, 1987) that there are now no excellent companies in the USA. The treatment of theory and evidence is similarly suspect, with eclectic and uncritical use of parts that suit particular arguments, even if they are not compatible with the general perspective. The use of Skinner in *In Search of Excellence* is a case in point. A further remarkable aspect is the failure to learn *from* their main inspiration, the human relations tradition.

There is no sign of recognition of the central flaw that arose from the Hawthorne Studies, that intervention based on 'attention to employees' produces independent effects on performance. At least some of the hoop-la and contrived events could produce a stream of Hawthorne effects of a short-lived and superficial nature.

The perspective is riddled with glaring contradictions. So we are told that 'in institutions in which culture is so dominant, the highest levels of autonomy occur' (Peters and Waterman, 1982: 105), while Deal and Kennedy assure us that companies with strong cultures can tolerate differences (153) and that outlaws and heretics are encouraged in companies such as IBM (50–1). At the same time, the latter authors tell us that managers did not tolerate deviance from company values and standards (14) and that middle managers as well as blue-collar workers should be told exactly what to do (78). The books are so anxious to convince us that these are anti-authoritarian, 'no-boss' set-ups that we are expected to accept that calling workers cast members (Disney) or crew members (McDonalds) in itself banishes hierarchy and class divisions. In Silver's (1987) brilliant demolition of the excellence genre, he reminds us of the reality of McDonald's 'people-orientation': 'Behind the hoop-la and razzle-dazzle of competitive games and prizes lies the dull monotony of speed-up, deskilled Taylorised work – at McFactory. And McFactory's fuel is cheap labour, part time, teenage, minimum wage, non-union workers' (110). Furthermore, as an ex-seagoing colleague reminded us, most crews still have captains!

The tragedy is that we have a lot to learn from studying organisational cultures (Frost *et al.*, 1985), particularly as culture mediates all change processes. Companies such as IBM and Marks and Spencers *do* have corporate cultures of a highly distinctive nature. Such companies have long used management styles based on 'sophisticated paternalism' which combine high levels of employment security and social benefits with careful screening of recruits, direct communication and in-house training, wrapped up in a 'philosophy' of respect for the individual (Miller, 1989). IBM carefully constructs its employment practices to individualise employees' relations with the company. Prominent features of this approach are personal wage 'negotiation' and performance evaluation, immediate grievance accessibility to management and an internal labour market which provides for mobility and security (Dickson *et al.*, 1988), and all this before any thought of corporate cultures and human resource management! Creating a culture resonant with overall goals is relevant to *any* organisation, whether it be trade unions, voluntary groups or producer-co-operatives. Indeed, it is more important in such consensual groupings. Co-operatives, for example, can degenerate organisationally because they fail to develop adequate mechanisms for transmitting the original ideals from founders to new members and sustaining them through new shared experiences.

But we can only genuinely learn by jettisoning impoverished notions of culture which mistake style as substance. A complex and realistic analysis would avoid treating culture as a catch-all for the soft aspects of management (Hammond and Barham, 1987: 10) or as a reified and monolithic phenomenon. There is some recognition of *sub-cultures* on functional or gender lines, but not enough, and anyway these can be *managed* to produce a healthy tension within the corporate framework (Deal and Kennedy, 1988: 152–3). Yet as Martin and Siehl (1983: 53) point out, in the context of a variety of often contradictory influences, cultural development is just not as amenable to direction as believed. Nor can it be simply fitted into overall strategic goals.

At the moment there is also 'a tendency in the organisational culture literature to treat workplace culture as independent of the labour process' (Alvesson, 1988: 3). This by no means rules out studying specifically *corporate* cultures as management strategies. But this has to be within the plurality of cultures and interest groups in the workplace. Without such a framework, organisational analysis continues to neglect the dimensions of conflict, power and even consent. Luckily there are rich sources to draw on such as Salaman's (1986) study of the occupational culture of the London Fire Brigade; accounts of making-out on the shop floor (Nichols and Beynon, 1977; Burawoy, 1979); and gender at work (Willis, 1977; Pollert, 1981; Westwood, 1984). Using such a framework, we can avoid nonsensical ideas that strong cultures produce conflict-free organisations (Kelly and Brannick, 1987: 1). After all, despite IBM's worldwide strategy for a union-free environment and sophisticated industrial relations system, it still has to contend with an international organisation of IBM workers opposed to its policies! (Howard, 1985). Even where IBM has been successful in securing employee identification with its individualistic culture, as in the West of Scotland, those same workers had *collectivist* attitudes towards general social issues and supported trade unionism, even if they felt a union was unnecessary in their particular circumstances (Dickson *et al.*, 1988). This illustrates a further important point, that any analysis should show what is unique about organisational as opposed to national, regional, family or other cultures; something that is largely absent from the management literature (Hofstede, 1986). On that basis it would be possible to examine how the societal and organisational cultures interact.

With all these faults, why then has the corporate culture literature been so successful? There are those who simply describe it as the emperor's new clothes. In *Management Today*, Thackray (1986) argues that the American manager needs a language that goes beyond particular functions. Buzzwords therefore come and go and culture has entered on the scene as Western pride has been shaken by Japan and old certainties have been eroded by economic and occupational shifts. New ideas are required to motivate the troops and a 'gaggle of culture consultants', as well as human resource and personnel teams and others whose empires expand with the literature, are feeding at the honey pot. It appeals to managers because it proclaims that their activity and skills can produce the results, as Mayo once did in relation to early human relations.

Silver adds a wider ideological and political dimension to the explanation. He describes it as 'Reaganism writ small', a glorification of entrepreneuralism and the capacity of America to stand tall again. It is certainly true that a clear sub-text of Peters and Waterman and Deal and Kennedy is that the discovery of excellent companies in the West means that all good things do not come from Japan. It is also true that the ideological content of most of the books often shows a sharp break with the old 'liberal' consensus. Deal and Kennedy say that the society suffers from too much uncertainty about values and that managers should have the conviction to set standards and not undermine them by being humane (1988: 22, 56, 76), while Naisbitt and Aburdene (1985: 161–4) enthusiastically endorse New Right ideas such as education vouchers. But this does not entirely explain the popularity of the genre outside the USA, or why *In Search of Excellence* sold 300,000 copies in Japan in six weeks.

It also isn't enough to refer to corporate culture as the latest attempt by management consultants to 'wrap each new technique in packaging slightly different from that of its predecessors' (Silver: 123). To describe management theories and in-vogue practices as a series of fads is to underestimate their significance and effects, and neglect the need to locate changes carefully in their political, economic and geographic contexts. If we take corporate culture, necessary though the debunking of its methods and coherence is, in some ways it misses the point. The relationship between management and theory is not passive or one-way. Consultants and theorists help to constitute and articulate managerial interests and action, and subsequent practices 'act back' on the processes of intellectual production. A critical analysis has to recognise that part of the picture is that many managers do actually believe the ideas and act on them, producing real effects. Management discourse is a legitimate object of analysis in its own right and with its own rules, even if it is not the primary level of investigation. There is a further reason in this case for taking the analysis seriously. For all the absurdities of content and presentation, the culture literature has touched on genuine issues that, as we argued at the start of this chapter, were partly neglected in the past. These need looking at in a context free from the merchandising process.

A RATIONAL CORE: CULTURE AND CONTROL

Corporate culture writers like to present their perceptions as an *alternative* to control (Naisbitt and Aburdene, 1985: 53; Kelly and Brannick, 1987: 8). Yet we can reconceptualise the process, not just in terms of management strategies but as compatible with the analysis of control outlined in Chapter 4. This is not foreign to the more academic of the culture literature that openly describes the process as a form of organisational control (Ouchi and Johnson, 1978; Martin and Siehl, 1983). Nor is it inconsistent with many of the statements from the more popular works, such as, 'Strong culture companies go into the trouble of spelling out, often in copious detail, the routine behavioural rituals they expect from their employees' (Deal and Kennedy, 1988: 15). In other words, cultural control is essentially concerned with the development of an appropriate social order which provides the basis for desired behaviour (Kelly and Brannick, 1987: 8). The difference is that it works less through formal structures and mechanisms than through informal processes, value systems and management of the emotions. It certainly does not eliminate the use of formal mechanisms. We have already spoken in Chapter 5 about the increased use of selection and training processes and these receive considerable attention in the culture literature.

Tandem Corporation's exhaustive selection process is likened to an 'inquisition' by Deal and Kennedy (1988: 12). One of the offshoots is that those who are chosen are likely to have a much more positive image of themselves and the company. There is also an increasing attempt to extend the culture of the corporation into other value-producing institutions. Naisbitt and Aburdene detail growing links between businesses, schools and universities in the US. The offer of financial inducements to higher education establishments by the Manpower Services Commission if they will incorporate the teaching of entrepreneurial values and enterprise skills on their courses is a further example.

Cultural controls also operate through expanding the sphere of social activities in the organisation. This is something which is often characteristic of Japanese corporations' methods of using the peer group as a means of integrating both shopfloor and managerial employees. Broad (1987: 11) refers to 'Social gatherings organised by team leaders and foremen are regularly held amongst all male employees'. The link to Japan is also made in Goldsmith and Clutterbuck's jolly account of management japes at Asda's social events: 'The schoolboy activities in these companies is strongly reminiscent of Japanese companies, whose evening carousels have traditionally been part of the cementing of the managerial team' (1985: 82). Many of the other books are similarly full of accounts of cultural extravaganzas that function to develop a sense of community through a form of *compulsory sociability*.

The above trends are given theoretical expression by Ray (1986), utilising a Durkheimian framework discussed earlier. She points out that bureaucratic controls, though an attempt to integrate employees positively through internal labour markets and the reward system, are still control by incentive. These may generate contradictions around the struggles of the workforce to establish work rules and job guarantees. In addition, 'while bureaucratic control may prompt individuals to act *as if* the company is a source of meaning and commitment, that is an entirely different matter from seriously believing it. In other words control remains externalised rather than internalised' (292–3). Even humanistic controls deriving from the various branches of the human relations tradition do not possess the real tools to generate sentiment or emotion. Ray's analysis can be implemented with the emergence of a small body of like-minded empirical studies such as Alvesson's (1988) account of a medium-sized computer consultancy organisation in Sweden. The founders established an open and charismatic managerial style capable of generating strong emotional ties among the consultants employed. A particular problem for the management was that the work was by its very nature variable and flexible, and therefore could not be controlled by conventional means. It was also largely carried out at the client's workplace, potentially undermining the consultants' sense of identity with their own firm. This is compensated for by a large number of social and leisure-time activities with the emphasis on fun, body contact, informality and personnel support, which in turn build social and emotional ties and a sense of company as community. Some of these are consciously linked to presentations of corporate performance to enhance favourable perceptions.

Corporate culture should not be isolated as the only element of the shift to new forms of control. We have already noted developments connected to the new HRM concerned with extending levels of identification between employee and organisation. But there are other important aspects, notably those connected to create a performance-conscious culture or environment (Fowler, 1988; Hendry *et al.*, 1988). Within the overall process of managing a culture change, *performance-related pay* is often seen as a key element in transforming employee attitudes. In these circumstances, as we have previously discussed, manual employees are assessed for their qualities as individuals, in addition to the traditional quantitative criteria. Ratings in such areas as relationships and co-operation means that 'subjectivity should not be scorned but rationalised' (performance management manual quoted in Fowler, 1988: 31).

A related example is the increased use of *staff development*. Staff development is essentially a parallel to organisational development, though drawing on a separate intellectual tradition (Teather, 1979). In business organisations staff development activities may be carried out in human resource development or assessment centres, located in the range of firms that sell corporate culture. McDonald's 'Hamburger University' is one example of the type of centre, with similar ones being run by IBM, Xerox, Kodak and other companies. Staff development is also the terminology often used in higher education and administration. But whatever the title it still involves:

> A systematic attempt to harmonise individuals' interests and wishes and their carefully assessed requirements for furthering their careers with the forthcoming requirements of the organisation within which they [are] expected to work. (Piper and Glatter, 1977, in Teather, 1979: 14)

Staff development uses individual profiling techniques which are said to assist in career planning and self-development. This operates through the self-assessment of needs, capacities and abilities; personal recording of appropriate training and professional activities for preparing job applications; and acting as pointers for discussion and remedial training within appraisal systems. Profiles work by breaking activities down into functional categories of activity and the skills necessary to perform them. They can act to deflect attention away from the resources and support necessary for employees to adequately perform their work. Employees are encouraged to perceive their performance and utility to the enterprise as their responsibility. Rather than looking for the best way of managing, it focuses on how the individual can find the best way to make themselves more manageable, essentially a form of management by objectives by stealth.

The limits to such systems lie in employee unwillingness to take them seriously or invest effort unless instrumental rewards are forthcoming, therefore contradicting the aims of the system. Contradictions are also raised by the clash between concerns for individual development in organisations and the continuous pressure for rationalisation of resources and for more effort and commitment. This can be linked to a variety of major qualifications that can be made to the reinvention of organisation man by any means. First, there are trends in corporate development which are working against the stability of cultures of company loyalty. Even some of the high priests of the free market are beginning to despair at the effects of merger mania and the acquisition and asset-stripping of companies. The consequent breakdown of co-operation in the organisation can be seen in examples such as the 1989 strike and dispute about the selling-off of Eastern Airlines in the USA. In addition, what the management pundits are calling 'downsizing' – the cutting out of middle layers of the company discussed in Chapter 5 – is hurting most the 'organisation men, conditioned to look to large corporations as the fountainhead of security' (Thackray, 1988: 80). Loyalty, obedience and goal identification are not easy to sustain when companies are scrutinising their policy manuals to remove implied promises of job security or even termination benefits.

Second, these are trends within some but not all organisations. Many companies, small and large, will carry on with 'weak cultures' and wouldn't recognise a culture strategy if it landed on the MD's desk. Third, even within those organisations that do implement cultural controls, they are intended to complement not eliminate the need for bureaucratic, technical or other systems. Lastly, the creative appropriation, modification and resistance to corporate cultures by employees means that they will never work as intended. Organisation man is back on the agenda, but that agenda cannot only be set in the corporate boardroom.

PART TWO

PART TWO

7

Issues in Organisational Behaviour

The 'subjective factor' in the study of organisations is manifested in the experiences of organisational participants and in the identities through which they transact with others in organisational environments. Our examination of these issues of subjectivity in Part Two is initially viewed through psychological approaches which tend to focus mainly on behaviour as opposed to experience. The intention here is not to ignore the sociological and structural accounts of subjectivity available in the areas covered in Part One. Rather, we begin by examining the deficiencies of behavioural approaches in order to indicate how a closer articulation of structural and behavioural explanations can benefit the understanding of organisational subjectivity.

The study of what has come to be termed 'Organisational Behaviour' (OB) does, in fact, incorporate elements of the full range of academic disciplines and subject specialisms which might reasonably be expected to have something to say about people's lives in organisations and the influences on their activities. The major foundations of OB and the major inputs to the content of texts in the area are, however, informed mainly from the perspective of 'organisational psychology', which is in turn founded upon the subject divisions within social psychology. The treatment of subjectivity in organisational psychology does not typically develop in any systematic sense upon the foundations of such issues within social psychology. Such concerns are generally subordinated to

OB's agency in legitimating, developing and refining the social practices within which subjective identities are continuously *recreated* in images appropriate to the relations of social production. This theme is followed up in detail in Chapter 8.

This chapter examines the explanations, along with some of the instruments and techniques, developed in OB. The aim is to assess the nature and adequacy of the traditional agenda in the mainstream study of OB for an understanding of our experience of organisational life and how this shapes the *construction* of the identities through which we face it.

In Chapter 8 we return to consider in more detail the nature of identity and the contrasting approaches and resources a redefined agenda would need to focus on to begin to address issues of subjectivity. In particular, we address social relations such as those of domination, gender and ethnicity which are central features of work organisation. Chapter 9 develops the perspectives explored in Chapter 8 to provide a closer analysis of how subjectivity is experienced, structured and *transformed* within organisations.

ORGANISATIONAL PSYCHOLOGY: THE MAINSTREAM AGENDA

In a review of the 'discipline' of organisational psychology as a professional practice, Blackler describes it as follows:

> The subject 'organisational psychology' can legitimately be understood to include all aspects of behaviour in organisations that may be studied from a psychological point of view. By common usage, however, the term is normally used to refer to applied social psychological studies of organisation. Important areas of practical and theoretical concern have included motivation, attitudes and job satisfaction, job and organisation design, interpersonal and group behaviour, leadership studies, approaches to participation and industrial democracy, conflict, decision-making, and the planning of change. (Blackler, 1982: p. 203).

This of course is by no means exhaustive of the work undertaken by organisational psychologists. Topics could be added from those more usually associated with occupational psychology such as selection, placement and counselling. Historically the subject has a *problem-centred* approach and at present issues such as the psychological consequences of new technologies and unemployment are provoking much research.

The areas from social psychology which have been enlisted into organisational psychology's project of understanding human behaviour are often limited to those which have some functional utility. Texts tend to be presented under chapters or headings focusing on topics such as learning, perception and motivation, reflecting psychological explanations of individual personality, and topics such as leadership and group processes, which incorporate social-psychological explanations of interpersonal dynamics. However, the topics in the sphere of aggression, affiliation and prejudice, which within social psychology are assumed to deal with influential determinants of human behaviour, are not routinely assimilated into organisational psychology: an odd separation given that such factors may be expected to have at least some bearing on practices within organisations. The difference is largely that the latter set reflects areas of subjective experience which, although of importance to individuals and groups in organisations, are not of direct relevance to the production process, except in so far as they might interfere with it. Rather, the factors are treated as *external* to what is considered necessary and appropriate behaviour at work. Similarly, issues of discrimination, though a structural feature of organisational life, are marginalised and not constituted as significant objects of study. Aggression is addressed obliquely in OB through the issue of organisational conflict. But the perspective used examines conflict as a problem to be resolved or avoided rather than to be understood as a possible consequence of inequalities of power and resources.

We will return to the general limitations of the mainstream agenda in the final section. In terms of its content, that agenda can be thought of as a journey through the processes by which individuals become social participants who perceive, learn and are motivated beings with individual personalities. Our intention here is to treat the mechanisms and processes identified by competing approaches as inputs to, rather than exclusive accounts of this developmental process. This is because the fragmented treatment of subjectivity in OB means that the implied journey through an individual's development into a social being never explicitly takes place.

The competing mainstream explanations of psychological and social processes are treated in OB texts almost as if they were discrete accounts of human development and activity. Taking an area such as learning (which must be integral to any account of psychological development), the mechanisms and processes of apparently mutually exclusive perspectives such as the cognitive and behaviourist models are categorised through the assumptions about human nature which underly them. Thus we get the 'models of man' approach to OB where theories are assessed through the assumptions they make and the implications of those assumptions for social behaviour. There is nothing intrinsically wrong with this as a method of analysis, but it does tend to reinforce the exclusivity of differing approaches, which are in fact no more than varying conceptions of the basic processes by which we all develop and negotiate our changing identities.

The fact that these approaches often make incommensurate theoretical assumptions does not prevent their conceptions from being appropriate to the experiences of individuals at some time in their lives or in the various situations they find themselves in. In this sense it is entirely possible that, for example, both the cognitive and behaviourist notions of learning (discussed later in this chapter) will hold some utility in explanations of individual behaviour and subjective experience. Their applicability will of course vary according to both a person's unique history of socialisation and the strategies they choose and develop both to cope with and possibly enhance their situation in life.

Our starting-point here is not in the area of learning, even though development is essentially a process of learning. For our purposes it might be more appropriate to begin with perception, as the process of learning is itself dependent on the development of the perceptual processes which shape our view of the world. In fact, the processes of perception and learning are so thoroughly interdependent that they might best be treated as a single area, but we maintain the traditional conceptual division in order to engage with the existng forms of explanation in OB. Of the other major topic areas common in OB, this chapter addresses personality and motivation. Two further topic areas from social psychology which have been important influences in the development of OB, the study of leadership and group processes, are not presented here as they form a significant part of the discussions in Chapter 8.

Perception: Learning What to See

Perception is defined in terms of 'the active psychological process in which stimuli are selected and organised into meaningful patterns' (Buchanan and Huczynski, 1985, 33). This is usually explained within a cognitive perspective which seeks to explain how our perceptions of ourselves, others and our environment shape our attitudes and behaviour. The utility of understanding perceptual processes lies in the fact that people's perceptions of themselves and others can be manipulated to change attitudes and behaviour to the situations and contexts within which work takes place. The practices associated with the 'Japanisation' of British industry, such as single status canteens and clothing, provide an example of this in that they are intended to alter perceptions of the divisions between management and labour in order to create attitudes more compatible with organisational goals.

Perception, then, is the umbrella heading for the processes through which we organise and interpret the range of visual, aural, tactile and chemical stimuli which impinge on us. As these processes enable us to comprehend and order the world around us, they must also underly the manner in which we go about constructing identities.

The organisation, processing and interpretation of incoming stimuli are the basic subject matter of cognitive psychology. Much material in this area deals with the neurophysiology of perceptual systems. But as our focus is on OB we do not intend to deal with the detailed cognitive processing of information as the ordering and organisation of these systems is not wholly determined by their structure. In social, interpersonal and self-perception, the determinants we are concerned with are the past and present influences and constraints on us and our actively directed interests. Perception, then, is not just the process of seeing but involves our other senses and is intimately connected with the notion of intention. In other words, what we see and hear is transformed according to how our system of values, attitudes and beliefs informs our actions. Identity could, in this light, be viewed as the filter through which our perceptions pass in order to select out what is of value to us.

Basically, to perceive something we have to be attending to it. This does not mean that we only take in those stimuli which we notice. Rather, we take in everything our particular range of senses allows us to. What it does mean is that we only actively process and act upon those parts of the incoming data which concern us. This concept of *perceptual selectivity* can be illustrated by a crowded and noisy office where we cut out much of the background noise in order to concentrate on the people we are listening to. Yet we can still pick out and shift our attention to references to ourselves or other things that interest us coming from other parts of the room, temporarily or permanently cutting out the immediate conversation we had been intent on a moment before. Hence we appear to have some mechanism which can shift our attention and select the stimuli which we attend to according to which appear of the greatest current relevance. Having to concentrate for long periods on a single type of stimulus, for example, components being inspected on a production line, requires effort in face of the distractions coming from other stimuli in our environment. The notion of perceptual selectivity underlines the *intentionality* of attention. We may not be consciously aware of directing our attention because we are predisposed to notice some things rather than others. Our perceptual systems are structured to pay attention to things that change and things that stand out from their surroundings, but we do adapt our perceptions to our immediate social situation on a subjective basis. For example, we perceive information as being more valid when it comes from what we consider to be an 'authoritative' source. Thus criticism of our work from a respected peer or a superior responsible for evaluating it will be taken more seriously than that from sources less close to our own interests.

This is taken further in the notion of *perceptual set*, which refers to our individual and unique readiness to perceive what we expect to perceive. Our perceptual set reflects our own perceptions of ourselves and our social position. For instance, we often appear to be set to perceive people of lower status to ourselves as less competent, inferior and more generally inadequate. This type of set extends to social groups and to wider social divisions; men, for example, generally perceive women as less competent than themselves, reflecting the social value placed on gender rather than any reliable sex differences. Likewise, men tend to attribute competence shown by women to luck rather than skill (Deaux and Emswiller, 1974), showing that their subjective adaption of their perceptions will tend to reinforce the security of their male identity.

The outcome of these processes is that we actually put effort into interpreting the world around us, rather than simply taking it all in as a camera might. But a haphazard interpretation of the myriad stimuli coming to us would be worse than none at all. We need a system of interpretation. Our perceptions need to be organised. For our purposes we need to look at the ordering of perceptions in terms of the way in which we categorise people and events. By placing perceptual stimuli into categories, we in effect take shortcuts in our comprehension of the world. We enable ourselves to deal effectively with the numerous stimuli which impinge on our senses by reducing the necessity to analyse each new stimulus as a unique object. This does, however, mean that we treat the things and people that we interact with through their relation to the subjectively determined but apparently objective categories into which we place them. Thus, to some extent, we *reify* everything and everyone we come across. We produce them as mental representations which are our own creation, yet we treat them as if these images were in fact real.

It is through this process of *categorisation* that the major perceptual processes dealt with in organisational behaviour texts can be understood. Categorising people on the basis of limited cues, such as gender, skin colour, bodily characteristics, social, regional and national identity, and then treating an individual as having the generalised traits associated with that category is the pervasive phenomenon known as *stereotyping*.

It enables us to make quick assessments of others and of situations. You can, for example, have a stereotype of what a particular kind of person or meeting will be like and react accordingly. Although it has psychological uses to the individual, stereotyping can also have negative social consequences, for example, as one of the mechanisms through which racism and sexism are socially enacted and given ideological justification. Thus a branch manager in a case study of the insurance industry comments on his perceptions of why women are unsuitable for sales work at 'Insco', 'Yes, it can be a soul destroying job, and women are either not hard bitten enough to ride off insults or those that can are pretty unpleasant people' (Collinson and Knights, 1986, 155). It would appear that in the face of an established stereotype, you just can't win! We will use the Insco case as a way of linking some of the issues in this and the following chapters.

Another process given force by our categorisation of stimuli is the so-called '*halo effect*', which is essentially another process of producing a stereotype. When we come across new persons or situations we can only assess them in terms relevant to our own experience and the limited cues we have about them. This initial assessment, whether positive or negative, tends to be carried over into the attitudes we build up to that person or thing. Thus, if we rate a new workmate in a positive fashion on the basis of our first impressions, we would tend to continue to rate them positively in the future. Of course, the fact that we rate them positively will probably in itself improve our relations with them. This may produce a self-fulfilling prophecy from our first impression and probably improve self-categorisation of our own ability to judge others. The halo effect can work against stereotyping, in that meetng a member of a group we hold stereotyped views about who makes a good first impression on us may weaken a negative stereotype. On the other hand we may simply view them as an exception. The experience of a new recruit in an organisation where the prevailing view of power relations is unitarist and hierarchical will heavily reflect categorising processes, in that their experiences will tend to be interpreted through the dominant attitudes of their peers.

We also have a tendency to categorise others in the same

light in which we categorise ourselves. Suspicious or aggressive persons, according to this principle of *projection* or *assumed similarity*, will view others as being more suspicious or aggressive in nature than will people who tend to be more trusting or placid. We can apply this notion to the kind of attitudes and values currently espoused in the 'new realism' which supposedly permeates industrial relations these days. To someone who sees themselves as 'looking after number one', those who stand for the values of class solidarity and loyalty to the union might be seen as stupid, unrealistic or hiding a lust for personal power behind a façade of caring for others. Identity in this sense becomes the standard of social comparison by which we judge the world and those in it.

To project categorisations onto others we must be categorising ourselves. We can produce stereotypes about ourselves, perhaps regarding our likely or favoured responses to certain people or things. We can also apply the halo effect to ourselves. If we perform well at a particular activity the first time we try it, we will tend to rate ourselves better in the future and vice versa. The major source of the categorisations we utilise are the various groups that we belong to, as the membership of these groups provides us with the basis of the identities which we take up in various situations. Thus the norms and standards of conduct of a group we belong to will inform both the kinds of stereotypes we use and the identity which recognises our right to make such judgements. If a group can be said to have an identity, then that identity is communicated to its members in their self-perceptions and becomes part of, possibly a major part of, their own identities. Given that the major groups that many of us belong to are work- and organisation-related, our identities will be constructed in terms of our perceptions of ourselves within work organisations. Even the identities of the unemployed will be defined to a great extent by their lack of attachment to work groups.

Organisation and categorisation of our perceptions enables us to comprehend and interpret our world and on this basis we are able to make judgements which depend on how we interpret the intentions of others. This is a crucial task for any individual as it is linked to the fashion in which we identify the links between cause and effect in events. *Attribution theory*, developed by Heider (1958), shows how we tend to be biased in our judgements of others' intentions. It is based on the notion that we rationally calculate whether the reasons for actions are due to internal or dispositional factors or to external or environmental factors. It appears that we have a tendency to judge people's intentions in terms of dispositional factors. We tend to attribute the causes of their actions to something based in their personality or nature. In the Insco case, women office workers are seen to require high levels of supervision and control. This is not attributed to their 'experience of subordination and blocked mobility but to their gender'. The 'discontented and moody' behaviour they are seen to exhibit is thus attributed to their gender-based disposition and is further used to disqualify them from jobs in sales (Collinson and Knights, 1986, 151).

Attribution theory conversely implies that the more information we have about the other person, the greater our capability of making accurate environmental attributions about their actions and the better able we are to see things as not necessarily intended or inherent in their nature but due to their social and personal circumstances. The choice to initiate a strike may be attributed by employers or managers whose knowledge of their employees consists mainly of stereotypes, to bloody-mindedness or their militant nature. In Lane and Roberts's (1971) account of the long strike at Pilkington's in St Helens, the tradition of paternalism meant that management could only interpret the action in terms of intruders such as scousers, revolutionaries or both. One would hope then that attribution theory implies a manager who knows something of what it is like to be at the lower end of an organisational hierarchy might be more likely to attribute their decision to factors relating to the workplace or its environment, making a more realistic assessment of the situation in the process!

To an extent, in making attributions we are making assessments of the personality or identity of others. But our ability to make consistently valid attributions is questionable. We constantly have to make judgements on the basis of too little or inaccurate information. Also, according to Langer (1981), we often behave in a less rational manner than assumed by attribution theory, using habituated scripts which we act out in appropriate situations. These factors, coupled with our tendency to make dispositional attributions, make both our perceptions of others and ourselves highly subjective and prone to fallibility. Thus in our construction of identities out of our perceptual world we need to make constant reference to sources of knowledge and comparison which we have built up over time. We need to learn in order to check on the validity of the identity we have secured for ourselves.

Learning and Socialisation: Seeing What To Do

Learning is normally defined in such terms as 'a relatively persistent change in an individual's possible behaviour due to experience' (Fontana: 1985, 64). Stimulus-response and/or cognitive models are usually given as the main explanations of this process, these attempting at various levels to account for how individuals come to gain the particular knowledge and abilities they possess. The use of learning theory is, on the other hand, tied to refining the processes by which individuals are socialised into the behaviour patterns reqired by organisations, for example, through prescriptions aimed at increasing the effectiveness of training programmes.

Our perceptual organisation enables us to comprehend our experience, but if we do not learn from it then our experience is of little use. The concepts and mechanisms of individual learning are of fundamental importance to the understanding of how we build up both unique identities and common behavioural patterns out of perceptual experience. Accounts of learning might then be expected to focus on how and where we acquire the behaviours appropriate and necessary to our social functioning and survival. In the psychological literature this is usually presented in terms of models based variously on *behaviourist, cognitive* and *social learning theory.*

The behaviourist model focuses on *associative* and *instrumental* learning. In the former process, proposed by Pavlov and refined by Watson, we learn to behave in a certain fashion because we identify and associate that behaviour with a particular stimulus. For example, a bell or buzzer signalling the end of a tea-break can cause us to stop what we are doing and go back to work even if there is no supervisor present to tell us to do so. We do this because we have identified the stimulus as signalling the danger of punishment for non-compliance and associate it with the behaviour of returning to work. We are thus conditioned to obey the buzzer. The process of instrumental learning takes this a stage further and provides more explanation of why we learn, in that it focuses not on the stimulus but on the consequences which follow the behaviour. This process, pioneered by Thorndike and refined by Skinner, focuses on the way in which the rewards and punishments which are the outcomes of a behaviour become associated with that behaviour. If we do not go back to work when the buzzer sounds and we get away with it, then we are rewarded by extending our rest period and by avoiding the associated punishment. Thus the likelihood of our doing the same thing in a similar situation is *reinforced* by the positive consequences of the behaviour.

These two mechanisms have been used at one time or another to explain the learning of just about every type of behaviour. They do not, however, tell us very much about the mental processes which allow us to associate stimuli and behaviour or to expect and assess consequences, given that behaviourism does not regard mental processes as open to examination. The positive (reward) and negative (punishment) aspects of reinforcement schedules do, however, neatly fit into what we term the '*technologies of regulation*' which back up the processes of control in organisations. The incentives to work harder and the disincentives to social and collective interaction with other workers, which a piecework system encourages, present a good example of these strategies of control. McKenna (1987, 182–4) notes that the techniques of organisational behaviour modification which use conditioning and reinforcement principles to attempt to 'shape' the behaviour of workers (for example, in areas such as safety practices and absenteeism) are mainly confined to 'highly controllable situations', the basic flaw in such techniques being that they ignore the 'interaction between situational and personal factors' which are 'encapsulated in social learning theory' (1987, 184).

The theoretical base of behaviourism also does not really explain how we acquire a new behaviour. It would not explain how someone would ignore the warning buzzer the first time in order to have the behaviour reinforced, beyond doing it accidentally. Social learning theory, on the other hand, could explain the novel behaviour on the basis of observing and imitating the behaviour of others. Thus we could become socialised into ignoring the buzzer and pushing the limits of how long we can take for a tea-break as part of a social process whereby we both reinforce our own actions and are reinforced by the successful actions of others in our workgroup.

To explain this we need some recourse to cognitive theory. For instance, we could learn to ignore the buzzer in the right circumstances on the basis of what are known as 'TOTE' units. These *Test-Operate-Text-Exit* units (Miller *et al.*, 1960) represent the pieces in which we learn a behaviour and process the information relating to it. The process involved is a simple feedback mechanism whereby we continuously monitor (test) the results of our actions (operations) until we successfully complete them (exit). Tote units build up behaviours as part of sub-plans which feed into wider plans. Thus we might continually test out the limits of how far we can extend our tea-break as part of trying to increase our time away from work we dislike, or as part of attempts to annoy a hated supervisor, or even as a formally constituted plan to resist management controls.

These behaviours can be built into scripts, so we utilise learned knowledge through applying categories of particular activities. This is the process involved in the notion of *action regulation* (Hacker and Volpert, cited in Resch *et al.*, 1984), whereby all action is hierarchically organised into sub-units representing sub-goals of the planned action. 'Actions are continually adjusted to changes in the environment' (Frese, 1982, 213) and are initially performed and learned at an *intellectual* level under conscious control. After time and practice they ecome more 'automatised' and are controlled at lower levels. *Flexible action patterns* are the middle level of control and represent standardised scripts which can be somewhat modified in the face of situational change; whereas at the lowest or *sensorimotor* level, actions are stereotyped, automatic responses. When actions are learned to this level, the higher levels are made available for pursuing other goals and tasks. Of course, in highly routinised work, although actions may be made at the sensorimotor level there is no concomitant 'freedom' to pursue personal goals. At the intellectual level such work only frees us to be frustrated or at best to daydream.

We can explain how we go about learning from the above perspectives. But it is more difficult to explain how we know what we need to learn and what the appropriate behaviours are in any given situation. If we are to link learning to the construction of identity in organisational settings, we need to know how the demands of that setting are communicated to us and why we internalise them. When we join an organisation there are demands on us to learn certain things (how to do our work, 'correct' attitudes and behaviour) and we need to learn how to survive in a new and possibly unfamiliar environment. This process can occur in a formal fashion, as in a training programme where we may learn about the work itself and the rules and procedures that surround it. But more importantly it can proceed in an informal fashion, stemming not from training but from our interaction with those we work with. Most people learn their work through observation and questioning of their workmates. In this way they also learn how to cope with work, the short-cuts, or how to 'make-out' by manipulating the bonus system.

The models and mechanisms of learning which it would be most appropriate to examine in this context are those which offer some account of the process of *socialisation*. Socialisation as a process fully reflects our focus in the next two chapters on the construction of subjective identity in both the sense of an individual becoming a subjective entity and that of the individual becoming subject to external influence. These two aspects of the socialisation process are not separate, although they are conceptualised differently in organisational literature and suffer the difficulty of being explained through psychosocial mechanisms rather than subjective experience. On the one hand there are the aspects of socialisation which deal directly with the psychological process of learning, notably the 'social learning' models characterised by Eysenck (1947), which focuses on inherited differences in a person's ability to build up conditioned responses, and by Bandura and Walters (1963) which focuses on how conditioned responses to external stimuli are mediated by internal psychological processes. On the other hand, there are those aspects which deal with the ways in which a person is tied to the demands of the groups they belong to, though these too can be approached through the notion of social learning.

Social learning theories combine elements of cognitive and behaviourist theory to produce a model of learning which focuses on interaction. From this the basic process of learning is the observation of the behaviour of others, the *selection, organisation* and *transformation* of the stimuli provided through observation and the subsequent identification with and imitation of selected parts of the observed behaviour. This process, known as *modelling*, goes further than mechanisms such as associative or instrumental learning, as it involves people generating their own rewards and reinforcements and selecting behaviours in line with their own expectations and desired consequences. We do not slavishly imitate the behaviour of those about us or even those who appear to act in the most appropriate fashion in the specific situation we are in. We select those aspects of the activity we observe which we can usefully incorporate into our own repertoire of appropriately scripted behaviours. By modelling our behaviour in this fashion we avoid both indulging in wasteful and possibly embarrassing attempts to fit ourselves to our surroundings by trial and error, while managing to exert some control and influence over our own activity.

The modelling process guides us to the appropriate behaviours demanded of us in our organisational '*role*'. The concept of 'role' has had too much interpretation for us to give a full account. But for our present purposes, roles can be seen as sets of self-categorised, stereotyped and scripted behaviours which enable us to act in a contextually consistent manner. Through modelling, our behaviour can be influenced by that of those we select as role models, those whom we perceive to be acting in a 'correct' or desirable fashion. By building our own behavioural repertoire out of selected actions of role models, we can fit our actions to those required by the organisational culture. We also utilise negative role models to define for us the types of behaviour we do not wish to imitate, or those we perceive as acting in inappropriate or socially disapproved fashions. In other words, what an individual gains from the social learning process are guidelines and a framework for self-evaluation and action in the production of an identity which can cope with and blend into its surroundings. Examples of this might be found in the way that newcomers are socialised into sexually stereotyped occupations. In the Insco case, for example, the branch manager explains that 'we try to keep people coming in at the bottom so that we can train them to our ways, get them used to the company' (1986, 161). The models newcomers are most likely to emulate and compare themselves to are those who appear situationally competent, who fit the appropriate stereotypes and who hold the right attitudes, thus reproducing, for instance, the 'macho' image of the construction worker.

Socialisation through social learning does not, however, simply transform an individual into an image of what an organisation requires, notwithstanding Handy's definition of socialisation in OB terms as 'the process by which an organisation seeks to make the individual more amenable to the prevalent mode of influence' (1976: 134). We certainly do learn to produce in ourselves normative characteristics and produce identities with consistent social meaning. At the same time we acquire and produce distinctive characteristics, those which define our identities. Even though social learning enables us to take on a normative role, our observations can just as easily lead us to enhance those things about ourselves which reinforce our personal rather than social meaning.

The role models we utilise are not only those people we are in immediate contact with. In producing an identity we also use individuals and reference groups with whom we may have little or no interaction. We may base the image we present not only on those behaviours and models appropriate to our present context but on those pertaining to roles and perceived identities which we aspire to. We may act in a way consistent with other shopfloor workers, but at the same time adopt some forms of behaviour which link us with superiors if we desire promotion, or perhaps the representatives of a professional or trade union organisation, if we see the possibilities of enhancing meaning and identity as lying in that direction.

The values we internalise, the attitudes we exhibit, will all

reflect the choices, however limited, we have made and the learned constraints which we act within. Our unique history of learning and socialisation enables us to produce a subjective identity which is malleable in both our own terms and those of the others and organisations we encounter. We produce something which others see as our 'personality' but which in effect is simply an actively managed and continually rehearsed manipulation of our identity, fitted to what we have to do and what we want to do.

Personality: Masks for Tasks

Personality is defined in terms of 'the physical, mental, moral and social qualities of the individual' (McKenna, 1987, 11), or whatever makes you different from other people. It is understood as a complex of characteristic features or traits which describe the particular types and/or dimensions through which personalities are categorised. This may be the ultimate contradiction in organisational psychology, in that the study of 'unique' personalities is placed almost wholly in the service of the production of standardised measures aimed at the categorisation and selection of individuals so that they can be fitted into their appropriate niches in organisational cultures.

The psychological understanding of how an individual develops a distinctive personality depends, like that of perception on the notion of categorisation. Because personality is generally understood within a series of categorisations, its relationship to the construction of identity cannot be separated from the activities of those who produce the categories. Hence the explanation of personality in an organisational setting is more directly connected to the use of personality theory by managers than is the case with perception and learning.

Describing personality as that which makes an individual different from others essentially defines it as that which sets the boundaries of what you are and what you aren't. However, the way the notion of personality is used in OB highlights this type of definition as an idealised, liberal conception which is in direct contradiction to operational concerns with the controlled performance of work. The study of personality from this angle centres around the identification and prediction of *consistent and/or distinctive modes of response* in individuals. Distinctive behaviours in this sense are not the same as uniquely individual behaviours. They would be typical ways of reacting to people or situations which would distinguish an individual as belonging to a category of persons. Thus a person who is seen to react in a consistently unco-operative fashion may be placed into a stereotypical category whereby their future behaviour will be assumed to be typical of that sort of person who is 'difficult'. The important point is in the assumptions that this form of personality theory makes about the nature of individuals and their activities. Behaviour is assumed to be inherent in the individual's make-up, biologically or genetically fixed. Being fixed it is possible to predict, and being possible to predict it becomes a useful tool in controlling behaviour. Personality theory becomes an exercise in discovering how these various modes of response vary over time and between situations in order to refine the levels of categories and prediction possible. For example, what kind of observed behaviour in a person is sufficient to label them as a troublemaker, or what type of situation will influence a person to reveal different aspects of or levels of their 'undesirable' behaviour?

For OB as a 'science', this process frequently results more in a battery of methodologies and techniques for selecting the 'right person for the job', than in an account of personality. These are used to select prospective employees or candidates for promotion into categories which will show how well they fit into the organisational culture, thus making it easier to take decisions about them. Personality tests and inventories effectively perform the same function for an organisation as stereotypes do for an individual or group. They help to sort out the bewildering variety of information available about organisational members into categories which can be easily comprehended and dealt with. The last thing which a science of personality of this sort is concerned with is that which makes us subjectively unique individuals. It might be interested in what makes a particular individual different from others, but only to the extent that it might be a pointer to a characteristic useful or damaging to the organisation.

In delineating categories of personality characteristics, psychologists tend to fall back on two main sets of concepts. The first of these, personality *types*, are predetermined categories which we 'fit' into and which represent broad generalisations of character such as moody or lively. The second, personality *traits*, are habitual behaviours or tendencies to behave in particular ways, for example, tendencies to react in an anxious, reserved or outgoing fashion. Types are generally used these days to refer to patterns or clusters of traits. The Eysenck Personality Inventory (EPI) (Eysenck and Wilson, 1975) groups clusters of traits, such as reserved, unsociable, quiet, passive, careful, into types such as introversion.

Personality inventories have been and still are widely used by organisations to determine, for example, who will make a good manager or is most eligible for promotion. Cattell's 16PF (Personality Factors) scale, which is based on the same basic types as the EPI, is widely criticised and yet still utilised because it appears to select people who will make good managers. Holloway (1984) notes that it does not really matter whether the 16PF tells us anything realistic about personality as it actually works by fulfilling the expectations of existing managers about what makes a good manager, that is, people like themselves. Since it is possible to work out which are the appropriate types of answer to the questions, it does not really matter if the respondent does not actually belong to the same social groupings as the dominant organisational culture they are trying to enter. It will help if they do, as it makes 'correct' responses easier to identify, but the ability to lie correctly is just as good a sign that the candidate is capable of or willing to become the kind of person who will fit. The candidate who is incapable or unwilling to frame the right kind of responses automatically selects themselves out, regardless of their actual managerial potential.

Personality testing is currently undergoing something of a revival as a new generation of computerised personality profiling systems are coming onto the market. Their ease and speed of use, combined with neat computer printouts detailing managerial potential, reinforce an air of spurious objectivity in their validity as managerial tools. Most of them are still, of course, based on systems such as the EPI, but do not impose the same levels of costs in licensing and in training for their administration and interpretation as the older paper-based systems. Their value is in their capacity to reduce complex factors to simple stereotypical categorisations. Thus they make the decision-making process for personnel departments simpler, more cost-effective and less dependent on skilled staff.

The underlying assumption behind techniques such as the 16PF, that managerial ability is somehow related to personality factors, would almost certainly ignore the kind of managerial ability it takes to say, hold down a job, run a household and bring up children. But, of course, the dominant cultures in most organisations and institutions are not composed of the working women who are generally the ones who have to display such abilities. The assumption is not about personality as such but about having or aspiring to the right kind of personality. In contrast to managerial assessment, the assessment of shopfloor workers has traditionally focused on tests of *capacities* and *aptitudes* rather than personality. Both kinds of test are tests of the ability to do the job, the difference being that it is assumed that only in the higher levels of organisational hierarchies does personality become a relevant factor. It is the pragmatic psychology of Taylorism which is at work here, though this may be changing as we examine in Chapters 5 and 6. As long as the person can do the job, who they are and what they are is of little importance. The personality of a manager is not important, as long as they have a 'managerial' personality.

In the area of personality assessment, as with the notions of stereotyping, projection and attribution, the assignment of categories on the basis of limited information can lead to damaging consequences. For example, the assigning to personality of a biologically fixed nature which can be assessed through the identification of types and traits can reinforce the notion that problems within an organisation are rooted in the pathological personality characteristics and behaviours of individuals. Thus the interpersonal, social and organisational problems that arise can be blamed on bad attitudes and in turn on bad personalities. The end result of this type of process is blaming the bad personalities on genetic inheritance and then we are one step from the attitude that says to resolve the problems you need to remove the people who cause them (see Chorover, 1979, and Henriques, 1984, for extended discussions of biological and cognitive determinism in social theory and practice). At a less extreme level the branch manager at Insco commenting on the traits appropriate to sales work in insurance delineates them in a sex-typed fashion which acts to render problematic the employment of women in this area,

> I'm looking for whether they've got drive, initiative and are basically a self-starter. So he must want to get on, and get on by his own efforts (Collinson and Knights, 1986: 156)

The focus on traits and types in OB is a function of their utility in making personality amenable to classification and manipulation. Yet personality to a great extent is simply the observable manifestation of identity. It is essentially similar to the notion of social identity, which a person develops and constructs through negotiation and interaction with others. In this sense personality cannot simply be a cluster of traits, it is a process. It is not something which can be measured in terms of the ways in which people tend to react. Personality is a proactive process in which people present to others the image which will most benefit themselves in the situation they are in. The process of acquiring a personality, a social identity, would itself be influenced by having to fill out an inventory such as the 16PF in applying for a post. It would necessitate giving over an impression of your personality which was appropriate rather than accurate. The personality exhibited in this situation would be a mask appropriate to the task at hand.

Personality, like perception, is linked to intention. It is constructed in relation to the goals one is trying to achieve, to developing strategies to survive the circumstances one has to endure. It is a tool which allows individuals to manipulate their own environment, even at the same time that it allows others to manipulate them in organisations. The personality component of our identities is the signal which indicates the types of influence we are open to. In the end the things which are the objects of the influences brought to bear on us are argu-ably the major components of the developing identity which are dealt with in the mainstream agenda of OB – our motivations.

Motivation: the Drive for Satisfaction

Motivation according to Dawson (1986: 7), 'refers to the mainspring of behaviour; it explains why individuals choose to expend a degree of effort towards achieving particular goals'. It is explained in terms of biologically based *needs* and *drives* and the selection of *goals* (content theories) and cog-nitively oriented notions of the *processing of information* on the rewards, costs and preferences for particular goal-related outcomes of action (process theories). The usage of knowledge of human motivation is linked to the service of organisational 'needs', in that motivation is understood in terms of the process of *social influence*. Even though Herzberg (1968) pointed out that in attempting to influence someone to work harder it is the manager who is motivated and not the worker, it is still the case that one of the principal concerns of organisational behaviour is to increase 'motivation' in the search for greater productivity.

Motivations are viewed as choices made about, or percieved predispositions to, certain behaviours and outcomes. They reflect the things we want and the strategies we choose to achieve or obtain them. Basically they can be explained in two ways. Firstly, in terms of instinctual drives which we are motivated to reduce, for example, when we are thirsty we are driven to seek drink. Secondly, they can be described in the mechanistic terminology of stimulus-response when we seek out those things which satisfy or reward us and avoid those which punish or cost us. However, since motivation also concerns choice and hence intention, it is necessary to explain how such choices are made. This explanation is given within cognitively oriented theoretical models which examine either the content of motivations, or the process through which they are expressed. The former examine what it is that motivates people through concepts such as goals, needs and 'motivators' and is exemplified by the work of Maslow, Alderfer, McClelland

and Herzberg. The latter examine how people are motivated through the processes by which behaviours are selected, directed, initiated and maintained. Included in this category is the work of Porter and Lawler, Adams and that of Vroom which is discussed in some detail in the conclusion to this chapter. The key concerns for organisational behaviour in these theories are those which relate the concept of *job satisfaction* to that of task performance.

Both types of theory outlined above are concerned with the notion that humans direct their behaviour towards goals. In the case of content theories, the concern is with the source of the goals towards which behaviour is directed and for process theories with the decision-making process by which goals are selected and pursued. There is another basic viewpoint on the importance of goals to motivation theory, which again reflects the managerial concern with satisfaction and performance. This is that motivation can also be viewed as the process of social influence by which agencies external to the individual can try to direct the selection and pursuit of desired goals by individuals. To a very great extent this aspect of motivation theory into which both content and process theories are incorporated is the practical focus of organisational behaviour as a whole. Thus practitioners in the area are concerned to understand the strengths and directions of human motivations in order to increase control over the performance of work-related behaviours.

The goals to which we direct our behaviour will constitute a formative influence in the identities we construct for ourselves. But this aspect of goal-related behaviour is not examined within organisational behaviour as a discipline, except to the extent that individual goals can be moulded or 'set' to fulfil organisational ends. Once again the branch manager in the Insco case provides relevant commentary.

> I'm looking for someone who will work with me. So I look for someone who I think I can mould to my own ways, but they must already have the necessary spark and drive (Collinson and Knights, 1986: 154).

Identity and related goals are treated as external to the position of workers in the productive process, in that goals are usually related not to intentions but to biologically derived drives, or more often needs such as those identified by Maslow (1954). These 'needs' for food, shelter, affection, self-respect and individual growth are seen as operating on the basis of either *intrinsically* or *extrinsically* derived stimuli. People are motivated and achieve satisfaction through factors which are internal or external to their work, from the work itself through the enhancement of skill, responsibility, status or authority, or from outside work through activities related to the family, leisure or other organisations they might belong to. Intrinsically motivated persons are assumed to be influenced through their attachment to their work, whereas it is assumed that extrinsically motivated persons will only be influenced by aspects of their work that facilitate their 'outside' interests, such as pay levels, perks and increased leisure time. Whether they are intrinsically or extrinsically motivated, however, they are still responding to the fulfilment of needs. They simply fulfil them differently.

Organisational behaviour texts almost always refer to Maslow and his 'hierarchy of needs' but very seldom consider the satisfaction of needs within the organisational environment, beyond the extent to which they can be manipulated to increase productivity. They are once again seen as external to the place of the worker in the productive process. Those in positions of control in work organisations do not see themselves as being in the business of comprehensively supplying the needs which Maslow hypothesises. They exchange financial and sometimes material benefits for the labour of employees, but beyond a minimal concern that workers should be satisfied with the conditions and rewards of work to improve performance, or at least not to disrupt production, little else is provided.

The hypothesised need for 'self-actualisation' and individual growth has repeatedly been incorporated into prescriptive packages, such as Herzberg's (1968) notion of 'job enrichment', which seek to improve the content of work to the point where workers will be self-motivated to improve their performance, However, as we saw in Chapter 5, such initiatives tend to fail on the basis that no real improvement is made in factors relating to the conditions of work and the job context or environment. For example, in Nichols and Beynon's (1977) study of job enrichment at Chemco, managers were motivated to pursue the 'New Working Agreement' on the basis that they were convinced that they would get at what makes workers 'tick' and thus be able to coax more work from them. For most of the workers involved, all that came out of this was an inadequate system of job rotation which was worse than the system they had evolved for themselves. Hence managers in this study were easier to 'motivate' because the context of their work was adequate.

Herzberg himself recognised this in saying that job rotation constituted 'job enlargement' rather than enrichment and this could result in no more than short-term improvements in productivity as it represented 'adding nothing to nothing' (1968: 263–4). Such prescriptions are still offered by organisational consultants and still bought by organisational managements, however, possibly because even short-term improvements in productivity offer some kind of competitive edge in the market. Motivation, in the above example, is reduced to the status of things or techniques which will motivate, a manipulative rather than an explanatory concept.

If motivation is linked to identity, we can focus on the content or processes of motivation as inputs to situationally determined strategies which people adopt to enhance the identities they have constructed. People would not be 'intrinsically' or 'extrinsically' motivated. Rather, they would take meaning from whatever sources are available, inside or out of the work environment, and use them to enhance both the image they have of themselves and those that others hold of them. In a work environment where possibilities for securing meaning were scarce, people might still be capable of taking meaning from the situation to the extent that they could gain some personal or collective control over their work. Strongly cohesive workgroup cultures might in this sense actually identify with working practices to the extent of feeling that they, and not management, 'own' them. Attempting to re-define working practices in such situations might only detract from the sources of meaning available in the workplace and in essence attack whatever portion of identity resides there. If this is the case, then compensations, even assuming they are

designed to satisfy both intrinsically and extrinsically motivated persons, would probably not overcome hostility to
changes and would therefore make them difficult to implement. The individuals and groups concerned would either
attempt to revert to their old practices or devise new strategies
for regaining some control over and meaning from their work.

As far as the practical use of motivation theory is concerned, identity is essentially an *intervening variable* which
acts to complicate applications. Taking account of individual
identities would introduce subjective factors which would
make motivations difficult to assess with standardised test
inventories such as interest questionnaires. Likewise, the
application of techniques based on the assumed relation
between satisfaction and performance, which is difficult to
define or measure in the first place, tends to ignore the
operation of social, cultural, organisational and environmental factors which will all intervene to make a simple 'more
satisfaction, more performance' relationship less likely.

Any meaningful view of the relation between job satisfaction and performance would have to recognise that alienated
responses are rooted in the estrangement of workers from their
creative capacities in the act of production, from ownership
and control of the workplace, and from fellow workers. As the
conditions and responses derive, at least in part, from the
basic structures of the capitalist labour process, changing
them would require more than tinkering with peripheral
aspects of work design. This does not mean that individuals
will not report some sort of increased positive satisfactions.
For example, Frese (1982) states that

> much of the work on job satisfaction has tapped an attitude
> which could be labelled resigned job satisfaction. Because of
> the unavailability of other jobs and ways to change the job
> situation, a worker has reduced his aspiration level over
> time and has become resigned to his job. (1982: 212)

Such feelings are directly related to powerlessness and lack of
control over the job situation. Reduction of aspiration levels
does not necessarily imply a lack of aspiration, however; it
could simply mean resignation to progression as defined by

the rules and procedures of the organisation, an acceptance of bureaucratic methods of control and the ideologies which underly them. At Insco, for example, one of the female clerks, who had been continually discouraged from applying for a position as a sales inspector, decided not to risk the security of her position as senior clerk and redefined her aspirations in terms of 'a woman's idea of going higher up within the company on the inside' (Collinson and Knights, 1986: 166). By considering the idea of progression into office management rather than sales, she has started the process of redefining her goals in line with the engendered job segregation fostered by the company.

People experiencing passive satisfaction with their lot rather than active satisfaction with their work, may possibly be open to the types of influence exemplified by attempts at job enrichment or similar schemes. Herzberg's (1968) two-factor theory of motivation suggests that the 'motivator' factors associated with job content and satisfaction are separate from the 'hygiene' factors associated with job context and dissatisfaction. The content factors, such as growth, responsibility, recognition, achievement and variety, are similar to those assumed to motivate people who value intrinsic rewards. The context factors, such as salary, conditions, security, relationships and possibly policy and status, are similar in effect to extrinsic rewards in that they make work either easier or more rewarding as they improve. Techniques such as job enrichment assume that if content and context factors are adequately met for individuals in organisations, then the motivation to work will be maintained. More importantly, they rely on the notion that people are passive recipients of organisational influences. If people do construct for themselves a passively resigned workplace identity, then the chances will increase that they will accept the redesign of their jobs on the basis that it will eventually improve their lot. The developments in flexible working practices and unitarist industrial relations in the 1980s may indicate that what has been identified as a 'new realism' is nothing more than the kind of coping engendered by having to adopt a passive workplace identity in response to environmental constraints such as high unemployment.

Job context and content factors are seldom if ever met adequately for everyone within the work environment, so attempts to influence motivation levels in individuals will always run foul of factors they do not take account of. Thus, in addition to active attempts to 'motivate' individuals, organisations take advantage of the socialising pressures of work to create a climate where people are open to these kinds of influence. However, attempts to motivate or socialise individuals into accepting the managerial direction tends to ignore the decision-making aspect of the process of becoming motivated. If motivation is indeed the 'mainspring of behaviour', then it not only refers to the selection of goals but to the selection and development of the coping strategies and skills that individuals use to achieve those goals. Lee and Lawrence (1985) identify four factors which underpin all 'political' models of motivation that focus on decision-making:

- *Goals* – relating to values, interests and perceptions of individual opportunities and possibilities;
- *Strategies* – formulated to achieve goals or to react to threats to capacities to achieve them;
- *Coalition* – exchanging commitment to group interests for support for goal strategies which cannot be achieved on an individual basis;
- *Power* – assessing success of goal strategies and membership of coalitions, arriving at estimates of personal power to affect events and revising goals in line with this.

The first three factors are dependent on the fourth in that, 'An individual's perception of his power will affect the goals he sets, the strategies he chooses and the nature of the coalitions he joins' (1985: 78). Likewise, in the construction of identities, perceptions of a person's situational power will determine the sources of meaning which are appropriate to the maintenance of a secure identity.

Motivation may be influenced by either interfering with or facilitating the individual's capacity to perceive, formulate or implement one or more of these factors. Organisational strategies which simply restrict the employees' capacity to act in these areas will, however, probably lead to individual and group attempts to circumvent them. Techniques aimed at the 'motivation' of groups and individuals may not in this sense achieve their aims. They may exacerbate the situations they were designed to ameliorate by reproducing or reinforcing existing areas of conflict, by re-opening old issues or by introducing new topics of dispute.

Current examples of strategies aimed at enhancing group motivation for managerial benefit include programmes such as quality circles at the behavioural level and autonomous workgroups at the level of job design. Aimed at increasing production quality, overall productivity, workforce flexibility and job satisfaction, they depend on the production of workgroup identities consonant with the collective goals of management. For them to work effectively through group identities remaining manipulable by management, there must be a continuing identification with organisational 'needs'. These in the end can only be sustained to the extent that the organisation enables group members to maintain comparative material benefits *and* secure identities. This, however, has long-term implications for job security which are in direct contradiction to the aim of producing a flexible workforce responsive to the short-term demands for changes in product lines, working practices and manning levels. The threat of a reserve pool of unemployed labour is not sufficient to maintain the levels of commitment required by these programmes. Commitment based on the fear of losing one's job is only equivalent to the type of motivation achieved by holding a gun to someone's head. As soon as the threat is removed, so is the motivation. All that is achieved is an increase in the likelihood of retaliatory action.

In essence, then, the study of motivation in OB is the study of the processes of organisational influence and a study in the exercise of power and domination. No matter what the intent of consultants and practitioners in the area in terms of increasing job satisfaction and the elusive 'quality of working life', to management these techniques are effectively 'technologies of regulation' aimed at increasing control over behaviour and performance. Unfortunately, from a managerial point of view at least, in the long run such programmes cannot survive exposure to the contradictions inherent in trying to control subordinates who are actively attempting to control their own environent.

Motivation as a Problematic Concept

Motivation as presented above lies at the heart of the explanatory project of organisational psychology and as such can be used to reflect generally on the limits and contradictions within mainstream theories and practices. At one level, motivation is a classic case of Adorno's concept of *'identity thinking'* (Rose, 1978), where a concept is used as if it denoted instances of something when it does not. For example, an individual is not 'motivated' to perform well at a particular task or 'satisfied' with their job when the underlying reason for their performance is to maintain a reasonable level of subsistence and not to lose their job by falling behind. In this sense, organisational psychology assumes an identity between being motivated to do something and being constrained to do it by physical and social necessity. In Adorno's terms one can only make proper use of a theoretical concept or construct in the context of the 'theory of society' through which it is itself constructed.

In taking the situational contexts in which behaviour within organisations takes place largely as given, the concepts used in mainstream analyses are often reified, involving 'the conversion of concrete social relations of production into abstracted, quantitative measures' (Wexler, 1983: 66). Reification can be viewed as a dual process. Firstly, the products of human thought and activity are treated as things in themselves and secondly, socially produced concepts are treated as being intrinsic to individuals and organisations. Thus, in relation to the first part of this process, organisations are often treated as actual entities or organisms with their own needs, drives and characteristics analogous to those of people, rather than as the continuously recreated products of human labour and organisational ingenuity. Returning to the concept of motivation, we can observe that it is often applied to organisations themselves, in that they are seen as having their own internally derived goals which can change to accommodate the environmenal contingencies that the organisation is faced with; for instance, the current fashion for management and staff 'development' programmes designed ostensibly to meet the 'training needs' of organisations but which serve mainly to locate organisational problems at the individual rather than the structural level (see Chapters 6 and 9).

The second part of the process can also be illustrated through the concept of motivation. Content theories such as that of Maslow (1954) utilise highly generalised typologies of needs which range from the satisfaction of 'lower order' needs relating to physiological and interactional factors, through needs for self-esteem, to 'higher order' needs for self-actualisation and development. This type of formulation seeks to explain the innate determinants of human behaviour in order that they might be better understood and directed by individuals. But they are developed in organisational psychology into measurement packages which seek to typify the range of needs applying to individuals in order to establish the minimum conditions for their compliance. This effort to more fully integrate human resources into the production process is similarly present in the usage of process theories of motivation, as can be seen in the application of the expectancy theory of Vroom (1964).

This seeks to quantify and predict the strength of an individual's tendency to behave in a particular way, as an assigned probability which is given by the equation: $F = \Sigma\ (E \times V)$: where F is the resulting motivation to behave in a particular way, E is the *subjective probability* or *expectation* that the behaviour will be followed by a particular outcome and V is the *valence* of the outcome or the *preference* that the individual has for that particular outcome. Since any particular behaviour has a number of possible outcomes, then the calculation depends on the sum of all the measured values of $E \times V$ and the sign Σ indicates that we should add the resulting values obtained for each outcome. The E value, being a probability, can vary between 0 and 1, 0 meaning that the individual estimates there is no chance of that particular outcome and 1 meaning that it is a complete certainty. The value of V is determined by asking the individual to rate the value they place on various outcomes along a dimension which would, for example, give those they preferred as $+1$, those they felt neutral towards as 0 and those they did not prefer as -1.

If, then, the problem is to discover the motivation that an individual has towards working harder, we must first identify the possible outcomes which might result from their working harder, such as more pay, increased prospects for promotion, increased stress, or a more positive attitude from the supervisor. Then the probability of and preference for each of these outcomes occurring must be assessed (the E and V values), and the resulting values must be added to give us a value for F. The assumption is that the *higher* the value of F, the *stronger* the motivation to behave in that particular fashion. Of course, the value of F must be compared to some sort of baseline and therefore we might compare the scores for a particular individual over a number of different behaviours or the scores for a number of individuals on the same behaviour.

On the surface this model appears to provide organisational psychologists with a simple and powerful *tool* for predicting behaviour. But the assumptions made in such a measurement present a number of problems. The first is that expectancy theory provides a *rational-cognitive* explanation of individual behaviour. Can we assume that individuals make rational calculations based on their cognitive input in deciding whether to act in a particular way? Even assuming that this is the case, do these form the major determinant factor in their subsequent actions? These questions are often posed in OB texts, but no adequate account is generally given of whether such assumptions are warranted. The question is simply stated prior to a discussion of what can be done with expectancy theory in terms of understanding motivational goals, in order to influence and alter people's behaviour.

An objection arises from those, including Langer (1981), who suggest that many of our behaviours are acted out in what they term a 'mindless' manner. Rather than behaving in an analytic, rational fashion, we in fact follow unconscious 'scripts' through which our actions are fitted to and determined as appropriate to the contexts they occur in. Thus in much the same way as we do not consciously think of the numerous and complex series of actions which we go through in performing even such an apparently simple task as making a cup of tea, we do not necessarily take an analytical and conscious part in performing many of the behaviours we must go through at work. Although we may consider and think about the options open to us and the best way of going about a particular task, the underlying motivation may simply be that we are following the script which we have come to learn as appropriate to that situation. The work of Roy (1973) provides examples of how both labour and social interaction in the workplace can take on the attributes of ritual. Roy's monotonous and fatiguing work of 'mincing plastic sheets into small ovals, fingers and trapezoids' (208) was made 'relatively satisfying' in Baldamus's (1961) terms by turning the production process into a series of 'games' which varied the colour, shape and ordering of the components turned out. The self-induced scripting of the work itself was accompanied by the breaking up of the working day into 'times', such as 'peach', 'banana' and 'pick-up time'. 'Times' were constructed around the ritualised social interactions and verbal interplay in the brief interruptions to production which were repeated on a daily basis. Thus the behavioural scripts built up around eating, drinking and visits from outsiders reintroduced some level of meaning and interest for the machine operators into a deskilled labour process. Interest was further enhanced by the continuous repetition during work of 'serious' and 'kidding' verbal 'themes' centered around the characteristics and problems of the operators involved. In this sense then, scripted behaviours become an effective, though not necessarily actively planned, mechanism for coping with the mundanity of working life.

A second and related problem for models of motivation are the narrow and over-deterministic accounts of experience which rational-cognitive theories of human behaviour produce. These place the responsibility for action on individuals rather than on the contexts they find themselves in. This tends to reinforce the view that the pathology of organisations is based on the irrational actions of individuals. In this view the problems and uncertainties faced by organisations are caused by the self-serving behaviour of those who do not appreciate the 'big picture' of organisational life.

In the simplified example of expectancy calculations given above, it is fairly easy to see how the categories which define the possible outcomes of a particular behaviour are arrived at.

What is also fairly easy to see is that there are almost an infinity of intervening variables or factors which, for the calculation to be carried out, would have to be taken into account. Even if the behaviour of individuals in organisations is largely carried out in the context of scripts which their socialisation into organisational life has taught them, they have still to bring to their working life an actively constructed identity which has been transformed within the organisation into an appropriate image. These behaviours and scripts do not exist in isolation. Even considering the possible outcomes of working harder on one particular task would involve an almost endless series of ramifications and secondary consequences. Thus to obtain a realistic prediction about how motivated a single individual would be to perform a particular behaviour would involve taking into account not only most of the behaviours applicable to their work and their life outside the organisation, but also those of similar individuals inside and outside the organisation to provide a basis of comparison. The project of fully understanding how people are motivated from this perspective would involve identifying and explaining all of the subjective and structural influences on their lives and those of the others surrounding them.

In this light, the functional utility of such models would appear to be in establishing the minimum conditions under which workers can be mobilised to consent to the nature of work that is demanded of them. This is achieved through a narrow means of conceptualising motivation, which supplies enough information about an individual to be useful in engaging their consent for working practices by actively manipulating their perceptions of expectations and preferences. Information about the social and material rewards available, or perhaps the danger of redundancy, can be manipulated to reinforce control practices by getting the worker to internalise the rationale for increasing productivity. What is effectively happening here is that extrinsic factors, those largely outside the control of the individual such as pay and conditions, are being translated into intrinsic factors. These include those processes assumed to be under individual control, for instance, satisfaction and motivation, thus making employees personally responsible for their own objective situation. Seivers (1986) goes further by arguing that motivation is not an intrinsic factor of individual personality, but an *artefact* produced by the science of organisational behaviour which acts as a *surrogate* for the meaning which people have lost from fragmented and dehumanised work.

> Motivation only became an issue – for management and organisation theories as well as for the organisation of work itself – when meaning was either lost or disappeared from work. ... In consequence, motivation theories have become surrogates for the search for meaning. (1986, 338–9)

That management has become such a great consumer of theories and techniques of motivation is in itself an indication that there is little in much work which can in itself act as a source of meaning and the basis for a secure identity. The attempts to introduce greater levels of participation, to 'humanise' work, to 'enrich' jobs, are in part a recognition that at least some level of commitment from workers is necessary to efficiently valorise capital. Attempts to 'motivate' are founded on the assumption that workers need to be led, but their theoretical bases do not examine the corollary that they need to be influenced to co-operate because of their essential alienation from the productive process. The fashionable view of the use of psychological knowledge in the area of motivation is generally that they are employed in order to produce greater harmony and integration in the workplace. However, the use of motivation as a manipulative concept implies not a lesser but a greater unitarism of outlook from management. The integration of individual and 'organisational' goals not only binds people ever closer to the productive process, but creates the climate where programmes such as the 'Total Quality Management' initiatives taken up by companies such as Philips and Jaguar make them responsible for monitoring their own performance. The 'motivations' served are the managerial aims of greater 'unit' productivity, the drive for more work and less waste operating under the cover story of a *consensus-based* participation provided by motivational techniques.

CONCLUSION: THE LIMITS OF SOCIAL AND ORGANISATIONAL PSYCHOLOGY

We have used the treatment of motivation to illustrate some of the general problems of organisational psychology and the social psychology that partly underlies it, but this limitation needs to be put in a broader context. Social psychology is concerned with individual behaviour as it exists in various contexts, but such behaviour is still what people do, not what they are. The discipline has tended to reduce its treatment of subjective experience to abstract and supposedly *quantifiable* traits and mechanisms which are compatible with practice-led assumptions as opposed to its dominant theoretical ideals.

This failure to address the issue of subjectivity adequately partly underlies one of the major problems which confronts social psychology, that is, the contradiction inherent in attempting to address both the individual and social determinants of human behaviour. Social psychology as a discipline purports to fill the divide between psychology and sociology, the tendency having been for the former to concentrate on the individual and the latter the social. But it does not escape the problem. Henriques *et al.* (1984) correctly identify the weakness as one of a *dualism* between individual and society. They argue that even when social psychology attempts to provide accounts of how the two sets of determinants interact in shaping behaviour, it tends to come down on the side of explanations which emphasise biology and/or individual rationality as causative agents. Social and structural factors are tacitly acknowledged as having some effects, but these are seldom treated in an explicit fashion. They are generally reduced to the status of intervening variables which complicate the action of the individually based mechanisms and determinants of behaviour.

Social psychology and its development can therefore be seen as a product of the tensions and debates between competing explanations of behaviour. In utilising perspectives such as social learning theory, social psychology tacitly incorporates the essential portions of prior perspectives, notably psychoanalytic and behaviourist theory. These perspectives embody contradictory assumptions about the nature of human behaviour. Yet critiques and reformulations of these assumptions form the very basis of the development of the discipline itself. These are refined over time by the cycle of critique and reformulation to produce a discipline responsive to the needs of its individual, organisational and institutional clients. However, these tensions and debates serve only in the end to mask the fact that no wholly consistent body of theory of behaviour has been developed which can explain the social construction of identity. What social psychology actually does is continually to reproduce and repackage the tensions between the dominant competing assumptions about human behaviour. The end product of this process is generally to reinforce the understanding of social problems as residing in the *deficiencies* of individuals. Within the workplace for instance, sabotage to machinery would be blamed on the deviant or even criminal tendencies of workers rather than on the working conditions or practices which they are often powerless to respond to in a more direct fashion. This kind of development and shaping of subjective experience in the workplace tends to be neglected or ignored.

Therefore the dependency of organisational psychology on social psychology for its theoretical resources is important in shaping its direction and application. The tensions may be partly avoided by maintaining a specific focus on individual and group behaviour within organisational contexts. An attempt is made to avoid confronting the main contradictions of the *individual–society dualism* which faces social psychology. Context is taken as a given or contingent factor which may be manipulated to alter behaviour. This conveniently leaves organisational psychology to deal with measurable and *marketable* packages of behaviour, which are easily incorporated into frameworks that of necessity theorise individuals as standardised social objects rather than specific social subjects with unique personal histories. The resulting treatment of individuals as subject matter rather than as subjective entities is commensurate with the dominant assumptions extant in social psychology as a whole.

Hence there is a double abstraction of behaviour from its social and structural contexts, and from much of its subjective content. The humanistic critiques within social psychology in the 1960s and 70s, which were concerned with the lack of social context and individual meaning in existing theory and methodological practice, have undoubtedly influenced organisational psychology. But the presentation of its traditional agenda has reproduced them as vague ideals rather than as core assumptions of the discipline. This remains a continuing contradiction between the way in which the major topic areas in organisational psychology are defined and the way they are utilised in the control and regulation of behaviour at work. We return to this issue of regulation in the following chapter.

8

Society, Psychology and the Individual

I have a reputation for getting people's backs up who work for me. I will help them if I consider they need it, but sometimes I give them the impression that I can't be bothered. I prefer them to learn by looking for themselves. So I'm fairly abrupt and indifferent. I'm not worried if they like me but I do want their respect ... I don't like them to take advantage ... they often say, 'Oh we can't understand you, Allan, we try to be nice to you but you're not nice back.' I think there's only one I've not made cry ... I don't think I have to do the job. My job is to keep them as busy as possible. I'd rather me be bored than them, otherwise if you do bring work for them again, it just leads to moaning and groaning. You can't keep all six happy at the same time. With some you can tell their monthly changes, even the other girls say so. Sometimes when they're having a good chunner about the inspectors I have to impress on them that if it was not for the men, there'd be no jobs for them, if the blokes don't go out and sell insurance (Collinson and Knights, 1986: 158).

Socially produced identities are a central factor delineating people's experience of work. As the authors of the Insco case study argue, Allan views his hierarchical position as a re-flection of his own personal status and dignity. In his dealings with his female 'subordinates' he utilises a mixture of patron-ising humour, sarcasm and indifference in order to maintain a symbolic distance of authority and 'motivate' them to work independently. His proud boasts also indicate the significance of gender to his work identity.

The case itself addresses the gendered aspects of job segregation and the social construction of skill in the insurance industry, where 'Conventionally, the task is described in terms of an heroic drama in which intrepid and autonomous males stride out into the financial world and against the odds return with new business'. These 'almost mystical perceptions' of male skills are contrasted to the 'internal staff of women clerks whose work is assumed to be dependent, supportive and secondary' (1986: 148). Far from the aggressive instincts of the hunter, success in selling is seen to be dependent on the *gendered interpersonal skills* which are employed to maintain 'exclusively male relationships' with insurance agents. At the same time, the devalued work of the female clerks is essential in the maintenance of long-term client support and after-sales service. Thus the success of the 'heroic' male is paradoxically dependent on the 'stock of working knowledge' possessed by the women which allows them to maintain their own personalised telephone relations with clients. The unacknowledged and differentially rewarded *'tacit skills'* employed in the administrative support role are 'further emphasised when women also act as caring ego-masseurs or office wives for sales inspectors who sometimes return to the office dejected after unsuccessful appointments' (1986: 150).

The continuation of such gendered job segregation is seen as being dependent on the continued acquiescence of the clerical staff to their subordination, even in conditions where

> Allan's highly coercive approach generates a level of anxiety or frustrated resentment which is expressed in internal conflict, poor standards of work, indifference, disenchant-ment or even resignation (1986: 168–9).

These reactions from the women underwrite the prejudicial attitudes used by the male managers to exclude the women from promotion to the sales force on the basis that they are 'naturally' unfit to handle such macho work. But such 'reactions' are not in fact problems in themselves, they are in effect the range of *coping* responses which the women see open to them in that they themselves have *internalised* the view that they are unfit to be sales 'reps'. By accepting the gendered definition of themselves the women are limited to striving for personal material gain, or 'symbolic security expressed either in resignation, indifference or the search for future promotion within the clerical ranks' (1986: 169). Such necessarily individualistic strategies are said merely to reproduce the contradictions of job segregation and effectively to block any moves towards collective action which would challenge their institutionalised subordination.

Issues of identity raised in the Insco case are therefore central, but cannot be dealt with without concepts deriving from the study of structural processes such as organisational design, control strategies or the impact of wider social formations. But they in turn will be incomplete without reference to the factors surrounding the *construction* of the subjectivity and experience of those involved. Organisational psychology should allow us to enter these areas necessary for a fuller account of 'organisational behaviour'. But as the discussions in Chapter 6 have begun to argue, the relation between organisational psychology and the subjective factor in the study of work organisations is, however, by no means clear. Though organisational psychology and its practitioners might be expected to have a natural concern with the identities and subjective experience of participants, the range of issues and topics traditionally presented in the area do not consistently address these concepts. Explaining Allan's relations to 'his staff' would thus be difficult using the theoretical models and concepts currently available.

SUBJECTIVITY AND IDENTITY

Definitions

Our approach to the 'subjective factor' in organisations focuses on the experience of people in work organisations through the two common themes of subjectivity and identity.

Both concepts present problems of interpretation and there is considerable overlap in their usage. Our use of 'subjectivity' follows Henriques *et al.*'s (1984: 2–3) twofold definition. First, the *'condition of being subject'*; the ways in which the individual is acted upon and made subject to the structural and interpersonal processes at work in organisational life. Second, the 'condition of being *a* subject': possessing individuality and self-awareness. Thus the term encompasses the fundamentally contradictory experience of work and the subjective development and regulation of people's 'emotions, desires, fantasies, a sense of self' (Banton *et al.*, 1985: 44).

The concept of identity commonly involves the notion that there is an irreducible core of social and individual being which uniquely identifies each of us. Psychologically, identity variously incorporates concepts of self and self-esteem; structures of values, attitudes and beliefs, personality and associated traits. Sociologically, it includes concepts of self and of roles and reference groups. Lasch (1984: 31–2), notes a shift of meaning that does not admit a fixed or continuous identity. What we do possess, however, is a *'minimal self'*, which because of our need for an 'emotional equilibrium', retreats to a 'defensive core, armed against adversity' (1984: 16).

Our usage, then, incorporates the notion of *self-aware* and *participative* subjects who maintain a valued part of their identity against the unpredictability of the external world, while at the same time being acted on and constrained by organisational ideologies and practices. These themes of subjectivity and identity are examined in the context of inter-related arguments which together provide a framework that is capable of addressing issues of structure, agency, individual action and experience.

We are concerned to maintain a perspective rooted in a materialist conception of social production and existence. Capital and management on its behalf manipulate, direct and shape the identities of employees. This reflects the need to mobilise the consent and co-operation of workers in order that effective control may be maintained over the productive process.

We also maintain a focus on the development of identity in individuals, and more especially the *reproduction* and *transformation* of those identities in the context of work organisations. Individuals are not the passive *recipients* or objects of structural processes but are constructively engaged in the *securing* of identities (Knights and Willmott, 1985) and the development of capacities (Leonard, 1984). These, although influenced and shaped by organisational contexts and practices, are at the same time the unique products of each person's history.

Explanations of identity

As we explained in the previous chapter, through a variety of interpretations the mainstream agenda can be shown to refer to common and basic processes through which individuals develop identities. Through these processes, notably learning, perception and socialisation, the individual is seen to develop a distinctive personality and patterns of motivation. There are many useful things to learn from examining that journey, but as an account of the development of subjectivity and identity within an organisational context it has distinct limitations. It fails adequately to understand individual identity as a social reality through which we transact with our environment. Hence we deal with objective reality through a subjective construction which interprets and shapes our whole world in terms of what we value about ourselves. Our focus on subjective identity lies in this process, because as individuals we guide our actions according to what will in our view best defend, enhance or *substantiate* our identities. As we have previously argued, each of us then is effectively engaged in securing for ourselves identities which provide both a sense of personal stability (Knights and Willmott, 1985) and a basis for setting the personal goals which direct our activity. Identity in this light is a tool which we use to present ourselves in, and possibly transform ourselves into, images appropriate to our social, cultural and work context.

Some theoretical sources within social psychology do develop aspects of an understanding of identity which are helpful. Unless one takes personality and identity as being an entirely genetically determined phenomenon, there can be little doubt that an individual's identity is to a great extent determined by social contexts and pressures. In researching differential socio-emotional development in male and female children, Lewis (1975) found that as early as biological influences can be distinguished, there are parallel differences in the treatment of the two sexes by adults and other children. Thus, though biological influences undoubtedly have some effects on personality in the same way that they have an influence on hair colour and general bodily characteristics, these effects are almost impossible to differentiate from social or environmental influences.

According to Weigert *et al.* (1986: 31), 'identity is a definition that transforms a mere biological individual into a human person. It is a definition that emerges from and is sustained by the cultural meanings of social relationships activated in interaction'. To extend the above example, if someone dyes or changes their hairstyle they have taken steps to place a self-directed social construction on the body they were born with. They are taking for themselves an identity produced out of what they select as attractive or appropriate out of the social values, expectations and fashions of their time. The tradition of sociological social psychology represented by Weigert and other writers tries to avoid the contradictions which have existed between notions of personal and social identity. They take the view that identity is a social product which is both bestowed on the individual by others and appropriated by the individual for themselves. It takes the form of a '*typified self*', in that it is a self-produced categorisation out of what is available to the individual within the various situations they participate in. In this sense individuals may construct for themselves any number of identities from the relationships encountered in their home, work and leisure activities.

If the focus is shifted from personal to social identity, it is possible to see that we are constantly representing our subjective selves to the others in our social environment. In the way we dress, speak and behave we present a changing image of who we are to those we interact with. Our identity is in this sense a *negotiated* construction. Depending on whom we are dealing with at the time, we can present an image which is intended both to appear appropriate to the situation and to appear consistent with the expectations of the other. Using a Symbolic Interactionist framework, Erving Goffman (1971) explored this conception of self within a dramaturgical metaphor, representation of social identity being a performance analogous to that of an actor. The image presented is not necessarily the 'real' self of the person but is a situationally appropriate image sustained both by the 'actor' themselves and those observing and/or interacting with the performer. The others involved collaborate with the actor to enable them to present a consistent performance and hence a social identity consistent within the situation. The students in a lecture theatre, for example, collaborate with the lecturer to maintain an image of authority for the latter and of subordination for themselvs, even though they may in no way consider themselves socially or intellectually inferior to the lecturer. They simply participate in the production of a performance which fits the perceived rules of the situation.

The interface between social and personal identity lies in this act of interpersonal negotiation. A social identity does not simply spring fully formed from the demands of the situation but requires effort and practice from the individual and appropriate feedback from others. Thus the contexts from which we are able to construct a unique subjective identity for ourselves consist mainly of 'rationalised' performances, and we construct our personal identity out of the strategies and responses we devise to deal with the situations we encounter. The problems which many people find in discovering their 'own' identity may in part arise from the consequences of trying to be consistent over time and from the wide range of images they have had to present to survive in a complex and changing social environment.

The idea that we each possess a core identity which relates to what we value about ourselves is examined in the social learning conception of identity (Miller, 1963). As a source of meaning, identity links us to others in the social structure through perceived similarities and processes of identification. As definition identity sets us apart from others, it is the basis of social comparison in that it shows us the things and people that our particular set of personal meanings debar us from identifying with. Personal, subjective identity consists of the

meanings and images we have found to represent us accurately
in the past. Social identity, where it is different from the former,
consists of the negotiated position between our personal identity
and the meanings and images demanded of us in our current
social context.

This leads us to a final aspect of identity as a linking
concept between differing levels of explanation. We gain
identities through interaction and association with others,
though the major source of these interactions and associations
is not other individuals in themselves but the social and
cultural groupings that we belong to. These groups provide us
with points of reference and comparison out of which we can
define ourselves. Social groupings are in turn defined in terms
of the social structure that they exist within. Through this
route identity is directly moulded by social structure. For this
reason Miller (1963) saw identity as the foundation of the
links between social structure and personality, and fundamental as such to the explanation of socialisation, motivation and
psychological conflict. Our personal transactions with social
structures are conducted in great part through the organisations we belong to, work for and with which we have to deal.
Organisations attempt to socialise people into their particular
workplace cultures. Management attempts to influence individual motivation to its advantage. The amelioration of the
psychological, interpersonal and group conflicts engendered
by these activities are the main rationale for the involvement
of social and behavioural scientists in organisations.

Redefining the Agenda

To understand more adequately the individual's development
towards a participant in organisations who is active, yet acted
upon, we also need to redefine further some of the issues and
agenda. For example, because so much of OB takes the structures, workings and goals of organisational life for granted, it
underestimates the degree that the environment restricts
sources of meaning for secure identities and imposes costs on
individuals. The resources which an individual can bring to
an *identity project* will depend on their *situational power* in the

organisation. Admittedly, this situational power does not depend simply on a person's place in an organisational hierarchy. An individual's perception of their own situational power, whether at an interpersonal, group or organisational level, will also condition how secure they feel. Thus a shop-floor worker can construct an identity jut as secure as, or even more secure than that of someone with more position power. These identities are also not necessarily situation specific. They can provide meaning and support outside the context they were constructed within, though there are of course limits. The 'organisation man', secure in his or her identification with organisational goals and objectives, may generalise associated attitudes and behaviours to situations where such an identity may be inappropriate. Yet the possession of a secure identity may still make them capable of acting confidently, even in situations where their power to effect events is not supported by their organisational position. 'Do you know who I am?' thus becomes a question which acts both to confirm the situational competence of an individual to themselves and to undermine the perceived situational power of another.

Nevertheless, the attitudes, behaviours and abilities through which our identities are externally communicated will reflect the constraints placed on us at work and the standards and values of the dominant organisational cultures we are in contact with. The individual and group identities we eventually secure will be favourable, neutral or antagonistic to organisations on the basis of the climate and context they are constructed in, mediated by our experiential base and the standards of comparison this gives us.

The treatment of identity in mainstream psychology also tends to neglect contextual issues because it treats identity in the same fashion as we tend to do in everyday life, as inherent in the person. Breakwell (1986: 95) argues that psychologists 'tend to treat identity as the origin of action'; they use it as a 'motivational variable'. In contrast, we have to see identity as the outcome of interaction within particular material contexts which act as constraints on available sources of meaning and on the process of identity construction.

The central limiting factor on available sources of meaning

is the context of *fragmented* and *commodified* work. Labour is reduced to abstract capacities which serve the ends of production rather than those of the person, as in the apropriation by work organisations of the *use-time* available to individuals for developing and pursuing their own capacities, abilities and interests (Séve, 1978). Subjectively, this reduction of the relations between people and things to their value in a system of exchange both increases feelings of powerlessness and decreases feelings of personal responsibility. In an externally controlled environment, the most individuals can often hope for is to maintain or increase their situational power and material resources. Our relationships with, and our attribution of motives to others are reduced to their instrumental function in the process of 'accumulation without regard to need' (Wexler, 1983: 122). Socio-psychological models of motivation continually reflect this, as in the rational calculations of personal advantage we are assumed to make in exchange and equity theory, or the assessments of personal power in Lee and Lawrence's 'political model' of motivation (see Chapter 7).

The instrumentality of relationships also extends into the definition of gender identities in the workplace. Hearn and Parkin (1987) identity the *'desexualised'* nature of work organisations as reinforcing patriarchy and sexism. Instrumentality in the continuing forms of fragmented, Taylorised work relations defines masculinity and reproduces organisational work as a male concern:

> The workman is, potentially at least, nothing more than the doer of the task, without feelings and emotions. The ideal workman would appear to almost lose physical presence, or be a mere disembodied bearer of role, in effect part of a machine system. (Hearn and Parkin, 1987: 19)

Women workers are in general separated from the dominantly male culture of organisations, and feminine gender identity is suppressed or at best marginalised. Women managers especially are often required to exhibit what is almost a male gender identity in work and are often viewed as exceptions to women in general. Hearn and Parkin (108) cite as an example the lack of appropriate female role models in management on which to base standards, and the subsequent development of the 'image' or clothing consultant to advise women in particular on what is termed 'executive' or 'power' dressing. Likewise, domestic labour is not viewed as 'real' work in the fashion that paid work is, the identity construct of 'worker' being reserved for the latter. Women's labour in organisations can often be an extension of domestic labour, as in the example of bosses' secretaries who act as 'office wives, protecting their charges from unnecessary interference and strain, making tea, buying presents, even cleaning their bosses' false teeth', (1987, 92).

Sexual and racial discrimination in labour markets is reinforced by stereotypical categorisations of women and black workers which portrays them as 'naturally' inferior in various abilities or only suited to certain types of work. Notions such as women being better suited than men to boring, repetitive tasks serve to legitimise restricted access to labour markets. Black workers in particular can be discriminated against in the recruitment and selection process on the basis of a stereotyped lack of acceptability in white workplace cultures. Jenkins (1986) notes that the causes of racism are often attributed to those who are discriminated against; 'managers do, in the main, see black workers as posing problems for their organisations. These problems were typically seen to be created by black workers, not by white racism' (1986: 114).

Predominantly white, male managers, whose workplace identities would be expected to be closely aligned with organisational goals, would not be expected to view problems as created by their own racism or by racism institutionalised into workplace cultures. Rather, they would be seen to reside in those who demonstrably deviate from the cultural standards they have come to see as 'natural'. White workers are viewed as individuals, whereas black workers are perceived as groups characterised by often contradictory stereotypes: 'if you've got a problem with one of them, you've got a problem with all of them, whereas with the whites, you're just dealing with an individual' (1986: 99). Of course, the fact that people tend to fall back on the resources of group identity in the face of discrimination and consequent situational powerlessness is wholly understandable. The unfortunate effect is that it simply acts to reinforce stereotypes. Falling back on group identity is also a perceived problem with white workers, especially when that identity is crystallised in trade union activity. But this type of resistance is at least seen as acceptable in the sense that its source is a competing power structure. Additionally, they are likely to be seen as part of the same socio-cultural framework and thus their actions are legitimised, though disapproved of.

It is important to recognise that any form of organisational domination does not only or primarily occur through overt coercion such as threats to job security. Consent has to be mobilised because domination by coercion is often 'inefficient'. It requires constant reinforcement of coercive pressures and extensive monitoring of reactions to them. Domination of the individual through self-limitation and constraint is far more effective. This is engendered through individual assimilation of, and accommodation to, dominant workplace cultures and ideologies. At its most visible level, this process can be seen in the internalisation of the norms and accepted standards of behaviour in workgroups which occurs in organisational socialisation. If consent is not present, the pressures to shape ourselves in appropriate images may not be perceived as legitimate and may actively promote resistance. In West-wood's (1984) account of the lives of women at 'Stitchco' the women participated in a patriarchal labour process which from the management view was 'harmonious' in its appeals to both common progressive goals and paternalistic values. The women, however, had a 'clear understanding that there were sides in industry and that these sides maintained an uneasy truce which was easily broken' (1984: 25). Westwood argues that the 'deprivation, pain and waste that black and white working-class women live with on a daily basis' can be 'a spur to action rather than defeat'. As such, domination becomes the source of an identity project which empower their creativity and resourcefulness, sisterhood being the focus of a resistance which does more than enable their survival in a hostile environment.

Where we do internalise the constraints of a dominant

ideology or workplace culture, it must either appear to have some value in terms of enhancing situational power and thus identity, or appear so powerful and pervasive that we have no option but resign ourselves to submission. Resignation and submission can still be seen as acts of consent in that they may require us to repress or deny feelings of anxiety, frustration and hostility in order to remain in a state of perceived powerlessness. However, this process of internalising external constraints is not necessarily experienced as repressive, it may simply be perceived as a realistic response to the demands of a situation. Our transactions with social reality lead us to the self-limitation of our activities in line with what is perceived as practical and/or correct. Whether by the Freudian process of identification or the social learning principles of imitation and modelling we may come to accept structured, environmental constraints as natural and/or inevitable.

A person may be aware of the fact that the personal and social identities they carry around with them have been influenced by the organisations they have belonged to. They may even be quite cognizant of the nature of the particular things, people and events that have influenced them. A student, for example, who appeared to prefer drinking, dancing and socialising to keeping up to date with their work might be completely aware of the peer pressures that have made them into what their tutors may think of as a problem student. They may also be aware later of the pressures which turn them into a hard-working and committed member of a commercial organisation. But unless they completely identify with 'their' organisation it will be the constructed identity itself which they will regard as holding meaning, and not the sources from which they have constructed it. For most people, then, it is ourselves that possess meaning. We feel ourselves to be more than the sum of our influences. To a great extent it is the fact that we perceive meaning and identity as being inherent in ourselves that allows us to act in our own interests, to comply and consent to organisational demands when we feel it will profit us and to resist them when we feel they will cost us. Yet this is also the genesis of the process by which we can be separated from others and from acting in our collective interests.

This is one of the ways in which existing transactions between individuals and work organisations impose identity costs. When we attempt to construct an identity that offers us a degree of protection from uncertainty (Knights and Wilmott: 1985), we often find ourselves in competition with others for sources of meaning. This may take the form of access to and 'possession' of material resources for living and the symbols we place value on. In order to maintain an identity we attempt to control our environment and those in it and to resist those pressures which act to define our identities for us. The sense of individual meaning we gain from identity gives us a basis to resist external manipulation, but at the same time places us in competition with those in a similar position to ourselves who could aid us in our resistance. Thus we could both resist the attempts to shape our identities made by groups in organisations, and yet use our positional or situational power in those groups to enhance our identities at the expense of others. The separation that this achieves acts to blind us to the fact that an organisation is a structure of *interdependence* and the success of systems of control depends upon our compliance with managerial demands. By neglecting the context in which we compete for sources of meaning we can become estranged from one of the major sources available to us, the collective identity and power of those with similar interests.

We have already recognised that, in terms of identity construction, the contextual issues raised above are not necessarily simply sources of constraint. They may for some individuals be the very factors which allow them to secure identity. The worker with worries over job security may find meaning in defining themselves in line with nationalist or traditionalist sentiments, which can give expression to their fears through hostility to 'immigrant' workers or women who should remain at home. Likewise, hostility and resistance to organisational goals and practices may arise out of the conditions of exploitation, domination and alienation which renders others submissive. It would appear that identities are constructed out of whatever meanings are readily available and are constrained only by the individual's ability to sustain them. Thus the construction of identity is a continuous process which has to be understood in the context of the workplace, where it is maintained and reproduced on a daily basis. Organisational psychology often plays a significant role in this process.

ORGANISATIONAL PSYCHOLOGY AND ORGANISATIONAL BEHAVIOUR: TECHNOLOGIES OF REGULATION?

The explanations, instruments and techniques developed from mainstream theories are active in sustaining and implementing a culture of domination in the workplace. Organisational psychology, though paradoxically informed by humanistic concerns, has both a role as an agent and a vested interest in mobilising the consent of organisational members. New practical and theoretical knowledge often becomes part of the repertoire of the science of organisational behaviour, functioning as *technologies of regulation* which are used to control and discipline employees.

Such practices were inherent in the origins and early development of the sub-discipline of *industrial psychology*. In the first two decades of this century, employers drew on the variety of psychological theories on offer (Bendix, 1956: 200–1). *Behaviourism's* orientation towards 'human engineering' was a particularly useful source of advice for managers seeking to manipulate environmental stimuli in the form of penalties and incentives in order to produce the appropriate worker-response. At the same time, rival schools such as *instinct psychology* could suggest means of employers meeting 'innate' needs, such as self-expression, which were being distorted by evil Bolsheviks and union organisers. Perhaps most practically, *vocational psychology* could provide a battery of tests and measurements for applications to selection and placement. It was in this latter sphere that industrial psychology really took off in the USA, boosted by the extensive use of tests for intelligence and other factors during the war.

Psychology in industry had in fact begun in the area of advertising, but it soon shifted from manipulation of consumers to workers. Most concepts and techniques were extremely primitive, but psychologists such as Munsterberg promoted the idea that they could be applied to the 'labour problem'. The accumulation of knowledge about individual differences provided the basis for a varied apparatus of testing and measurement techniques geared to vocational counselling, placement testing and job analysis, with suggested correlations between factors such as intelligence, personality and potential work performance. Munsterberg summed up the general aim as finding 'those personalities which by their mental qualities are especially fit for a particular kind of economic work' (quoted in Baritz, 1965: 3). There was a widespread tendency to claim bogus relationships between national or racial characteristics and suitability for jobs (Kamin, 1979). In Britain, organisational psychology was relatively isolated from its American cousin. The National Institute of Industrial Psychology, founded under the leadership of Charles Myers in 1921, took a painstaking and broader interest in the related issues of training, rest, monotony and fatigue at work. But even here, a considerable number of programmes of vocational guidance, selection and testing were dictated by consultancy pressures.

It was these kind of developments that led Baritz (1960) to develop his famous analysis of psychologists and other industrial social scientists as *servants of power*. The science of behaviour was seen as giving management 'a slick new approach to its problems of control' (209). Included in the bag of schemes were attitude surveys, selection devices, motivation studies, counselling and role-playing. Events in the 1930s, notably the Hawthorne Studies, discussed in Chapter 2, were a particularly powerful confirmation of the social engineering role that could be played by social scientists, in this case under the framework of human relations theory. Those kind of superficial and manipulatory practices are still being recycled today, for example, where the reaction to objective problems employees face in their work, recognised in the stress research literature, has led to the astonishingly innovative introduction of ... employee counselling programmes! Baritz's great insight was to recognise that the service provided by social scientists to industry meant that 'control need no longer be imposed. It can be encouraged to come from within'. Workers could be manipulated to internalise the very ideologies and practices that ensured their domination.

A perfect modern example of this is the role played by industrial psychologists in some of the new human resource management techniques. The American writer, Grenier (1988), worked as part of a team hired by Johnson and Johnson, the medical products company, to create the required conditions for the setting up of a new plant on a greenfield site in New Mexico. This involved many of the elements discussed in Chapters 5 and 6: quality circles and semi-autonomous workteams, status and symbolic harmonisation of conditions, and extensive socialisation into a corporate culture facilitated by psychological testing at the selection and hiring stage. None of this, of course, is necessarily negative or manipulative, not even the secret tape recordings of workteam meetings to help identity success in fostering group identity and dynamics. But the hidden agenda of the whole project was a 'union avoidance' campaign, and this came to light when some of the workforce began an organising drive. The social psychologists became active and central participants in the struggle inside the heads of employees. All the supposedly innocent information collected became a means of screening workers and their attitudes. Team meetings in particular played an important role in identifying pro-union workers, Grenier being asked to develop an index through which to rank workers in their degree of support. Grenier later publicly reveals this process and himself becomes subject to surveillance and intimidation.

The important point here is that the techniques themselves are not the problem, but their uses that are conditioned by the client role. Not all social scientists, of course, have been concerned with such manipulatory practices and there has been a considerable amount of useful work done on employee satisfaction. The modern equivalents of Baritz's servants of power are not necessarily 'on the payroll', but still have a tendency to accept managerial norms as the parameters of their activities. In the same way as the newspaper owner does not have to threaten journalists to toe the editorial line, mainstream behavioural scientists generally internalise controls and largely unacknowledged self-censorship becomes the order of the day. In other words, the institutional relationship between the disciplines and their client groups remains a crucial problem.

Figure 8.1   'Psychological warfare'

Source: CAITS (1986), *Flexibility, Who Needs It?*, London, p. 34

Later, in developing out of industrial and human relations psychology in the 1950s and 1960s, organisational psychology brought to the study of work organisations an emphasis on descriptive and experimental research incorporated from social psychology. This was allied to the concern with applied work within organisations that had given impetus to indust-rial psychology in the early part of the century and the human relations tradition discussed in earlier chapters. Later inputs to organisational psychology from areas such as socio-technical systems theory and operations research have further cemented the relationship of the subject with the interests of power-groups in organisations.

That the practitioners of organisational psychology and organisation theory are mainly located in such institutions as business schools rather than in industry or psychology depart-ments, also reinforces the conception of the subject as a discipline in its own right, with its own client groups and professional concerns. At the same time, this distances them enough from their clients and subject matter to enable them to concentrate more on the theoretical understanding of organisations than was the case with the more strictly application – led industrial psychology. In turn, this enabled a retention of much of the humanistic theoretical orientation derived from social psychology. Theoretical ideals of this nature do not, however, often survive exposure to the needs of the main client group. As with industrial psychology before it, this results in the subject becoming chiefly directed towards the practical needs of management. A humanistic perspective, fully cognizant of the effects of organisational work on the subjective identities of individual employees, is unlikely to promote harmonious relations with clients whose major tasks include the deployment and control of an organisation's 'human resources'. Nor would an organisational psychology that grounded its theory and practice in an understanding of the politics of production, be likely to be in a position fully to give itself over to the demands of these clients.

The Roles of Organisational Psychologists

The relations between the practitioners of organisational psychology and their clients have thus formed a major influence on the development of the discipline, and we can further our understanding through an examination of the complex and interrelated roles which they take up in these relationships. Blackler (1982: 204–6) provides a useful framework for the discussion identifying four roles taken up by organisational psychologists:

- *Role as social critic*: evaluating organisational practices and predicting and studying the human consequences of organisational decision-making.
- *Role as social policy adviser*: evaluating the criteria that govern organisation in general and exploring alternatives.
- *Role as change agent*: evaluating and exploring ways in which alternatives identified in the light of the above two roles may be practically implemented.

● *Role as management consultant*, assisting and facilitating the efficient and effective management of organisations and social resources in respect of both routine tasks and non-routine contingencies.

These roles are qualified by the identification of a number of shifts in the approaches taken by organisational psychologists. There has been a recognition that in serving various interest groups in organisations, a claim to 'scientific' impartiality is difficult to sustain. Their interests must to some extent follow those of their clients. A role of *'specialist helper'* has generally replaced that of expert advisor. In addition, there has been a move away from trying to implement widespread changes in organisations towards attempting more incremental changes which rely on 'securing structural supports for changes at the interpersonal level' (Blackler, 1982: 206). Lastly, they are beginning to recognise that they can make no claims to certain knowledge or laws of organisational behaviour, and that the concepts and models generated by them are mainly relevant in localised contexts. Overall, the effect of these qualifications would appear to be a shift to a far closer involvement and identification with the client.

Although tending to serve particular client and/or interest groups, the products of organisational psychology, the prescriptive packages are presented as being of potential general benefit to organisations, or specifically to some groups or individuals within them. Even if practitioners are aware of the contextual limitations of the knowledge they produce, such awareness is not necessarily reflected in the attitude of their clients to them and the discipline they represent. To the client, the impression is of a unitary discipline, supplying analysis, advice and practical techniques in support of their own goals and tasks. The function of the organisational psychologist is seen as a 'therapeutic' one, treating the pathological problems of the organisation in much the same way as psychoanalysts treat those of their patients. In turn, this can further reproduce and reinforce in the client a unitary, rational conception of organisations which is supportive of dominant ideological assumptions, for example, that organisations are entities with common internal processes and socially necessary functions, duties and rights. If organisational psychologists are becoming more closely involved with their clients, their problem is the risk of becoming locked into a self-fulfilling prophecy in which they are viewed and treated as the doctors or maintenance technicians of the organisational world and are forced to conform to this image in order to survive. This latter shift is readily appreciated in the current pressure on academic institutions to become both more involved with and dependent on industry in the scramble for funding.

How then should we evaluate the general relations between the four roles of social critic, policy advisor, change agent and consultant assigned by Blackler? The view of practitioners as belonging to a professional discipline responsive to the needs of the client, tends to subordinate the first three of the roles to the fourth. The critical role is to be distinguished from a genuinely critical theory. Although organisational psychology can present a humanistic critique of the consequences of particular organisational practices, it seldom produces a critique of the dominant social relations within the mode of production itself. Furthermore, the approach does not include a reflexive critique of its own role in producing and reproducing practices and techniques. The result is more an analysis of how subjective influences on production can be *controlled out*, than of how they can successfully be used to create democratic forms of work organisation and socially useful work. The role of social policy advisor is the arena in which the above is sold as a commodity of value to the client. Advice is supplied not on alternatives to existing practices but on how reappraisals of them might be utilised and implemented in line with managerial goals.

Similarly, the role of change agent tends to avoid concern with alternatives in favour of technologies of regulation. This is not intended in a negative fashion, but the effects are frequently such for lower-level employees. Holloway (1984: 37–42) cites the techniques of job analysis and evaluation (such as those developed by consultants like Hay-MSL and Urwick, Orr and Partners) as examples of how systems designed to aid organisations in specifying critical requirements for adequate worker performance have their main consequences for the workers involved 'in the direction of the increasing rigidity of work' (1984: 37). These three roles thus become indicators of the divisions of intellectual labour which are necessary to the work involved in the fourth role of management consultant. The true paradigm of the organisational psychologist is that of ensuring *'effective resource use'*: supplying advice, resources and training which are aimed at assisting organisations in efficiently managing the conflict and resistance which is a predictable consequence of hierarchically organised production.

The 'science' of organisational behaviour would appear, then, to embody a fundamental contradiction in the relation between the benign and humanistic assumptions which inform its 'critical' theory and its assimilation into and accommodation of managerial ideology and practice. It is employed in a project of fitting the lived experience of other organisational employees into marketable and manipulable categories. The irony is that in fulfilling this task it manages to market itself in such a way that it becomes one more tool for the transformation into appropriate images of all those, including itself, who deal with work organisations. This leads almost inevitably to the situation where the very nature of the initiatives and interventions which practitioners put forward for the betterment of organisational life acts to block their possible success in a 'Catch-22' fashion. The programmes are short-circuited by their own actions.

Value-free organisational psychology is not possible, but there is a difference between a grounded theory approach which takes full account of the practical reality in which it operates, and a functionary service which is subject to the demands of its client to the extent that it distorts analytical tools to no one's ultimate benefit. It is for this reason that in attempting to redefine the agenda of organisational psychology, it is not enough to simply provide an adequate explanation of subjectivity. The need is also for critical perspectives which can integrate an understanding of the social construction of subjectivity, with explanations of how organisational practices develop and the role of social scientists in producing and refining them.

Importing critical theory and practice into the areas of organisational psychology and behaviour? To say that the discipline cannot adequately acount for subjective experience because it is subordinate to capital will mean little to people who have to earn their living within such regulatory structures. In such a context it appears reasonable that the rationale for the discipline is in making organisational processes both more effective and more tolerable. After all, its practitioners, like everyone else, can normally only work within the constraints of reality as it is, not as they might like it to be. Criticism may appear to be useful only to the extent that it aids the relationship between understanding and practical application. Ultimately this is true and we discuss some of the possibilities for organisational change in our concluding chapter. However, we have to recognise that part of the limitations of the behavioural sciences derives from the very fact of a practical, problem-centred orientation. To change realities we have to start from developing the necessary theoretical resources.

RESOURCES FOR A CRITICAL THEORY

The sciences of organisational behaviour have managed to produce better ways of manipulating the identities and behaviour of employees, but have not succeeded in addressing the problems that make such manipulation necessary. A redefinition of the traditional agenda of organisational psychology requires that individual, group and organisational behaviour be placed in a wider context, particularly the social relations of production. Specifically, this would account for subjective experience, while avoiding the over-utilisation of rational-cognitive explanations which focus on the individual determinants and constraints of purposive activity. Instead, we seek to maintain a focus on how subjectivity is constructed within social and organisational structures.

   Given these requirements and the limitations of existing perspectives, it is understandable that we have seen the development of a variety of critical social psychologies. This label covers a multiplicity of radical viewpoints which have utilised concepts from mainstream western social psychology, Marxist and humanist perspectives and Freudian theory. The attempts to formulate 'Marxist psychologies' (Schneider, 1975; Séve, 1978; Leonard, 1984; Hacker, Volpert and Von

Cranach, 1982) are of particular interest to us because the explanation of social behaviour is located specifically in an understanding of work organisations. It is certainly necessary to have an account of the material structures which shape our experiences and personalities. This does not claim that attitudes and behaviour can be 'read-off' from the material circumstances but the that individual is not constituted prior to them (Leonard, 1984: 25). This production of subjectivity and consciousness in the wider social world is also explored by Henriques *et al.* (1984) through an articulation with psychoanalysis and discourse theory which attempts to move beyond both individual and social determinisms.

Critical Social Psychologies

Social psychology has historically encompassed a wide variety of critical traditions differing mainly in their concerns for internal critique of methodology and content, as opposed to critique of the socio-cultural relations of the knowledge they produce (Wexler, 1983). From work such as that of Moscovici (1972), Gergen (1973) and Rosnow (1981), we gain a focus on the methodological limitations of social psychology and its lack of relevance to social issues. These are essentially calls for reform, which in their understanding of human social relations in terms of relatively fixed characteristics and roles follow the liberal tradition of social emancipation through individual transformation. Alternatively, we have the vein of critique characterised by Armistead (1974), Archibald (1978) and Larsen (1980), which focuses on examining radical alternatives within social psychology. Although not always consistent with each other, these critiques do maintain a perspective on the often repressive nature of socially organised relationships. Appealing to both humanist and Marxist theory they are concerned with social transformations leading towards human emancipation, and like the more conventional methodological critique they also appeal to internal procedural reform. Being essentially theoretical critiques, their focus is outside the specific contradictions of social existence, tending to enshrine critique as a principle in itself.

The tradition of the Frankfurt School, for example, in the work of Horkheimer, Adorno, Marcuse and latterly Habermas, examines the role of ideologies in the production of our knowledge of the social contexts in which we exist. This provides a self-reflexive critique of how social psychology operates both to uphold the current social order and to work against the possibility of a socially transforming discipline. The image produced is of an instrumentalised culture where psychology, in servicing and refining control procedures, acts to blind individuals to their capacities and lock them into dependence on commodity relations by presenting them as the inevitable 'natural order'. According to Van Strien (1982: 18), the conceptual framework developed by the Frankfurt School is of importance in moves towards an emancipatory social science as it 'puts science directly at the service of Man's consciousness of his own possibilities, interests and values'. Like critique based on radical alternatives though, it does have a tendency to be 'broadcast without a specific audience at the receiving end' (18), criticism again being elevated as an emancipatory practice in itself, without linking it to the everyday experience of those whom it was assumed to benefit.

Social Action

There is another critical perspective on offer, that of social action theory. In a manner which parallels our account of this theory in Chapter 1, we would argue that the stress is on the intersubjective nature of social behaviour as a form of negotiated order. The useful contribution of social action theories is in the methodological emphasis that they maintain in rooting their work in accounts of subjective experience and, secondly, in the linking of accounts of how subjectivity is constructed to accounts of structures of control, culture and ideology in organisations. The various conceptions of social action theory and the roles these play in maintaining critical alternatives to mainstream organisation theory is, as we said, discussed in Chapter 1. In relation to organisational psychology they represent that part of the domain of analysis characterised by subjective, partly rational action processes based on phenom-

enological, social constructionist models. They provide a link
to the ethnomethodological tradition in sociology and to
symbolic interactionism which has been influential in both
sociology and social psychology.

Symbolic interactionism following from Mead (1934) has
long been the area where an interface between sociological
and socio-psychological conceptions of identity has existed.
The construction of identity and the social milieu within
which individual identity exists is, in this model, dependent
on interaction with others and through others with the self.
Subjectivity, then, is mainly a product of *intersubjective*
processes and is constructed through the negotiation of social
rules and conventions. The social production of subjectivity,
though acknowledged, is addressed through an understanding
of how the formal and informal processes of culture and
ideology impinge upon individual functioning. This phenomenological emphasis on situated meaning in the construction
of subjectivity is a necessary methodological focus in providing a reflexive account of organisational behaviour, and
informs much of our account of the securing and reproduction
of identity in Chapter 9. What it lacks is the framework for
understanding the social order which conditions action inside
the organisation. Indeed, neither critical social psychologies
nor social action theories present consistent theories of either
subjectivity or its structural location. To expand on this theme
we turn to consider further the relations between Marxism
and psychology.

Marxism, Psychology and Beyond

Marxist understandings of subjectivity at work, whether
described as psychologies or not, begin with the concept of
alienation: the estrangement of creative capacities that means
that 'work is external to the worker, that it is not part of his
nature, and that, consequently, he does not fulfil himelf in his
work but denies himself' (Marx, 1963: 124–5). The reference
to a 'human nature' is not to an eternal set of values or
behaviours such as aggression or jealousy beloved of reactionary thinkers, but rather to certain characteristics which

distinguish man's species-being, such as the capacity for purposeful and reflective action.

Simply stated, what Marx meant when he talked of alienation was this: it is man's nature to be his own creator; he forms and develops himself by working on and transforming the world outside him in co-operation with his fellow men. In this progressive interchange between man and the world, it is man's nature to be in control of this process, to be the initiator, the subject in which the process originates. However, this nature has become alien to man (McLellan, 1973: 110).

Though referring to social life in general, this relation between man and nature is focused on the labour process, where man necessarily reproduces the conditions of existence. Labour epitomises the potential for creative and purposeful activity, as evidenced by Marx's comparison of the architect and the bee. What distinguishes the former from the latter is the necessity to raise the structure in the imagination before erecting it in reality. For some writers (Willmott, 1989) the concept of species-being is problematic because it gives the impression of a universal human essence, whereas the reality is that people value self-expression or exercise of skills simply because they have been constituted to do so. But the idea is not meant to be used in this sense. Marx made clear that human nature and needs were never independent of history or culture (Geras, 1983). Such criticism is better directed at perspectives such as the neo-human relations of Maslow. This does argue that man has a set of universal and unchanging set of needs, such as those for self-actualisation, which are largely unmet by existing work organisations, but which provide no account of the material structures which shape and constrain them.

Utilising a Marxist framework, we can grasp that alienation is given specific and concrete form by its location in the capitalist labour process. When the worker no longer owns or controls the products of labour, individual needs and capacities are subordinated to the requirements of capital accumulation, with the psychological consequence that the worker feels a stranger in his or her work. Alienated labour deepens with the further development of capitalism, as new forms of science, technology and management are used to incorporate skills and knowledge. This ties in with the analysis of Braverman

(1974), particularly the emphasis on the separation of conception and execution. Volpert, Hacker and other German organisational psychologists have produced some useful specific concepts in this area, particularly those of action regulation and the partialisation of action (Resch *et al.*, 1984). These integrate models of the cognitive structuring and regulation of work with the context-bound restriction of labour in fragmented and alienated activities. However, we should remember the qualifications made in Chapter 5. Management still need to engage the subjectivity and tacit skills of the workforce at some level to ensure profitable production, for example, through quality circles. But as a tendency running through management's structuring of work, it is a valuable point which confirms Marx's general analysis. Linked to the concept of alienation is that of *commodity fetishism*. The socially constructed relations between labour and capital embodied in the organisation of production and exchange are experienced as an alien power and as the natural order of things. This is then reinforced by the dominant ideologies which proclaim, for example, that the operation of the market is determined by laws of supply and demand that are beyond human planning and control.

The problem with constructing a critical psychology from Marxism, however, is that there are no adequate tools for understanding how alienated social relations are subjectively experienced and acted on by the individual. Marxism tends to deal with individuals only as bearers of economic categories such as labour and capital. This is alright at the structural level, for instance, when analysing changes in patterns of ownership and management (see Chapter 4), but is little use for any understanding of the individual subject.

In their analysis of the Insco case, Knights and Collinson recognise that Marxist and labour process literature tend to produce critiques of social structures and institutions which take as given the behavioural practices that reproduce our concerns with identity. Such structures are both consequences of and give rise to the behavioural routines through which we generate secure identities for ourselves. Without accounts of identity then, analysis of structures and the power relations and strategies through which they are maintained will always be incomplete. Moreover:

The absence of this social psychology from labour process theory means that it is unable to recognise how individuals such as the men and women in our case study, seek security either through controlling, and/or subordinating themselves to, others. (Collinson and Knights, 1986: 171)

The absence of such tools of analysis helps explain why Marxists have had a tendency to try a forced marriage with Freudianism in order to borrow ideas, such as that of the unconscious and the dynamic model of personality (Schneider: 1975; Deleuze and Guattari: 1977), which was for some an attempt to reconcile the irreconcilable (O'Neill: 1985). Furthermore, if individuals do not recognise their common class interests within these categories, they are deemed to be suffering false consciousness. This concept denies the validity of what people think or feel merely because it does not correspond to a set of imputed interests.

The only modes of reaction allowed are *habituation* to the demands of capitalist production or to collectively *resist* and seek to transform society (Leonard, 1984: 164, 206). While we do not doubt either the existence or desirability of various forms of worker resistance, there are a far greater number of responses to alienated work. As Willmott (1989) observes, wage labour does not always destroy or deny the subjectivity of employees. The worker has an identity as labour and, indeed, other identities such as gender and ethnicity. He or she may become attached to and seek to develop the valued aspects, such as the skilled image of the craft worker or the service to the community of the nurse. These processes are not unambiguously positive. Attachment to routines can diminish creative capacities. A popular story at Ford Halewood was of the man who left Ford to work at a sweet factory where he had to divide up the reds and blues, but left because he couldn't stand the decision-making (Beynon, 1975: 109). Identity projects can also be dominated by anxieties and constrained within the range of known possibilities, such as the aggressive salesman or feminine secretary. The search for a secure identity or sense of solid self can be self-defeating, either because the individual occupies a range of positions which pull identity in different directions (Henriques *et al.*, 1984), or because the identity, like commodities, becomes fetishised (Willmott, 1989), treated as a thing to which there is no alternative. This may lead individuals to a self-defeating project of continual reinvestment in the search for security, which in turn reproduces the very institutions which constrained their experiences in the first place.

CONCLUSION

The problems of developing the perspectives outlined in the preceding sections are obviously of daunting theoretical and practical complexity. In Chapter 7 we charted the often contradictory mainstream psychological theories contributing to OB, but characterised them as inputs to common, basic processes. Furthermore, we endorse Van Strien's argument that to develop emancipatory projects, mainstream social science can be 'ransacked for their practical experience and theories of practice' (1982: 24). The methodological, ideological and theoretical inputs from critical sources are often equally diverse and contradictory. But we have tried to tie together some of the common themes through situating the concept of identity within structures of organisational domination and exploitation.

In using the concept of identity as a linking concept, we are in no way claiming that it is the complete answer to understanding issues connected to the subjective factor; rather, that it is one means of taking our understanding further. Nor do we claim that it is possible at this stage to use identity or any other means to produce an integrated critical social psychology. Unfortunately, in redefining the agenda there is no new and improved magical ingredient which will wash away all the contradictions between these perspectives and provide us with a realistic, emancipatory paradigm to proceed with. What we aim to do is use the discussion of identity and subjectivity to address issues that arise in and across mainstream and critical theories and research, reassessing and integrating material within some consistent focus. The approach taken, though focusing mainly on the experiential level, is, we believe, compatible with the structural framework deriving from the perspectives informed by labour process and Weberian concepts in Part One. Chapter 9 furthers this process by focusing on the dialectic between the shaping of identities and the forms of resistance and coping which arise out of that domination.

9

Identity Work

If our society is characterised by the involvement of individuals in organisational structures, then organisations are characterised by their attempts to *control the performance and behaviour* of the individuals they consist of. It is this rule-bound control of individual behaviour which distinguishes organisational behaviour from other forms of social organisation. Home and family life, for example, are undoubtedly organised, and controls and sanctions are placed on the behaviour of family members. But this control is in no sense as systematic as that existing in even a small commercial organisation. On this basis, for work organisations of any type to maintain their present forms of authority, hierarchy and control it becomes necessary to produce some kind of change in the types of regulation employees will consent to. There is, of course, a great amount of prior socialisation for work contained in our experience of schooling, and this is presently being extended in the kinds of job training discussed in Chapter 3 to better 'fit' youth for work. This, however, merely serves to illustrate that organisations depend on being able to mould people into the kind of workers they need.

Organisations do not simply transform individual identities at work by some form of brainwashing. Neither do they simply depend on the individual's recognition of economic necessity to ensure their consent to the control of their performance in their work. The concept of 'economic man' is not adequate to the explanation of how a worker's consent to change and rationalise their working practices can be obtained. It is simply not enough to explain the range of variations in the

314

motivation and performance of, and the amount of super-vision necessary over, different individuals. In order to gain a person's consent within a hierarchical control structure it is in the end necessary to have at least some tacit form of collabora-tion from them. Attempting to transform the perception and conception by individuals of their social and work-related identities into forms which will not conflict with, and will hopefully reinforce organisational control is a major strategic element in obtaining such collaboration.

The rules and procedures used to control work-related behaviour will often conflict with the individual's attempt to secure a stable and favourable identity, unless, that is, the person can manage to construct for themselves a workable identity out of the very rules which constrain them. Alterna-tives can include becoming an 'organisation man', setting themselves up in opposition to their emloyers, or distancing themselves from the whole affair and concentrating their lives on external interests. Whatever the tactics emloyed by in-dividuals as mechanisms for survival and coping, they may in time transform themselves into an image which functions in a way that is useful to the organisation they work for. Even the deviant or militant worker is useful in this sense in terms of providing an image of what the 'good' employee should not be, and in providing a focus for the attribution of blame.

Identity becomes not only the basis of individual involve-ment in organisations but also the basis for manipulation by them. This is achieved through a negotiated transaction between organisational strategies of control and individual strategies for securing identity. The consequences of this negotiation are not always positive for the organisations concerned. We all to some extent cope in a creative fashion with the constraints of work or unemployment. Strategies used to survive can become powerful tools for extending our own abilities and capacities. Those who try and manipulate our behaviour must face the fact that they are attempting to interfere with the self-perceptions and judgements that actually make us what we are. If manipulation is perceived as going too far, it may do no more than encourage employee identities more resistant to organisational control.

Identity work and situational power

Subjective experience in organisations consists of lived relationships bounded by social, organisational and workgroup cultures in the context of structural and ideological constraints. These form the three basic contexts within which individual identity is continually reproduced. Lived relationships are the subjective arena of identity construction. Even though our subjective 'now' is informed by our past experience and moulded by the pressures brought to bear on us, we still act as if we are independent and self-directed entities. Thus our everyday existence can continue as if it largely bypasses the influence of cultural and structural constraints on our behaviour.

Social, organisational and workgroup cultures are the arenas in which 'fitting behaviour' is moulded and regulated and in which we perform 'identity work' (Cohen and Taylor, 1978). Just as our perceptions of the world are simplified by the use of stereotypical categories, the activities we carry out in the workplace are simplified by the use of stereotyped categories of behaviour. This process of constructing and enacting scripts we shall refer to as *'scenariotyping'* (the term was accidentally coined at Lancashire Polytechnic as a mistyping on an exam paper). These various cultural contexts also represent the medium of communication and *translation* of structural contexts to everyday existence. These are the limiting factors on identity construction in work and social life. They act to define possible sources of meaning and activity in hierarchical organisations and also provide the contextual limitations on what is acceptable practice for those who study, design and intervene in organisations.

Individual and group concerns with job security, status, promotion, conflict and satisfaction can be characterised under a number of related categories. Included are the prediction and control of reality, coping with uncertainty, retaining autonomy and discretion, and maintaining or enhancing individual assessments of situational power. For the individual these represent the tensions created by trying to maintain and monitor the *strategies* through which we enact behaviours. A secure identity, or at least an identity which is not too severely threatened, forms both a bulwark against threats and provides personal standards for social comparison and action. The ability to control the various categories of individual and group concerns can also represent sources and reflections of organisational or situational power. The strategies utilised by individuals and groups to secure or appropriate identity will seek to control sources of power and meaning. As a consequence, identity construction may threaten the organisation of work (Weigert, 1986; Knights and Willmott, 1985; Breakwell, 1987).

Organisations, in trying to reduce uncertainty, are willing to allow room for the maintenance of worker identities in so far as they make the control of behaviour and production processes more effective. In implementing the introduction of CNC machine tools, firms such as Westland Helicopters have allowed an element of manual input from operators on the basis that human intervention is necessary in automated processes because they are not absolutely error-free (Corbett, 1985). Such decisions allow operators to exert some levels of skill and discretion within labour processes with increasing tendencies towards deskilling. Thus, alongside gains in the reduction of uncertainty in the production process there may also be benefits to the organisation in reducing the level of threat to skilled identities implied by automation.

The greater the effort put into attempts to define employees' work life, the greater the use of undefined areas by workers to develop 'informal workgroup cultures'. Cultures of this type can provide workers with a degree of autonomy and a basis for active resistance. By the same token, membership of sub-cultural groups in organisations may provide the benefits to threatened identities which they do for sub-cultures in wider society; 'the threatened can regain self-esteem, generate positive distinctiveness and promote continuity' (Breakwell, 1986: 141). Although Breakwell argues that societal sub-cultures have virtually no impact on power structures, they are, she maintains, the focus of possible social concerns and the associated 'moral panics' (Cohen, 1973) which identify them as being 'scheduled for control'.

This is not to say, of course, that managers never recognise this tendency and take steps to short-circuit the development of informal groups which may in time, become hostile to organisational goals. Drago and McDonough (1984: 67) quote a management planning document from the General Foods Topeka plant where they were initiating a controlled participation experiment: 'No power groups will exist within the organisation that create an anti-management posture'.

In trying to predict and control reality, for most of us it is our subjective concepts and values that are most amenable to change as we cannot on our own hope to change the structural framework which surrounds us in the organisations we work within. Even for those with the power to change the form of, and processes within, organisations there is still no absolute security of position or certainty that their actions will produce results fully in line with their goals. Thus, in coping with the uncertainties of organisational life, most individuals are forced either into a strategy of *accommodation* which necessitates a gradual redefinition of self and subjective reality, or a strategy of *assimilation* which requires these to be subjected to the superordinate goals of the group.

PUTTING THE PRESSURE ON

All people working in organisations face pressures to mould their identities to fit normative expectations. Although these expectations originate within the goals, strategies or policies of the various individuals and groups in an organisation, in subjective terms they can also appear to originate in the organisation itself. In the OB literature, expectations are mainly dealt with through the notion of *role*; the roles we wish to play ourselves, the roles others wish or expect us to play and the roles demanded of us from our relations with work organisations. The total number of *role expectations* which impinge on any individual is referred to as a *role-set* and can comprise of contradictory demands from workmates, supervisors, management, customers or clients and from home or social life. The role expectations are not separate and neutral consequences of status, position or skill. Rather, they are *specific* and interdependent products of a social organisation of work which depends for effective production on the internalisation of role demands. The divisions of labour which result in fragmented work are likewise dependent on *role specialisation* being perceived as a natural social order.

Role Control

Salaman (1979: 133–6) raises the possibility that variations in role discretion and role expectations may be linked to strategic decisions on the forms of control exercised over different categories of workers. Professional employees face contradictory expectations arising from their peers, their external professional associations and from the organisation itself. These have to be handled by the individual and managed by the organisation. Direct control by managers over professionals, involving rule-bound job definitions and tightly regulated behaviour, may conflict with the latter's values and socialisation. A more effective form of control can be achieved through a focus on their role as a professional, performing their organisational duties to the satisfaction and benefit of their masters or clients.

In contrast to the forms of control appropriate to professionals, 'Role type control is less commonly employed with workers because senior members of organisations (and, possibly, the workers themselves) see the workers as being in conflict with the goals and reward system of the enterprise' (Salaman, 1980: 136). The moulding of workers' attitudes and behaviour can be identified with 'adjusting one's perspectives on what one will be able to achieve' (Frese, 1982: 210). Since such 'adjustments' necessitate at least some internalisation and legitimation of structures of regulation, it may be expected that role-type control would be possible at most levels of organisations. But, of course, not everyone in an organisation 'knows their place' or is resigned to powerlessness and helplessness. The informal socialisation of workers, or 'learning the ropes', will consist largely of learning the shortcuts around and resistance to, organisational controls. Such knowledge and its associated activities confer at least some small sense of personal autonomy, meaning and hence identity to workers. Consequently, direct controls, combined with

elements of technical and bureaucratic control where possible
or appropriate, are more often employed by managment at
lower levels of organisations.

Socialisation within work is not necessarily directed at the
technical aspects for other grades. When examining the
socialisation of skilled manual workers into their workplace
identities, Penn argues that such socialisation is more directed
at 'instruction into the appropriate actions of the trade' (1986:
4). Such instruction and the identities it produces are aimed at
generating scripts for interaction in the workplace. They deal
with 'Norms and procedures held to be appropriate for
dealing with three groupings found in the workplace: fellow
workers, other workers and management' (1986: 4).

This process builds on *anticipatory socialisation* into work in
the home and at school, in that apprentices require a commitment to deferred gratification and continued learning after the
end of formal schooling. Hence there is a form of pre-selection
for skilled manual work, in that those who have previously
internalised appropriate forms of meaning are preferred: 'a
certain degree of seriousness and moral uprightness is required by a sponsor who already works in a firm' (1986: 4). In
contrast, 'tearaways' who define their identities as inimical to
authority and those who seek immediate extrinsic gratification
in work are not wanted (Willis, 1987). Organisations, then,
try to get the right kind of material to mould into the images
they require.

The types of assessment techniques utilised in recruitment
and selection procedures also reflect differential concerns, this
time with the personality dimension of identity. The study by
Holloway (1984), cited in the section on personality in
Chapter 7, shows that the assessment of managers, and hence
the forms of control used over them, are related to the 'fit' of
their personalities into dominant organisational cultures.
When reviewing organisational recruitment procedures in the
British Army and Ford UK, Salaman (1979) also notes that
this 'fit' is shown by the candidates' willingness to demonstrate an 'appropriate' range of attitudes.

In this sense, roles are scenariotyped scripts which are
themselves as essential to the labour process as the working
practices, labour and machinery through which they are

played out. Attempts to increase worker 'participation' can thus be seen not only as efforts to place individual goals more in line with organisational goals, but as attempts to produce role-based control of workers. The aim is to produce workers who will themselves initiate the enactment of the correct scripts, rather than having to be directed to do so. This produces savings for the organisation in terms of the amounts of direct supervision necessary and, of course, in terms of the number of supervisors needed. There is currently a parallel emphasis on the operational skills 'content' seen as necessary to make management education more responsive to the 'needs' of business. The management trainee is assumed to have the necessary role commitment and motivation to consent to organisational control structures. Thus 'education' becomes a process of exposing the trainee to the 'skills', techniques and attitudes which will be required of them and then teaching them how to recognise the appropriate contingencies in which particular scripts should be enacted.

Role Stress

The psychological pressures on individuals have been well-documented, not in terms of pressures to mould identity but in terms of the *intrapsychic* conflicts they can produce. Interpersonal conflicts and conflicts between role expectations are seen as causative factors in producing anxiety and stress. *Role conflicts* between differing expectations from the various parts of a person's role-set (those that play a part in determining an individual's intra- and extra-organisational roles) are inevitable with the level of pressure that most of us are exposed to in or out of work. A person cannot always fulfil the demands of all their roles. Role conflicts can also exist between external role demands and personal values and beliefs, or between a person's gender, ethnic or skilled identity and their treatment by other workers or by management.

An example of the conflicts which fulfilling a role may induce is seen in Hochschild's (1983) notion of *emotional labour*. This occurs in occupations where individuals have to manage their emotions in order to serve the commercial purposes of the enterprise. Using flight attendants and debt-collectors, she shows how people are constrained to maintain emotions in their work – friendliness for the stewardness, suspension of trust and sympathy for the debt-collector – which relate only to the requirements of the job. This requirement extends beyond individuals and includes collective emotional labour:

> It is not simply individuals who manage their feelings in order to do a job; whole organisations have entered the game. The emotion management that keeps the smile on Delta Airlines competes with the emotion management that keeps the same smile on United and TWA. (Hochschild, 1983: 185–6)

In such situations, where management attempts to mould the social identities of individuals and groups into images consonant with commercial demands, people often become estranged from their own feelings. As an interdependent process, emotional labour requires both the collaboration of the client and the adjustment of personal feelings to accommodate the client's demands. For the emotional labourer, identification with the job itself can lead to difficulties in making constant adjustments to situations. Considerable socio-emotional costs may be incurred, which will be further examined later in this chapter.

Many people may experience *role ambiguity*, where the demands of a role or roles are unclear and norms and standards of social comparison are lacking. In addition, such pressures may originate in role overload or unload, where the demands of a role are greater or lesser than expected. The problem with role-based stress as an explanatory concept is that it has the effect of portraying the process as natural and individually based, instead of a product of the historically produced conditions of work. In his study of responses to the pressure of work in 'Powerco', Sturdy (1987) notes that management are aware of the negative effects that such pressures have on employee morale and yet would not want completely to remove backlogs of work since it would portray their sections as overstaffed and on occasion leave people with little or nothing to do!

The anxieties and pressures of work at Powerco led to the practice of 'shifting' in the employees, where people, even in conditions where motivation and commitment might not be expected, indulged in 'unceasing effort beyond what would be expected from even the most committed worker' (1987: 35). Their compulsion to keep ahead of the work and not let backlogs build up, to relieve pressure by getting work 'shifted', extended to refusing breaks and feeling frustrated rather than relieved when interruptions such as computer breakdowns stopped the work. Though partially based in the desire to increase security in work, shifting, according to Sturdy, acts for the individual not only as a relief for the helplessness they feel but as a mechanism which obscures the experience of subordination itself. By using shifting to cope with the pressure of work, the individual co-operates with the structures of workplace control to produce a sense of identity which offers some level of autonomy and responsibility. At the same time, shifting paradoxically increases the pressures employees feel as both management and themselves come to depend on the gains stemming from their increased productivity. Identities can, then, be reactively moulded as a response to situational stress factors and in directions which reproduce the experience of subordination and domination in work.

Situational stress factors are in general less directly identifiable as consequences of the organisation of work than are environmental stress factors (e.g. noise, chemicals or working with VDUs). This is precisely because they are attributed to an individual's incapacity to cope with the demands of work. The work of nurses and social workers provides a good example of organisations exploiting a person's ability to cope with untenable situations to the limit, and only becoming concerned when the rate of turnover or lack of efficiency of skilled staff becomes difficult to manage. As with emotional labour, work in the 'caring' professions requires that people identify closely with their work and that they exercise self-control over their role-based work. The responses people make when they cannot take the demands that their work places on them are examined in the section on individual responses to pressures on identity.

Stress Control?

Estimates vary on the cost of stress-related illness to industry, but figures in excess of 40 million lost working days (Lucas: 1986) have led to an increasing concern with organisational programmes to help individuals cope with work-related stress, as well as conflicts between work and home life. Examples of these 'wellness' programmes include Pepsico's multi-million dollar 'fitness' centre, and the stress management programmes developed by the Trustee Savings Bank and Digital Equipment in the UK (Cooper, 1984). The 'Staywell' programme and Employee Advisory Resource of the Control Data Corporation in the USA offers 24-hour advice on assessing health risks, medical screening and health education to help people change life and work styles in healthy directions (Lucas, 1986; McKenna, 1987). 'Companies have a major stake in promoting a healthier life-style for employees, because of the potential benefits in reduced insurance costs, decreased absenteeism, improved productivity and better morale' (McKenna, 1987: 403).

The role of the organisation in producing unhealthy systems and conditions of work is in danger of being ignored. In its place we get systems reinforcing the *self-attribution* of stress and anxiety as personal problems to be coped with rather than structural issues to be contested. There is nothing new here of course. Baritz's interpretation of the Hawthorne research points out that the outcomes of the research on employee counselling led some to the conclusion that 'workers did not have compelling objective problems' (1960: 201). The rationale for this, according to a counsellor cited by Baritz, was that their grievances could be dealt with by allowing them to 'talk them out':

It may not be even necessary to take any action on them. All that they require is a patient and courteous hearing, supplemented when necessary, by an explanation of why nothing can be done. ... It is not always necessary to yield to the worker's requests in order to satisfy them (201).

In respect of corporate responses to the 'problem' of stress the 'talking out' of employee problems has by now become big business in itself!

In order for such programmes to succeed they have to change both attitudes and cultural factors in the workplace and become part of managerial strategies for moulding the identities of workers. The Control Data Corporation places great emphasis on group sessions where 'eventually group members learn to help one another to sustain the changes in their behaviour, and they practice various techniques and strategies to avoid failure' (McKenna, 1987: 402). The feeling that a person can cope with adverse situations can both be a source of meaning and danger to them in, for example, working in difficult and dangerous occupations such as construction or agricultural work. The result would be to divorce a person's view of their working conditions from their desire for personal safety to the extent that they take unncessary risks or adhere to dangerous practices.

Managerial work was one of the first areas to be associated with the negative effects of stress, especially through personality traits linked with supposedly high rates of coronary heart disease (Rosenman *et al.*, 1964). These are associated with people with high levels of personal investment in their work, as is expected to be the case with those in managerial grades. Although it has since been established that stress-related illness is more likely to vary inversely rather than positively with organisational status, position and job-related skills (Cooper, 1985), there is still a great concern with managerial stress and its possible effects on organisational effectiveness. The ability to deal with and to some extent actually relish a high-pressure working environment is seen as a valued characteristic in managers. The person who is able to cope with the conflicting demands of a managerial position is encouraged to view this capacity as a personality trait which indicates their suitability as a leader. Through such a process it is no surprise that organisational élites come to view themselves as those most 'fit' to lead and survive in the given environment.

Such legitimations, though active in the securing of managerial identities, are not necessarily part of any conscious conspiracy of control or domination. They may simply be the habitual response with which managers have learned to cope with various situations where their identities are threatened.

Domination and control would thus be outcomes of the scripts managers use in their daily activities, these outcomes requiring some level of self-justification from managers, which ideologies can supply.

It does appear that material on the moulding of identities in organisations tends to focus on professional, skilled and managerial workers. However, such concepts as emotional labour and the utility of 'wellness programmes' would indicate that organisations may routinely attempt to mould the identities of all levels of employees. Aichholzer and Schienstock (1985) examine opportunities for maintaining identities in the face of the intensification of control surrounding the introduction of new technologies. Such intensification is seen in 'tighter binding of human actions with machine processes, an increasing transparency of the labour process as a whole, a rising vertical integration and extension of technological control to white collar work' (1985: 20). They also note a number of apparent 'counter-tendencies' to increased control. These include the reintegration of fragmented work roles, the revaluing of 'marginal' human functions in work and an emphasis on problem-solving activities. Aichholzer and Schienstock argue that these counter-tendencies in effect pressurise workers to internalise controls in order to soften the new problems of control raised by new forms of technology and work organisation, and that this questions the 'maintenance of individual and collective identities in the modern labour process' (1985: 81).

It is, however, possible to identify aspects of the analysis of the shaping of work around technologies which do offer redefinition of psychological pressures and stresses in directions that integrate notions of psychological well-being and growth into the design of work. In particular, the identification of dimensions (see Figure 9.1) through which the degree of flexibility and discretion available to employees can be analysed offers insights into how workers can have inputs to the process of shaping their work-related behaviour, objectives and environment (Rauner *et al.*, 1988: 55–7).

● *Time structure*; time pressures imposed and possibility of individual or group planning use of time themselves.

Figure 9.1 The interrelation of dimensions of experiencing and shaping of work

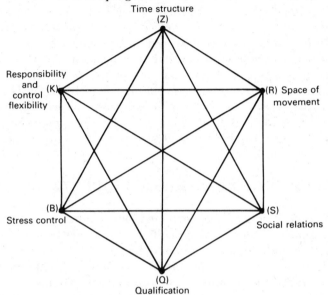

Source: F. Rauner, R. Rasmussen and J. M. Corbett, 'The Social Shaping of Technology and Work: Human Centred CIM Systems', *Artificial Intelligence and Society*, vol. 2 (1980), p. 56.

- *Space for movement*; degree of formalisation versus choice governing movement of workers within and between job functions.
- *Social relations*; degree of formalisation versus informal possibilities in workplace interactions and organisational communications.
- *Responsibility and control flexibility*; scope and degree of responsibility available to workers and possibilities for self-management and control.
- *Qualification*; range of functional abilities related to task and work processes, and possibilities of learning and personality development.
- *Stress control*; degree of control over physical and psychological pressures resulting from work organisation and human-machine interactions.

All six dimensions are to be viewed through their relations to the others. This allows analysis of, in the first instance, the extent to which a labour process permits 'humane' work and, in the second, of the dimensions along which increased flexibility and discretion would most benefit psychological well-being. These six interrelated dimensions should enable both more precise determinations of the restrictiveness inherent in a labour process and a focus which emphasises the necessity of designs that enable subjective as well as operational flexibility, thus allowing room for the constructive use of subjective variables in analysing individual experience.

RESPONSES TO PRESSURES ON IDENTITY

The production of scenariotyped behaviours and the ideological formulations which justify them enables people, collectively or individually, to enact their own situational power and resist controls. This does not, however, explain why individuals and groups try to resist organisational controls. Resistance is in itself both a *source* of meaning and a *pressure* on identity. This is founded on the perception by individuals of contradictions between the goals, ideologies, approved identities and required behaviours which are exhibited in organisational settings. Leonard (1984: 116–18) identifies four sources of pressures leading to resistance, avoidance and dissent, which provide a useful framework for discussion and reaction.

● *Contradictory consciousness*; This arises from competing ideologies based on the material interests of groups and classes. Because dominant ideologies partly clash with people's actual experiences of everyday life, they can never have more than an imperfect influence on identities. Leonard cites class, gender and ethnic struggles as examples of the conflicts which produce psychological disturbances in individuals and can produce acts of deviance, while at the same time still result in a general submission to the demands of the dominant order. These acts of deviance may be directed towards material gains, individual protest or to fulfil particular values not acceptable to the social order. There may be important consequences for organisations in the form of theft, industrial sabotage or other 'destructive' actions.

● *Unconscious resistance*; Lenoard represents this partly in Freudian terms as the struggle of id against ego and superego. The individual attempts not to repress or bury those impulses which 'are unacceptable or inconvenient to dominant social forces' (1984: 117). However, impulses to act against the social order may be renounced and buried in the unconscious because the obstacles to action are too great or perceived situational power is too little. Anxiety and frustration are the likely results of everyday unconscious resistance, though at its extreme, internal conflicts could result in forms of mental disorder. Leonard identifies tendencies to neurotic and psychotic illness with social class position. In organisational terms, neurotic reactions could be characterised as consistent with the frustrations caused by conflicts around the role-based control and supervisory responsibilities of professional and managerial classes. Psychotic reactions, characterised as escapes into alternative realities, are associated with the 'working classes'. In a parallel concept, the Hungarian psychologist, Laszlo Garai (see Eros, 1974), refers to individuals having recourse to 'fictive satisfactions' when the specifically human 'need' for self-realisation and non-alienated activity is blocked. These can take the form of destructive impulses, cynicism or the ritual affirmation of helplessness, all of which are likely to be perceived as unmotivated or individually deviant.

● *The development of individual capacities*; This arises from the attempt to avoid the dehumanising effects of alienated labour. It may lead to the development of personal activities either within work or outside it, which are directed at benefits for the individual rather than the organisation. Outside work they may develop artistic, literary, craft or sporting skills which 're-humanise' their lives, making active and identity-enhancing use of their time rather than merely recuperating from work. Within the workplace, people can develop capacities from the exploration and development of their skills which extends beyond what is demanded by wage labour. Wilkinson (1983b) provides an example of CNC machine tool operators, some of whom effectively redefined the technology which had deskilled them and brought some interest back into their work by teaching themselves to programme the computers and to edit computer tapes.

However, just as in the world of fashion or popular music, where people's creative and autonomous control over their own image and expression are eventually incorporated into commercial products, the smart company will incorporate the efforts of individuals to indulge in non-alienated activity into the organisation of the labour process. In the world of the work organisation the 'revolt into style' may be transformed into the instrumental rewards of the suggestion box.

● *Participation in collective action;* This 'contains contradictions between hope and despair, optimism and depression, depending on the balance of political forces at any given time' (Leonard: 118). Capacities are further developed through joining informal coalitions to pursue some more or less specified goal, or becoming formally involved in unions, professional and other associations. The immediate benefit is in an enhancement of situational power through collective strength. Leonard sees benefits in collective resistance, in that it counters individualistic impulses and moves towards altruistic activity which attempts to transform social relations into forms beneficial to the individual and group. It also raises consciousness about forms of change that are available, associated with a redefinition of self that can counter subordination.

These forms are neither exhaustive, nor mutually exclusive. Nor does it necessarily follow that resistance is inevitable, even though it may be structured into the forms and processes of organisations. Where there are no overt conflicts, it is possibly easier for individuals to accept managerial definitions of reality, to become 'organisation people' and to gain meaning from their appointed role. For the purpose of clarity our further examination of responses to pressures and threats to identity is divided into responses at individual and group levels. It must be remembered, however, that these responses are interdependent processes which can be conceptually separated but are all part of the cycle of organisational control and resistance.

Individual Responses

In securing and maintaining a stable and meaningful identity an individual is faced with the difficulty of presenting consistent images to the other people they must deal with. The pressure engendered by the necessity to perform both organisational and interpersonally derived roles involves a continuous process of identity management to maintain situational fit or appropriateness. As long as this does not threaten core identity, people can follow the scripts they learn from others in order to fulfil their various role expectations. When threat does arise they are left with the choice to submit or resist. Both involve possibly substantial redefinitions of the identities they have secured.

The management of identities has been explored in work such as that of Goffman (1971) on *impression management*. The individual, like an actor on stage, attempts to maintain a consistent and believable performance for their audience, those who have a significant influence over the role they play. When used in this sense, identity is malleable and instrumentally defined. However active and manipulative such identities are, they are still dependent on the collaboration of others not to interfere with the performance. We know that the performance of an actor is not real. But according to Goffman we exercise 'tact' to allow the performance to proceed, as in the case of a management 'pep-talk' (see Chapter 7).

The management of impressions is one example of the process of identity work referred to earlier. But such performances may break down in the context of threats and constraints in the work environment, and we may be forced to respond with impressions and performances which are 'out of character' for the expected role. Similarly, individuals may experience difficulty in coping with situations where our projected images are not adequate to achieving some measure of control or meaning. For example, Hochschild in examining the supervision of emotional labour cites the reaction of a flight attendant whose paycheck had been mishandled, 'I can't take this all day and then come back here and take it from you! You know I get paid to take it from the passengers, but I don't get paid to take it from you' (1983: 18).

The scenariotyped behaviour demanded of those Hochschild examines can, like those demanded of people in the caring professions, conflict with the levels of commitment involved in their work. Such constrained responses can have serious consequences for mental health and social relationships. In order to respond to conflicts between commitment and capacity to act, people may *burnout*. Storlie (1979) argues that this occurs where the individual confronts an intractable reality which cannot be changed, so that the only effective response is to change themselves; the end result being that they continue to 'go through the motions' but remove any emotional or identity investment they had in their work. This acts as a defence mechanism against the stresses that may result from the conflicts between their own tendencies and their role demands. Emotional labour can thus lead the individual into a removal of emotion, labour being reduced to mere activity. This could have some benefits to the employer, but for the employee such numbing of emotional response leads to a loss of a central source of meaning for them.

The identity work we perform depends a great deal on our ability to utilise and manage the scripts available to us. Conversely, we need to break free of the habituated scripts we use to '*make out*' when the conditions under which we employ them become untenable. Opportunities to secure new or enhanced meanings, symbols, capacities and goods are as much pressures on our identities as they are threats to them. The types of opportunity we will respond to will depend upon the current identities and strategies we employ, our perceived power and ability to take them and our expectations concerning what benefits we can hope to obtain. Breaking free from established patterns of identity work can therefore be difficult, as Sloan's (1987) study of sales work illustrates. The salesmen had invested a great deal in a conception of professional identity which could legitimate the arduous work and their manipulative relations with customers. Professionals did not need unions. There was also a gendered dimension whereby masculinity was central to the identity; 'A little alcohol and a lot of imagination reproduced a culture in which reps were not only professional salesmen, but were also professional lovers' (31); the 'heroic' males of Insco are apparently not alone!.

All of the above are responses to the identity concerns of individuals. It is difficult to locate them in a framework which is solely based on different categories of resistance or dissent. The relatively unconscious coping strategies identified by Roy (see Chapter 7) can be seen as responses to identity concerns, but are essentially strategies of accommodation rather than resistance. Typical forms of individual response to pressure contain a combination of coping strategies, instrumentally derived tactics and accommodation to the dominant culture, as well as different types of resistance. As far as the individual is concerned they are making out in the best fashion possible in the given circumstances, the form of response being determined in subjective terms by what appears to work. As long as there are available scripts which satisfy goals and identity concerns, there are no real bars to an individual fitting in to whatever forms of work and survival they have access to.

Such strategies or responses could in one sense be said never entirely to fail. With the capacity to redefine meanings and manage impressions, human beings are capable of creating their own self-fulfilling prophecies, shifting the ground on which they stand to justify both success and failure. We do not only manage the impressions we give to others but those we produce of ourselves. Central to this are self-attributed judgements which justify our actions in terms of our current identity concerns and environmental influences.

In counterpoint to strategies which lead to extremely negative consequences for the individual, there are forms of making out which can lead more unambiguously to social recognition, approval and self-justified identities. Recognition as a leader in an organisation is one such form. Pressure to define identity in line with the assumed leadership qualities would in turn lead to behaviours and self-perceptions supportive in subjective terms. The failure of others to recognise an individual as a leader, or attempts to undermine their leadership, might lead to perceived contradictions with their self-justified role. These could be handled by more autocratic attempts at control, justified by attributions of deviant characteristics to those causing the disturbance. Conversely, if strategies to cope with the situation fail and put the identity of the ostensible leader at risk, they could distance themselves from the role on the basis that dealing with such people was impossible or not worth the effort.

The section on organisational responses to and uses of pressures on identities will return to this notion in examining the role of leadership in mobilising consent.

The strategies suggested in the example above are two of those that Knights and Willmott (1985) identify as being used by individuals to secure identities and reduce anxiety. These are described as *domination* and *distancing*. In organisations a strategy of domination would involve those with power over the distribution and possession of scarce resources using it to give themselves the illusion of independence and security. It is partially an illusion because such reliance acts to obscure the interdependence of social relations. Managers or others can then ignore the fact that their power is dependent on the *compliance* of their subordinates.

Compliance in this sense is related to Rotter's (1972) notion of internal and external *loci of control*. People who feel that they are externally controlled may also put themselves into a state of '*learned helplessness*' where the tendency to comply becomes part of the way the individual defines themselves (Seligman: 1975). To subordinates, however, compliance may simply be their way of making out and avoiding 'identity damaging disciplinary controls' (Knights and Willmott, 1985: 25). Strategies which employ the 'cynical distancing of self from the activities and social relations within which individuals are immediately involved' (27) reinforce individualism and subordination.

Distancing is also one of the main forms of identity work identified by Cohen and Taylor (1978). Unlike Knights and Willmott, their focus is not on power and interdependence but rather on 'escape attempts' from, or resistance to the mundanity and unpleasantness of, everyday life; in other words, on subjectively making out. However, the strategies they see as employed in identity work can still have relevance to the understanding of how making out is incorporated into the social relations of production. Cohen and Taylor start out at the level of the 'regularities which we happily accept as part of life' (1978: 26). These regularities are not necessarily tedious behavioural repetition but are scripts to which we *unreflexively accommodate* as a method of managing the 'paramount reality' of our objective world. Scripts in this sense are more than the 'mindless' behaviour posited by Langer or the 'sensorimotor' activity posited by Hacker and Volpert (see Chapter 7).

The habitual dependence on scripts referred to by Cohen and Taylor can be a defence against uncertainty and provide meaning through their very regularity. However, our capacity for self-reflection allows us to create a 'zone for self' or *'identity domain'* (1978: 32) which enables us to distance ourselves from those who appear to be committed to the scripts which they live by. The capacity to be self-reflexive can effectively remove the need to actually *do* anything about the conditions of our existence because we critically separate ourselves from them in our thoughts. At the same time we often deprecate those we see as not having our own level of critical self-aware-ness, defining them as something less than ourselves. The paradox here is the likelihood that our fellow workers are having the same thoughts as and about ourselves. But they do not see our thoughts, only our still-regulated actions.

A concomitant capacity which self-reflexiveness endows us with is the release of the *escape into fantasy* where we can alter the conditions of our life to our own satisfaction. This form of escape is akin to the strategy of unconscious resistance identified by Leonard. Leonard's identification of these escapes with position in the organisational hierarchy can now be understood, in that fantasy is free.

Cohen and Taylor also note socially institutionalised routes of escape which are seen as legitimate self-expression, and where 'assertions of meaninglessness of the activity are vir-tually taboo' (1978: 95). These *activity enclaves* give us free areas in our lives where, in the terminology of Séve and Leonard, we can develop 'personal concrete capacities'. Such socially approved escapes from work or the lack of it include hobbies, games, sports, holidays and the attractions of mass culture.

On the other hand, there are less socially approved activity enclaves which resemble more Garai's fictive satisfactions, in that they are often socially viewed as self-obsessive or destructive. 'Preoccupations' with sex, gambling, drugs and even dependence on therapy are examples of this form of escape. They are, however, only different from other forms in terms of the social, legal and historical contexts they are carried out in. Again, self-reflexiveness carries its own internal contradictions. Distancing ourselves from the roles we play is, in the end, another limited and passive strategy which tends to confirm existing organisational structures and separates the individual from the possibilities inherent in social relations.

Finally, to escape from this vicious spiral of making out through reconstruction of identity concerns, Cohen and Taylor identify the strategy of *self-conscious reinvestment*. The individual becomes recommitted to aspects of the very regularities – language, rituals, clothes – from which they are escaping. Within work organisations this represents the return to the fold, making something of one's life or the rescue of career. All of these means of psychic escape can be utilised to further managerial control, either by employees' dependence on the financial and social supports necessary to pursue them, or, in the case of reinvestment, the cleaving back to the very structures of control themselves. For those who run organisations the problem is to monitor the identity work of employees to ensure that they do not overstep the bounds of the acceptable. For the employee the problem is to discover the appropriate mode of escape, enjoyment and making out for the subjective and objective conditions pertaining at the time.

Group Responses

Groups in general are defined in terms which vary according to the aspects which are being studied. However, a composite definition would define a group as a collection or coalition of people who interact meaningfully in the pursuit of common goals or objectives and have at least a tacit sense of agreed standards, values and common identity (based on Schein, 1965, and Drake and Smith, 1973). Groups are often referred to as the 'building blocks' of organisations and are studied in terms of the roles and associated norms generated within them, their role and communication structure, their interpersonal dynamics and their relations to other organisational coalitions and interest groups. Whether formally or informally constituted, cohesive or loosely associated, groups could be viewed in many situations as responses to pressures. Whether by individual design, accident or external determination, we live out much of our existence in the contexts of varying coalitions to which we are attached for a purpose. Groups in this sense are social and interpersonal *tools*, or even possibly *technologies of action*, through which we achieve ends which are beyond our perceptions of personal power. At the same time, our activities are circumscribed by and directed towards whatever goals or ends the group exists to serve.

Groups in organisations are seen by Handy (1985: 154–60) to serve both socio-psychological and instrumental functions. Socio-psychologically they act to provide a sense of belonging and identity, affiliation with others, guidelines for behaviour and a basis, and as a means for altering the formal structures of an organisation to suit group members better. An example of this is seen in Nichols's and Beynon's (1977) 'Chemco' study. A formal job rotation system was introduced under a job enrichment programme which only allowed them to move from one routine job to another. Yet the workgroups had already organised informal job rotation which allowed members to rest while others covered for them.

Groups can also be highly effective mechanisms for making out and directly instrumental for their members' capacity to control the wage-effort bargain, as research like Burawoy's (1979) shows. Handy's notion of instrumental functions, however, refers to the purposes groups serve for organisations as a whole and by implication for the dominant power groupings within them. In this sense they are the basis for the distribution of work, the units of monitoring, control and data collection and an integral part of many organisational decision-making processes. Groups and looser coalitions are also the arenas within which individuals secure identities and of management attempts to regulate them. As interest groups, such as trade union, professional or employers' associations, they set the contexts within which individuals and smaller groups compete for power over the structures and processes of organisations and for access to the material and psychic rewards they can supply.

Groups can also be viewed as sites of socialisation. The identity constructs which are of great importance to individual meaning and social definition based on class, race, gender, or religion are communicated to us through our participation in groups. This occurs through the behaviours and beliefs we internalise. The processes of socialisation through which the appropriate behaviours which an organisation demands are dependent on the operation of intra-group processes for their effectiveness. Thus an individual entering an organisation becomes attached, or is assigned to, a particular group wherein they 'learn the ropes' of how to survive and what is expected of them. As direct influence and hierarchical control is a possible source of threat to identity, it is possible that such moulding into appropriate images could be better pursued through the influence of peers. This can be seen clearly from the examples of use of peer-group pressures as a form of social control in Japanese management techniques, discussed in Chapter 5. Similarly, when using the 'sitting with Nellie' approach to job training, companies try to be sure that 'Nellie' is someone whose own workplace identity is at least roughly compatible with managerial objectives.

The extent to which we are influenced or affected by the particular groups we belong to is generally seen to be associated with the relative *cohesiveness* of different groups. Cohesiveness is both a function and consequence of the individual's attraction to a group. The motivation to remain a member stems from their subjective expectations concerning the personal, social or material rewards which are to be gained. It is not necessary, however, that we rationally calculate differential attractiveness and the rewards available. We might become members of various groups simply as a result of following appropriate scripts for making out in various social situations. Calculations of advantage and disadvantage may only actually apply when we become self-reflexive about our membership of a particular group. Most of the time we will probably construct our own identity in line with the identity of the group on the basis that such an identity is appropriate to the scenariotyped behaviours which the group carries out. When reflexiveness does occur we may respond with exactly the range of coping strategies which we can employ as individuals, but with the added possibilities of rejecting one group membership for another, attempting to redirect the group and thus reconstruct its identity or trying to redefine our own position in the group.

Individuals do of course use groups actively to transform their personal and social identities. For example, the reflexiveness involved in the raising of consciousness of disadvantage in social groups can be the spur for responses to pressures which direct the use of groups as technologies of action. Thus interest groups can actively promote not only the material interests of members but also promote their development of positive identities as mechanisms for making out. The patriarchal nature of power relations in organisations is currently being contested throughout industry, commerce and the professions by women's groups which rely on their own systems of '*networking*' to counter the male cliques who generally control their destinies. Such networks provide both a forum for ideas and information and work to heighten awareness of the position of women in organisations. Their capacity for social transformation will be dependent not only on the extent and nature of the contacts they can build up but also on the extent to which they can empower women to develop strong individual and group identities. On this basis they are often more than promotional or defensive interest groups in that they act to foster the recognition and self-development of the capacities of all women. 'Our purpose is to help women to develop their potential – not to foster élitism' (North-West Women into Management, 1987).

The recognition of group identity by members and those outside group boundaries will be a major determinant of the kinds of response groups will make to threats to their identity. The better defined the identity of a group is, the greater will be the value of the group to its members as a source of social support, comparison and evaluation. The more effective these processes are, the greater will be the range of external pressures which can be perceived as affecting the group, and thus the more likely that some kind of collective response will be demanded. Likewise, the stronger the identity of a particular group is, the more likelihood there is of other competing groups perceiving them and their actions as sources of threat, and thus the more likely that competitors will take action which once more demands some form of response.

An important factor is the extent to which group identity is constructed around a coherent set of values; common instrumental strategies for maximising extrinsic rewards or the needs and desires of group members for affiliation and interaction. This is most visible in the contestation over control of the labour process between management and workers. But that conflict is also manifested within intergroup relations. Thompson and Bannon (1985) show that the instrumental and anti-authoritarian attitudes of the better paid 'high flying' groups caused friction not only with management but with lowly rewarded and traditional craft workgroups. Each group identity was strengthened by the conflict and the prime target of resentment was more often other workgroups rather than management. Individual identities can, of course, suffer in intergroup struggles, but this is a measure of the extent to which group membership provides a powerful means of resisting pressures from outside. The pressure to conform can outweigh the pressure to secure oneself against uncertainty and damage. Brown confirms the above example, arguing that intergroup conflict acts to strengthen group and intra-group identities and when groups do resist management, 'the psychological satisfactions an individual may gain from his group membership may be more potent than the rewards (or threats) the management can hold out' (1980: 167). For management the problem of how to disrupt, short-circuit or redirect group identities is central for securing organisation goals, mobilising consent, exerting influence and promoting 'motivation' and organisationally directed goals. The types of response made are examined in the next section.

Even when there is only a tacit, unacknowledged sense of group identity, the stereotyped judgements of power-holders about particular groups may lead them to form sub-cultural units. They are likely to be based around resistance to managerial activities rather than in a coherent ideology of their own. Individual cohesion within such a group may be low and resistance may not be co-ordinated in any sense. It may not even be visible as such, but manifested in jokes at the expense of superiors, general stubbornness and lack of co-operation (Nichols and Beynon, 1977). At this level, pressure on individual identity may be no more than disapproval at not joining in, or at worst definition as being somehow different. Over time, the benefits, in terms of access to sources of meaning, of belonging to such a group may coalesce it into a true sub-culture with the ability to protect members against threats to identity.

Much of the informal organisational processes, including sub-cultural groupings, are generated within the free areas which groups and their members carve out for themselves within labour processes. Whether formally or informally constituted, such groups have to, in some fashion, reduce the possible internal tensions which might develop out of any contradictory goals and identity concerns of their members. The internal dynamics of groups have been seen largely to consist of role-based mechanisms and processes directed at the maintenance of the group. According to Breakwell 'group dynamics are the most frequent sources of threats to identity. These threats need not be personalised: they are directed at the individual as a group member, a cipher in a social category, not as a personality' (1986: 128). The detailed operation of such processes will be group-specific. But like the actions of individuals, it will be oriented towards identity securing strategies. Just as the construction of individual identities depends in part on competition with others for sources of meaning, the production of group identities depends on gaining access to symbols and resources or behaviour patterns which serve to distinguish the group from others.

At the extremes of group response to pressures on identity are traditional forms of industrial action and attempts at 'self-management'. The first could be seen in accounts by skilled workers involved in the 1987 British Telecom strike. A persistent theme was that the background to the action was as much a 'gut reaction' to the way in which management attitudes and behaviour represented an attack on their self-perceptions and identities as skilled workers as it was about pay and conditions. Pressure of this sort on individual identities can be the triggering factor which alerts workers to the possibilities and benefits which Leonard identifies in collective action.

Self-management as a strategy for making out ranges from the individual setting up in business to 'be your own boss', to large-scale worker-co-operatives. The use of group and inter-group self-management as a strategy could be seen as evidence of Garai's hypothesised need for non-alienated activity to motivate people towards transformations of work in the direction of self-control. Such efforts would act initially to reinforce the interdependence of productive relations and reinforce the security of previously constructed workplace identities, such as the craft pride of workers in the Triumph Meriden co-operative in the 1970s. However, attempts to secure autonomy and self-direction may be simply part of strategies to defend existing work against movements of capital, no matter how alienating. Unless the financial and management processes under which co-operatives operate are constructed differently from conventional businesses, the only extra source of meaning available in such work may be a collective identity and a set of common goals.

Self-management, though, is not restricted to the total direction of a business which a sole trader or co-operative must contend with. It can just as readily be a tactic within overall struggles to achieve control of the portions of the labour process. In attempting to control the speed of a production line or the throughput of work in a particular department, a group is actively trying to manage its environment. A parallel for professional groups are the 'collective mobility projects' (Armstrong, 1984) discussed in Chapter 4. Claims on access to decision-making power by professional groups such as accountants, engineers and personnel specialists rest in part on their ability to restrict sources of meaning to members and to utilise specialised knowledge to downgrade the competence of other groups.

In the above sense any form of resistance to external control, by groups or individuals, is a type of strategy for increasing the scope of self-management. It could thus be seen as a basic response, at different levels of the organisation, to constraints embodied in the work situation. Describing such action as resistance runs the risk of being a purely ideological judgement based on the damage done to existing structures of power and reward. But dominant groups do have their own needs for autonomy, discretion and non-alienated activity. It is therefore probable that they will define other people's self-management as a threat to their identities and produce regulatory responses. The activities of managerial groups in this area are the focus of the next section.

Management: From Response to Regulation

The form and content of control processes are influenced by the responses of managerial groups to pressures on the identities produced in their role as agents of capital. Mobilising their consent to expose themselves to the threats and pressures of management roles has its own particular place in the labour process. It also underpins the mobilisation of consent of production workers to comply with that supervision. Resistance and contestation by other individuals and groups are threats to managerial identities which are only somewhat ameliorated by the situational power they wield. As we reported in Chapter 4, managers have been reported as often feeling frustrated and ineffectual in their workplace roles and having little control over the strategic policies which determine their activities. This will depend, of course, on the position and situational power of the managers involved but does point to the fact that managerial work has its own levels of alienation and partialisation. If this is so, then dominant organisational groups will also expend effort and devise strategies to secure and defend their identities.

Effective managerial identity work can utilise worker resistance and associated damage to productivity and profitability as an ideological justification for their own strategies to enhance identity. By being perceived by peers and superiors as capable leaders who are able to contain, regulate or negate disturbances to the efficient flow of work, managers are able to secure sources of meaning which in turn reinforce their ideological supports.

The fashion for reorganising production processes into

semi-autonomous workgroups can provide examples of the way in which interventions by management act both to secure managerial identities and short-circuit potential worker resistance. As we saw in Chapter 5, such workgroups give employees some latitude of decision-making over operational matters and integrate different levels of production-related skills into more flexible working on more 'natural' units of work, turning production-line assembly into a semblance of unit or small-batch production. Wall *et al.* (1986), in a long-term study of autonomous workgroups, identified the justifications underlying their implementation as being in their assumed effects in increasing intrinsic motivation to work, enhancing employee satisfaction, improving group performance and reducing labour turnover, as well as suggested increases in organisational commitment and improvements in mental health.

The results of this study indicated that 'employees clearly appreciated the autonomous work system. On balance managers did too, through clearly there were costs in terms of personal stress arising from the difficulties involved in managing and maintaining the system' (1986: 298). Of the assumed effects, only intrinsic job satisfaction and productivity were significantly increased along with reported perceptions of increased autonomy. Labour turnover actually increased through increased dismissals of those who could not or would not fit in to the new systems. The increased productivity was not due to employees working any harder. If anything, their individual productivity was lower in comparison to those working on more traditional lines. Improvements largely flowed from reduced indirect labour costs owing to decreases in the need for direct supervision of the workgroups. This organisational benefit can be seen as a gain at the expense of increased managerial effort, with greater responsibilities being generated in monitoring and managing the new system.

Although suffering increased stress, the fact that managers thought the effort worthwhile indicates that associated productivity benefits provide enough possibilities for enhanced situational meaning to offset personal costs. When such a system becomes established, it is also possible that managers may gain from new sources of meaning. As they are directly responsible for co-ordinating teams of workers who are more satisfied in their work, it is likely to enhance self-perceptions of managerial effectiveness; though this potential is limited by possible conflicts with existing managerial ideologies, as we shall point out below. Increased intrinsic worker satisfaction is also a potential source of meaning to managers because greater intrinsic satisfaction may reduce the scope for contradictory consciousness arising in workers. If this leads to short-circuiting of potential resistance in employees, then managerial identities are further secured.

However, in one of the most widely studied implementations of autonomous working, conflicts with ideological conceptions of managerial control were seen to interfere with the factors which made such systems of work more effective. In a case study based on this material, the experimental assembly of trucks within an autonomous workgroup system in the Volvo company between 1974 and 1976, Blackler and Shimmin (1984: 117–19) note that workers finishing their daily quota of work were allowed some relaxation around their work station. Senior managers, however, saw this relaxation as 'slack' which could be taken up and controlled by increasing work quotas. This obviously produced demoralisation in the workforce. Allowing slack time is contrary to the managerial conception of how productivity is to be maximised, even though it may be one of the major factors which produces the sense of autonomy for workers that allows the system to succeed. An enhanced source of workplace meaning for one group appears in this case to be an unacceptable threat to the processes of control which supply meaning to another group. This example illustrates the point that the ideological underpinnings which control-systems provide for managerial identities may, in some circumstances, be more central to them than the control outcomes in increased profit. In this sense, strategies of control, regulation and discipline become part of the *instrumental transformations* of social reality which managerial groups set as the goals of their own identity work.

Strategic choices about organisational design can, however, be reinforced by a level of *indoctrination* into the dominant organisational goals. Such indoctrination may be a primary level of response to the attempts of members to secure a measure of autonomy and discretion within their work and to create free areas where they can develop their own identities and capacities. Lynne (1966) argues that the behaviours of even 'democratic leaders' can approximate to the principles of 'brainwashing'. Prescriptions to maintain warm and friendly relations with subordinates go hand-in-hand with maintaining a social distance between themselves and the group.

> We see here the dual role of the brainwasher: the aloofness corresponds to the threatener role, the friendliness to the protector role. The authoritarian leader is only playing the threatener role and misses out on the friendlieness. Vice versa with the laissez-faire leader. It is the brainwashing, democratic leader who plays both roles who is the most effective. (1966: 270)

Such indoctrination can take place within both formal and informal socialisation, and function to reinforce self-control rather than self-management. The study of bakery salesmen by Ditton (1974) showed how the salesmen were trained to cheat their customers in order not to lose out themselves when they ended up short in their takings. Supervisors both tacitly and overtly encouraged this activity as it short-circuited possible conflicts with workers, such as those that could be caused by the firm trying to recoup loses from the drivers' pay. The socialisation process also worked to weed out salesmen who wouldn't or couldn't collaborate in theft and to legitimise it to others as the only real means for making out in the job. Hence there was no objection to them making a little for themselves on top of balancing their books. Comments from a sales manager such as 'They're not real salesmen if they can't make a bob or two on the side, are they?' (1974: 36) indicate that the ability to steal was linked to job competence, the same manager being noted for encouraging valued salesmen to 'use fiddled cash personally'.

This socialisation into theft was of course only sanctioned by management to the extent that salesmen did not begin to steal from their employers as well as their customers. Mars (1983) has claimed that fiddling can increase job satisfaction, raise work rates and productivity by making the process of work more interesting, and binding those involved together. It can be used by management as a reward, as in Ditton's example, as long as they 'turn a blind eye', or can still be used as a method of 'cracking the whip'.

The final irony for management is that they lose control of the fiddle that they themselves have started. The workforce then seize it and use its unofficial and unsanctioned ability to increase their wages (especially in times of national restraint) as a basic condition of employment (Ditton, 1974: 36).

The strategies and identity work of managerial groups are likewise incorporated into organisational processes through ideological legitimations which can supply positive self-attributions. One of the major elements of these legitimations is the notion of leadership. Leadership is defined in terms of 'a social process in which one individual influences the behaviour of others without the use or threat of violence' (Buchanan and Huczynsci, 1985: 389). Explanation in this area has focused on personality traits, styles of leadership, and more recently on *situation-contingent* styles, and the relations between leaders and group members. Although the threat of violence is not commonly relied upon nowadays to maintain positions of leadership, the continuing use of threats to and sanctions on financial and job security in organisations means that the 'social process' of leadership must be understood in its intimate relationship with the exercise of power. According to Fiedler (1976: 108), 'the acid test of leadership theory must be in its ability to improve organisational performance'. The study of leadership is then directly related to the improvement of management control strategies and to the refinement of the tactical options open to managers in the day-to-day practice of regulating workplace behaviour, for instance, the Vroom-Yetton (1973) 'path-goal' model of leadership which attempts to provide options for the 'leadership styles' to be adopted by managers in dealing with problems and subordinates in varying situations.

Leadership in Selznick's terms, however, is partly founded on 'morally sustaining ideas' and 'socially integrating myths' (1957). The former mobilises support for the notions of compromise and restraint which underpin management's search for meaning and security. The latter are the superordinate

goals which leaders appeal to in order to unite organisational
members behind managerial strategies. Currently fashionable
'Japanese' management styles (discussed in Chapter 5) can
work to lock both managers and workers into appearing to
make the organisation successful for the good of all. This is
manifested in the single-status canteens and dress and the
workgroup-based discussion circles that channel perceptions
of the organistion towards superordinate goals.

Organisational ideologies play a crucial role in underpinning identities, particularly those of management. Salaman (1979: 199–212) locates five. *Structuralism* presents
organisational processes as outcomes of politically neutral
principles of management and achievement based on merit,
with 'managers operating as referees of a variety of competing
demands and pressures' (199). Markets complement internal
hierarchies as functionally necessary principles. The ideology
of achievement within structuralism links it to the approch of
psychologism, where organisational performance is the responsibility and outcome of individual behaviour. People are
resources and where their qualities, abilities and goals are not
in line with neutral structures they must be moulded to fit.
Conflicts of interest are avoided through the rational application of objective and neutral procedures for assessment and
feedback. *Consensualism* presents the specialised division of
labour and differentiated rewards as a necessary precondition
of the achievement of overall organisational goals benefiting
all members. The organisation survives by virtue of consensus, whilst conflict is due to the pathological personalities and
behaviours of individuals or to inadequate communications.
Welfareism focuses on integrating the commitment of employees through concern for their well-being and happiness.
The emphasis is on 'personal relations at work, on less onerous
and oppressive forms of control, on more relaxed supervisory
methods, on some changes even in the organisation of work'
(209). *Legalism* presents the social relations of production as
being determined by the binding contractual agreements between the parties involved in the enterprise. Conflict is handled
through negotiation and appeals to the obligations, rights and
duties of participants. The contrast implies consent to direction
of effort by those who are assigned 'the right to manage'.

Whether or not such ideologies in practice act as coherent guiding principles of organisations, they do present some common themes, notably the *neutrality* of managerial practices, the rational and consensus-based form of organisations and the emphasis on *individual responsibility* for exhibiting appropriate behaviours and identities. If internalised by employees, they have the effect of reducing uncertainty for dominant groupings and thus increasing their situational power in securing strategic identities. They risk failure in the light of the contradictory consciousness raised by perceived conflicts between espoused values and actual practice. Knights and Collinson give the example of a US-owned firm in Britain that directed its communicative efforts through a house magazine which

> simply exacerbated the 'them and us' attitudes since the harmonious and efficient image of Slavs depicted by it conflicted dramatically with the experience of shop floor workers. The shop floor was insulted by what it saw as the deceptive 'propaganda' in the magazine. (1987: 9)

Ideologies of this sort survive in part because dominant groupings have the power to shape cultural meanings in the workplace, and also because they can call on the expertise of their peers and outside professionals to justify them or supply the technologies of regulation to make them applicable to changing circumstances.

Organisational development is a good example of these strategic interventions in the organisation of work. 'Technologies' employed in OD interventions include team reviews, sensitivity training, performance counselling and the redesign of jobs. They largely depend on *social facilitation* effects for their operation, in other words, on pressures brought to bear on individuals through the effects of social comparison processes, group norms and the perceptions of expected rewards. An important aim is the achievement of a 'best fit' between the policy goals of the oranisation and the workplace identities of both employees and those who manage them. The latter is important in that successful interventions have to convince the managerial client that they have bought the right strategy

(Evden, 1986). Any doubts, or sophisticated ideas such as failure being a valuable learning experience, undermine the positive identities such interventions can reinforce. OD is discussed in greater detail in Chapter 6.

The utility of managerial education outside, though sponsored by, organisations, could also be said to be based on reinforcing the ideological identity work required of managers. A secure cultural identity is an important factor in reducing employee uncertainty and thus in increasing organisational cohesiveness. The content of managerial education is effectively directed at making concrete the notion that systematic control over complex and variable processes is possible. The reduction of uncertainty provided by the ideas themselves, backed up by the demonstration of techniques which purport to provide reliable diagnostic and control procedures, acts as a powerful enabling factor in the maintenance of ideological structures. The expected payoffs for the employee in both financial terms and in terms of career mobility are thus bought through a process of personal identity work. This increases the employee's self-perceived competence at handling the contingent uncertainties of organisational life, with the concomitant organisational gains of increased effort and commitment in overcoming goal barriers.

STRATEGIES OF SELF-REGULATION

The desire to improve the 'quality of working life' for employees, which has served as a justification for much research in organisational psychology, is by no means false and has resulted in many such improvements. But such improvements – based themselves on a questionable link between satisfaction and productivity – would be unlikely to take place unless they were supportive of managerial strategies. As was argued in Chapter 8, the involvement of organisational psychology and behavioural theory in supplying prescriptions and social policy advice to organisations is always going to raise contradictions with attempts to facilitate the social growth of individuals. This can be readily seen in a final example:

attempts to use *goal-setting* and related techniques to direct motivation and identity into 'functional' channels.

Goal-setting as a technique is said to be not only effective with scientists, managers and blue-collar workers; it is also said to work with (and on) minorities;

> Uneducated black workers in the south (USA) have reported feelings of greater self-confidence, pride in achievement, and increased willingness to accept future challenges as a result of goal setting. (Locke and Latham, 1984: 19)

Goal-setting is thus assumed to extend earlier techniques such as 'Management by Objectives', in that it is claimed to work beyond supervisory and managerial grades. It is claimed by the above authors to be a *core motivational technique* (121) that can underpin job enrichment, behaviour modification or other processes. Human resources are fully utilised by directing attention and action, mobilising energy and effort, increasing persistence and motivating the development of appropriate task strategies. It operates by breaking down goal-related behaviour into simpler sub-routines in the way that scientific management does with physical operations, thus reducing the stress of dealing with complex goals. Locke and Latham portray it as a tool which 'gets results' but when used improperly can result in 'conflict, feelings of failure, increased stress, dishonesty' (171).

Goal-setting is an example of the extension of technologies of regulation into what has been termed a '*behaviour technology*' which replaces 'impractical models and theories' with 'a technological approach to using human resources effectively for the creation of industrial wealth' (Wellin, 1984: 4). This aspires to integrate the whole body of knowledge in industrial and organisational psychology into contingent strategies for increasing effectiveness or: 'a practical bag of tools for solving human problems in organisations' (183). For such as Wellin we may be witnessing the coming of age of Baritz's 'bag of schemes' (see Chapter 8). Behaviour technology is thus a putative attempt to integrate the disparate technologies of regulation developed under the banner of OB into a 'unified field theory' of domination over workplace behaviour and identities. Such a conception of intervention is placing behavioural science directly at the service of those who wish to create a climate where conformity outweighs possible resistance and where compliance with strategies of domination is presented as offering the benefits of belief in consensus. Goal-setting and problem-solving approaches supply the context and diagnostic tools. Techniques such as *transactional analysis* supply the analysis of subjective variables. Then the whole barrage of technologies of regulation are applied through these to control behaviour. Coupled with attempts to shape the culture of organisations examined in Chapter 6, such initiatives are projected as an 'answer' to the organisational problems which arise out of the contradictions of modern capitalism.

The systems of staff development discussed in Chapter 6 provide an example of the extension of goal-setting techniques into attempts at the systematic regulation of workplace identities. Miller and Verduin (1979) place the theoretical base of staff development in perceptual psychology, assuming attitudinal and behavioural changes to be dependent on changing perceptions, as was argued in Chapter 7. The element of goal-setting involved makes staff development the natural heir to MBO but takes the notion one stage further. Instead of setting goals monitored by senior managers to ensure compatibility with organisational objectives, individuals are required to set goals compatible with their own aspirations and 'needs'. By emphasising the intra-organisational construction of individual identity, managerial strategies for transforming motivation and identity into influence and productivity are hopefully disguised.

In many ways the systems of profiling work utilised in staff development act as self-administered and continuously assessed personality, attitude and aptitude inventories, providing feedback both to management and staff that is useful in the moulding of functional identities. Thus functional activities are integrated into social comparison processes, into hierarchical relationships and even into the way in which individuals allocate their use-time within work.

Profiling can be reinforced by courses, trips and exchanges which act both as rewards and as reinforcers of group and organisational norms. Team-building exercises, where members of the same group or organisation are required to dress similarly and indulge in activities designed to increase group identification, can produce further facilitation effects. Employers such as Ford Motors also offer exchanges to production workers. They visit and work in plants employing new production processes and those which are said to have good productivity and industrial relations records. Return visits presumably imbue others with the values which have made particular plants 'successful'. It is also possible, of course, that such visits highlight workers' perceptions of their dispensability within the international division of labour.

Staff development works by encouraging self-attributions which reinforce organisational objectives and by focusing social comparison on functional activities. It can break down managerial, professional and supervisory work into operational units just as scientific management does with production work. Instead of appeals to ideologies of rationality, neutrality, objectivity and efficiency, it appeals to the subjective ideologies which support individual identities. It is an implementation of the role-based control and psychologism discussed earlier and an attempt to control not just the behaviour but also the identity work of employees. The probability is that the success of staff development is like that of organisational development: dependent on the expectation effects that can be induced in participants.

As we argued in Chapter 6, such strategies will probably never work as intended. Even if individual subjectivity can act, as Knights and Willmott argue, to separate people and blind them to their collective interests, it will still operate to motivate and enable them to circumvent such technologies of regulation for their own purposes. You can in no way guarantee that staff will develop the goals set for them, only that they will develop goals. The kind of goals they develop will depend on the interaction of factors such as the six dimensions shaping workplace behaviour identified earlier in this chapter. It is through analytic conceptions such as these that the possibilities inherent in an OB that takes full account of issues of subjectivity can make inputs to the process of changing organisations, as outlined in the concluding chapter.

PART THREE

10

Conclusions: Changing Organisations

The study of *organisational change* is a narrow and rather technical specialism. In this concluding chapter, we want instead to focus briefly on issues concerned with changing organisations and, in particular, the relationship between theories and practices. That must begin with an attempt to reflect on what we can learn from the growth of large-scale enterprise and the development of organisational theories. How have 'practitioners' used theories and how and why have they changed? But more than this, questions need to be asked about the possibilities for new forms of oranisation. Whyte's call in *Organisation Man* for the individual to fight a lonely battle against conformity was never going to get very far. Individuals already did and still do. But the capacity to change realities is partly dependent on the availability of alternative models of behaviour and structure. For the organisational participant in normal circumstances, such alternatives are inevitably restricted by their experience and the tendency to take what exists as natural, though constraining.

One of the purposes of this book is to puncture those images of normality. By showing the socially constructed character of existing forms and practices, we hope to have raised issues about how things could be done differently. On the other hand, it would be foolish to mirror the prescriptive orientation of mainstream perspectives. As Watson comments, 'It is not up to social scientists to tell us how best to organise work. But they should assist the opening up of possibilities' (1986: 14).

Unfortunately he then adds, 'They should help inform the choices that are made by those with the responsibility for decision-making'. What about empowering the vast majority currently excluded from such responsibilities? In our view one of the tasks of analysis should be to enable those who work or are entering work, to survive, improve and transform organisations. Survival hints are useful but people will invent their own means anyway. Employees will also go on finding the spaces inside management initiatives to improve them, without succumbing to the illusion that they are a major and lasting source of advancement. Transformation is the difficult bit. But critical theory has mostly avoided that part. It is easier to engage in critique. That is understandable. So have we. It is easier to proclaim solutions in terms of vague overthrowing of the system in some unspecified and ill-defined future. We have tried to avoid that pitfall. But as we said earlier, it is necessary to start from existing theories and practices.

MANAGEMENT AND THEORY

If we examine the interaction between theories and practices described in previous chapters, no mechanical and few direct relationships can be found. Above all, organisational theories are a *resource* for practitioners, mostly of course employers and managers. Taylor and Mayo, for example, were great synthesisers of ideas and practices in a way that management found useful, not just as a guide to action but as a way of clarifying and legitimating their role. Yet theorists, and Taylor was a prime case, frequently rail against companies that do not swallow their whole package but rather apply them selectively. As Chandler (1977: 277) observes, 'No factory owner ... adopted the system without modifying it'. This should come as no surprise. Employers and managers are pragmatists and, with some exceptions such as the Quaker-owned companies in the UK, seldom show any intrinsic interest in ideas in themselves but rather for their 'use value'. Or, as one senior manager is quoted in Gowler and Legge (1983: 213), 'There's no good ideas until there's cash in the till'.

This is one of the main reasons why, as Watson (1986: 2) correctly notes, there will never be a full and generally acceptable organisational or management theory. But it is not merely a case of a plurality of competing perspectives. The *partiality* of such theories is inherent in their use in control and legitimation processes. It is in the nature of theories of and for management that they give incomplete pictures. The perspectives and accompanying prescriptions only address aspects of the basic contradictions in capitalist work organisation. Therefore, at one level both theorists and practitioners respond within a continuum that has Taylor's minimum interaction model at one end and varieties of human relations at the other. Employers, of course, would like it both ways. Bendix gives an example of a management journal in 1910 calling for 'absolute authority as well as the willing co-operation of the workers' (1956: 272).

To some extent they can do this by *combining* theories and practices within the continuum. So we saw in Chapter 2 that human relations did not challenge Taylorism on its own terrain of job design and structures, but rather sought to deal with its negative effects and blind spots. That story of combination to deal with different dimensions of organisational experience is repeated through every period and sector. It is, of course, the case that management is not only trying to deal with the contradictory aspects of utilising human labour. Variations in strategy and practice reflect broader problems, such as harmonising different functions and sites of decision-making. But the resultant difficulties in managing the contradictions are similar – different routes to partial success and failure, as Hyman noted in Chapter 4.

It would be wrong to give the impression that the choice and use of theories is solely an internal matter. This would reinforce the erroneous view that organisational theories are an historical sequence of 'models of man', the new naturally replacing the old as grateful managers learn to recognise the more sophisticated account of human needs and behaviour. Selectivity is also conditioned by *circumstances*, involving a number of key 'macro' and 'micro' dimensions. At the broadest level, organisational theories interact with the political economy of broad phases of capital accumulation. Taylorism and classical management perspectives emerged at a time when the scale and complexity of organisations and of markets were undergoing a fundamental change. The globalisation of markets and intensified competition, particularly from Japan, has stimulated major shifts in management thinking in the more recent period. Ideological conditions are also influential, as evidenced by the spillover of entrepreneurial values from the political to the managerial sphere. At a micro-level, the choices made by particular companies reflect even more complex factors. In particular, the *sector*, with its specific product market and labour market, technological framework and political context, is a vital consideration.

Each country, too, has its own unique configuration of intellectual, social and economic conditions mediating the form and content of organisational change. But just as there are global markets for products, so there are increasingly for ideas. This process is enhanced by the spread of pop-management and 'airport lounge' books, as the success of the excellence genre is testament to. Unfortunately it reinforces the tendency for academics to form alliances with sections of management around particular perspectives or techniques as solve-all solutions. So much ideological investment is made in the process that the chosen vehicle can seldom meet the burden placed on it. hence burn-out, cynicism and later fortunate loss of memory, until, that is, a new solution comes along!

But why do managers so often become locked in this fatal embrace? One explanation is that as an interest group management requires a means of defining and expanding its activities. Referring to the recent spread of interest in corporate culture, Thackray comments, 'Culture is particularly seductive because it appears to open up a new frontier of managerial activism' (1986: 86). This option is particularly attractive to the personnel or human resource teams of large corporations, reminding us that the adoption of theories and practices is also likely to be affected by the internal fissures within the managerial labour process. With the demise of the great practitioner-theorists such as Taylor and Fayol, and the growth of more specialised academic production, management are also in a more *dependent* position.

But the attraction is also a reflection of the fact that the meaning of management is inseparable from the management of meaning (Gowler and Legge, 1983). Organisational theories become part of a language and a sub-culture through which management tries to understand itself and legitimate its activities to others, even when those ideological resources are used in a contradictory and rhetorical way. The essence of these points is that regardless of the social influences, organisational and management theory has a level of autonomy and its own rhythm of development. Regardless of the cycles of interest in ideas and imitations of the fashion cycle, they have their own very real effects. And as they are grappling with genuine problems it is possible to draw positive lessons, even for those of us who want to take the process of organisational change much further.

LEARNING FROM PRESENT AND PAST

It is important for critical theory not just to proclaim the limits of existing organisational forms and practices. Those constraints arising from dominant relations of wealth, power and control are real enough, as observation of the very partial progress of QWL programmes or employee participation illustrates. But solely 'negative learning' implies an *essence* to work organisation under capitalism which denies it any significance. For instance, the *Work Relations Group* led by the noted American radical scholar Jeremy Brecher (1978: 20) argues that the history of such research 'exposes the shallow conceptions of "job enrichment", "workers' control" and the like as window dressing which leaves untouched the essential tyranny of the capitalist labour process'. Certainly many aspects of work reorganisation have been and still are based on increasing the intensity of labour, tightening controls and marginalising sections of the workforce. But when Marx wrote that the logic of competition between companies compels them constantly to revolutionise the means of production, he was recognising that by its very nature capitalism is a dynamic system.

The search for profitability involves innovations in

technology, co-ordination of resources and utilisation of people's skills and knowledge that offer positive lessons relevant to any more democratic and egalitarian social order at work. This is not the same as the orthodox Marxist view, expressed by the founders of the Soviet Union, that a socialist society simply 'adds on' the techniques of capitalist work organisation to new property relations. Those techniques rather have to be added *to*, rethought and resituated in a new context of a fully democratic economy. for job enrichment or modern forms of QWL, however flawed, are also indicators of the great potential of human labour to create more efficient and satisfying forms of work. To argue that all this is mere superficial window dressing is to fly in the face of the reality that we all find some work situations more creative and rewarding than others. Furthermore, there appears in some spheres to be a lot more to learn about innovative forms of work organisation from capitalism than from existing state socialist societies.

A further reason for not regarding the worlds of today and tomorrow as wholly sealed off from one another is that there is much to learn from the existing practices of *employees*. As Brecher rightly says, there is a massive 'hidden history of the workplace' which needs to be recognised and uncovered. That history is based on the self-organisation of workers trying to resist and transform work relations. Admittedly that was easier to see when craft labour was dominant and many workers genuinely felt that they could run the factories better than their bosses. Old-style movements for workers' control are no longer feasible in a world of transnationals, global production and semi-skilled labour. But there remains a wealth of untapped experience and knowledge in employees' informal job-controls and patterns of organisation.

Though measures like QWL are back-handed compliments from employers, little is learnt because workers' self-activity is seldom given institutional form. Discussions of alternative forms of organisation often depend on examples such as producer co-operatives. Such initiatives have grown rapidly in recent years, partly as a response to the economic recession and restructuring. As collectivist and democratic forms of management and ownership, co-operatives constitute an important experience, despite their critics from left to right who predict inevitable degeneration into traditional structures (Cornforth: 1988). But the fact remains that they are relatively marginal in the economy. With a few well-known exceptions such as the large-scale Mondragon movement in Spain, most are small, labour-intensive and self-financed and they flourish in areas of the market where there is little competition from mainstream organisations (Rothschild-Whitt, 1979).

Alternatives within the mainstream economy are few indeed and those that have taken place, such as the UK Lucas workers' alternative plan, have had to bear a heavy burden as exemplar and hope for the future (Collective Design Project: 1986). This initiative arose as a strategic means of local trade union organisation to provide a positive alternative to dependence on making armaments, based on production that was both socially useful and economically viable. Predictably, though highly praised by all and sundry, it did not get very far with management. But it did provide a model of *popular planning* which was at last given some institutional support through the enterprise boards set up by some Labour local and regional authorities. Mike Cooley, the key figure from Lucas, became the Director of the Technology Division of the Greater London Enterprise Board (GLEB). A technologist and critic of the uses of science under capitalism (Cooley, 1987), he is an exception to the previously noted absence of theorist-practitioners.

The priorities of the Division were to develop human-centred technologies which retained and expanded labour skills in a way often denied in conventional enterprises, and Technology Networks which provided resources, expertise and finance to link community, educational and industrial projects. Unfortunately, as one of its leading figures admits (Palmer, 1986), the concrete achievements of GLEB overall were small. But the emphasis on alternative technologies has perhaps had a more lasting impact and is tied into further design work done by the Control Systems Centre at UMIST (Corbett, 1985). Such initiatives illustrate one of our central points, that positive connections can be made between the kind of theoretical critiques of technological determinism and deskilling made by labour-process and other writers, and practical initiatives in new forms of work design.

We would also do well not to forget that the mainstream world of large-scale organisations includes the public sector. Such services in the UK, notably those in local government, have been given a rough ride in recent years, both with respect to their funding and sharp attacks on their efficiency. Some of the criticisms have been well deserved. Much local authority service provision has been characterised by over-centralisation, a lack of flexibility in meeting diverse consumer demands and poor managerial direction in setting and attaining goals. But the innovative organisational response, mainly from Labour local authorities, has been neglected (Goss and Parston, 1989). There have been significant experiments in decentralising service delivery and management, particularly in housing, and in greater consumer choice and involvement. Initiatives such as self-managing teams of workers certainly need further development, but the new forms of organisation often have far greater substance with respect to redistributing power and decision-making than their much-hyped private sector equivalents.

All these examples illustrate the need and potential for organisational theorists to broaden their conception of practitioners and extend contacts and collaboration to broader groups of clients, including those in the voluntary and public sectors, and to trade union and other employee organisations. Nevertheless, practice without theory is blind and such activity has to be underwritten by more extensive analytical work directed towards developing new thinking on alternative organisational forms.

RETHINKING ORGANISATIONAL FORMS

The capacity of critical theory to develop alternative models has been limited by two interrelated factors: an inability to reconceptualise the management of work organisations and to develop feasible modes of decision-making and involvement. In the 1960s and 1970s the attitude of management as a neutral technique was replaced by an equally unhelpful hostility that failed to distinguish between particular forms of authority expressed through existing structures and systems, and the necessity for co-ordination and control of resources. Or as, Landry *et al.* (1985: 61) put it:

> There is a vital distinction to be made between 'management' and those people who hold managerial positions, and 'management' as an assortment of integrative functions which are necessary in any complex organisation – planning, harmonising related processes, ensuring appropriate flows of information, matching resources to production needs, marketing, financial control, linking output to demand, etc.

This is part of an excellent dissection of the weaknesses of many community and other organisations in the radical movements in this period. Frequently they rejected any form of specialised division of labour and formal structures of decision-making, in favour of informal methods and rotation of all responsibilities. The result was seldom democratic or efficient. Sirriani (1984) also criticises such 'productive integrity' models in which all forms of involvement in the organisation must be total and holistic in character. Genuine criticisms of hierarchies and alienated work are thus lost in an attempt to put them into complete reverse. Desirable goals such as sharing and learning of skills to overcome fragmented labour are not given an adequate framework of expertise to sustain them. In fact, the political culture from which the organisations emerged 'made it difficult to conceive of the genuine importance of skills such as financial planning ... management and entrepeneurship. These skills were seen as capitalist and reactionary by their very nature' (Landry *et al.*, 30).

The difficult relationship between organisational cultures and the development of appropriate management forms and skills can also be seen in the relative failure of the early period of GLEB. Though its supporters bemoan the dearth of *personnel* with business or industrial experience in the labour, co-operative and radical movements (Palmer, 1986), the dominant internal culture was hostile to such skills, leading to a failure to establish effective means of monitoring investment and develop training within the new business initiatives. As a consequence, a shake-up was necessary in the leadership and running of the organisation which is now functioning more successfully as Greater London Enterprise, despite a number of attempts by the Conservative Government to kill off a public sector success story.

A similar problem arises in coming to terms with bureaucracy. Some of the radical writers we have discussed, such as Clawson, have made useful analyses and criticisms of the development of industrial bureaucracy. Unfortunately, the associated work structures are then argued to have been developed and introduced for solely capitalist purposes. The difficulty is that in the desire to explain the social origins of organisational forms, bureaucracy and efficiency are simply reduced to specific class interests. This is reinforced by giving alternative socialist production relations a utopian capacity to avoid bureaucratisation altogether in a model of 'total democracy' based on:

> the election of everyone above the level of ordinary worker, with no fixed hierarchy and no-one having the right to give commands (except insofar as this right is temporarily delegated, with the commands always subject to the review of the group as a whole). Moreover, instead of a plethora of rules and an illusory focus on bureaucratically defined expertise ... regulations are reduced to a minimum, freedom is maximised, and everyone becomes technically competent to do the work. (1980: 16–17)

At best such practices may be possible in a small co-operative, though even this is extremely doubtful. In any large-scale and complex organisation the efficiency and energy costs would soon make it impossible to operate. In his attempt to develop a viable model from the experience of workers' self-management in Yugoslavia, Horvat (1983) carefully avoids such ultra-democratic excesses. Though the basis of organisational democracy is the work unit, representatives form a general workers' council which makes the broader decisions. The system builds in sanctions against as well as rights for work units; clearly demarcates the democratic content of decision-making from the professional expertise necessary for implementation through administrative structures; and recognises the need for specialised policy development through commissions which combine experts and elected lay-members.

Clearly, Yugoslavian self-management has had a difficult time in a country beset by a variety of political and economic problems, but Horvat's work is an attempt to build from, not propagandise about, those experiences. It can be supported by a small but growing body of theoretical work, for example, Sirriani (1984) and Clegg and Higgins (1987). The goal is to think through the problems of developing democratic work organisation that is also pluralist in nature, in that it recognises a variety of possible organisational forms of decision-making, ownership and involvement. Emphasis is put on feasible levels of task-sharing, egalitarian reward systems, democratic controls and participation and co-operative cultures. This would result in what we call a *minimal bureaucracy*. Only by recognising certain necessary and distinct functions for bureaucracy can we begin to control and transform them. Clegg and Higgins comment that such arrangements:

> will neither eliminate rules nor the division of labour; in this sense it will not eliminate bureaucracy at all. To presume to do so would be chimerical. What we will achieve is a form of bureaucracy – administration by office and rules – which is not premised on hierarchy, but on collectivity; not on authoritarianism but on democracy; a new ideal type of a bureaucratic, democratic and collectivist organisation. (1987: 217)

Models of this nature would pose a major challenge to much of the existing forms of ownership, management and power discussed in this book. But perhaps it is time that organisation studies rediscovered a genuinely critical relationship with its environment.

A Guide to Further Reading

No matter how detailed or comprehensive its descriptions of the literature, no textbook is an island. It cannot and should not stand alone and hopefully one of its functions is to stimulate those who use it to read further. The literature on work organisations is a large and diverse one. With over 500 references in the bibliography we are somewhat spoiled for choice. Below are some of the books and articles we found useful, occasionally essential and sometimes stimulating. They are necessarily things we agree with, but may be representative of perspectives that cannot be ignored. We have not generally included sources which, though they meet the above criteria, are difficult to get access to.

General Texts and Theory

Though most orthodox general texts are fairly standard in ideas and coverage, two of the better UK examples are from McKenna (1987) and Buchanan and Hucznyski (1985), the former having a better treatment of psychological theories and their applications than found in most OB texts. At the more critical end of the mainstream, Watson (1986) provides a text which usefully overlaps into personnel and industrial relations issues, while Dawson (1986), though aimed mainly at service courses, has lively discussions in neglected areas such as power and technology as a social product. Perrow's (1979)

Complex Organisations is still one of the most readable and provocative commentaries, particularly on the American debates. In contrast, two of the more blatant examples of explicit prescriptive 'technologies of regulation' are Wellin (1984), *Behaviour Technology* and Locke and Latham :1984), *Goal Setting: a Motivational Technique that Works!*

The writings of Salaman (1979) and Clegg and Dunkerley (1980) were path-breaking contributions to putting radical organisation theory on the map, and still repay reading. Reed's (1985) *Redirections in Organisational Analysis* is heavy theory, but is a valuable account and reinterpretation of critical and mainstream literature. Reworking theories through a series of metaphors, Morgan's (1985) *Images of Organisation* has been described as a masterpiece by its fans, but we are not convinced that it represents a substantially different approach. From Donaldson (1986) we get an aggressive reaffirmation of the virtues of orthodoxy in *In Defence of Organisation Theory*. There is a symposium on this in the journal *Organisation Studies* (1988, vol., 9, no. 1). The second edition of Rose's *Industrial Behaviour* (1988) has added a lively account of more recent radical theories to a reworking of earlier management thinking.

One of our main themes has been the necessity to see theories in their practical and historical context. We have found a number of books essential for that task. One of the oldest, but still a good source of information on managerial ideologies, is *Work and Authority in Industry* from Bendix (1956). On similar territory, it is possible to learn much from Child's (1969) *British Management Thought* and Chandler's (1977) business history of the USA. Three radical writers deserve mention for their historical accounts. Clawson's (1980) study is marred by a rather crude Marxism, but its focus on the genesis of industrial bureaucracy up to and beyond the turn of the century is still valuable. Moving the emphasis to the UK and further into the 1920s and later is Brown's *Sabotage*. This could win a prize for the title least representative of the content of a book. But it's an important source of information on management and shopfloor practices in areas such as the implementation of Taylorism and human relations. Edwards (1979) also contains a lot of valuable material on the contested terrain of the shop floor, as well as being a noted contribution to labour process theory in its own right.

Specific Issues

On *organisations and their environments,* Perrow again and the second edition of Child's (1984) *Organisation: A Guide to Problems and Practice* are useful for evaluations of the traditional literature, as are many of the readings collected together by Salaman and Thompson (1973). Yet another Thompson – the American, J. D. – is commonly held to provide the key text of the open systems approach in his 1967 book. Wood's article (1979) provides one of the best critiques, mainly of contingency theory. On the population ecology perspective, Hannan and Freeman's (1977) article gives a lucid exposition.

Recommending things in the sphere of the *political environment* is difficult as much of the writing consists of highly specialised theories of the state. A good collection is in Held *et al.* (1983). Readers may prefer a shorter, though highly compressed account of recent theoretical work in the Pierson (1984) article 'New Theories of State and Civil Society'. Essential reading on the public sector is *Controlling Social Welfare* by Cousins (1987). Her readable book is very good on wider theoretical debates about bureaucracy, the labour process and gender.

In the area of *management, power and control,* most of the things we found useful were articles in journals. For an excellent summary and evaluation of the literature on managerial work, start with 'What do Managers Do?' by Hales (1986). Willmott's (1984, 1987) two articles on similar issues are also valuable. Some of these articles can be found in a special issue of the *Journal of Management Studies* (vol. 21, no. 3). The collection of articles *Introducing Management* edited by Elliot and Lawrence (1985) is very uneven, but contains some useful contributions. Armstrong's work (1984 is the most accessible) is the best account of the relations between management, control and the business professions.

On *management strategies,* two recent articles in the excellent new journal *Work, Employment and Society* offer a stimulating survey of current issues and research. These are from Hyman (1987) and the German writer, Streek (1987). A survey of labour process debates on management strategies of control can be found in Thompson (1989, 2nd edn), while some of the newer empirical work is collected together in readers edited by Knights and Willmott (1985, 1986b). The latter has a dense but very good introduction to the debates by the editors.

Knights and Willmott (1986a) have also edited a useful collection on *gender and the labour process*. The question of gender obviously traverses the different issues, but though there is a lot of material on labour markets and employment, there isn't much written directly on organisational matters. However, Hearn and Parkin (1987) offer a fascinating and unique account of the interrelationships between sexuality and organisational life.

As we said in Chapter 4, *power* is a neglected issue. A useful account of internal politics and decision-making can be found in Lee and Lawrence's (1985) *Organisational Behaviour – Politics at Work*. Clegg's new text, *Power*, (1989), is a comprehensive though difficult account.

Moving to issues of *design*, Mintzberg's *Structure in Fives: Designing Effective Organisations* represents the advance guard of mainstream thinking. Again, Child (1984) gives a comprehensive and practical account of a wide range of issues and research. Essential readings for the newer debates on *flexible working* are Atkinson (1985) for the model of the flexible firm, and Piore and Sabel (1984) for the theory of flexible specialisation. The collection edited by Clutterbuck (1985) is lightweight but useful for an understanding of a section of management thinking. Excellent critiques are provided by Williams *et al.* (1987) and Pollert (1988b), and there are wider discussions on new directions in work in the collections edited by Hyman and Streek (1988), Pahl (1988) and Wood (1989).

On the other current design favourite – *Japanese Management Method* – Pascale and Athos (1982) and Wickens *The Road to Nissan* (1987) are at the better end of the pop-management school, while the articles by Wood (1986), Sayer and Meyer (both in the same issue of the journal *Capital and Class*, no. 30, 1986) offer a more critical and realistic account of different aspects. A very good starting-point would also be a special issue of the *Industrial Relations Journal* (Spring 1988), which brings together some of the best contributions from a conference on Japanisation of British Industry. An antidote to the hype about Japan itself is Kamata's (1982) account of working on the track at Toyota.

Organisational culture has been the 'hottest' topic of discussion in organisational and management writing in the recent period. One place to start is *Corporate Cultures* by Deal and Kennedy (1988). The quality of evidence is often abysmal but the flavour of the argument is there. Peters and Waterman's (1982) *In Search of Excellence* is more famous and is a bit more theoretical, as is Ouchi's (1981) *Theory Z*. The deeper theoretical roots are explained in a useful article by Ray (1986). For a swingeing and entertaining radical critique of the literature, see the article by Silver (1987) – though you may have some problem getting hold of the source: the journal *Studies in Political Economy*.

Critical Psychologies

We have already given references for some of the key mainstream behavioural texts. What about the critical sources we have found useful? The first thing that must be said is that many of these are fairly difficult pieces but nevertheless repay reading. One of the more accessible is Leonard's (1984) *Personality and Ideology*. Though we do not share its view that Marxism is a viable basis for a theory of the individual, it does a good job in situating psychological theories within a materialist account of the social order. From a different tradition – Foucault and discourse theory – *Changing the Subject* by Henriques *et al.* (1984) is heavy-going in parts. But it has a useful emphasis on the production of subjectivity and psychological knowledge, with a wealth of material on applications to gender, work and other areas.

Even heavier is Wexler's (1983) comprehensive and reflexive critique of social psychology in the tradition of the Frankfurt School of Marxism. Articles by Seivers (1986) and Van Strien (1982) provide critical discussions of the issues of *motivation* and *practical interventions* by psychologists respectively.

On the question of *identity*, Weigert *et al.* (1986) provide a detailed treatment of the theories and applications of the concept from a 'sociological social psychology' perspective. We extensively used the article by Knights and Willmott (1985) on 'Power and Identity in Theory and Practice'. Two other more empirically based contributions in this area are *Coping with Threatened Identities* by Breakwell (1986), which provides useful models of the process, and Cohen and Taylor's (1978) witty and readable *Escape Attempts: the Theory and Practice of Resistance to Everyday Life*. For those who wish to go deeper and further into the debate, the best current work on discourse and identity is J. Shotter and K.J. Gergen, *Texts of Identity* (1989).

Bibliography

ACAS (1988) *Labour Flexibility in Britain: The 1987 ACAS Survey*, London, ACAS Occasional Paper 41.

Ackroyd, S. *et al.* (1987) 'The Japanisation of British Industry', Paper presented at Conference on Japanisation of British Industry, UWIST, also in *Industrial Relations Journal*. Spring 1988, vol. 9, no. 1.

Aichholzer, G. and Schienstock, G. (1985) 'Labour in Conflict: Between Capital Interests and the Maintenance of Identity', Paper for 20th Annual Meetings of the Canadian Sociology and Anthropology Association, University of Montreal.

Albrow, M. (1970) *Bureaucracy*, London, Pall Mall.

Albrow, M. (1973) 'The Study of Organisations – Objectivity or Bias?' in G. Salaman and K. Thompson (eds).

Aldrich, H. E. (1979) *Organisations and Environments*. Englewood Cliffs, Prentice-Hall.

Aldrich, H. E. and Pfeffer, J. (1976) 'Environments and Organisations' in G. Inkeles *et al.* (eds) *Annual Review of Sociology* 2.

Aldrich, H. E. and Stabler, U. (1987) Organizational Transformation and Trends in US Employment Relations, Paper at ASTON-UMIST Labour Process Conference.

Allen, S. and Wolkowitz, C. (1987) *Homeworking: Myths and Realities*, London, Macmillan.

Alvesson, M. (1985) 'A Critical Framework for Organisational Analysis', *Organisation Studies*, vol. 6, no. 2, pp. 117–38.

Alvesson, M. (1988) 'Management, Corporate Culture and Labour Process in a Professional Service Company', Paper presented at Conference on the Labour Process, ASTON-UMIST.

Archibald, W. P. (1978) *Social Psychology as Political Economy*, Toronto, McGraw-Hill Ryerson.

Argyris, A. (1967) 'Today's Problems with Tomorrow's Organisations', *Journal of Management Studies*, vol. 4, no. 1, pp. 31–55.

Argyris, C. (1970) *Intervention Theory and Method*, Reading, Mass., Addison-Wesley.

Armistead, N. (ed.) (1974) *Reconstructing Social Psychology*, Baltimore, Penguin.

374

Armstrong, P. (1984) 'Competition between the Organisational Professions and the Evolution of Management Control Strategies', in K. Thompson (ed.) *Work, Employment and Unemployment*, Milton Keynes, Open University Press.

Armstrong, P. (1986) 'Management Control Strategies and Inter-Professional Competition: the Cases of Accountancy and Personnel Management', in D. Knights and H. Willmott (eds).

Armstrong, P. (1987) 'The Divorce of Productive and Unproductive Management'. Paper at ASTON-UMIST Labour Process Conference.

Armstrong, P. (1987a) 'Engineers, Management and Trust', *Work, Employment and Society*, vol. 1, no. 4, pp. 421–40.

Armstrong, P. (1987b) The Abandonment of Productive Intervention in Management Teaching Syllabi, Warwick Papers in Industrial Relations.

Armstrong, P. (1989) 'Management, Labour Process and Agency', *Work, Employment and Society*, vol. 3, no. 3 pp. 307–22.

Atkinson, J. (1984) 'Manpower Strategies for Flexible Organisations', *Personnel Management*, August.

Atkinson, J. (1985) IMS Report no. 89, IMS, Falmer, Sussex.

Atkinson, J. and Gregory, D. (1986) A Flexible Future: Britain's Dual Labour Force, *Marxism Today* April.

Bachrach, P. and Baritz, M. S. (1962) 'Two Faces of Power', *American Political Science Review* 56: pp. 947–52.

Baldamus, W. (1961) *Efficiency and Effort: An Analysis of Industrial Administration*, London, Tavistock.

Bandura, A. and Walters, R. H. (1963) *Social Learning and Personality Development*, New York, Holt, Rinehart & Winston.

Banton, R., Clifford, P., Frosh, S., Lousada, J. and Rosenthall, J. (1985) *The Politics of Mental Health*, London, Macmillan.

Baran, B. (1988) 'Office Automation and Women's Work: The Technological Transformation of the Insurance Industry', in R. H. Pahl (ed.) (1988) *On Work*, Oxford, Basil Blackwell.

Baritz, L. (1960) *The Servants of Power*, Middletown, Wesleyan University Press.

Barnard, C. (1938) *The Functions of the Executive*, Cambridge, Mass., Harvard University Press.

Basset, P. (1989) 'All Together Now', *Marxism Today*, June.

Batsfore, E. Ferner, A. and Terry, M. (1984) *Consent and Efficiency*, Oxford, Basil Blackwell.

Beckhard, R. (1969) *Strategies of Organisational Development*, Reading, Mass., Addison-Wesley.

Beer, M. *et al.* (1985) *Human Resource Management: A General Manager's Perspective*, Glencoe, Ill., Free Press.

Bell, D. (1960) *The End of Ideology*, New York, Collier Macmillan.

Bellaby, P. and Orribor, P. (1977) 'The Growth of Trade Union Consciousness Among General Hospital Nurses', *Sociological Review*, vol. 25.

Bendix, R. (1956) *Work and Authority in Industry*, New York, Harper and Row.

Bennis, W. (1966) *Changing Organisations*, New York, McGraw-Hill.

Benson, J. K. (1977) 'Innovation and Crisis in Organisational Analysis', in J. K. Benson (ed.).

Benson, J. K. (ed.) (1977a) *Organisational Analysis: Critique and Innovation*, London, Sage Contemporary Social Science Issues 37.

Berg, M. (1985) *The Age of Manufactures*, London, Fontana.

Berger, P. L. and Luckman, T. (1967) *The Social Construction of Reality*, London, Allen Lane.

Berle, A. A. and Means, G. C. (1935) *The Modern Corporation and Private Property*, New York, Macmillan.

Beynon, H. (1975) *Working for Ford*, Wakefield, E. P. Publishing.

Beynon, H. (1987) 'Dealing with Icebergs: Organisation, Production and Motivation in the 1990s', *Work, Employment and Society*, vol. 1, no. 2, pp. 247–59.

Bittner, E. (1967) 'The Police on Skid Row: A Study of Peace Keeping', *American Sociological Review*, vol. 32, no. 5, pp. 699–715.

Bittner, E. (1973) 'The Concept of Organisation', in G. Salaman and K. Thompson (eds).

Black, J. and Ackers, P. (1989) 'Between Adversarial Relations and Incorporation: Directions and Dilemma's in the US Auto Industry', Paper at UWIST Flexibility Conference.

Blackler, F. (1982) 'Organisational Psychology', in S. Canter and D. Canter (eds) *Psychology in Practice: Perspectives in Professional Psychology*, Chichester, John Wiley.

Blackler, F. and Brown, C. A. (1978) *Job Design and Management Control*, Farnborough, Hants., Saxon House.

Blackler, F. and Shimmin, S. (1984) *Applying Psychology in Organisations*, London, Methuen.

Blau, P. M. (1955) *The Dynamics of Bureaucracy*, Chicago, University of Chicago Press.

Blau, P. M. (1964) *Exchange and Power in Social Life,* New York, Wiley.

Blau, P. M. (1970) 'A Formal Theory of Differentiation in Organisations', *American Sociological Review*, 35, pp. 201–18.

Blau, P. M. and Scott, W. (1963) *Formal Organisations: a Comparative Approach*, London, Routledge & Kegan Paul.

Blau, P. M. and Schoenherr, R. A. (1971) *The Structure of Organisations*, New York, Basic Books.

Blauner, R. (1964) *Alienation and Freedom*, University of Chicago Press.

Boreham, P. (1980b) 'The Dialectic of Theory and Control: Capitalist Crisis and the Organisation of Labour', in D. Dunkerley and G. Salaman (eds).

Bosquet, M. (1977) *Capitalism and Everyday Life*, Brighton, Harvester, Press.

Bradley, H. (1986) 'Work, Home and the Restructuring of Jobs', in K. Purcell *et al.* (eds).

Bramble, T. (1988) 'The Flexibility Debate: Industrial Relations and the New Management Production Practices', *Labour and Industry*, vol. 1, no. 2.

Brannen, P. (1983) *Authority and Participation in Industry*, London, Batsford.

Braverman, H. (1974) *Labor and Monopoly Capital: The Degradation of Work in the Twentieth Century*, New York, Monthly Review Press.
Breakwell, G. M. (1987) 'Identity', in H. Beloff and A. M. Colman (1987) *Psychology Survey 1987*, Leicester, British Psychological Society.
Brecher, J. (1978) 'Uncovering the Hidden History of the American Workplace', *Review of Radical Political Economics*, vol. 10, no. 4, Winter.
Briggs, P. (1987) 'The Japanese at Work: Illusions of the Ideal', Paper presented at Conference on Japanisation of British Industry, UWIST. Also in *Industrial Relations Journal*, Spring 1988, vol. 19, no. 1.
Broad, G. (1987) 'Beyond Quality Circles: A Critical Review of Employee Participation in Japanese Industry', Paper presented at Conference on Japanisation of British Industry, UWIST.
Brown, G. (1977) *Sabotage*, Nottingham, Spokesman.
Brown, H. (1980) 'Work Groups', in G. Salaman and K. Thompson, (eds).
Brubaker, R. (1984) *The Limits to Rationality: An Essay on the Moral and Social Thought of Max Weber* London, George Allen & Unwin.
Bruner, J. S. (1968) *Towards a Theory of Instruction*, New York, Norton.
Buchanan, D. (1986) 'Management Objectives in Technical Change', in D. Knights and H. Willmott (eds).
Buchanan, D. and Huczynski, A. (1985) *Organisational Behaviour: An Introductory Text*, London, Prentice-Hall International.
Bumstead, D. and Eckblad, J. (1985) 'Meaning Business: Values in the Workplace', in D. Clutterbuck (ed.).
Burawoy, M. (1979) *Manufacturing Consent: Changes in the Labour Process Under Monopoly Capitalism*, Chicago, University of Chicago Press.
Burawoy, M. (1985) *The Politics of Production*, London, Verso.
Burgoyne, J. G. and Germain, C. (1984) 'Self Development and Career Planning: An Exercise in Mutual Benefit', *Personnel Management*, April.
Burnham, J. (1945) *The Managerial Revolution*, Harmondsworth, Penguin.
Burns, T. (1982) *A Comparative Study of Administrative Structure and Organisational Processes in Selected Areas of the National Health Service* (SSRC Report, HRP 6725), London, Social Science Research Council.
Burns, T. and Stalker, G. M. (1961) *The Management of Innovation*, London, Tavistock.
Burrell, G. (1980a) 'Radical Organisation Theory', in D. Dunkerley and G. Salaman (eds).
Business Week (1983) 'A Work Revolution in US Industry', 16 May.
CAITS (1986) *Flexibility, Who Needs It?*, pamphlet, London.
Cameron, S. (1973) 'Organisation Change: A Description of Alternative Strategies', London, Work Research Unit Occasional Paper.
Campbell, A. and Currie, B. (1987) 'Skills and Strategies in Design Engineering', Paper presented at Conference on the Labour Process, ASTON-UMIST.
Campbell, J. P. and Dunnette, M. D. (1968) 'Effectiveness of T-Group Experiences in Managerial Training and Development', *Psychological Bulletin*, 70, pp. 73–104.
Carchedi, G. (1977) *On the Economic Identification of the Middle Classes*, London, Routledge & Kegan Paul.

Carey, A. (1967) 'The Hawthorne Studies: A Radical Criticism', *American Sociological Review* 32, pp. 403–16.

Carr Mill Consultants (1973) Report on the Herzberg Seminar, Blackpool.

Carter, R. (1985) *Capitalism, Class Conflict and the New Middle Class*, London, Routledge & Kegan Paul.

Cattell, J. M., Eber and Matsuoka (1970) *Handbook for the 16PF*, Colombia, IPAT.

Cavendish, R. (1982) *Women on the Line*, London, Routledge & Kegan Paul.

Chandler, A. (1962) *Strategy and Structure*, Cambridge, Mass:, MIT Press.

Chandler, A. (1977) *The Visible Hand*, Cambridge Mass: Harvard University Press.

Cherry, L. (1978) 'On the Real Benefits of Eustress', *Psychology Today*, March, pp. 60–70.

Child, J. (1969) *British Management Thought*, London, Allen & Unwin.

Child, J. (1972) 'Organisation Structure, Environment and Performance: the Role of Strategic Choice', *Sociology*, vol. 6, no. 1, pp. 1–22.

Child, J. (1973) (ed.) *Man and Organisation*, London, Allen & Unwin.

Child, J. (1982) 'Professionals in the Corporate World', in D. Dunkerley and G. Salaman (eds).

Child, J. (1984) *Organisation: a Guide to Problems and Practice*, 2nd edn, London, Harper & Row.

Child, J. (1985) 'Managerial Strategies, New Technology and the Labour Process', in D. Knights *et al.* (eds).

Child, J. (1987) 'Organisational Design for Advanced Manufacturing Technology', in T. D. Wall *et al.* (eds).

Child, J. *et al.* (1983) 'Professionalism and Work Organisation: a Reply to Kevin McCormack', *Sociology*, vol. 20, no. 4, pp. 607–14.

Child, J. and Smith, C. (1987) 'The Context and Process of Organisational Transformations – Cadbury Limited in its Sector', *Journal of Management Studies*, vol. 24, no. 6, pp. 565–93.

Chorover, S. L. (1979) *From Genesis to Genocide: Meaning of Human Nature and the Power of Behaviour Control*, MIT Press.

Cicourel, A. V. (1968) *The Social Organisation of Social Justice*, New York, Free Press.

Clairmonte, F. and Cavanagh, J. (1981) *The World in Their Web: the Dynamics of Textile Multinationals*, London, Zed Press.

Clawson, D. (1980) *Bureaucracy and the Labour Process: The Transformation of US Industry, 1860–1920*, New York, Monthly Review Press.

Clegg, S. (1977) 'Power, Organisation Theory, Marx and Critique', in S. Clegg and D. Dunkerley (eds).

Clegg, S. (1988) 'The Good, the Bad and the Ugly', *Organisation Studies*, vol. 9, no. 1, pp. 7–13.

Clegg, S. (1989) *Power*, London, Sage.

Clegg, S., Boreham, P. and Dow, G. (1987) *Class, Politics and the Economy*, London, Routledge & Kegan Paul.

Clegg, S. and Dunkerley, D. (eds) (1977) *Critical Issues in Organisations*, London, Routledge & Kegan Paul.

Clegg, S. and Dunkerley, D. (1980) *Organisation, Class and Control*, London, Routledge & Kegan Paul.

Clegg, S. and Higgins, G. (1987) 'Against the Current: Organisational Sociology and Socialism', *Organisational Studies*, vol. 8, no. 3, pp. 201–21.

Clutterbuck, D. (ed.) (1985) *New Patterns of Work*, Aldershot, Gower.

Cochrane, A. and Dicker, R. (1979) 'The Regeneration of British Industry: Jobs and the Inner City, in Community Development Project, *The State and the Local Economy*, Newcastle.

Cockburn, C. (1983) *Brothers: Male Dominance and Technological Change*, London, Pluto Press.

Cockburn, C. (1985) *Machineries of Dominance: Men, Women and Technical Know-how*, London, Pluto.

Cohen, S. (1973) *Folk Devils and Moral Panics*, London, Paladin.

Cohen, S. and Taylor, L. (1978) *Escape Attempts: The Theory and Practice of Resistance to Everyday Life*, Harmondsworth, Pelican.

Collective Design Project (eds) (1986) *Very Nice Work if You Can Get It: The Socially Useful Production Debate*, Nottingham, Spokesman.

Collins, R. (1986) *Weberian Sociological Theory*, Cambridge, Cambridge Univerwity Press.

Collinson, D. and Knights, D. 'Men Only: Theories and Practices of job segregation in Insurance, in Knights, D. and Willmott, H. (eds) (1986a).

Control Data Corporation (1985) 'Telecommuting', in D. Clutterbuck (ed.).

Cook, K. (1977) 'Exchange and Power in Networks of Interorganisational Relations' in J. K. Benson (ed.).

Cooley, M. (1987) *Architect or Bee?*, London, Hogarth.

Cooper, C. L. (1984) 'What's New In ... Stress', *Personnel Management*, June, pp. 40–4.

Cooper, C. L. and Smith, M. J. (1985) *Job Stress and Blue Collar Work*, Chichester, Wiley.

Cooper, R. and Barnell, G. (1988) 'Modernism, Post-Modernism and Organisational Analysts', *Organisation Studies*, vol. 9, no. 1, pp. 91–112.

Corbett, J. M. (1985) 'The Design of Machine-Tool Technology and Work: Technical Science and Technical Choice', Unpublished Draft, Sheffield, MRC/ESRC Social and Applied Psychology Unit.

Corbett, J. M. (1985a) 'Prospective Work Design of a Human-Centred CNC Lathe', *Behaviour and Information Technology*, vol. 14, no. 1, pp. 201–14.

Coriat, B. (1980) 'The Restructuring of the Assembly Line: a New Economy of time and Control', *Capital and Class*, 11, pp. 34–43.

Cornforth, C. (1988) 'Patterns of Cooperative Management: Revising the Degeneration Thesis', Paper to a Conference on New Forms of Ownership and Management, Cardiff Business School.

Cousins, C. (1986) 'The Labour Process in the State Welfare Sector', in D. Knights and H. Willmott (eds).

Cousins, C. (1987) *Controlling Social Welfare: a Sociology of State Welfare Work and Organisation*, Brighton, Wheatsheaf.

Coventry, Liverpool, Newcastle and N. Tyneside Trades Councils (1980) *State Intervention in Industry: a Workers' Inquiry*, Newcastle.

Cressey, P. and MacInnes, J. (1980) 'Voting for Ford: Industrial Democracy and the Control of Labour', *Capital and Class*, no. 11, pp. 5–37.

Crompton, R. and Jones, G. (1984) *White Collar Proletariat*, London, Macmillan.

Cross, M. (1985) 'Flexible Manning', in D. Clutterbuck (ed.).

Crouch, C. (ed.) (1979) State and Economy in Contemporary Capitalism, London, Croom Helm.

Crozier, M. (1964) *The Bureaucratic Phenomenon*, London, Tavistock.

Crowther, S. and Garrahan, P. (1987) 'Invitation to Sunderland: Corporate Power and the Local Economy', Paper presented at Conference on Japanisation of British Industry, UWIST, also in *Industrial Relations Journal*, Spring 1988, vol. 9, no. 1.

Cummings, T. and Blumberg, M. (1987) 'Advanced Manufacturing Technology and Work Design', in T. D. Wall *et al.*.

Cyert, R. M. and March, J. G. (1963) *A Behavioural Theory of the Firm*, Englewood Cliffs, N.J., Prentice-Hall.

Dahl, R. (1957) 'The Concept of Power', *Behavioural Science*, 2: pp. 201–15.

Dahl, R. (1978) 'Pluralism Revisited', *Comparative Politics*, 10: pp. 191–204.

Dahrendorf, R. (1959) *Class and Class Conflict in Industrial Society*, London, Routledge & Kegan Paul.

Daily Telegraph (1987) 'Workers Quit as Low Morale Hits Nissan Car Plant', 6 May.

Daniel, W. W. (1987) *Workplace Industrial Relations and Technical Change*, London, Francis Pinter.

Daniel, W. W. and McIntosh, N. (1972) *The Right to Manage?*, London, MacDonald.

Daniel, W. W. and Millward, N. (1983) *Workplace Industrial Relations in Britain*, London, Heinemann.

Dankbaar, B. (1988) 'New Production Concepts, Management Strategies and the Quality of Work', *Work, Employment and Society*, vol. 2, no. 1, pp. 25–50.

Davies, L. E. and Taylor, J. C. (eds) (1979) *Design of Jobs*, 2nd edn, Santa Monica, Goodyear.

Dawson, S. (1986) *Analysing Organisations*, London, Macmillan.

Day, R. A. and Day, J. V. (1977) 'A Review of the Current State of Negotiated Order Theory: An Appreciation and a Critique', *Sociological Quarterly* 18 (Winter), pp. 126–42.

De Vroey, M. (1975) 'The Separation of Ownership and Control in Large Corporations', *Review of Radical Political Economics*, vol. 7, no. 2, pp. 1–10.

Deal, T. and Kennedy, A. (1988) *Corporate Cultures: the Rites and Rituals of Corporate Life*, Harmondsworth, Penguin.

Deaux, K. and Emswiller, T. (1974) 'Explanations of Successful Performance on Sex-Linked Tasks: What is Skill for the Male is Luck for the Female', *Journal of Personality and Social Psychology*, 24, pp. 30–85.

Delamarter, R. T. (1988) *Big Blue: IBM's Use and Abuse of Power*, London, Pan Books.

Deleuze, G. and Guattari, F. (1977) *Anti-Oedipus: Capitalism and Schizophrenia*, New York, Viking.

Dent, M. (1986) 'Autonomy and the Medical Profession', Paper at the ASTON-UMIST Labour Process Conference.

Dickens, P. and Savage, M. (1987) 'The Japanisation of British Industry?: Instances from a High Growth Area', Paper presented at Conference on Japanisation of British Industry, UWIST. Also in *Industrial Relations Journal*, Spring 1988, vol. 19, no. 1.

Dickson, T. *et al.* (1988) 'Big Blue and the Unions: IBM, Individualism and Trade Union Society', *Work, Employment and Society*, vol. 2, no. 4, pp. 506–20.

Dill, W. R. (1962) 'The Impact of Environment on Organisation Development', in S. Mailick, and E. H. Van Ness (eds) *Concepts and Issues in Administrative Behaviour*, Englewood Cliffs, N.J., Prentice-Hall.

Ditton, J. (1974) 'The Fiddling Salesman: Connivance at Corruption', *New Society*, 28 November.

Domhoff, G. (1967) *Who Rules America?* Englewood cliffs, N.J., Prentice-Hall.

Donaldson, L. (1985) *In Defence of Organisation Theory*, Cambridge, Cambridge University Press.

Donovan, Lord (Chairman) (1968) *Report on the Royal Commission on Trade Unions and Employers' Associations*, London, HMSO.

Doray, B. (1988) *A Rational Madness: From Taylorism to Fordism*, London, Free Association Books.

Drago,R. and MacDonough, T. (1984) 'Capitalist Shopfloor Initiatives, Restructuring and Organising in the '80s,' *Review of Radical Political Economics*, vol. 716, no. 4, pp. 52–77.

Drake, R. I. and Smith, P. J. (1973) *Behavioural Science in Industry*, London, McGraw-Hill.

Drucker, P. (1955) *The Practice of Management*, Harper & Row, New York.

Drucker, P. (1977) *People and Performance*, London, Heinemann.

Drucker, P. (1979) *Management*, London, Pan.

Drucker, P. (1981) *Managing in Turbulent Times*, London, Pan.

Dunford, R. and McGraw, P. (1986) 'Quality Circles or Quality Circus? Labour Process Theory and the Operation of Quality Circle Programmes', Paper presented at Conference on the Labour Process, ASTON-UMIST.

Dunkerley, D. and Salaman, G. (eds) (1980a) *The International Yearbook of Organisation Studies 1979*, London, Routledge & Kegan Paul.

Dunkerley, D. and Salaman, G. (eds) (1980b) *The International Yearbook of Organisation Studies 1980*, London, Routledge & Kegan Paul.

Dunkerley, D. and Salaman, G. (eds) (1982) *The International Yearbook of Organisation Studies 1981*, London, Routledge & Kegan Paul.

Dunkerley, D. and Salaman, G. (1986) 'Organisations and Bureaucracy', in M. Haralambos (ed.) *Developments in Sociology*, vol. 2, Ormskirk, Causeway Press.

Dunning, J. H. (1986) *Japanese Participation in British Industry*, London, Croom Helm.

Economic Progress Report (1986) 'A More Flexible Labour Market', no. 182, the Treasury.

Eden, D. (1986) 'OD and Self-Fulfilling Prophecy: Boosting Productivity by Raising Expectations', *Journal of Applied Behavioural Science*, vol. 22, no. 1, pp. 1–13.

Edwardes, M. (1978) *The Dark Side of History: Magic in the Making of Man*, St. Albans, Granada.

Edwards, P. K. (1987) 'Control, Compliance and Conflict', Paper to be published in D. Knights and H. Willmott (1989) *Labour Process Theory*, London, Macmillan.

Edwards, R. (1979) *Contested Terrain: The Transformation of the Workplace in the Twentieth Century*, London, Heinemann.

Edwards, R., Reich, M. and Gordon, D. M. (1975) *Labour Market Segmentation*, Lexington, Mass., D.C. Heath.

Ehrenreich, B. and Ehrenreich, J. (1979) 'The Professional-Managerial Class', in P. Walker (ed.) *Between Labour and Capital*, Brighton, Harvester.

Elbaum, B. and Lazonick, W. (eds) (1986) *The Decline of the British Economy*, Oxford, Clarendon.

Eldridge, J. E. T. and Crombie, A. D. (1974) *A Sociology of Organisations*, London, Allen & Unwin.

Elger, T. (1987) 'Flexible Futures? New Technology and the Contemporary Transformation of Work', *Work, Employment and Society*, vol. 1, no. 4, pp. 528–40.

Elliot, D. (1980) 'The Organisation as a System', in G. Salaman and K. Thompson (eds) *Control and Ideology in Organisations*, Milton Keynes, Open University Press.

Elliot, K. and Lawrence, P. (1985) *Introducing Management*, Harmondsworth, Penguin.

Emergy, F. E. and Trist, E. L. (1965) 'The Causal Texture of Organisations', *Human Relations*, vol. 18, no. 1, pp. 21–32.

Eros, F. (1974) 'Review of L. Garai's Personality Dynamics and Social Existence', *European Journal of Social Psychology*, vol. 4, no. 3, pp. 369–79.

Esland, G. (1980) 'Professions and Professionalism', in G. Esland and G. Salaman (eds).

Esland, G. and Salaman, G. (eds) (1980) *The Politics of Work and Occupations*, Milton Keynes, Open University Press.

Etzioni, A. (1961) *A Comparative Analysis of Complex Organisations*, New York, Free Press.

Evden, d. (1986) 'OD and Self-Fulfilling Prophecy: Boosting Productivity by Raising Expectations', *Journal of Applied Behavioural Science*, vol. 22, no. 1, 1–13.

Eysenck, H. J. (1947) *Dimensions of Personality*, London, Routledge & Kegan Paul.

Eysenck, H. J. and Wilson, G. (1975) *Know Your Own Personality*, Harmondsworth, Penguin.

Fevre, R. (1986) 'Contract Work in the Recession', in K. Purcell *et al.* (eds).

Fiedler, F. E. (1967) *A Theory of Leadership Effectiveness*, New York, McGraw-Hill.

Fiedler, F. E. (1976) 'Situational Control: A Dynamic Theory of Leadership', in King, B., Steufert, S. and Fiedler, F. (1978) *Managerial Control and Organisational Democracy*, Washington, Winston & Wiley.

Finlay, P. (1985) 'Control', in K. Elliot and P. Lawrence (eds).

Finn, D. (1986) *Training Without Jobs*, London, Macmillan.

Fischer, F. (1984) 'Ideology and Organisation Theory', in F. Fischer and C. Sirriani, (eds).

Fischer, F. and Sirriani, C. (1984) *Critical Studies in Organisation and Bureaucracy*, Philadelphia, Temple University Press.

Fleishman, E. A. (1974) 'Leadership Climate, Human Relations Training and Supervisory Behaviour', in Fleishman, E. A. and Bass, A. R., *Studies in Personnel and Industrial Psychology*, New York, Dorsey.

Fontana, D. (1985) 'Learning and Teaching', in C. L. Cooper and P. Makin, *Psychology and Managers*, London, BPS and Macmillan.

Fowler, A. (1988) 'New Directions in Performance-Related Pay', *Personnel Management*, November, pp. 30–4.

Fox, A. (1974) *Beyond Contract: Work, Power and Trust Relations*, London, Faber & Faber.

Fox, A. (1980) 'The Meaning of Work', in G. Esland and G. Salaman (eds).

Francis, A. (1986) *New Technology at Work*, Oxford, Clarendon: OUP.

Freedman, M. (1984) 'The Search for Shelters', in K. Thompson (ed.) *Work, Employment and Unemployment*, Milton Keynes, Open University Press.

French, J. R. P. and Raven, B. H. (1959) 'The Social Bases of Power', in D. Cartwright (ed.) *Studies in Social Power*, Ann Aror, University of Michigan Press.

French, W. L. and Bell, C. H. jnr. (1973) *Organisation Development*, Englewood Cliffs, N.J., Prentice-Hall.

Frese, M. (1982) 'Occupational Socialisation and Psychological Development: An Underdeveloped Research Perspective in Industrial Psychology', *Journal of Occupational Psychology*, 55, pp. 209–24.

Fridenson, P. (1978) 'Corporate Policy, Rationalisation and the Labour Force-French Experiences in International Comparison, 1900–29', Paper presented at Nuffield Deskilling Conference.

Friedman, A. (1977) *Industry and Labour: Class Struggle at Work and Monopoly Capitalism*, London, Macmillan.

Friedman, A. (1986) 'Managerial Strategies Techniques, Activities and Technology: Towards a Complex Theory of the Labour Process', Paper presented at ASTON-UMIST Labour Process Conference.

Friedman, A. (1987) 'The Means of Management control and Labour Process Theory: A Critical Note on Storey', *Sociology*, vol. 21, no. 2, pp. 287–94.

Frost, P. J. *et al.* (eds) (1985) *Organisational Culture*, Beverley Hills, Sage.

Galbraith, J. K. (1967) *The New Industrial State*, Harmondsworth, Penguin.

Galbraith, J. R. (1984) 'Organisation Design: An Information Processing View', in Paton, R. *et al. Organisations: Cases, Issues, Concepts*, London, Harper & Row.

Garnsey, E. Rubery, J. and Wilkinson, F. (1985) 'Labour Market Structure and Workforce Divisions', Unit 8 of Open University course *Work and Society*, Milton Keynes Open University Press.

Geary, R. (1985) *Policing Industrial Disputes: 1893–1985*, London, Methuen.

George, M. and Levie, H. (1984) *Japanese Competition and the British Workplace*, London, CAITS.

Geras, N. (1983) *Marx and Human Nature: Refutation of a Legend*, London, Verso.

Gergen, K. J. (1973) 'Social Psychology as History', *Journal of Personality and Psychology*, vol. 26, no. 2, pp. 309–20.

Giles, E. and Starkey, K. (1987) 'From Fordism to Japanisation: Organisational Change at Ford, Rank Xerox and Fuji Xerox', Paper presented at Conference on Japanisation of British Industry, UWIST.

Gill, C. (1985) *Work, Unemployment and the New Technology*, Cambridge, Polity.

Giordano, L. (1985) 'Beyond Taylorism: Computerisation and QWL Programs in the Production Process', Paper presented at Conference on the Labour Process, ASTON-UMIST. Also published in D. Knights and H. Willmott (eds) (1988).

Glenn, E. K. and Feldberg, R. L. (1979) 'Proletarianising Office Work', in A. Zimbalist (ed.).

Glover, I. *et al.* (1986) 'The Coming Proletarianisation of the British Accountant?', Paper presented at Conference on the Labour Process, ASTON-UMIST.

Goffman, E. (1971) *The Presentation of Self in Everyday Life*, Harmondsworth, Pelican.

Goldman, P. and Van Houten D. R. (1977) 'Managerial Strategies and the Worker: A Marxist Analysis of Bureaucracy', in J. K. Benson (ed.).

Goldman, P. and Van Houten, D. R. (1980a) 'Bureaucracy and Domination: Managerial Strategy in Turn-of-the-Century American Industry', in D. Dunkerley and G. Salaman (eds).

Goldman, P. and Van Houten, D. R. (1980b) 'Uncertainty, Conflict and Labor Relations in the Modern Firm 1: Productivity and Capitalism's Human Face', *Economic and Industrial Democracy*, vol. 1, pp. 63–98.

Goldsmith, W. and Clutterbuck, D. (1985) *The Winning Streak*, Harmondsworth, Penguin.

Gordon, D. M., Edwards, R. and Reich, M. (1982) *Segmented Work, Divided Workers*, Cambridge, Cambridge University Press.

Gorz, A. (ed.) (1976) *The Division of Labour*, Brighton, Harvester Press.

Goss, S. and Parston, G. (1989) *Public Management for New Times*, London, Labour Co-ordinating Committee.

Gouldner, a. (1955) *Wildcat Strike*, London, Routledge & Kegan Paul.

Gouldner, A. W. (1954) *Patterns of Industrial Bureaucracy*, New York, Free Press.

Gowler, D. and Legge, K. (1983) 'The Meaning of Management and the Management of Meaning: A View From Social Anthropology', in M. J. Earl, (ed.) *Perspectives on Management: A Multidisciplinary Analysis*, Oxford, Oxford University Press.

Grant, W. (1983) 'Representing Capital', in R. King (ed.), *Capital and Politics*, London, Routledge & Kegan Paul.

Greenwood, R. and Hinings, C. R. (1987) 'Organisational Transformations', *Journal of Management Studies*, vol. 24, no. 6, pp. 561–4.

Grenier, G. J. (1988) *Inhuman Relations: Quality Circles and Anti-Unionism in American Industry*, Philadelphia, Temple University Press.

Grieco, M. and Whipp, R. (1986) 'Women and Control in the Workplace: Gender and Control in the Workplace', in D. Knights and H. Willmott (eds) (1986a).

Grossman, R. (1979) 'Women's Place in the Integrated Circuit', *Radical America*, vol. 14, no. 1, pp. 29–48.

Guest, D. (1989) 'Personnel and HRM: Can You Tell the Difference?', *Personnel Management*, January.

Guest, R. H. (1983) 'Organisational Democracy and the Quality of Working Life: the Man on the Assembly Line', in C. Crouch and F. Heller (eds), *Organisational Democracy and Political Processes*, London, John Wiley.

Habermas, J. (1971) *Toward a Rational Society*, London, Heinemann.

Hacker, W., Volpert, W. and Von Cranach, M. (eds) (1982) *Cognitive and Motivational Aspects of Action*, Amsterdam, North-Holland Publishing Company.

Hackman, J. R. (1978) 'The Design of Work in the 1980s', *Organisational Dynamics*, summer, pp. 3–17.

Hackman, J. R. and Oldman, G. R. (1980) *Work Redesign*, Reading, Mass., Addison-Wesley.

Hain, P. (1986) *Political Strikes*, Harmondsworth, Viking.

Hales, C. P. (1986) 'What do Managers Do? A Critical Review of the Evidence', *Journal of Management Studies*, vol. 23, no. 1, pp. 88–115.

Hales, C. P. (1988) 'Management Processes, Management Divisions of Labour and Managerial Work: Towards a Synthesis', Paper presented at Conference on the Labour Process, ASTON-UMIST.

Hall, R. H. (1973) 'Professionalisation and Bureaucratisation', in G. Salaman and K. Thompson (eds).

Hall, R. H. (1977) *Organisations: Structure and Process*, 2nd edn, Englewood Cliffs, N.J., Prentice-Hall.

Hall, P. A. (1986) 'The State and Economic Decline', in B. Elbaum and W. Lazonick (eds).

Hallet, S. (1988) 'Privatisation and the Restructuring of a Public Utility: A Case Study of BT's Corporate Strategy and Structure', Paper to a Conference on New forms of Ownership and Management, Cardiff Business School.

Hamilton, P. (1980) 'Social Theory and the Problematic Concept of Work', in G. Esland and G. Salaman (eds).

Hammond, V. and Barham, K. (1987) *Management for the Future: Report on the Literature Search*, Ashridge Management College.

Handy, C. (1984) *The Future of Work*, London, Basil Blackwell.

Handy, C. (1985) *Understanding Organisations*, Harmondsworth, Penguin.

Hannan, M. T. and Freeman, J. H. (1977) 'The Population Ecology of Organisations', *American Journal of Sociology*, 82, pp. 929–64.

Harris, R. (1987) *Power and Powerlessness in Industry: An Analysis of the Social Relations of Production*, London, Tavistock.

Harrison, R. G. (1984) 'Reasserting the Radical Potential of OD', *Personnel Review*, vol. 13, no. 2.

Hearn, J. and Parkin, W. (1987) *Sex at Work: the Power and Paradox of Organisation Sexuality*, Brighton, Wheatsheaf Books.

Heider, F. (1958) *The Psychology of Interpersonal Relations*, New York, John Wiley.

Held, D. (1983) 'Central Perspectives on the Modern State', in D. Held *et al.* (eds), *States and Societies*, Oxford, Martin Robertson.

Hendry, C. *et al.* (1988) 'Changing Patterns Of Human Resource Management', *Personnel Management*, November.

Henriques, J. (1984) 'Social Psychology and The Politics of Racism', in Henriques, J. *et al.*

Henriques, J. *et al.* (1984) *Changing the Subject: Psychology, Social Regulation and Subjectivity*, London, Methuen.

Herzberg, F. (1966) *Work and the Nature of Man*, Cleveland, Ohio, World Publishing Company.

Herzberg, F. (1968) 'One More Time, How Do You Motivate Employees?', in Carroll, S. J., Paine, F. T. and Miner, J. B. (eds) (1977), *The Management Process*, 2nd edn, New York, Macmillan, pp. 256–69.

Herzberg, F. *et al.* (eds) (1959) *The Motivation to Work*, New York, John Wiley.

Heydebrand, W. 77) 'Organisational Contradictions in Public Bureaucracies: Toward a Marxian Theory of Organisations', in J.K. Benson (ed.).

Hickson, D. J. (1971) 'A Strategic Contingencies Theory of Interorganisational Power', *Administrative Science Quarterly*, 16, pp. 216–29.

Hickson, D. J. (1973) 'A Convergence in Organisation Theory', in G. Salaman and K. Thompson (eds).

Hickson, D. J. and A. F. McCullough (1980) 'Power in Organisations', in G. Salaman and K. Thompson (eds).

Hickson, D. J. *et al.* (1973) 'A Strategic Contingencies Theory of Intra-organisational Power', in G. Salaman and K. Thompson (eds).

Hinings, C. R. (1988) 'Defending Organisation Theory', *Organisation Studies*, vol. 9, no. 1, pp. 2–7.

Hitt, M. A. *et al.* (1986) *Management Concepts and Effective Practice*, St Paul, West Publishing Company.

Hobsbawm, E. J. (1975) *The Age of Capital: 1845–1875*, London, Weidenfield & Nicolson.

Hochschild, A. R. (1983) *The Managed Heart*, Berkeley, University of California Press.

Hofstede, G. (1977) *Humanisation of Work: the Role of Values in a Third Industrial Revolution*, Working Paper, EIASM, Brussels.

Hofstede, G. (1986) 'Review of E. H. Schein, Organisational Culture and Leadership: a Dynamic View', *Organisation Studies*, vol. 7, no. 2.

Holland, S. (1975) *The Socialist Challenge*, London, Quartet Books.

Holloway, J. (1987) 'The Red Rose of Nissan', *Capital and Class*, no. 32, pp. 142–64.

Holloway, W. (1984) 'Fitting Work: Psychological Assessment in Organisations', in Henriques, J. *et al.*

Hopper, T. *et al.* (1986b) 'Management Control and Worker Resistance in the National Coal Board: Financial Controls in the Labour Process', in D. Knights and H. Willmott (eds).

Horne, J. H. and Lupton, T. (1965) 'The Work Activities of Middle Managers', *Journal of Management Studies*, vol. 2, no. 1, p. 14–33.

Horvat, B. (1983) 'The Organisational Theory of Workers' Management', in *International Yearbook of Organisational Democracy*, C. Crouch and F. Heller (eds), London, Wiley.

Howard, S. (1985) 'Big Blue's Big Family', *International Labour Reports*, March–April.

Hunt, J. (1984) 'The Shifting Focus of the Personnel Function', *Personnel Management*, February, pp. 14–18.

Hyman, R. (1982) 'Whatever Happened to Industrial Sociology?', in G. Salaman D. Dunkerley (eds).

Hyman, R. (1986) 'Trade Unions and the Law: Papering Over the Cracks?', *Capital and Class*, no. 31, pp. 93–114.

Hyman, R. (1987) 'Strategy or Structure: Capital, Labour and Control', *Work, Employment and Society*, vol. 1, no. 1, pp. 25–55.

Hyman, R. (1988) 'Flexible Specialisation: Miracle or Myth?' in R. Hyman and W. Streek (eds), *Trade Unions, Technology and Industrial Democracy*, Oxford, Basil Blackwell.

IPM Digest (1986) 'Flexibility: In Search of a Definition', no. 253, August.

Israel, J. and Tajfel, H. (eds) (1972) *The Context of Social Psychology: A Critical Assessment*, London, Academic Press.

Itoh, M. (1984) 'Labour Control in Small Groups', *Radical America*, vol. 18, no. 2/3.

Jenkins, D. (1973) *Job Power: Blue and White Collar Democracy*, Garden City, Doubleday.

Jenkins, R. (1982) 'Management, Recruitment Procedures and Black Workers', Working Papers Ethnic Relations, no. 18, Birmingham, Research Unit on Ethnic Relations.

Jenkins, R. (1986) *Racism and Recruitment: Managers, Organisations and Equal Opportunities in the Labour Market*, Cambridge, Cambridge University Press.

Johnson, A. and Moore, K. (1986) The Tapestry Makers, pamphlet, Merseyside Docklands Community History Project.

Johnson, T. (1972) *Professions and Power*, London, Macmillan.

Johnson, T. (1980) 'Work and Power', in G. Esland and G. Salaman (eds).

Johnston, L. (1986) *Marxism, Class Analysis and Sociaist Pluralism*, London, Allen & Unwin.

Jones, A. N. and Cooper, C. L. (1980) *Combating Managerial Obsolescence*, Philip Allan.

Jones, G. (1978) 'Ideological Rsponses to Deskilling of Managerial Work', Paper presented at Conference on Deskilling, Nuffield.

Kamata, S. (1982) *Japan in the Passing Line*, London, Pantheon.

Kamin, L. (1979) *The Science and Politics of IQ*, Harmondsworth, Penguin.

Kanter, R. (1984) *The Change Masters*, London, Allen & Unwin.

Karmel, B. (ed.) (1980) *Point and Counterpoint in Organisations*, Illinois, Dryden.

Katz, D. and Kahn, R. L. (1970) 'Open Systems Theory', in O. Grusky, and G. A. Miller (eds), *The Sociology of Organisations: Basic Studies*, New York, Free Press.

Katz, F. E. (1968) *Autonomy and Organisations: The Limits of Social Control*, New York, Random House.

Kelly, A. and Brannick, T. (1987) 'Personnel Practices and Strong Organisational Cultures in Ireland', Paper presented at Conference on Japanisation of British Industry, UWIST.

Kelly, G. A. (1955) *The Psychology of Personal Constructs* (2 vols), New York, Norton.

Kelly, J. E. (1980) 'The Costs of Job Design: A Preliminary Analysis', *Industrial Relations Journal*, vol 11, no. 3, 22–34.

Kelly, J. E. (1982) *Scientific Management, Job Design and Work Performance*, London, Academic Press.

Kelly, J. E. (1985) 'Management's Redesign of Work, in D, Knights *et al.* (eds).

Kern, H. and Schumman, M. (1984) *Das Ende der Arbeitesteilung? Rationalising in der Industriellen Produktion*, München, C. H. Beck.

Kerr, C. *et al.* (1960) *Industrialism and Industrial Man*, Cambridge, Mass., Harvard University Press.

Khandwalla, P. N. (1973) 'Viable and Effective Organisational Design of Firms', *Academy of Management Journal*, September.

Knights, D. and Collinson, D. (1987) 'Shop Floor Culture and the Problem of Managerial Control', in J. McGoldrick (ed.) *Business Case File in Behavioural Science*, London, Van Nystrand.

Knights, D. and Willmott, H. (1985) 'Power and Identity in Theory and Practice', *Sociological Review*, vol. 33, no. 1, pp. 22–46.

Knights, D. and Willmott, H. (eds) (1986a) *Gender and the Labour Process*, Aldershot, Gower.

Knights, D. and Willmott, H. (eds) (1986b) *Managing the Labour Process*, Aldershot, Gower.

Knights, D. and Willmott, H. (eds) (1988) *New Technology and the Labour Process*, London, Macmillan.

Knights, D. and Willmott, H. (eds) (1989) *Labour Process Theory*, London, Macmillan.

Knights, D., Willmott, H., and Collinson, D. (eds) (1985) *Job Redesign: Critical Perspectives on the Labour Process*, Aldershot, Gower.

Kotter, J. (1982) *The General Manager*, New York, Free Press.

Kouzmin, A. (1980) 'Control in Organisational Analysis: the Lost Politics', in Dunkerley, D. and Salaman, G. (eds).

Kraft, P. and Dubnoff, S. (1986) 'Job Characteristics in Computer Software', *Industrial Relations* (USA), vol. 25, no. 2, pp. 179–195.

Kreiger, J. (1983) *Undermining Capitalism*, London, Pluto.

Labour Research Department (1986a) 'Flexibility Examined', *Bargaining Report*, London.

Labour Research Department (1986b) 'Franchising – Who Really Benefits?' August, London.

Landes, D. S. (1969) *The Unbound Prometheus*, Cambridge, Cambridge University Press.

Landry, C. *et al.* (1985) *What a Way to Run a Railroad: An Analysis of Radical Failure*, London, Comedia.

Lane, T. and Roberts, K. (1971) *Strike at Pilkingtons*, Glasgow, Fontana.

Langer, E. J. (1981) 'Rethinking the Role Of Thought in Social Interaction', in, J. H. Harvey, W. Ickes, and R. F. Kidd, *New Directions in Attribution Research*, vol. 2, New York, Erlbaum.

Larsen, K. S. (1980) *Social Psychology: Crisis or Failure?*, Monmouth, Oregon, Institute for Theoretical History.

Lasch, C. (1984) *The Minimal Self: Psychic Survival in Troubled Times*, London, Picador.

Lawlor, E. E. (1976) 'Control Systems in Organisations', in H. D. Dunnette (ed.), *Handbook of Industrial and Organisational Psychology*, Rand McNally Publishing, Chicago.

Lawrence, P. R. and Lorsch, J. W. (1967) *Organisation and Environment*, Cambridge, Mass., Harvard University Press.

Layton, E. T. (1969) 'Science, Business and the American Engineer', in R. Perruci and J. E. Gersth (ed), *The Engineer and the Social System*, New York, John Wiley.

Lee, B. (1985) 'Internal Politics', in K. Elliot and P. Lawrence (eds).

Lee, R. and Lawrence, P. (1985) *Organisational Behaviour: Psychology at Work*, London, Hutchinson.

Legge, K. (1978) *Power, Innovation and Problem-solving in Management*, London, McGraw-Hill.

Lehman, C. and Tinker, T. (1985) 'The Not-So-Great Society: the Role of Business Literature on Reshuffling Johnson's New Deal', Paper Presented at Conference on the Labour Process, ASTON-UMIST.

Leonard, P. (1984) *Personality and Ideology: Towards a Materialist Understanding of the Individual*, London, Macmillan.

Lessem, R. (1985) 'The Enabling Company', in D. Clutterbuck (ed.).

Lessem, R. (1986) *The Roots of Excellence*, London, Fontana.

Lewis, M. (1975) 'Early Sex Differences in the Human: Studies of Socio-emotional Development', *Archives of Sexual Behaviour*, vol. 4, no. 4, pp. 329–35.

Likert, R. (1961) *New Patterns of Management*, New York, McGraw-Hill.

Likert, R. and Likert, J. G. (1976) *New Ways of Managing Conflict*, New York, McGraw-Hill.

Lindblom, C. E. (1959) 'The Science of Muddling Through', *Public Administration Review*, vol. 19, pp. 79–88.

Littler, C. R. (1982) *The Development of the Labour Process in Capitalist Societies*, London, Heinemann.

Littler, C. R. (1985) 'Taylorism, Fordism and Job Design', in D. Knights, H. Willmott and D. Collinson (eds).

Littler, C. R. (1980) 'Internal Contract and the Transition to Modern Work Systems', in D. Dunkerley and G. Salaman (eds).

Littler, C. R. and Salaman, G. (1982) 'Bravermania and Beyond', *Sociology*, vol. 16, no. 2, pp. 251–69.

Locke, E. and Latham, G. P. (1984) *Goal Setting: A Motivational Tecnique that Works!*, London, Prentice-Hall.

Loveridge, R. (1982) 'Business Strategy and Community Culture', in D. Dunkerley and G. Salaman (eds).

Lucas, M. (1986) *How to Survive the 9–5*, Thames, Methuen.

Lukes, S. (1974) *Power: A Radical View*, London, Macmillan.

Lupton, T. and Gowler, D. (1969) *Selecting a Wage Payment System*, London, Kogan Page.

Lupton, T. and Tanner, I. (1980) 'Work Design in Europe', in K. Duncan *et al.* (eds), *Changes in Working Life*, London, John Wiley.

Luthans, F. (1981) *Organisation Behaviour*, 3rd edn, New York, McGraw Hill.

Lynn, R. (1966) 'Brainwashing Techniques in Leadership and Child-rearing', *British Journal of Social and Clinical Psychology*, 5, pp. 270–3.

MacInnes, J. (1987) *Thatcherism at Work*, Milton Keynes, Open University Press.

Maguire, M. (1986) 'Recruitment as a Means of Control', in K. Purcell *et al.* (eds).

Mangham, I. (1978) *Interactions and Interventions in Organisations*, Chichester, John Wiley.

Mangum, G. L. and Mangum, S. L. (1986) 'Temporary Work: the Flip Side of Job Security', *International Journal of Manpower*, vol. 7, no. 1, pp. 12–20.

March, J. G. and Simon, H. A. (1958) *Organisations*, New York, John Wiley.

Marchington, M. (1982) *Managing Industrial Relations*, London, McGraw-Hill.

Marchington, M. and Parker, P. (1987) 'Japanisation: a Lack of Chemical Reaction?' Paper presented at Conference on Japanisation of British Industry, UWIST.

Marglin, S. A. (1974) 'What do Bosses Do? The Origins and Functions of Hierarchy in Capitalist Production', *Review of Radical Political Economics*, 6, pp. 60–102.

Mars, G. (1983) *Cheats at Work: An Anthology of Workplace Crime*, London, Unwin.

Martin, J. and Siehl, C. (1983) 'Organisational Culture and Counterculture: An Uneasy Symbiosis', *Organisational Dynamics*, Autumn, pp. 52–64.

Martin, P. and Nicholls (1987) *Creating a Committed Workforce*, London, Institute of Personnel Management.

Marx, K. (1963) *Early Writings*, trans. T. B. Bottomore, London.

Marx, K. (1984) 'The Spirit of Bureaucracy and Beyond Bureaucracy: The Paris Commune', in F. Fischer and C. Sirriani (eds).

Maslow, A. H. (1954) *Motivation and Human Personality*, New York, Harper & Row.

Mather, C. (1987) 'Disposable Workers', *New Internationalist*, July.

Mayo, E. (1946) *Human Problems of an Industrial Civilisation*, New York, Macmillan.

McCullough, A. and Shannon, M. (1977) 'Organisation and Protection', in S. Clegg and D. Dunkerley (eds).

McGregor, D. (1960) *The Human Side of the Enterprise*, New York, Harper and Row.

McKenna, E. (1987) *Psychology in Business: Theory and Applications*, London, Lawrence Erlbaum Associates.

MacLean, A. (1981) 'OD. A Case of the Emperor's New Clothes?' *Personnel Review*, vol. 10, no. 1, pp. 3–14.

McLellan, D. (1973) *Karl Marx: His Life and Thought*, London, Macmillan.

Mead, G. H. (1934) *Mind, Self and Society*, Chicago, Chicago University Press.

Mechanic, D. (1962) 'Sources of Power of Lower Participants in Complex Organisations', *Administrative Science Quarterly*, no. 7, pp. 349–64.

Melling, J. (1982) 'Men in the Middle or Men on the Margin?', in D. Dunkerley and G. Salaman (eds).

Merton, R. K. (1949) *Social Theory and Social Structure*, Chicago, Free Press.

Meyer, P. B. (1986) 'General Motors' Saturn Plant: a Quantum Leap in Technology and its Implications for Labour and Community Organisations', *Capital and Class*, 30, pp. 73–96.

Miliband, R. (1969) *The State in Capitalist Society*, London, Weidenfeld & Nicolson.

Miller, D. R. (1963) 'The Study of Social Relationships: Situations, Identities and Social Interaction', in, Koch, S. (ed.), *Psychology: a Study of a Science*, vol. 5, New York, McGraw-Hill.

Miller, E. J. and Rice, A. K. (1967) *Systems of Organisation: the Control of Task and Sentient Boundaries*, London, Tavistock.

Miller, G. A., Galanter, E. and Pribram, K. H. (1960) *Plans and the Structure of Behaviour*, London, Holt.

Miller, H. G. and Verduin, J. R. (1979) *The Adult Educator: A Handbook for Staff Development*, Houston, Gulf.

Miller, N. E. and Dollard, J. (1953) *Social Learning and Imitation*, New Haven, Yale University Press.

Miller, P. and O'Leary, T. (1987) 'The Entrepreneurial Order', Paper presented at Conference on the Labour Process, ASTON-UMIST.

Miller, P. M. (1989) 'Strategic HRM: What it Is and What it Isn't', *Personnel Management*, February.

Mills, C. W. (1959) *The Power Elite*, New York, Oxford University Press.

Mills, T. (1975) 'Human Resources – Why the New Concern?', *Harvard Business Review*, March–April.

Mintzberg, H. (1973) *The Nature of Managerial Work*, New York, Harper and Row.

Mintzberg, H. (1983) *Structure in Fives: Designing Effective Organisations*, Englewood Cliffs, New Jersey, Prentice-Hall.

Mitter, S. (1986) *Common Fate, Common Bond: Women in the Global Economy*, London, Pluto.

Mitter, S. (1988) 'Flexible Casualties', *Interlink*, no. 5.

Montgomery, D. (1976) 'Workers' Control of Machine Production in the Ninteenth Century', *Labor History*, vol. 17, no. 4: pp. 486–509.

Morgan, G. (1985) *Images of Organisation*, London, Sage.

Morgan, G. and Hooper, D. (1987) 'Corporate Strategy, Ownership and Control', *Sociology*, vol. 21, no. 4, pp. 609–27.

Morgan, K. and Sayer, A. (1984) A 'Modern' Industry in a 'Mature' Region: the Re-making of Management–Labour Relations, Working Paper, Urban and Regional Studies, University of Sussex.

Morris, J. (1987) 'The Who, Why, and Where of Japanese Manufacturing Invstment in the UK', Paper presented at Conference on Japanisation of British Industry, UWIST.

Moscovici, S. (1972) 'Society and Theory in Social Psychology', in J. Israel and H. Tajfel (eds).

Mullins, L. (1985) *Management and Organisation Behaviour*, London, Pitman.

Mulgen, G. (1988) 'The Power of the Weak', *Marxism Today*, December.

Murray, F. (1983) 'The Decentralisation of Production and the Decline of the Mass-Collective Worker', *Capital and Class*, 19, pp. 74–9.

Murray, F. (1987) 'Flexible Specialisation and the Third Italy', *Capital and Class*, no. 33, pp. 84–95.

Murray, P. and Wickham, J. (1985) 'Women Workers and Bureaucratic Control in Irish Electronic Factories', in H. Newby, *et al.* (eds), *Restructuring Capital: Recession and Reorganisation in Industrial Society*, London, Macmillan.

Murray, R. (1985) 'Bennetton Britain', *Marxism Today*, November.

Myers, S. (1976) *Managing Without Unions*, Reading, Mass., Addison-Wesley.

Nadworny, M. (1955) *Scientific Management and the Unions*, Cambridge, Mass: Harvard University Press.

Naisbitt, J. and Aburdene, P. (1985) *Reinventing the Corporation*, London, MacDonald.

NEDO (1986) *Changing Working Patterns*, Report prepared by the Institute for Manpower Studies for the National Economic Development Office in Association with the Department of Employment, NEDO, London.

Neimark, M. and Tinker, T. (1986) 'On Rediscovering Marx: Dissolving Agency-Structure in Dialectical Unity', Paper presented at Conference on the Labour Process.

Nelson, D. (1975) *Managers and Workers: Origins of the New Factory System in the United States 1880–1920*, Madison, University of Wisconsin Press.

Newman, R. and Newman, J. (1986) 'Information Work, the New Divorce', *British Journal of Sociology*, vol. 36.

Nichols, T. (1986) *The British Worker Question*, London, Routledge and Kegan Paul.

Nichols, T. and Beynon, H. (1977) *Living With Capitalism*, London, Routledge and Kegan Paul.

Noble, D. (1979) 'Social Choice in Machine Design', in A. Zimbalist (eds) *Case Studies in the Labour Process*, London, Monthly Review Press.

North-West Women Into Management (1987) Newletter, Manchester, June.

Nyland, C. (1987) 'Scientific Management and Planning', *Capital and Class*, 33, pp. 55–83.

O'Neill, N. (1985) 'Marxism and Psychology', in M. Shaw (ed.), *Marxist Sociology Revisited*, London, Macmillan.

OECD (1977) *The Development of Industrial Relations Systems: Some Implications of the Japanese Experience*, Paris, OECD.

Offe, C. (1984) *Contradictions of the Welfare State*, London, Hutchinson.

Ouchi, W. G. and Johnson, J. B. (1978) 'Types of Organisational Control and Their Relationship to Emotional Well-Being', *Administrative Science Quarterly*, vol. 23, June, pp. 293–317.

Ouchi, W. G. (1981) *Theory Z*, Reading, Mass., Addison-Wesley.

Pahl, R. H. (ed.) (1988) *On Work*, Oxford, Basil Blackwell.

Palmer, B. (1975) 'Class Conception and Conflict', *Review of Radical Political Economics*, vol. 17, no. 2, pp. 31–49.

Palmer, G. (1983) *Industrial Relations in Britain*, London, Allen and Unwin.

Palmer, J. (1986) 'Municipal Enterprise and Popular Planning', *New Left Review*, no. 159, Sept–Oct, pp. 117–24.

Parker, M. (1985) *Inside the Circle: A Union Guide to QWL*, Boston, Labor Notes.

Parsons, T. (1951) *The Social System*, New York, Collier Macmillan.

Parsons, T. (1956) 'Suggestions for a Sociological Approach to the Theory of Organisations', *Administrative Science Quarterly*, 1, pp. 63–85, 225–39.

Parsons, T. (1960) *Structure and Process in Modern Societies*, Chicago, The Free Press.

Pascale, R. T. and Athos, A. G. (1982) *The Art of Japanese Management*, Harmondsworth, Penguin.

Paul, W. J. and Robertson, K. B. (1970) *Job Enrichment and Employee Motivation*, Aldershot, Gower.

Pearson, R. (1986) 'Female Workers in the First and Third Worlds: the "Greening" of Women's Labour', in K. Purcell *et al.* (eds).

Penn, R. (1985) *Skilled Workers in the Class Structure*, Cambridge, Cambridge University Press.

Penn, R. (1986) 'Socialisation into Skilled Identities: an Analysis of a Neglected Phenomenon', paper presented at Conference on the Labour Process, ASTON–UMIST.

Perrow, C. (1961) 'The Analysis of Goals in Complex Organisations', *American Sociological Review*, 26, pp. 854–66.

Perrow, C. (1979) *Complex Organisations: A Critical Essay*, Illinois, Scott Foreman.

Peters, T. J. (1987) 'There Are No Excellent Companies', *Fortune*, 27 April.

Peters, T. J. and Austin, N. (1985) *A Passion for Excellence*, New York, Random House.

Peters, T. J. and Waterman, R. H. (1982) *In Search of Excellence: Lessons from America's Best-Run Companies*, New York, Harper & Row.

Pettigrew, A. (1973) *The Politics of Organisational Decision-making*, London, Tavistock.

Pettigrew, A. (1985) *The Awakening Giant: Continuity and Change at Imperial Chemical Industries*, Oxford, Basil Blackwell.

Pfeffer, J. (1981) *Power in Organisations*, London, Pitman.

Pfeffer, J. (1982) *Organisations and Organisation Theory*, Boston, Pitman.

Phizacklea, A. (1987) 'Minority Women and Economic Restructuring: The Case of Britain and the Federal Republic of Germany', *Work, Employment and Society*, vol. 1, no. 3, pp. 309–25.

Pierson, C. (1984) 'New Theories of State and Civil Society', *Sociology*, vol. 18, no. 4, pp. 563–71.

Pinchot, G. (1985) *Intrapreneuring*, New York, Harper & Row.

Piore, M. J. (1986) 'Perspectives on Labour Market Flexibility', *Industrial Relations*, vol. 25, no. 2, pp. 146–66.

Piore, M. J. and Sabel, C. F. (1984) *The Second Industrial Divide: Possibilities for Prosperity*, New York, Basic Books.

Polan, A. J. (1984) *Lenin and the End of Politics*, London, Methuen.

Pollard, S. (1965) *The Genesis of Modern Management*, London, Edward Arnold.

Pollert, A. (1981) *Girls, Wives, Factory Lives*, London, Macmillan.

Pollert, A. (1988a) 'Dismantling Flexibility', *Capital and Class*, 34 Spring, pp. 42–75.

Pollert, A. (1988b) 'The Flexible Firm: Fixation or Fact?' *Work, Employment and Society*, vol. 2, no. 3, pp. 281–316.

Poulantzas, N. (1975) *Classes in Contemporary Capitalism*, London, New Left Books.

Pugh, D. S. (ed.) (1971) *Organisation Theory*, Penguin, Harmondsworth.

Pugh, D. S. and Hickson, D. H. (1973) 'The Comparative Study of Organisations', in G. Salaman and K. Thompson (eds).

Pugh, D. S. and Hickson, D. J. (1976) *Organisation Structure in its Context: the Aston Programme 1*, London, Saxon House.

Pugh, D. S. *et al.* (1963) 'A Conceptual Scheme for Organisational Analysis', *Administrative Science Quarterly*, vol. 16.

Pugh, D. S. *et al.* (1968) 'Dimensions of Organisation Structure', *Administrative Science Quarterly*, vol. 13, pp. 65–103.

Pugh, D. S. *et al.* (1969) 'An Empirical Taxonomy of Structures of Work Organisations', *Administrative Science Quarterly*, vol. 14.

Purcell, J. and Sissons, K. (1983) 'A Strategy for Management Control in Industrial Relations', in J. Purcell and R. Smith (eds), *The Control of Work*, London, Macmillan.

Purcell, K. *et al.* (eds) (1986) *The Changing Experience of Employment, Restructuring and Recession*, London, Macmillan.

Ramsay, H. (1983) 'Evolution or Cycle? Worker Participation in the 1980s', in C. Crouch and F. Heller (eds), *Organisational Democracy and Political Processes*, London, Pitman.

Ramsay, H. (1985) 'What is Participation For: A Critical Evaluation of "labour process" Analyses of Job Reform,' in D. Knights *et al.*

Rauner, F., Rasmussen, L. and Corbett, M. (1988) 'The Social Shaping of Technology and Work: Human Centred CIM Systems', *Artificial Intelligence and Society*, vol. 2, pp. 47–61.

Ray, C. A. (1986) 'Corporate Culture: the Last Frontier of Control', *Journal of Management Studies*, vol. 23, no. 3, pp. 287–97.

Reed, M. (1984) 'Management as a Social Practice', *Journal of Management Studies*, vol. 21, no. 3, pp. 273–85.

Reed, M. (1985) *Redirections in Organisational Analysis*, Tavistock, London.

Resch, M., Hacker, W., Leitner, K. & Krogoll, T. (1984) 'Regulation Requirements and Regulation Barriers: Two Aspects of Industrial Work', in M. Thomas (ed.), *Design of Work in Automated Manufacturing Systems*, Oxford, Pergamon.

Roeber, J. (1975) *Social Change at Work*, London, Duckworth.

Roethlisberger, F. G., and Dickson, W. J. (1939) *Management and the Worker*, Cambridge, Mass:, Harvard University Press.

Roethlisberger, F. G., and Dickson, W. J. (1984) 'Human Relations and the Informal Organisation' in F. Fisher and C. Sirriani (eds.).

Rogers, C. (1969) *Freedom To Learn: Studies of the Person*, Columbus Ohio, Charles Merrill & Co.

Rose, G. (1978) *The Melancholy Science: An Introduction to the Thought of Theodore W. Adorno*, London, Macmillan.

Rose, M. (1975) *Industrial Behaviour*, Harmondsworth, Penguin, 2nd edn 1988.

Rose, M. and Jones, B. (1985) 'Managerial Strategy and Trade Union Responses in Work Reorganisation Schemes at Establishment Level', in D. Knights *et al.*

Rosenman, R. H., Friedman, M. and Strauss, R. (1964) 'A Predictive Study of CHD', *Journal of the American Medical Association*, 189, pp. 15–22.

Rosnow, R. L. (1981) *Paradigms in Transition: The Methodology of Social Enquiry*, New York, Oxford University Press.

Rothschild-Whitt, T. (1979) 'The Collectivist Organisation: An Alternative to Rational Bureaucratic Models', *American Sociological Review*, 44, pp. 509–27.

Rothwell, S. (1987) 'Selection and Training for Advanced Manufacturing Technology', in T. D. Wall *et al.* (eds).

Rotter, J. B. (1972) 'Generalised Expectancies for Internal versus External Control of Reinforcement', in J. B. Rotter *et al.* (eds), *Applications of a Social Learning Theory of Personality*, New York, Holt, Rinehart & Winston.

Roy, D. F. (1973) 'Banana Time, Job Satisfaction and Informal Interaction', in, Salaman G. and Thompson, K. (eds).

Rueschemeyer, D. (1986) *Power and the Division of Labour*, London, Polity Press.

Sabel, C. F. (1982) *Work and Politics and the Division of Labour in Industry*, Cambridge University Press.

Salaman, G. (1979) *Work Organisations: Resistance and Control*. London, Longman.

Salaman, G. (1981) *Class and the Corporation*, London, Fontana.

Salaman, G. (1986) *Working*, London, Tavistock.

Salaman, G. and Thompson, K. (eds) (1973) *People and Organisations*, Harlow, Longman.

Salaman, G. and Thompson, K. (eds) (1980) *Control and Ideology in Organisations*, Milton Keynes, Open University Press.

Sayer, A. (1984) *Method in Social Science: A Realist Approach*, London, Hutchinson.

Sayer, A. (1986) 'New Developments in Manufacturing: the Just-in-Time System', *Capital and Class*, no. 30, pp. 43–72.

Sayles, C. R. (1958) *Behaviour of Industrial Work Groups*, New York, Wiley.

Schein, E. H. (1965) *Organisational Psychology*, Englewood Cliffs, N.J. Prentice Hall.

Schein, E. H. (1969) *Process Consultation: Its Role in Organisational Development*, Reading, Mass., Addison-Wesley.

Schein, E. H. (1985) *Organisational Culture and Leadership: A Dynamic View*, San Francisco, Jossey-Bass.

Schneider, M. (1975) *Neurosis and Civilisation: A Marxist/Freudian Synthesis*, New York, Seabury.

Schutz, A. (1967) *The Phenomenology of the Social World*, Evanston, North Western University Press.

Scott, J. (1979) *Corporations, Classes and Capitalism*, Hutchinson, London.

Scott, J. (1985) 'Ownership, Management and Strategic Control', in K. Elliot and P. Lawrence (eds).

Scott, W. R. (1978) 'Theoretical Perspectives', in M. W. Meyer *et al.* (eds), *Environments and Organisations*, San Francisco, Jossey-Bass.

Seivers, B. (1986) 'Beyond the Surrogate of Motivation', *Organisation Studies*, vol. 7, no. 4.

Seligman, M. E. P. (1975) *Helplessness*, San Francisco, Freeman.

Selznick, P. (1949) *TVA and the Grass Roots*, Berkeley, Ca., University of California Press.

Selznick, P. (1957) *Leadership in Administration*, Evanston, Row Peterson.

Séve, L. (1978) *Man in Marxist Theory and the Psychology of Personality*, Sussex, Harvester Press.

Shaiken, H. *et al.* (1986) 'The Work Process Under More Flexible Production', *Industrial Relations* (USA), vol. 125, no. 2, pp. 167–83.

Shotter, J. and Gergen, K. J. (1989) *Texts of Identity*, London, Sage.

Shutt, J. (1985) 'Tory Enterprise Zones and the Labour Movement', *Capital and Class*, no. 23, pp. 19–44.

Silver, J. (1987) 'The Ideology of Excellence: Management and Neo-Conservatism', *Studies in Political Economy*, 24, Autumn, pp. 1;05–29.

Silverman, d. (1970) *The Theory of Organisations*, London, Heinemann.

Silverman, D. and Jones, J. (1976) *Organisational Work: The Language of Grading and the Grading of Language*, London, Macmillan.

Simon, H. A. (1960) *Administrative Behaviour*, New York, Macmillan.

Sirriani, C. (1984) 'Participation, Equality and Opportunity: Towards a Pluralist Organisational Model', in F. Fischer and C. Sirriani (eds).

Skocpol, T. (1979) *States and Social Revolutions*, Cambridge, Cambridge University Press.

Slaughter, J. (1987) 'The Team Concept in the US Auto Industry: Implications for Unions', Paper presented at Conference on Japanisation, UWIST.

Sloan, M. (1987) 'Culture and Control at Salesco: A Participant Observation Study', unpublished BA Dissertation, Lancashire Polytechnic.

Smith, C. (1987) 'Flexible Specialisation and Earlier Critiques of Mass Production', Paper presented at Conference on the Labour Process, ASTON-UMIST.

Smith, D. (1987) 'The Japanese Example in South West Birmingham', Paper presented at Conference on Japanisation of British Industry, UWIST.

Sorge, A. *et al.* (1983) *Microelectronics and Manpower in Manufacturing*, Aldershot, Gower.

Special Task Force to the Secretary of Health, Education and Welfare (1973) *Work in America*, Cambridge, Mass., MIT Press.

Staber, U. and Aldrich, H. (1987) 'Organisational Transformation and Trends in US Employment Relations', Paper presented at ASTON–UMIST Conference on the Labour Process.

Standing, G. (1986) *Unemployment and Labour Market Flexibility: the United Kingdom*, International Labour Office, Geneva.

Starkey, K. and McKinlay, A. (1989) 'Between Control and Consent? Corporate Strategy and Employee Involvement in Ford UK'. Paper presented at UMIST Conference on Flexibility.

Steiner, T. and Miner, B. (1978) *Management Policy and Strategy*, West Drayton, Collier-Macmillan.

Stewart, E. (1970) *The Reality of Organizations*, London, Macmillan.

Stewart, E. (1976) *Contrasts in Management*, Maidenhead, Berks, McGraw-Hill.

Stodgill, R. M. (1948) 'Personal Factors Associated With Leadership: A Review of the Literature', *Journal of Psychology*, 25, pp. 35–7.

Stodgill, R. M. (1976) *Handbook of Leadership*, Glencoe, Free Press.

Stone, K. (1973) 'The Origins of Job Structures in the Steel Industry', *Radical America*, vol. 7, no. 6.

Storey, J. (1983) *Managerial Prerogative and the Question of Control*, London, Routledge & Kegan Paul.

Storey, J. (1985) 'The Means of Management Control', *Sociology*, vol. 19, no. 2, pp. 193–211.

Storlie, F. J. (1979) 'Burnout: The Elaboration of a Concept', *American Journal of Nursing*, December, pp. 2108–111.

Strauss, A. *et al.* (1963) 'The Hospial and its Negotiated Order', in E. Friedson (ed.), *The Hospital in Modern Society*, New York, Macmillan.

Streek, W. (1987) 'The Uncertainties of Management in the Management of Uncertainty: Employers, Labour Relations and Industrial Adjustment in the 1980s', *Work, Employment and Society*, vol. 1, no. 3, pp. 281–308.

Stringer, P. (ed.) (1982) *Confronting Social Issues: Applications of Social Psychology*, vol. 2, London, Academic Press.

Stuart, R. (1988) 'Big is Back and Beautiful', *The Economist*, Review of the Year.

Sturdy, A. (1987) 'Coping with the Pressure of Work', Paper presented at Conference on the Labour Process, ASTON-UMIST.

Tailby, S. and Turnbull, P. (1987) 'Learning to Manage Just-in-Time', *Personnel Management*, January.

Taylor, F. W. (1947) *Scientific Management*, New York, Harper & Row.

Teather, D. C. B. (ed.) (1979) *Staff Development in Higher Education: An International Review and Bibliography*, London, Kogan Page.

Teulings, A. (1986) 'Managerial Labour Processes in Organised Capitalism: the Power of Corporate Management and the Powerlessness of the Manager', in D. Knights and H. Willmott (eds).

Thackray, J. (1986) 'The Corporate Culture Rage', *Management Today*, February, pp. 67–70.

Thackray, J. (1988) 'Flattening the White Collar', *Personnel Management*, August.

Thomas, R. J. (1988) 'What is Human Resource Management?', *Work, Employment and Society*, vol. 2, no. 3, pp. 392–402.

Thompson, E. P. (1967) 'Time, Work Discipline and Industrial Capitalism', *Past and Present*, 38, pp. 55–97.

Thompson, J. D. (1967) *Organisations in Action*, New York, McGraw-Hill.

Thompson, J. D. and McEwan, W. J. (1973) 'Organisational Goals and Environment', in G. Salaman and K. Thompson (eds).

Thompson, P. (1983, 1989 2nd edn) *The Nature of Work: An Introduction to Debates on the Labour Process*, London, Macmillan.

Thompson, P. (1984) 'The New Vocationalism: the Trojan Horse of the MSC', *Social Science Teacher*, vol. 13, no. 2.

Thompson, P. (1988) 'The End of Bureaucracy? New Developments in Work and Organisation', in *Developments In Sociology*, vol. 5, M. Haralambos (ed.), Ormskirk, Causeway Press.

Thompson, P. and Bannon, E. (1985) *Working the System: The Shop Floor and New Technology*, London, Pluto.

Thurley, K. and Wood, S. (1983) *Industrial Relations and Management Strategy*, Cambridge, Cambridge University Press.

Tichy, N. and Devanna, M. A. (1986) *Transformational Leadership*, London, John Wiley.

Tichy, N. *et al.* (1982) 'Strategic Human Resource Management', *Sloan Management Review*, pp. 47–61.

Toffler, A. (1970) *Future Shock*, New York, Bantam Books.

Tomlinson, J. (1982) *The Unequal Struggle? British Socialism and the Capitalist Enterprise*, London, Methuen.

Towers, B. (1987) 'Managing Labour Flexibility', *Industrial Relations Journal*, vol. 18, no. 2, pp. 79–83.

Transnationals Information Centre (1987) *Working for Big Mac*, pamphlet, London, TICL.

Trist, E. L. and Bamforth, K. W. (1951) 'Some Social and Psychological Consequences of the Longwall Method of Coal-Getting', *Human Relations*, vol. 4, no. 1, pp. 3–38.

Trist, E. L. *et al.* (1963) *Organisational Choice*, London, Tavistock.

Turnbull, P. J. (1986) 'The Japanisation of British Industrial Relations at Lucas', *Industrial Relations Journal*, vol. 17, no. 3, pp. 193–206.

Turnbull, P. J. (1987) 'The Limits to Japanisation: Just-in-Time, Labour

Relations and the UK Automotive Industry', Paper presented at Conference on Japansation of British Industry, UWIST.

Ursell, G. and Blyton, P. (1988) *State, Capital and Labour*, London, Macmillan.

Van Strien, P. J. (1982) 'In Search of an Emancipatory Social Psychology', in, P. Stringer (ed.).

Vroom, V. H. and Yetton, P. W. (1973) *Leadership and Decision Making*, Pittsburgh, University of Pittsburgh Press.

Vroom, V. H. (1964) *Work and Motivation*, New York, John Wiley.

Wainwright, H. (1987) 'The Friendly Mask of "Flexibility",' *New Statesman*, 11 December.

Walker, C. R. and Guest, R. H. (1952) *Man on the Assembly Line*, Cambridge, Mass., Harvard University Press.

Wall, T., Kemp, N. J., Jackson, P. R. and Clegg, C. W. (1986) 'Outcomes of Autonomous Workgroups: A Long-Term Field Experiment', *Academy of Management Journal*.

Wall, T. D., Clegg, C. W. and Kemp, N. J. (eds) (1987) *The Human Side of Advanced Manufacturing Technology*, Chichester, John Wiley.

Wardell, M. (1986) 'Labor and Labor Process', paper at ASTON–UMIST Labour Process Conference.

Watson, T. (1980b) 'Understanding Organisations: The Practicalities of Sociological Theory', in Dunkerley and Salaman (eds).

Watson, T. (1986) *Management, Organisation and Employment Strategy: New Directions in Theory and Practice*, London, Routledge & Kegan Paul.

Weber, M. (1968) *Economy and Society*, New York, Bedminster Press.

Weber, M. (1984) 'Bureaucracy', in F. Fischer and C. Sirriani (eds).

Weigert, A. J., Smith Teitge, J. and Teitge, D. W. (1986) *Society and Identity: Towards a Sociological Psychology*, New York, Cambridge University Press.

Weitz, S. (1977) *Sex Roles: Biological, Psychological and Social Foundations*, New York, Oxford University Press.

Wellin, M. (1984) *Behaviour Technology: a New Approach to Managing People at Work*, Aldershot, Gower.

Westwood, S. (1984) *All Day, Every Day: Factory and Family in the Making of Women's Lives*, London, Pluto.

Wexler, P. (1983) *Critical Social Psychology*, Boston, Routledge & Kegan Paul.

Whitaker, A. (1986) 'Managerial Strategy and Industrial Relations: a Case Study of Plant Relocation', *Journal of Management Studies*, vol. 23, no. 6, pp. 657–78.

Whitehead, T. N. (1936) *Leadership in a Free Society*, Cambridge, Mass., Harvard University Press.

Whitehead, T. N. (1938) *The Industrial Worker*, London, Oxford University Press.

Whitely, R. (1984) 'The Fragmented State of Management Studies', *Journal of Management Studies*, vol. 21, no. 3, pp. 31–48.

Whitely, R. (1987) 'Taking Firms Seriously as Economic Actors: Towards a Sociology of Firm Behaviour', *Organisation Studies*, vol. 8. no. 2, pp. 125–47.

Whittington, R. (1988) 'Environmental Structure and Theories of Strategic Choice', *Journal of Management Studies*, vol. 25, no. 6, pp. 521–36.

Whyte, W. H. (1956) *The Organisation Man*, New York, Simon & Schuster.

Wickens, P. (1987) *The Road to Nissan*, London, Macmillan.

Wilkinson, B. (1986) 'Human Resources in Singapore's Second Industrial Revolution', *Industrial Relations Journal*, vol. 17, no. 2, p. 99–114.

Wilkinson, B. (1983b) 'Technical Change and Work Organisation', *Industrial Relations Journal*, vol. 14, no. 2, Summer.

Wilkinson, B. (1983a) *The Shopfloor Politics of New Technology*, London, Heinemann.

Williams, K. *et al.* (1987) 'The End of Mass Production?', *Economy and Society*, vol. 16, no. 3, pp. 405–39.

Williams, R. (1988) 'The Development of Models of Technology and Work Organisation with Information and Communication Technologies', Paper presented at Conference on the Labour Process, ASTON–UMIST.

Willis, P. (1977) *Learning to Labour*, Farnborough, Saxon House.

Willmott, H. (1984) 'Images and Ideals of Managerial Work', *Journal of Management Studies*, vol. 21, no.3, pp. 349–68.

Willmott, H. (1987) 'Studying Managerial Work: A Critique and a Proposal', *Journal of Management Studies*, vol. 24, no. 3, pp. 249–70.

Willmott, H. (1989) 'Subjectivity and the Dialectics of Praxis: Opening up the Core of Labour Process Analysis', in D. Knights and H. Willmott (eds).

Wilson, F. (1988) 'Computer Numerical Control and Constraint', in D. Knights and H. Willmott (eds), *New Technology and the Labour Process*, London, Macmillan.

Winstanley, D. (1986) 'Recruitment Strategies as a Means of Control of Technological Labour', paper at ASTON–UMIST Labour Process Conference.

Witz, A. (1986a) 'Patriarchy and the Labour Market: Occupational Controls and the Medical Division of Labour', in D. Knights and H. Willmott (eds).

Wood, S. (1979) 'A Reappraisal of the Contingency Approach to Organisation', *Journal of Management Studies*, vol. 16, no. 3, pp. 334–54.

Wood, S. (1986) 'The Cooperative Labour Strategy in the US Auto Industry', *Economic and Industrial Democracy*, vol. 7, no. 4, pp. 415–48.

Wood, S. (1988) 'From Braverman to Cyberman', paper presented at ASTON–UMIST, Conference on the Labour Process.

Wood, S. (ed.) (1982) *The Degradation of Work: Skill, Deskilling and the Labour Process*, London, Hutchinson.

Wood, S. (ed.) (1989) *The Transformation of Work?*, London, Hutchinson.

Wood, S. (1989) 'The Japanese Management Model', *Sociology of Work and Occupations* (forthcoming).

Woodward, J. (1958) *Management and Technology*, London, HMSO.

Woodward, J. (1965) *Industrial Organisation: Theory and Practice*, London, Oxford University Press.

Woolf, J. (1977) 'Women in Organisations', in S. Clegg and D. Dunkerley (eds).

Wright, E. O. (1976) 'Contradictory Class Locations', *New Left Review*, no. 98.

Yates, D. (1986) 'Is Dual Labour Market Theory Dead? The Changing Organisation of Work: the Employer's Perspective', paper presented at ASTON–UMIST Conference on the Labour Process.

Zeitlin, M. (1974) 'Corporate Ownership and Control: the Large Corporation and the Capitalist Class, *American Journal of Sociology*, vol. 79, no. 5, pp. 1073–119.

Zimbalist, A. (1975) 'The Limits to Work Humanisation', *Review of Radical Political Economics*, 7, pp. 50–60.

Zimbalist, A. (ed.) (1979) *Case Studies on the Labour Process*, New York, Monthly Review Press.

Zimmerman, D. (1971) 'The Practicalities of Rule Use', in J. Douglas (ed.), *Understanding Everyday Life*, London, Routledge and Kegan Paul.

Zummato, R. (1988) 'Organisational Adaptation: Some Implications of Organisational Ecology for Strategic Choice', *Journal of Management Studies*, vol. 25, no. 2. pp. 105–20.

Name Index

Subject Index